MW00872989

Beyond the Fire and the Rain

My Journey

An intimate story of the struggle of an African-American youth to become a medical doctor, as he overcomes racism and the resistance of the establishment.

Wilbert Williams Jr., M.D.

Wilbert Williams Jr., M.D.
40 Underhill Road
Middletown, New York 10940

Trafford rev. 02/05/2013

 www.trafford.com

North America & international
toll-free: 1 888 232 4444 (USA & Canada)
phone: 250 383 6864 ♦ fax: 812 355 4082

ALSO BY WILBERT WILLIAMS JR., M.D.

Petals

Dancing in Fire

Shouting at the Rain

The Secret Place

In Memory Of

Dr. Robert V. Vaughn

FOR

My father, who was born in Chesson, in Macon County, Alabama, I remember your long quiet moments looking through our living-room windows at the people. I admired your indulgence with God's Creation. I am proud that in the midst of racism, which you encountered almost everywhere, you did not allow it to destroy you. Because of your strength, I am the man-child that will always respect, honor, and adore you. I am proud that you were my earthly father.

My mother, who was born in Baltimore, Maryland, I am indebted to you for telling me about life. I will always remember you're sharing with me the story of Harriet Tubman and the Underground Railroad. Thank you also for sharing with me the beauty of Baltimore. I am grateful that you exposed me to what you felt would benefit me the greatest. When I think of Baltimore, I see your beautiful soft brown face smiling at me.

My beautiful and faithful wife, you have always loved me dearly and honestly. I thank you for giving me, you. I am blessed and rich that you are my wife. You gave me seven beautiful children who fascinate me and whom I adore. Thank you for reviewing the revised manuscript and giving me your honest opinion. Thank you for allowing me the time to work on and finish our story.

To my sisters, I love you. I thank God for you. Thank you for encouraging me to aspire toward greater heights. I pray that this memoir will reflect an expression of our love to our parents, who raised us well.

My late friend Dr. Robert Vaughn, thank you for your determination to be my stepfather. Thank you for the many hours you labored with me to complete my manuscript from the inception of this body of work. Thank you for the many hours you shared with me in your beautiful warm home as you encouraged me to hold on to my faith in God. I learned many things from you that will last me a lifetime. Enjoy your fellowship with God. I love you.

To Beryl Shaw, thank you for taking your precious time while you studied in college to help me with the manuscript. You raised it to a higher level of acceptance and professionalism. Your soft-spoken words to me encouraged me to hold on to my dreams and goals and move forward.

Thanks to my children for tolerating my absence while I labored over my writing. Thank you for allowing me to speak to you for long periods of time, although you had things to do. Thank you for showing me your Agape love, mercy and forgiveness.

To my beautiful daughter, Shoshanna, thank you for correcting many of the mistakes in the manuscript.

To Mildred, thank you for reading the manuscript and giving me important critical advice.

To Domitilia, thank you for listening to why I had to publish my manuscript. I am indebted to you for giving me endless hours to review, edit and discuss my life.

Thank you Charlotte for your advice on the manuscript and always telling me how you feel about my behavior.

Thank you Amelia for your ability to search and find what needed important attention and correction when I thought I was finished with the manuscript.

"Men do not live by bread alone; so with nations, they are not saved by art, but by honesty; not by the gilded splendors of wealth but by the hidden treasure of manly virtue; not by the multitudinous gratification of the flesh, but by the celestial guidance of the spirit."

Frederick Douglas

Contents

Foreword

Some stories need telling. "Beyond the Fire and the Rain" is such a story. It is a story of success, and of overcoming challenges and prejudices from without and from within. Herein we follow the trials in the life of a young man whose father was a barber, and his mother a domestic worker. They lived where gangs notoriously spawned, an area from which this author "graduated," or perhaps better stated, "Escaped."

This is the inspirational story of a young African-American man. With the dedicated assistance and support from his parents, and his ever-loving wife, he has achieved a major goal in his life. It is the story of a young man who left the "safety" of his birthplace to seek an education in the "foreign" areas of long-established schooling systems. He often experienced hostile racial attitudes.

Inspiration should be the cornerstone of those who are privileged to read this intimate and very personal account. I hope many of these readers will be young people of different colors, cultures, religious beliefs, locales, etc. It is a lesson in overcoming the development of hatred and fear, which result from illogical discrimination; especially that of racial prejudice.

This book, too, should be an inspiration to those who have been engendered with prejudice as young people, and who have grown to adulthood, carrying those prejudices with them. It is another chance to look at ourselves, and to see others in light of our similarities, rather than our differences. This work is a message of hope in a "minefield" of racial prejudice, fear, and hatred.

Wilbert Williams Jr., M.D.

Dr. Wilbert Williams Jr., M.D. is a role model for young people of all hues. He is a dedicated physician that alleviates the illnesses of people wherever he goes, including the poor and the disadvantaged. He is living proof that one can make it "Beyond the Fire and the Rain."

Robert V. Vaughn, Ed. D.
Christiansted, St. Croix, VI

Introduction

"Beyond the Fire and the Rain" is a fascinating and compelling story of a young African-American who grew up in a South Brooklyn, New York public housing project. He beat overwhelming odds to become a medical doctor. His story will take one meandering through valleys and mountaintop experiences. He will journey from the streets of New York, and a housing project called Red Hook in South Brooklyn, to the beautiful Caribbean island of St. Croix in the United States, Virgin Islands. He will share his joy, and his pain and agony to overcome anxiety, depression, and a near nervous breakdown. He struggled to deal with racism, lost and broken relationships, and trying to become a physician. His journey through medical school may exhaust you. His revealing hurt when he faced racism, and the forces behind it, which threatened his life, may bring you to tears. Beyond the Fire and the Rain speaks to all of us. It gives us a mirrored reflection of our strengths and weaknesses in the presence of our challenges. It tells us that in spite of everything short of death, we can overcome anything in our lives by faith, hope and trust in God and in ourselves. Dr. Williams proclaims that perseverance and commitment are keys to conquering our tallest and most rugged mountains, and still grow. Beyond the Fire and the Rain is not only a success story of an African American youth from Brooklyn, New York. It is the story of a person's refusal to give up his dream to become a medical doctor, while facing tremendous odds. It is a statement to all of us that we do not have to let the existing society mandate or dictate our destiny. We can soar like eagles, to conquer our goals and dreams.

Robert V. Vaughn. Ed. D
Christiansted, St. Croix, VI

Preface

Some names in this journey have been altered. The situations and places; however, except to express them in proper conceptualization have remained the same. Some names, on the other hand, have not been altered, since they are a matter of a public record.

The audience for which this memoir has been written is the public, Blacks and whites, medical and non-medical persons, traditional and non-traditional religions and philosophy. This memoir is intended to portray the feelings and experiences as a Black person from childhood to adulthood, college, medical school and actual medical practice. It illustrates the revelations of prejudice and discrimination exerted on Blacks and whites, by the establishment.

Faced with the dilemma concerning terms used, such as African American, Black, Negro, white, Caucasian, etc., I have taken poetic license and have used the term "Black" for it was generally in use at the time of this memoir. African American, while perhaps more definitive and politically correct, was too cumbersome, just as the word "Caucasian" was cumbersome.

Both of those terms, Black and African American, would have been capitalized. 'Black' as a common noun capitalized and 'white' lowercase are being used here, as it appears as 'standard' in similar contemporary literature.

Capitalization, which was a dilemma in relation to "Black," was also a problem in relation, in other words, such as academic and medical areas of study, such as Philosophy, Chemistry, Obstetrics, Gynecology,

Hematology, Cardiology, and for acronyms such as OB/Gyn, IV, ICU, etc. Titles and positions, such as Chief of Obstetrics, Assistant Chief, Administrator, etc., have been generally capitalized. Capitalization in all the cases does not imply greater or lesser importance than if it was un-capitalized.

Because most medical terms that might not be known as the public have used, I have included a glossary in this account.

This is an ongoing saga. There is no logical ending, except that this account ends on a happy note.

Robert V. Vaughn. Ed. D
Christiansted, St. Croix, VI

Author's statement:

Beyond the Fire and the Rain may be perceived as one of the most negative books you will ever read. It took many years to present my journey to the general public. My intention is not to share with you a negative perspective but to share with you the life of one African-American male who life's external and internal forces shape him.

I have tried to be honest and true to all the circumstances that I have encountered on my journey. Allowing the truth to be my guide is an important foundation of my book. Some of the things that I have written about have been painful. The pain of the journey relates to the reality that we must make an effort to accomplish our goals, dreams and aspirations. Our desires may not readily be available, and at times we will have to be patient and delay gratification.

I tried to convey racial issues clearly and fairly but who can say what is fair? Race is still an issue in America, and it shapes the outcome of situations that affect many people. Race affects all of our lives. So, from an African American view being a male, my life has had many moments of who I thought I was to who I am as a Black male growing up in America.

There are intimate moments on my journey. I have shared these with you because without them; you would only see a part of a whole person. Most people do not share the intimate parts of their lives. Intimacy sometimes reveals hidden parts of a person. It may be important that some concealed things be revealed for a deeper understanding of the why. Why certain things unfolded on the journey or what something may indicate.

The pleasant, happy and positive parts of my journey may not be seen readily while reading Beyond the Fire and the Rain. I encourage you to look at the moments when I had a chance to reflect on accomplishments. I have enjoyed my journey in spite of the challenges I created or the challenges I faced.

It is important to me that you are encouraged by my journey. It is my desire for you to accomplish all of your goals, dreams and aspirations. I hope and pray that you will be all that you desire to be and live a full and productive life.

Wilbert Williams Jr., M.D.
Middletown, New York

Praise For Beyond the Fire and the Rain

"Dr. Williams' inspiring story . . . takes the reader with him from boyhood and youth in a housing project to the rigors of medical school and early practice . . . We are with him in every step on his journey. I highly recommend this uplifting autobiography."
Susan Thornton, Ph.D., Binghamton, NY

The author survived racism before, during and after medical school as well as threats against his life and that of his family. He lived among his wife and family in the Virgin Islands on the island of St. Croix for 30 years where he had a successful practice. His story is one of a person's refusals to give up his dreams while facing immense odds. You will experience his tears and joys and discover how his faith in God and mankind triumphed over tremendous odds.
Robert V. Vaughn, Ed.D., USVI

Dr. Williams' style is riveting—forthright and in your face. His first volume [Dancing in Fire] traced his years of dancing in the flames of America's social fires from Red Hook Housing Projects in Brooklyn, New York to St. Croix as a Christian physician. This page-turner will draw you into the fires as Dr. Williams unflinchingly confronts his insecurities and misgivings until a timely visit to relatives has him shouting at the rain.
Mr. Mario Moorehead, Historian

"Dr. Williams speaks the language of his people with an intent that is supernatural, his soft voice, his humble attitude and loving action dripping wet in compassion with a message of hope from "Beyond the Fire and the Rain." He is a highly skilled achiever who has hurdled over the same difficulties you, and I may be experiencing or someone we know. Personally, I saw his heart of honesty, asking can I help. I saw personal collateral damage to his sincerest intentions as he went through the fire and shouted at the rain, he offers you a soaking wet view into the interiors of his life.
Raymond Scott, Th.B., Th.M., New Jersey

Nebuchadnezzar the King made an image of gold,
whose height was three score cubits,
and the breadth thereof six cubits:
he set it up in the plain of Dura,
in the province of Babylon.

Daniel 3

Part I

The Fumes of Babylon

Chapter 1

Danger

Nebuchadnezzar the king made an image of gold, whose
Height was threescore cubits, and the breath thereof six cubits:
He set it up in the plain of Dura, in the province of Babylon.

Daniel 3:1

It was July 13, 1978. I was standing on Seventy-Eighth Street between
Fourth and Fifth Avenues in Brooklyn, New York, afraid for my life. It had
not been three months since I was awarded the Doctor of Medicine and
Surgery degree at the prestigious Albany Medical College in upstate New
York. Some angry people were yelling racial slurs at me. They were sitting
on cars, standing, and some were walking in my direction. The police were
guarding me from their fury. I wondered if their hatred for me, because I
was Black, was real. Racism affected my life at times, but not like this. I
heard someone say, "We don't want that nigger living here; we'll kill him
and his family. He can go back where he came from."

The New York City Assistant Commissioner of Human Rights was
standing by my side, as he encouraged me to take this duplex apartment
in that racist neighborhood. "They're only bluffing," the Commissioner
said. "Don't worry, you'll get the apartment, and they won't hurt you or
your family." I stood next to a police officer that had a gun strapped to
his ankle, as he protected me from the crowd. I thought when the people
saw me in my white intern clothes; they would realize that I was a medical
doctor and calm down.

A casually dressed man grabbed his penis and shook it at me. A woman named O' Keefe, with red hair, stood in my presence and told the commissioner that they did not guarantee my safety. She said if my family or I got hurt, our blood would be on the hands of the Commissioner of Human Rights and the police. I feared for my wife Iris, and two children Shoshanna and Taina, as the commissioner begged me to walk up the stairs to the duplex apartment.

When the crowd got out of control, the police officer stood closer to me. The other police officers pushed the crowd back. I told the commissioner that I didn't want the apartment, and he got upset. "What do you mean you don't want the apartment; we've come too far to turn around now?"

I replied, "It's not worth the destruction of my family, to live in a neighborhood with people who hate me for being Black."

He put his hand on my shoulder and nudged me forward. I resisted. "I am telling you," he said, "it will be OK. They're just bluffing."

I gave in and walked up the stairs, which lead to the apartment. I thought that someone was going to kill me. I braced my body in anticipation of being shot. When we got inside the apartment, wires were hanging from the ceiling and walls, and the light fixtures were not in place. The sliding glass doors were broken, and a brick was on the new carpet floor. Those racist people outside, who were full of prejudice and hatred for Black people, were serious. They were willing to kill my family and me.

The contractor, Mr. Hansen, was with me. The Assistant Commissioner of Human Rights asked Mr. Hansen, "When are you going to have this apartment ready for Dr. Williams?"

"If you want it finished," he said, "I'll give you the money, and you can finish it yourself. I'm not going to get killed." The police officer that was standing by my side looked at Mr. Hansen.

We learned that Mr. Hansen sent his thirteen-year-old daughter to Norway because they threatened her life. Someone phoned his house and told him if he finished the apartment for those "niggers," his daughter would be raped. They informed him of his daughter's panty and bra size over the telephone.

If those racists had handed me, the keys to the apartment on a golden platter, I would not have taken them. The commissioner was disappointed with me, but I didn't care how he felt. They humiliated and emotionally broke me.

The Fishing Trip

I was angry with the Swift Real Estate Company in the Bay Ridge section of Brooklyn for being racist. Mr. Swift claimed to be a Christian. He deceived me. He had a real estate agent take me to two roach-infested apartments, one in Brooklyn, and the other in Staten Island, as he tried to get me to rent one. He didn't want me to rent the apartment on 78th Street. I was angry and hurt.

Seemingly, as a gesture of friendship, Mr. Swift invited me on a fishing trip near Staten Island, New York on a late afternoon with his friend. They took me out in their boat and then stopped it. I thought that they were going to throw me overboard. They scared me. When we returned ashore, it was dark, and they drove me to a dreary isolated street on Second Avenue in Brooklyn. Mr. Swift yelled at me in an uncontrollable rage while his pale face turned red, saying over and again, "You better not take that apartment." He had foam forming on the sides of his mouth, and as he opened it, his saliva sprinkled my face. He wouldn't let me out of his car until I said, "OK, I won't take it." When I finally got out of that car, I thanked God for my life. I was mad but still scared.

Iris was in upstate New York camping with her family and when she came home, I told her what happened, and she begged me to forget the apartment. She said that we could find another apartment in a neighborhood where people did not care about our color and race. I understood her fear because I was frightened for our family. I questioned myself-worth, and my pride was ripping at me while I was struggling with my manhood. I tried to go on with my life. I felt ashamed that at this point in my life, after I had proven myself, having struggled hard to become a medical doctor, that anyone in his or her right mind would make my color and my race a focal point. They called me a "nigger." I never felt so low and broken in all of my life.

Running

Chesson, Alabama could not have been more than eight hundred miles from Brooklyn, New York. Both states swelled like a dead animal on a hot day with racial prejudice and hatred for Black people. It was so bad in Chesson that some white people gave the only black doctor in town twenty-four hours to get out, for attending to a white woman.

5

My father, Wilbert Williams, was a little boy growing up in Chesson, when they ran the black doctor out of town. He told me, "Those white crackers got up early in the morning and threatened to hang the doctor."

When my father was a teenager, he hunted raccoons and squirrels in the woods. He enjoyed the outdoors because it helped him feel free around all the oppression black people suffered in Alabama. They troubled his memories of his hometown with racial slurs, discrimination, lynching and mobs of hateful people threatening the existence of Blacks. When he spoke of Chesson, Alabama his face twisted and his eyes fixed in one area. He would not divert his eyes unless another subject was mentioned. I asked my father if he would return to Chesson to visit. He said, "What the goddamn hell for? Those racist bastards were no damn good, and if I had stayed at that place, those racist white crackers would have had to kill me. I was not going to let them treat me like a low down no-good nigger." He told me that the armed service was just as racist as the state of Alabama. They drafted him into the United States Army and put him in a segregated barrack, and treated the white soldiers with respect while they ridiculed the Blacks. When my father was told to stand guard duty at night, he replied, "If you want this goddamn place guarded, you better guard it your own goddamn self, because I am not doing it." My father believed he was disregarded by the United States government because of the way they allowed black soldiers to be treated in an inferior manner as compared with the white soldiers. He wanted to get out of the military because he believed that the United States did not care about him or any other black citizen. He rebelled against authority whenever he had a chance. He refused to put his life on the line for America, because black people in Alabama and throughout the country, were discriminated against and treated worse than animals. He wrapped it all up in telling me that, "those racist's white crackers, can take the whole goddamn country and go to hell with it."

The Other Side

My mother, LaVerne Smith Williams, did not have the kind of racial scar my father had. Her childhood in Baltimore, Maryland was pleasant. Racial prejudice and hatred were in Baltimore, but it did not change the way she felt about life and people. She spoke to me about a place called "Pig Town," in the southeast section of Baltimore, where her grandfather had horses and sold its droppings for fertilizer. The horses all mysteriously died one by one, and my mother believed that he was killing them. Some horses' legs got broken, and my grandfather put them to sleep. Whenever someone questioned him about the horses, he would make some excuse for why they were dying. She believed that he got tired of that business.

My mother loved Baltimore. She told me about the beautiful white marble steps in front of almost every house in her neighborhood and how the people cleaned it meticulously. My mother told me about famous Black people whom she learned about in school like Harriet Tubman and Sojourner Truth, how Harriet ran the Underground Railroad, and took many slaves to freedom from the South to the North. She told me that Sojourner was the first black woman to speak out against slavery. My mother never spoke to me about anything negative without showing me the positive side of it. Even the time that she had to eat horsemeat during the depression was told to me. She often told me of people standing on line to get a cup of soup. When I asked her how she dealt with it, especially eating horse meat, she said, "That's just the way it was."

Desire

When my father met my mother in Brooklyn, New York, he liked her at first sight. She told me that he was handsome and aggressive. He frequently roamed her block and asked about the girl with the big legs. When she saw him, she didn't think much about romance; although she liked the way, he looked physically. He was proud of his himself, while he paraded around as if he owned the world. My grandmother, Queen Victoria Smith, had a few negative words for my mother, about my father, but my father pursued my mother regardless whenever and wherever he could. I don't know what it was that my grandmother didn't like about my father, but she was not in favor of my mother being with him. My mother told me that she didn't want to be bothered by him, but he insisted in making contact with her. He sported fancy clothes, wore expensive shoes, and kept money in his pocket. After World War II, he opened a barbershop business in the Bedford-Stuyvesant section of Brooklyn, near Fulton and Nostrand Avenues. My mother named it "Tonsorial Studios." My grandmother continued to warn my mother about seeing him, but my mother fell in love with him. My parents got married, and they moved into a one-bedroom "flat" on Pacific Street in Brooklyn. They shared the bathroom that was in the hallway with other people inside the building.

Moving On

Less than ten months after her marriage, my mother gave birth to my sister Janice by C-section, because she couldn't advance in labor. When it was time for my sister to be delivered, the doctor had to cut into my mother's abdomen and womb, and pull my sister out. It was one of three C-sections my mother would have. She showed strength, and ability to face odds and survive just as she did while she was growing up during the Depression. My parents needed more room after my sister's birth, and couldn't stomach the one-bathroom deal anymore. They moved to Canarsie, New York, in Brooklyn, into an old World War II army barracks, which the government converted to public housing.

My father was a long way from Chesson, Alabama, but the memories of it haunted him. Although opportunities were better for him in New York, and he could make a decent living cutting hair, he faced racial challenges. He was just another Black man in America struggling to take care of his family, and survive the racist system. He still was not going to allow any person to treat him disrespectfully. My father was determined to be a free black man, in spite of racism. He understood if he returned to Alabama with such an attitude, his life would be in danger.

Negro

Sometimes the only thing that gave a Black man any kind of control that satisfied him was to love his woman and raise his family. My father was no different, and my mother was both the object of his love and the target of his frustration. In his mind, to be a man while challenging the system was consuming, but he knew he had to feed, clothe, house, and protect his family. Many Black men have fared well trying to overcome the racist system, and my father did the best that he could. Every Black man understands this dilemma and what it costs to be a strong black man in America.

My mother and my father loved each other, and they continued to share their affection in the center of things that challenged them. Fair housing, good jobs, and respect from people were challenges that faced most black people.

When I Was Born

My mother was pregnant with me and on February 11, 1948, entered Kings County Hospital in Brooklyn, to deliver me by C-section.. While she lay on the operating room table, the nurses and doctors were preparing to open her up with a scalpel (knife). It was all planned due to her first C-section when she had my sister Janice. No labor was involved, just the anesthesia, the nurses, the doctors and the knife.

I was born healthy. My mother named me after my father, and I became a junior, but one of my cousins said, "Let's call him Buddy." They wrote on my birth certificate "male Negro." I don't know who told the vital statistics employees at Kings County Hospital that I was a "Negro." My father's father looked white, and people called him "pecker wood," and we have Native American Indian in our family. My father's sister had fair skin with freckles and long straight hair, which extended to her waist. I don't pretend to be anything other than what I am. It was not my choice to be called a "Negro" baby boy; it was the decision of the system that failed to find out who my mother and father really were.

When my mother took me home, she knew her brand new healthy "Negro" baby boy would face challenges, being male and being "Negro."

My father and my two-year-old sister Janice waited anxiously at our house to greet us. Our house in Canarsie was comfortable. We had a back yard and a porch. My father was living in an Army barrack for the second time in his life. He didn't have to stand against the cold while guarding and cursing America for being racist. He was in a rented home, owned by the federal government, protected, and he felt good about it.

My mother told me about a family who lived next door to us and the children frequently had lice. My father was furious concerning those children with head lice. He did not want me or my sister to be infested as well. He cut off their hair.

The only thing I remember about Canarsie, New York, is a picture of me in my father's arms. He stood on the back porch and held me proudly, like a precious gift. I had on a little one-piece top and bottom with straps coursing over my shoulders. My hair was bushy and thick, and it looked like a mini-Afro. My father stood like a king on his throne holding me, surveying his wealth. My mother stood at the left of him. She had a sweet smile on her face, and her hair was full, just like mine.

Polio Virus

My father worked hard in his barber's business. He understood the responsibility of taking care of us. He did well financially cutting hair, until he was infected by the polio virus that crippled him in his right leg. He stayed at the hospital for months. My mother took care of us while he recuperated, and she had enough money saved to take care of our financial needs until my father came home from the hospital. When he came home, he had difficulty's bathing in the shower. It was trying for my mother to take care of my sister Janice and me after my father's paralysis. It was a full-time job for her, but she handled it well.

Two years after I was born; my mother was pregnant with my sister Shelly. She had her third C-section, and the doctor told her that she could not have any more children. She did not particularly want more. I never heard her comment that she was disappointed with the doctor's decision.

Red Hook Projects

We moved to Red Hook housing projects in South Brooklyn, because my father could not stand under the shower, and he needed a bathtub. They built Red Hook many years before I was born, sometime after the Great Depression, when my mother ate horsemeat. It looked like a colony of skyscrapers. The buildings numbered more than fifty. They were six stories tall, in that little corner of Brooklyn near the famous Brooklyn Battery Tunnel, which connects Brooklyn with lower Manhattan. It really was a unique place to live because it had almost everything the people who lived there needed. Red Hook projects even had a theater, and an Olympic-size swimming pool. One pool was sixteen feet deep and had a ten-foot diving board. Red Hook had a beautiful manicured lawn with a chain-link fence, and tall trees spaced along each side of it. The community respected the police. If someone was caught riding a bike onto the sidewalk, climbing a tree, or walking across the grass, the police notified your parents, and they gave the people a fine for breaking Red Hook projects' laws. Racial prejudice was not an issue then, and people spent their energy and time being neighbors and helping each other. We borrowed bread, milk, sugar and eggs from each other. I remember my father bringing home a fifty-pound bag of potatoes. He would tell my mother to round up the neighbors in the building and let them know that they could have some. Watching my mother's response was funny. She just looked at me, then at the ceiling, in disapproval of his suggestion. It wasn't that she didn't want to share, but my father did this each time he brought some extra food home to us.

Gangs

Red Hook had a gang called the "Kovons." They would walk in the middle of the street singing some dumb gang song, marching like soldiers, putting their weight on their left leg, (which gave them the "bee bob" walk), "doing the bad walk," and literally stopped traffic. The power, they had was amazing. I knew a guy in it named "Nero," his real name was Neal Wooden. He was a hefty-looking guy who scared me if he made an ugly face. He had a large square head, a wide mouth, and puffy lips. Neal told me often to behave, because he knew that I was a terror on the block. When he came to my house, he saw me in action creating confusion and would look at me and shake his head. Red Hook's elevated train station at Smith and Ninth Streets had his name written upon the wall with paint, in bold letters, "Nero." It remained there for many years, along with the names of other devious kids. I never looked up to Neal because I knew he was wayward in his behavior. I did enjoy watching him write because he had a beautiful handwriting.

The only rival gang in Red Hook the "Kovons" had to deal with was the "Black Diamonds," a Puerto Rican gang full of delinquents. Occasionally, someone was shot with a homemade zip gun. The guys made the guns by using a car antenna for a barrel, and a deadbolt door latched as a hammer, with fifty million rubber bands as a spring. This gadget, made from a piece of wood, could fire a .22-caliber bullet. Their other weapons were knives, bats, chains, rocks, and anything else that they could find. The "Kovons" never bothered children. Some of them told us kids to stay in line and do well in school.

Chapter 2
Affection and Protection

O Lord, thou hast searched me, and know me.

Psalm139: 1

My father made lots of money cutting hair in his barbershop. When he came home on Saturday night from work, he prepared himself to cut hair in our apartment on Sunday morning. We had constant traffic through our small living room into my parents' bedroom. He used our dining room table chair for his customers. Many people sat on that chair, while he reached for his barber tools that were in a cardboard box on his dresser.

He stood for hours cutting hair. The hair piled up in bunches on the floor, and sometimes hair was along the floor leading to the entrance door. My mother complained about the dirty hair in our apartment. My father would not let anything stop him from cutting hair, unless he got sick (which was not often). He worked long hours in his barbershop. His paralysis didn't stop him from making a living for us. He stood all day. His right hand was strong, because he used it to support his weight on his right side. I watched his hands, especially when he used them to cut hair; the veins bulged, and it made them look muscular. My father cut my hair almost every two weeks. I did not enjoy the haircuts, because he would twist my head when I was not paying attention to his commands to turn it. After he close-cropped my hair, he washed it. He massaged my scalp with his strong muscular hands, and it made me feel protected by him. I especially liked watching him wring out a washcloth with one hand, because the muscles on his arm bulged. He washed my hair with Ivory soap, then took the soiled washcloth and squeezed it with one hand. My father flipped the washcloth in his hand until it was almost dry.

My mother took us to the Baptist church every Sunday. Often when we arrived home, my father was sitting on the couch in our living room as he looked out the window to the people in the courtyard. He liked watching people and followed a person's every movement if he could. My father was a no-nonsense kind of guy who spoke very pleasantly and calmly. If crossed, he would curse while the veins on his forehead and neck bulged. If he liked a person, but something they did annoy him, he would not tell them, unless he felt that they gave him a reason. Even then, he would be very quiet until he could not take it anymore, and he would tell us about it as he sprinkled his feelings with "choice" curse words. I never understood his attitude towards his family. He would not talk to me about them except to say that they were "no good." He had ten brothers who were older than he and one sister who lived in Indiana. Once, his brother Louis came to our house in an old 1920s Model-T Ford with the skinny tires, and the Crank in front of the radiator. My uncle impressed me, but I could not figure out how that thing made it hundreds of miles on the roadway from Alabama. He came walking toward our apartment building with a guitar under his arm, dressed in a black suit. My uncle looked like he just came off a long journey. I never remembered seeing my father's brother before. When he saw me, he gave me a big hug. I didn't see any great reception between him and my father. After he settled down in our living room, he lit up a cigarette.

Those cigarettes and all the smoke that they made in our little apartment made me sick. Every time I turned around; cigarette butts were everywhere. One day our uncle took us to Coney Island in his 'Roaring' 20s car. It was great riding the Brooklyn Belt Parkway, watching people in faster cars looking at us black folk rolling to Coney Island. I never did get to know him well, although he was friendly. Respecting and loving my uncle Louis was easy because he was family. When he went to Alabama, I stood on our sidewalk and warmly waved him off. My father's relationship to his brother did not seem very close, though they talked seriously about life. I'm sure my father loved his brother, but a gulf was between them. My father's life never seemed exciting, unless he called a guy whom he knew, named Mr. George Washington. Mr. Washington had a Cadillac to take him out for a drive. My father didn't have the desire to buy his own car, although he had the money. I think he was afraid to drive. It was probably due to his paralysis, but a neighbor of ours who was paralyzed in both legs drove his own car by hand controls. Mr. Washington was a kind man. My father trusted him and enjoyed his company. Occasionally, he asked me to go along for the ride. I enjoyed sitting in that big car. During the week, my father spent an average of ten to fourteen hours per day working. He stood on his bad leg, taking occasional breaks to rest on a hard wooden chair. His barber chair was in the back of a long storefront. Six other barbers were there. My father chose the chair at the back, so he could easily get into the bathroom when he needed. Sometimes during the winter, when it snowed and was slippery, he stayed in the barbershop all night, sleeping in a dull-looking cot at the back. I missed my father when he didn't come home. I wanted him to be home with us, though he never wanted to talk much. The times he did come home, he was so tired dealing with people and exhausted from standing all day that he just wanted some peace and quiet. He liked to lie in bed and listen to religious stations all night until the morning. His radio would hardly ever go off from 9:30 p.m. until he went to work, which was usually at 5:15 a.m. Sometimes I watched him walk slowly on his bad leg with that brown scratched up cane of his, as he tried not to slip in the snow. I knew that I would not see him again for many hours.

Once, my father asked a neighbor to take me to his barbershop. My father wanted to give me affection. When I walked through the shop, all eyes were on me. The other barbers greeted me as if I were special. I had never seen them before. I'm sure that my father told them that I was coming. I know that he was proud of me. He told my neighbor to take me across the street to the toy store and buy me anything that I wanted. My father loved me special that day. I forget what I picked out, but it was a red toy; maybe a fire truck. Fire trucks fascinated me.

My father was working hard for us. He appeared strong, as he stood behind his barber chair, and he had the most customers waiting for him.

Finding Trouble

My mother had her hands full with us because we were constantly asking for something, and she never refused us. She cooked some great meals, and she enjoyed watching us gulp them down. From time to time, my father's absence was a burden for her because I, in particular, gave her a hard time. She endured my father's absence as a strong soldier. I never heard her complain, although at times I knew, she was lonely, when he stayed in the barbershop if it snowed heavily. She sat with us sometimes and told us stories in order to amuse us and make us laugh. My mother loved to see us laughing and enjoying each other's company. I remember her telling us always to be pleasant to each other. Her love was healing for our souls, and she hugged us a lot and made sure we never wanted for anything. The foundation for my love began to grow in my mother's arms. It wasn't that my father didn't love us; he did, but my mother expressed it more openly, and as children, we received it just as freely as it came. When I went outside to play, my father sat near the window, on our French provincial couch, which my mother cherished. If I did something, he didn't like, he would yell at the top of his voice from three stories high, and many yards away, in order to get my attention. Whenever he did, my heart pounded, and I shook because he usually called me upstairs and cursed me out. He would say, "What the hell is wrong with you, didn't you hear me calling you?" I stood before him, and listened to anything he wanted to say. When he finished with me, he would roll his eyes and say, "You can go."

When I went downstairs to play again, I found a spot where he could not see me creating confusion. I was a bad little boy (in the sense to the word), and I learned how to curse a person's ears right off their head. I didn't care who the person was; I spoke my mind. The neighbors were always complaining to my mother about my foul mouth. My mother washed my mouth with Ivory soap many times. She told me each time she caught me cursing; she would wash my mouth with soap.

The Psychiatrist

My mother took me to a psychiatrist at the county health clinic when I was four years old. I was devious. She couldn't control me, and she thought that some psychiatrists could. My mother thought that I was crazy. She told the doctor that I wouldn't sit still and every moment, I was doing something upsetting. My mother was at the end of her rope with me, but I had no idea that she was in torment. The psychiatrist looked at me. I looked at him. I thought that he just wanted to talk to me. I had no idea that he wanted to pick my brain and control my behavior. When he saw me, he made direct eye contact and didn't deviate. When he finished speaking with me, he told my mother that I had too much energy. He suggested that she put me to bed at 6:00 p.m. and awaken me at 6:00 a.m. in order to calm me down. It only helped for a few weeks, and it was just a matter of time before I acted up again.

15

I remember the first time my mother took me to school. I saw all these books and things. The first thing that I picked up was a wooden block with a red letter on it. As I held it in my hand, I felt like throwing it. I wasn't upset about being there. I just didn't want my mother to leave me alone. I stood in the middle of the floor, while my mother spoke with the kindergarten teacher.

While the kids sat on the floor and played with the books and things, I was thinking how to sneak out with my mother. When she left the classroom, I felt abandoned and lonely. I didn't want to play with the other children. When noontime arrived, my beautiful mother was waiting to take me home. I couldn't wait to get out of there and forget much about kindergarten, books, and things. Nevertheless, I do remember when I didn't have to go there anymore.

When my mother got her first job working in Jewish homes, she had my cousin Leray child-sit. Leray didn't put up with any foolishness. I gave her a hard time. We sat in the dark all evening when Leray came to sit with us. She watched TV, and I hated it. She, however, kept me in line. Her eyes and harsh voice intimidated me. I was frightened of her.

When my mother came home, I gave her the hard time that I couldn't give Leray. My mother stayed home with us when she didn't have any houses to clean in the Jewish neighborhoods. I enjoyed myself by jumping on my mother's bed from the shaky wooden headboard. "Buddy," she would say, "Are you jumping on the bed?" I wouldn't answer. My mother would continue whatever she was doing. Once I was practicing swan dives on her bed. After two good dives, she yelled, "Buddy, are you jumping on the bed again?" I didn't answer. Bang, the box spring hit the floor. "Buddy, I know you're jumping on the bed. I'm going to come in there and whip you." I ignored her, and did another dive on top of the bed. She dashed in my direction with a shoe in her hand and started swinging it at me, hitting me on my arms, shoulders, and butt. I tried to guard my head, but she found everything else without much effort. She never hit me on my head with anything unless it was soft. She must have felt I was missing enough brains. I rarely cried when she beat me, but I knew not to ask for any more.

When my mother was at work, after school, I roamed our little two-bedroom apartment and looked for anything that I could play with. We had the family's favorite fish with big eyes in a fish tank in our living room. It was a bad fish. It killed every fish in the tank. I was determined to kill that joker. I went into our kitchen cupboard and found vinegar and food coloring. Then, I went to the bathroom cabinet and got some iodine and alcohol. I put all the ingredients in the tank, and I stood with my nose, and forehead pressed against the glass, as I watched the skin peel from its eyes. It wouldn't die and float to the top. I pulled it out and stabbed it with a kitchen knife; then, I flushed it down the toilet bowl. When my mother asked about the fish, I told her it died, and I threw it away. My mother took us to many places. I remember the time that she took my sisters and me to the neighborhood theater (Clinton Movie House) in order to see a picture called "Hi Lilly." We sat in the movie theater; proud to be with our mother. When she spent recreational time with us, I felt very special. We sat in the balcony eating popcorn and candy, and the big screen was larger than life. Each spring she even took us to the Barnum and Bailey Ringling Brothers' Circus at Madison Square Garden. I always asked her to buy me a light that the circus ringmaster asked that everybody twirl when the high-wire act came on. The lion act was my favorite. I liked to see the lion tamer snap his whip and command those big beasts to roll over and jump over barrels. The high-wire act always tensed me. I believed each year that someone was going to plunge to his death. What really thrilled me was when a man was shot from the cannon into a net. I wouldn't have let anybody put me in a tube with gunpowder, light it, and propel me through the air. The clowns were great. They had a tall skinny one every year that uncurled out of a little car. I laughed hard when the clowns ran around and hit each other on the head with rubber bats. They had an act where a clown picked up a bucket of confetti water that was confetti paper, and tossed it on the crowd.

I always wished that I was sitting on the path of it. The circus was great, and my mother knew I loved it. One year at the circus, my mother bought a white cowboy hat for me, and I was proud to wear it. We did more than most of the kids on my block. My mother tried to expose us to as many things as she believed would stimulate healthy growth. She was always talking to us about loving people, and caring about each other.

Stealing

My father showed his affection for my sisters and me when he walked into our apartment after working a full ten to thirteen hours in his barber shop. He would bring us Chinese food, ice cream, or chocolate candy. My mother occasionally got upset with him for doing it, because she spent hours getting us to calm down, take a bath, and go to sleep. Often, we were in the bed when he came. He would stand at our dining room table, put the goodies down, and call our names. I was the first one to jump up. It was great when he brought old-fashioned vanilla ice cream for us. It was hard like a rock, and he would beat it until it got soft. I would watch those veins pop up in his strong hands while he whipped it. After we had our treat, my mother had a job getting us back to sleep. My father did this about once every week, and I loved it. He called during the day from his barbershop and asked me what I wanted him to bring home. Usually, whatever I told him, he walked into our apartment with it. (I should have told him once to bring me a real car, so we could go out together as a family, as my father did with Mr. George Washington), He never made me a promise that he did not keep, and this was one of many things that I respected about him.

My father understood the importance of being truthful with me. That is why it upset him when I stole some of his money. My sister Janice asked me to steal some of it in order to go into the movies. He usually allowed me to count his money on Friday nights. He would throw some cash on his bed and call me in order to count it. This time I put quarters in my pockets, shoes, and under my belt. He let me walk out of his room and did not say a word to me; then, he called me back while I was showing Janice some loot. My father asked me if he had more money than what was left on the bed. I told him "No." He said, "Empty your pockets." Tons of quarters came out. "Is that all you have?" he said. I replied, "Yes." He told me to take off my belt and tons of quarters dropped on the floor. He told me to take off my shoes, and I had more quarters.

He was infuriated. "Go and get my razor strap, I'm going to whip you." While I went for his weapon, I was afraid. He beat me like his arm needed exercise, and while he was beating me, he kept calling me a liar. If I had a quarter for each time he called me a liar, I could have taken the whole family to the movie theater. I didn't mind the beating nearly as much as my father calling me a "liar." I knew I hurt him and pushed a raw nerve. He believed that stealing was taboo, and he was right. I just got caught and had to pay the price. My sister Janice denied the whole thing. My father didn't say whether he believed her or me, but I paid for being a thief and a liar.

After a couple of days, my father apologized for beating me, and told me that I was never to lie again. It was rare when he beat me and didn't call the following day to apologize. It hurt my father to chastise me, but he knew I needed it. He understood my being a Black boy would make life hard enough for me, and I didn't need the added burden of getting locked up or killed for stealing. Christmas in my house was wonderful. I got almost everything that I asked for, unless I told my parents too late what I wanted Santa Claus to bring me. It was exciting hunting for a Christmas tree. I loved the evening, my mother and my sisters got together and dressed the tree with lights, bulbs, icicles, and angel hair. When the angel hair touched my skin, I would itch all night. I especially liked placing the main ornament on the top of the tree. When we turned the lights on, the tree looked pretty in our living room. My father never spent time decorating the Christmas tree with us. I missed him. He spent so much time making a living in his barbershop and doing whatever else, that all of us suffered from not doing important things together. I don't know how much he thought of his absence from us because he never spoke about it.

The things I missed doing with my father were substituted with plenty of things I did with my friends. Many things I did with my friends I would have never done in my father's presence. I don't know why, but I never spoke with my father about his staying in the barbershop so many times and believe it affected me in a negative way. Every child, especially every Black male child, needs his father to interact with him. Black males need their fathers to be their role models in order to show the side of Black worth. Therefore, my father's greatest influence on me was when I was in his presence.

Friends

My friends of my age were full of energy. I was not interested in girls other than to laugh at them and pick fights. They had no purpose or interest to me. My friends were various races, and it at no time dawned on me that it made a difference to either of us. We didn't talk about how we looked, about race or color.

One of my friends was Jewish, Herman. He lived across the hall from me. Herman was a rude boy, always cursing at his parents. His mother was constantly calling his name, and Herman ignored her. If I had done that, I would have been set on fire by my father's razor strap. My father had a big fat leather strap that he used to sharpen his straight razors, and if I was bad, he made me fetch it. He beat me with it often, until he got tired. I don't think Herman's parents ever beat him. He was out of control. I was not much better than he was, because often I was also out of control.

My father did not allow my sisters or me to do certain things that he felt would set a bad trend. My parents did not allow me to play marbles, because my father believed it would encourage me to gamble when I was older. Nevertheless, when the marble season came, my friends got their marbles, and I wanted some. My mother told me that I could not have any, because my father had forbidden it. I bought some anyway. A friend of mine named Eric was skilled at playing marbles, and he won all of mine. I started a fight with him because I wanted them back, and he refused. He held me in a headlock and would not let go until I gave up. When my mother heard about it, she made me throw all my marbles in the incinerator of our building. I, nevertheless, purchased more marbles, and I won a lot. When she heard about that, she made me get rid of my marbles again. No matter what she did with my marbles, I kept buying more, because I often had money to buy candy. I didn't fight with Eric again over marbles for two reasons: he was bigger than I was, and it would only get back to my mother.

I had lots of fun amid my friends. Richard was my friend, who wore thick glasses. Richard's father was paralyzed like mine, but his father was paralyzed in both legs. Richard was funny. When something was done, which he did not like, he would just stand on one spot and look at you. I teased him about his thick glasses. He never seemed bothered by my actions. Richard would laugh most of the times when I joked about him. We spent much time together, and our color was never an issue between us. One incident between our parents almost put a wedge in our friendship. One day Richard was teasing my little sister Shelly. My mother yelled to his mother, "You better tell Richard to leave my Shelly alone." Richard's mom yelled back at her, "Ah, shut up."

My mother dashed down the stairs like a football star. Without breaking her pace, she grabbed a paddle bat from a little girl and went to beat Richard's mother with it on her head, saying, "Ah, shut up?! Ah, shut up?"

I was in a state of shock. I could not believe my sweet little mother had assaulted and battered my friend's mother. That catastrophe took a back seat in my relationship with Richard, and we went on with our lives.

Steven was my best friend. He was chubby, light-skinned, and had curly hair. I liked Steven's family because they were always laughing, especially his father, whom they called "Danny Boy." Steven and I were prone to misbehaving. Steven's father thought I was the troublemaker. I encouraged some foul behavior, but Steven was not exactly an angel. Once

I gave Steven a wrench to open the water hydrant. I ran and hid among the bushes, while Steven slowly turned the nut. A police car rolled up, and a police officer caught him. I laughed at what happened, not taking seriously the consequence of the crime. Steven's father prohibited him to be with me, because I cursed and was a bad influence. The separation hurt us. Steven obeyed his father's wishes. I continued mischief wherever I went. I fought with girls in the block. I was constantly teasing my neighbors, Brenda, Patty, Sherlina, Gloria, and Sheila. Most of my fights with these girls were with Sheila. She was bold enough to fight me if I bothered her. Our fights ended with my face scratched and her ears hurting, and some of her hair would be gone. Sometimes we locked like two horned goats with my right hand in full contact with her left ear, while she scratched my face, neck, and arms. Once I punched Brenda in her chest for butting in while I was bothering her sister Patty. Brenda and Patty came into my house and complained to my mother. While they were leaving the building, I tossed dirty kitchen water down on them from my third-floor kitchen window. They hollered and ran next door where they lived.

I started turning on all my neighbors, and no one knew what to expect from me at any moment. My neighbors branded me as a terror, and most people felt I was either crazy, or possessed by the devil.

One day I was in my apartment with some firecrackers that I purchased with some money that my father gave me. I tossed a lighted one into a baby Carriage under my kitchen window. It blew up before it hit the Carriage. No baby was in it, and it was not my intention to hurt one. I was just bad.

When my mother found out about the firecracker incident and the baby Carriage, she scolded me verbally and asked me if I were insane. It was her way of communicating to me. She reminded me that she had previously taken me to a psychiatrist once and would do it again. I even roamed the streets looking for cigarette butts to straighten out and smoke in order to pass the time. I tried smoking a mini-cigar one day and near choked to death. One of my wildest adventures was when I went off with some guys whom I didn't know and scaled a large fence. We went into the famous Todd Shipyard, where lumber was kept. They had some bad dogs in there, and we all knew it. Halfway into the yard these dirty-looking dogs charged us. I barely grabbed onto the galvanized fence before one of those dirty dogs tried to rip into me. I took many chances and put my life on the line. My life was in danger of extinction until I almost lost my left eye. I was in Coffee Park, the neighborhood park, clowning around as usual. I grabbed my friend Tyrone's hat from his head and ran into an occupied swing. The swing struck me above my right eyebrow and exposed my skull, and the blood gushed out like a fountain. A person took me to the first aid building. When my mother arrived, she screamed when she saw me. It hurt me to see her frightened and crying. After they took me to the hospital, they stitched me. I vowed never to hurt my mother again. I behaved on holidays when the little family we had in New York got together. Thanksgiving was one of those times. My aunt Doris, Leray, Leray's husband Louie, my cousin Sarah who we called Aunt Sarah, her husband Douglas, and all their children with a host of other relatives flooded our little project apartment. The men would sit with my father and discuss all kinds of things. The women would talk between themselves and serve the men food and drink. It was the only time my parents allowed me to drink alcohol (12% grape wine). Once I drank a whole 8-oz. glassful as if I were drinking milk, got drunk, and fell in the clothes closet. My cousins who were my age loved to joke and have fun. We got along well. I forgot if I fought with any of them, although I probably did. I enjoyed Thanksgiving almost as much as Christmas because I felt secured by being with my relatives. When the evening ended and everyone got restless and started going home, I wanted them to stay. I will never forget these special times that we stayed together.

Chapter 3
Books and Things

Thou knowest my down sitting and mine uprising,
Thou understandest my thoughts afar off

Psalm 139:2

I was in love with my fourth-grade teacher, Mrs. Aronawitz. She was Jewish. When she gave us our assignments on the blackboard, she tiptoed in order to reach the top and the muscles in her legs bulged. She was short like my mother. Her hair was dusky brown and neatly styled to her neck. Her nose was long and fat, and her eyes and lips were large. Except for her pale skin, she looked like a Black person to me. She could not have been more than four and one-half feet tall. I thought that she was beautiful, but most of the kids in my class thought that she was ugly. I spent more time looking at her than I did in learning my lessons. Mrs. Aronawitz never gave me any reason to believe that I was special to her, but that did not matter.

The first girl to come into my life and cause me pain was Francis. Francis was not bad looking. Much of her beauty was hidden beneath her evil, lying nature, which she practiced on me. She turned my world upside-down emotionally, and Mrs. Aronawitz became allies with her. Francis sought my attention. I was, however, much too in love with the teacher to think about Francis.

At my age, the only female I liked, other than my mother and sisters, was Mrs. Aronawitz. She was the first female I thought of romantically, and I don't know why. I convinced myself that I was special to her.

We had mock fire drills. One day Francis had a brand new white wool hat that her mother bought her. During the drill, her hat fell on the floor, and she accused me of deliberately stepping on it. Francis knew I didn't step on her hat, but she wanted to blame me with hopes of getting my attention. When she told Mrs. Aronawitz, Mrs. Aronawitz demanded that my mother take me to Francis's house to apologize.

I told my mother, I didn't do it, but she wouldn't believe me. She knew that I could do anything, and she made herself allies with Francis, but this time Francis was framing me. "Nevertheless, Ma," I said, "I didn't do anything."

"Buddy," she said, "You're always doing something."

I pleaded with her to believe me, but she carted me down the beautiful manicured lawn in Red Hook Project to Francis' apartment. My mother had no idea that she had picked up the wrong banner, believing Francis' lie. She didn't know that what she was going to make me do would create a hate in me for Francis for many years. When we got to Francis' apartment, Francis was waiting as if someone was bringing her a prize for winning a contest. They were shuffling me like a pawn. Francis repeated in front of both of our mothers the same lie that she told my teacher. "He knocked my hat off my head and got it dirty," she said.

I yelled, "I did not dirty your white hat, Francis."

"You did too dirty my white hat," Francis yelled back. She was lying.

I wanted to choke her until her eyeballs rolled down her cheeks past her lying mouth. I even wanted to wash her mouth out with Ivory soap like my mother did to me once. My mother made me apologize to Francis for something I did not do, and I decided never to speak to Francis again. I hated her. Not even the lie that my sister told on me about not telling me to steal my father's money was worse than Francis' jumbo lie.

Mrs. Aronawitz gave me less attention after the incident with Francis. Her lack of attention caused double jeopardy between Francis and me.

The secret romance, which I had with my teacher, all vanished away after that lie. I wouldn't look at Francis, unless she showed up unannounced before my eyes. My behavior became more aggressive because I felt abused. My studies were less important to me, and I became a problem in school. I don't mean to suggest that anyone was responsible for my early rebellion or lack of interest in school. What happened with Francis and I served to distract me from the important issues of life for a nine-year-old.

When I finished the fourth grade, I didn't care much for school. It wasn't Francis' fault (although she gave me a reason to be angry), Mrs.

Aronawitz's belief of Francis, or my mother believing Francis; it was a rebellion against what I felt was dishonest and unfair in this life. I spent much time at the Clinton Street movie house. Every Saturday I went into the movies, especially if Tarzan or Superman was playing. Superman influenced my behavior. I imagined myself being Superman, by putting a red cape around my neck. I fantasized that I could run faster than a locomotive, fly faster than a speeding bullet, and leap tall buildings in a single bound. When I came home from school, I'd put the red cape around my neck and would walk outside my window three stories high. My mother was at work, but sometimes the neighbors saw me and told my mother when she came home. I knew that I couldn't fly, but I imagined that I could, as I was three stories from the ground. My mother asked me often if I were crazy. I tried flying all the time in my parents' bedroom. Standing on the top of the headboard, I'd launch myself in the air and plunge to the mattress, wishing to fly.

My mother quickly got tired of my acting out my fantasy about Superman, and bought an authentic Superman costume for me. After another few hundred dives to the mattress, Superman finally fell to his death. I imagined that someone killed me with krypton, because that was the only way Superman could die.

When Superman died, Tarzan came to life in my house. I would sit in the movie house and watch Tarzan command the animals, and those Africans with bones through their noses, and paint upon their bodies, to behave. I saw Tarzan as being one lonely man in a loincloth as he overpowered all of those strong-looking Africans and spoke in their language. I wanted to be like him. He fascinated me.

When I took a bath, which was only every Saturday (because I didn't feel any more frequent was necessary because I didn't smell), I would put on my bathing suit, strap a rubber knife to my side, and imagine myself fighting alligators and snakes. Splashing water all on the floor and on the walls, I imagined that I had an alligator in a headlock, stabbing it with my knife, just like Tarzan. My mother would come to the door and ask me why I was taking so long to bathe. I couldn't tell her that I was killing alligators. I always gave her another excuse; other than that, I was playing Tarzan. I imagined myself trapped by vicious Africans, with bones pierced through their noses, who tried to hurt me. They had large wooden spears, and I was protecting myself from them with my knife.

I was convinced the people who were white, strong and beautiful, had power. I didn't know that this was the way Hollywood made them, and it wasn't the way it really was. When I saw a romantic picture, I never saw any display of affection between people who looked like me in a movie. It was Hollywood's way of telling Blacks, "You are not a part of our group." It offended me to believe this. However, I continued to frequent the movies, like the rest with my Black friends.

Hollywood

By now, I was sensitive about my color. I didn't know anyone who was like me who was strong and in a position of power other than my father. I did see black people sometimes in the movies and on television, but they seemed weak. They were cast as servants, maids, and butlers. Hollywood was playing a game on Black folks, and we were buying it. My color became a burden to me. I wondered what it would be like to be white. All of my wondering and wishing couldn't change what I was; a Black boy.

The Colored Mask

The picture "Imitation of Life" wounded me racially. It was a story about a woman who looked white, but was Black. Hollywood was slick. The woman was ashamed of being Black, and she crossed the color line. She rejected everything about herself that was Black in any way, including her mother who loved her dearly. She escaped the bitterness of bigotry, and racial hatred. I felt rejected as I watched that picture. It had a lasting negative effect on my mind. It was at this point that I became angry about being Black. It felt as if I had on a "colored mask," because, I did not feel Black. The color of my skin marked me, and that was the only way anyone knew that I was a Black.

My friend Richard left Red Hook projects without giving me his address. It did not dawn on me that Red Hook Projects was changing. The whole country, for that matter, was changing; concerning the races. Life began polarizing. One by one, white people started moving out of Red Hook projects. The color and race issues fully invaded my life, and being a black male became a burden.

Mrs. Aronawitz, my fourth-grade teacher, was still fresh in my mind and Francis, destroyed the romantic fantasy fling that I had with her. I hated Francis and anyone who looked like her. I didn't hate being Black. I just wanted to feel free and not locked into a race color mode. I wanted to remove my "colored mask."

My fantasy world became larger and so did all the lies about most of the things that I thought were true. I continued to frequent the movies, and all those people that I saw as heroes, were not heroes at all. They were Hollywood's fabricated heroes, and they were nothing like me. The fact that Hollywood did not portray black people as heroic, strong role models hurt me, and the lie continued to get bigger. My fantasies were out of control, and I became hostage to being Black. The movies engrossed me, and I fed on Hollywood's cancerous "junk food" almost every weekend. When I went into the movies, I watched the picture about one and one-half times, and then created confusion. I ran up and down the aisles to be noticed. If the usher didn't catch me and throw me out, I would dash to the staircase that led into the balcony bathroom. After that, I would grab a roll of toilet paper, wet it, roll it up in pieces, and throw it into the projector movie light in order to watch it glitter.

I slid down the huge wooden staircase banister from the second floor, and when I reached the bottom, tumbled onto the carpeted floor. Then, I would run inside the theater smacking people on the back of their heads, or throwing paper balls or empty candy boxes at them. I never got caught by the ushers and would exhaust myself clowning around until it was time to go home.

My First Girlfriend

Major events were taking place in the world, but I had no idea what was happening. Red Hook projects were my worlds. Except a few outings, visits to the movies, and The Ringling Brothers' Barnum and Bailey Circus with my mother, all was well around me. It was 1957. Two years after Emmett Till, a 14-year-old black boy from Chicago, Illinois was murdered in Mississippi for saying, "Hey Baby" to a white woman in a grocery store. Emmett didn't know his life was in danger of extinction for just being a Black boy like me, growing up in America. He had no idea that racist people would torture and murder him, and throw him into a river. I, like Emmett, acted out my romantic fantasies with Hollywood's women of the screen and fell in love with my Jewish teacher, Mrs. Aronawitz. I also had a thing about Tarzan's wife, Jane, and even wanted that woman in "Imitation of Life."

I had no idea what it would cost me to act out my greatest fantasies in certain parts of the United States. For romance, there was innocence in me. I never thought of the opposite sex with any sexual intimacy until

I was about nine years old, sitting in the movie house, looking at all those women.

My first attraction to a Black female was Beverly. She was a fair-skinned nine-year-old who had fine hair and a big dimple on her chin. She was much lighter than I in complexion. It was an immediate attraction, and Beverly felt the same way about me. I walked home from school with her often when my friends were not around (because I was teased if seen with any girl by the guys). Beverly lived across the street from me, and before we reached our block, we had to separate, because she lived with her aunt, who was strict. Her mother and father lived in Germany because her father was in the Army. Beverly was leaving for Germany the summer of 1957, but the date was not exact. I wanted to take her to the Clinton Theater to be alone with her. My friends and I were close, and it was hard getting away from them, especially on Saturdays, without their asking a whole bunch of questions. I finally worked it out with Beverly to meet during the Saturday show. When I got to the movie house, I sat next to her and did not say a word. I looked at her and smiled. For over an hour, I didn't have the nerve to place my arm on her shoulder. I sat there thinking of the big dimple on her chin and her pink lips and wanted to kiss them. I was marveling at her beauty, looking at her long hair. She was the prettiest girl whom I ever saw; even prettier than Tarzan's wife was, Mrs. Aronawitz was, or any woman who I saw on the silver screen. As I pulled her closer to me, she didn't resist, and I knew that I had her approval. Leaning over to her, I put a closed-mouth kiss on her lips. I instantly fell in love with her. I stayed with Beverly through the entire picture and even remained after, in order to watch it again. I didn't think about running around the theater or throwing wet toilet paper on people, or smacking anyone on the back of his head. The world was a safer place in which to live because I was in love.

When the school year ended, so did my relationship with Beverly. She left Red Hook and went to Germany. She never said good-bye, and it hurt me. I couldn't believe what she did, and I don't know why. I wanted to believe that her aunt did not give her a chance to say good-bye. My heart was broken, and I felt cheated and lost. I knew that I wouldn't see her again. It was painful. Beverly was on my mind every day, for more days than I care to remember. I hurt so badly. It took me a long time to heal.

School became an issue in my life. I just wanted to have a good time. It wasn't anything, in particular, that finally turned me away from school. I just didn't care. The lost relationship with Beverly may have had something to do with my hurt. All I wanted was to draw attention to me. It was as if I needed something or someone special in my life, other than my parents, sisters and a host of relatives. I needed someone to help make me feel special.

I was the class clown, who made my classmates laugh. My name, Williams, rendered me last at many things. I got the last seat in the back of the class. I was the last one to get my test paper returned, the last one to walk out of the classroom at the end of the day, and the last one noticed if I needed something. Sometimes I would misbehave in class just to change my seat. Most of the time when I was bad in class, my teacher put me under her desk. We had a substitute teacher who tried her best to control the class. The teacher asked me to stop talking, and I refused. The teacher came toward me, and I got up and ran around the classroom. Students were in an uproar. I was having a ball, by not letting her catch me. She had her handbag with a long strap dangling from it in her hand. It was caught on some clothes hangers in the student closet. She continued to run and fell backward. She lay on the floor and played, dead. When I walked to her, she grabbed me by my collar and smacked me in my face a few times. The principal called my mother to the school and told her. It was the decision of a few faculty members to leave me in the fourth grade. My mother looked at me, next to him and said, "If you are going to leave him back, then leave him back." I stood spellbound, while my mother changed the course of my life with just a few simple words. I was angry with her for letting those people do that to me, but she didn't care. She knew that she was doing the right thing. She knew that it was for my own good. My mother was just tired of my foolishness.

Before the school year was over, a "gorilla" named Ronald beat me. For no reason known to me, he punched me in my stomach, and I fell on the school yard ground. When I hit the ground, he stomped on me, and hurt me badly. While I was on the ground, having surrendered, he continued to beat me. Some kids came to my aid and picked me up. It was the first-time anyone hurt me viciously. Emotionally, it created a fear in me because I didn't fight him back, and I knew how to fight. Ronald was the second person that I hated, besides Francis. I hated him for violating me, and I vowed to hurt him, even if I had to do it from a distance.

Desire

My mother decided to put me in the Cub Scouts. That blue uniform with the yellow and blue scarf made me feel special. I enjoyed the Cub Scouts' meetings because I had a chance to be noticed. I memorized the Cub Scouts' slogan and motto and found pride in reciting them. I didn't grasp fine tasks like the rest of the boys, and that challenged me to do better, because I wanted to do as well as all of them. I didn't like reading the booklet and the text, but I enjoyed listening to our scout master, Mr. Skipper. He was a tall, light-skinned, thin man who was very gentle. I liked him, and he and his wife took a special interest in me. They held our meetings in the Police Athletic League building in the projects (they held many community activities there). Every week, I learned what it meant to be a good Cub Scout, and it helped discipline me. The Cub Scouts gave me a different direction and created positive motivation in me. The most memorable thing I remember about the Cub Scouts was meeting a guy named Raymond, who was the Boy Scout leader, who took a liking to me. I was the only Cub Scout whom they allowed to go on an overnight camping trip in New Jersey. We all slept in a huge cabin in the woods, and it was the first time I was ever without electricity or heat from a radiator. The cabin had a massive fireplace, and we burned wood in it and used Coleman lanterns for light. We slept in a "bunk," which was a piece of canvas stretched between two steel pipes. I couldn't get comfortable in that thing for anything. The pipes were freezing cold, and the canvas sagged in the middle. They teased me because I was the youngest among them and the smallest of all the guys. It was a great experience, but at the end, I was glad to go home.

Doing Wrong

I had a fascination with fire alarm boxes and always wanted to pull the little red handle to see the fire trucks come screaming down the street. The guys in the black rubber suits with the yellow broad stripes on their pant legs and arm sleeves were great. The fire truck that came to Red Hook had one of those white dogs with the black dots who was supposed to be brave in fires. We called it a "fire engine dog." One day I slowly walked to a fire alarm box and pulled down the huge red handle. It started making this clicking sound, and my heart raced as fast as I ran to hide behind a car. Within moments, I could hear the fire trucks with the sirens coming closer to my block. I stood in excitement while the trucks pulled up, and the firefighters searched for the fire. It was a big joke to me. I felt bad about it later when I realized that someone may have needed those firefighters to save his or her life in a real fire. I looked for anything to keep me busy. Sometimes I walked the streets, picked up cigarette butts and smoked them. When I got tired of that, I would find old peach nuts in the street, break open the shell with a red hammer, which I stole from a fire alarm box, and eat the fruity center. I had become a bad little guy, and my biggest problem was me.

The Hard Way

The summer of 1958, I spent much time at the Red Hook swimming pool. I clowned around with my friends, and tried to look at the girls' breasts. My interest in the opposite sex became more focused on intimate body parts, and I enjoyed looking at all the different shapes, sizes, and colors. Once I saw a guy and a girl doing some funny things in the water, they pushed against each other back and forth. The guy had a serious look on his face. The girl had her eyes closed. It didn't take me anymore visits to the pool in order to figure out what they were doing, because many people were doing it. After the summer was over, I was convinced that people had sex in the water at Red Hook's public swimming pool. When I returned to school that September, I had to repeat the fifth grade, my parents, as usual, bought brand-new clothes for my sisters and me . . . returning to school, very sharp, was customary for the kids in my neighborhood. I had a thick tan wool sweater with a pair of dark corduroy pants and new black shoes. The first day of school was always great. I got to see people whom I had not seen all summer, because many went on vacations to relatives; sometimes down South. We would gather in the school yard with our unused notebooks with our names neatly written on them. Only a few unfortunate kids would be without any brand-new book or new clothes. The first day of school, Ronald didn't jump on me, and give me kicks to my stomach. I'm sure I would not have laid on the ground and taken a beating from him again. I would have tried to stomp him as he did to me. I still disliked him, and I would have fought him with hatred in my heart. For the first couple of weeks all was well for my studies. I really wasn't up to redo my class a second time. They didn't place me in the back of the classroom again, nor was I considered last at everything. They knew I had a strong deviant history behind me, and they were watchful of my behavior.

Chapter 4

Stealing Again

Whither shall I go from thy Spirit?
Or whiter shall I flee from thy presence?

Psalm 139:7

I knew that stealing was wrong. I got beat by my father when I stole his money. Ossie was a friend. He came to my house almost every Saturday, and we would, on occasion, go to the downtown shopping district. We weren't going to buy anything, but just look around. My mother told me often not to steal. She would say, "Buddy, watch your hands, do you hear me?" I didn't understand why she wouldn't just tell me not to steal. I was in the habit of picking things up, which weren't mine. Once I shaved down some pennies on the asphalt street until it had the shape and size of a dime, and used it to make telephone calls. I was caught putting one in a soda machine at a gas station. The owner shook me up a bit and told me never to come back to his place again. When Ossie did something, people blamed me, and when I did something, they thought that it was him. Many people believed we resembled each other. Ossie became one of my best friends, and every weekend; we roamed the projects and shopping districts together. Marvin was a strange guy. He was cocky. He looked older than he really was, and he was my age and grew hair on his face. Most people respected him because he had a deep voice and walked around as if he owned the world. One Saturday he came to my apartment and asked me if I wanted to go to the Brooklyn downtown shopping district and steal. He didn't say what we were to steal, and I jumped to it. I don't know why I was in a stealing mood because my parents gave me almost everything I asked for. We went to a department store called Abraham & Strauss. It was an exclusive store where many wealthy people shopped. My mother frequently shopped there, and I could easily have asked her to give me some money in order to buy things. I chose to steal instead. When we got in the store, security guards were everywhere. We caught the elevator to the famous 8th floor toy level. When we got off the elevator, I saw toys stacked up on counters, and the bright lights made it enticing. They really didn't have to entice me, because like most kids, I loved any kind of toy. Marvin went behind the toy counter and lifted a large shopping bag. We walked around the store picked up things and dropped it into the bag. I took a Remco science kit and a small radio. Marvin lifted a baseball glove. We walked out of the store as honored shoppers with our stolen goods. We were fortunate not to be caught. One day I was sitting at the dining room table in my apartment listening to the stolen radio, and my mother was cooking at the kitchen. A friend of mine named Donald said, "Isn't that the radio you stole?" My mother's head spun about its axis, and she said, "What?" I didn't say a word. I acted as if I never heard him. My mother asked me later if I stole anything, and I told her no. My relationship with Ossie ended without any fanfare. I forgot why, but maybe we grew out of our reasons to be together. I did not have a relationship with Marvin and didn't care; I was glad that we didn't cross stealing paths again. All the time I was being a thief, I remembered that my father hated thieves.

Being Bad

I caught a scalp infection early in the school year. I had to wear a female stocking on my head because I had sores that were very contagious. My father cut all my hair off, as he did our neighbors in Canarsie, and I was embarrassed and didn't want to go to school. The kids teased me and told me that I smelled like something dead. I could smell the mess myself, steaming from my head like a heating blanket. Sometimes those scabs would cause the stocking to stick to my scalp. When my father pulled it off my head, I felt as if my scalp was on fire. I suffered with the infection for weeks, until my father, in his barber's wisdom, could clean it with scalp medication and continuous washing.

I became a rebellious terror in school after my scalp cleared up. I don't know if it were because they teased me without mercy, or if it was just my time to create confusion on earth again. One time the teacher put me out of the classroom into the hallway for misbehaving. It was cold outside with ice and snow on the ground, and the heat in the hallway was piping hot from the large radiator. It dawned on me how I could make some urine smoke and stink up the whole hallway; I urinated on the radiator. It smelled so bad that I had a hard time staying there. My teacher made me stay in that hallway until the school day ended. She got tired of my foolishness.

One day while I was clowning around in class and being disruptive, the teacher called my mother to the school. I have no idea how my teacher engineered notifying my mother to come to the school. I never remember my teacher leaving the classroom. I was creating so much confusion that I didn't realize when she left the classroom it was in order to call my mother at home. When I saw my mother's face, I was shocked. She motioned to me to leave the classroom and beat me so bad I cried real tears. When I went back into the class, no one teased me as the tears streamed down my face. I believe that for the first time, my classmates felt sorry for me.

Academically I was not doing up to standard, and I was facing being left back again. My mother kept telling me that I had to do well in school, and she begged me to take my school work seriously. When she talked to me, I would promise her that I would do better. I had a rebellious streak running through me as big as a superhighway, and it seemed to control me. I know now that I was angry and hurt, and had not recovered from Hollywood's assault on my mind, and from the lost and broken relationships. The whole thing did something to me, and twisted me. I wanted to react as most of the people I knew and hung out with, but I was sensitive, super-reacting to the world around me. Everybody else did not seem bothered by it. I wondered why no one that I hung around with questioned why they were Black, who they were, or why the world worked the way it did. I felt as if the world around me was on fire, and its fumes were smothering me. My mother repeatedly told me that she had her education, and if I wanted to get mine, I would have to work for it.

My father never knew about most of the things, which I did because my mother would not tell him. She knew he would beat me bad, so she saved me from his sting many times. She did threaten me and say, "Buddy, I'm going to tell your father about you." I at no time took her seriously because she usually never told him. She watched my father beat me and my sister Janice with his razor strap, and felt sorry for us. Once she had to stop him because he accidentally hit my sister Janice in her face with the belt. He was so engaged in tearing her hefty frame up that he didn't realize it. My mother got between them and said, "No more, Wilbert!" It was rare when my mother could stop him from doing anything. When he chastised, it was without mercy. So either he would tell us to get the hell out of his face, or he would say, "Go get my razor strap." Sometimes he would get angry at my mother for what appeared to me to be something pointless. My grandmother, in her wisdom, tried to warn my mother about my father when they were dating. My mother never told me what my grandmother said to her about him. My mother followed her heart, and married my father. I guess that's what we're supposed to do in this life. Whatever my mother received from my father, in a sense, was hers to bear, because she "fixed her own bed" and was lying in it. Whenever he got angry, he accused her of doing something against him. If she was not kind to him, I didn't see it. I believed she was a victim of his mental cruelty. I never understood why he treated my mother this way. I know that he was angry and sometimes in a rage. Nevertheless, I believe that he truly loved my mother.

Many black men swallow a bitter pill in order to provide for their families, because of added pressure of dealing with the system. The system does not encourage our survival. Sometimes my father talked to me about how some people were no good. He still wouldn't talk to me about his family. He would, however, speak of his sister in a warm and passionate way. I'm sure she was his favorite because when I asked him about her, he never frowned or cursed.

He didn't talk about his paralyzed leg. I at no time saw him cry, and I think he was the strongest man, whom I knew. He worked long hours in his barbershop that was doing well. I was getting to the point of not wanting him at home, so we could have more peace. A few times, I saw him in such an uncontrollable anger and rage that he took his brown cane in order to strike my mother, and each time she would grab a big black iron frying pan and would tell him to come on and hit her, and she would tear his head up. Though my mother was short, she stood tall emotionally when my father backed her against a wall. I never saw him take her upon her offer. He would stand motionless, breathing hard, with his eyes fixed on her. I'd look at him frightened, and stare at him while he contemplated his move. I hated when he was this way, but I loved my father. When the eye game was over, he would put his stick down and walk away. He was so predictable after a crisis, no matter how bad it was. When he came home from work, he tried to compensate for his behavior. He brought us Chinese food, ice cream or chocolate candy, and on occasion, flowers to my mother. I loved my father, and though I believed our house at times was more peaceful without him; I wanted him by our side.

Raymond

In the summer of 1960, I joined the Boy Scouts of America. Raymond Scott became a major player in my life. He became my role model. Raymond loved kids and was the only adult I knew who played with us on our level. He graduated from Fort Hamilton High School in Brooklyn. From the first time, I met him as a Cub Scout, Raymond worked at least two jobs. He loved electronic things such as short-wave radios and stereo component sets. Swimming and bicycling were his two favorite sports. He could swim like a fish, and you would have believed he had been born on a bicycle. He had a bike made of aluminum, and I could pick it up with one hand. It had ten speeds, which was a big thing in 1960. It had a "Compenolla" gear changer which was one of the best made. Once, Raymond rode his bike to Philadelphia, Pennsylvania from Brooklyn, New York. He took some of us on a bike trip to a Boy Scout camp to Alpine, New Jersey. We rode over the Brooklyn Bridge to lower Manhattan, New York, past Central Park, through Harlem, across the George Washington Bridge, then ten miles to the camp. It was great until we had to ride back to Brooklyn. Half of us struggled to make it, but Raymond and his light-frame bike eased on home. It wasn't only his bike that gave him an edge over us. It was those strong muscles in his skinny legs. Raymond had a way of teasing us when he knew he had challenged us. We struggled to meet the challenge, and he won. He would start laughing and telling us that we were tough and "out of sight" (that we were very good). It was his way of embracing us and giving his approval. Approval from Raymond was important. We wanted him to be proud of us.

The first camping trip that I had with him is still fresh in my mind. I made some new friends, which included Clinton, Randy, Butch, Sam, Abney and Philip. Each week we met and had our Scout meeting. Steven was in my sixth-grade class. Though his father split us up because of my cursing when we were younger, his father allowed him to be a friend with me again.

My language had improved, and my mother didn't have to use Ivory soap to wash my mouth anymore. I decided to change my attitude in sixth grade. I was embarrassed over having to repeat the fifth grade, and now and then Ronald reminded me how stupid I was. I hated him with a passion, and I wanted to hurt him.

I admired and was jealous of a class that had academically gifted kids in it. They were some smart kids, and the teachers and faculties were noticing them. I wanted to be recognized as they were, but I had not done anything academically exceptional to earn it. My mother told me in many ways that I could be special as those kids, but I never took her seriously. I believed that I didn't have what it took to be special at anything. I was determined to change the course of my life.

Steven was also an encouragement to me, for although he liked to have fun, he was a good student, and I admired him and his handwriting. On our first math test, I struggled with it because I didn't know my time tables and counted on my fingers. I didn't have enough fingers or toes to do the computations, and I was doing terribly. Division was a block in my mind. I just couldn't do the stuff. My parents asked a friend of theirs to come to the house and help me. That man was so frustrated trying to help me understand the simple rules of division that he had to take coffee breaks and smoke tons of cigarettes. Week after week, he tutored me free of charge until I was finally able to do the problems alone. Learning fractions was another part of math with which I had trouble. I didn't understand proportions. I hated math because I couldn't count fast enough in order to do as well as my classmates.

I enjoyed being with my friends. It was a serious break from my studies. When I was with them, I concentrated on having fun and tried not to think about school. Ronald was still teasing me. I wanted to fight him. Nevertheless, I knew that I couldn't beat him, unless I first kicked him between his legs, but then I would have been considered a punk. If it didn't kill him, he would only knock me down and stomp on me another time. I knew that my day would come. I would hurt him, and I looked forward to it.

Boy scouting was exciting. Raymond took a special liking to me. Raymond was in his twenties and lived at home with his mother. Many Scouts didn't know it, but Raymond was having problems at home. His mother, Angelina, was a strong devout born-again Christian, who lived by the rules and teachings of the Holy Bible. She wouldn't even allow Raymond to play checkers in his bedroom. Once I was in their apartment in Red Hook. She nagged him so much that he in frustration hurled the checker board (with the checkers in their respective places) against the wall. His mother had a way of riding him when she believed he was in error. She didn't mean any harm to him. She loved Raymond. Raymond disciplined himself around his mother and always tried to respect her, so Raymond surprised and shocked me when he did that with the checkers.

He realized that I had an inferiority complex. He never let me get away with displaying fear, anxiety, or rage without confronting me. When I was frustrated and creating an atmosphere of confusion, Raymond would stare at me until I noticed him and say, "What's wrong with you, bonehead?" He made me laugh, and then he would deal with me and make my problem look petty. I loved airplanes, and Raymond liked to tease me about my attachment to them. Anytime an aircraft flew above me; I looked at the sky, and Raymond would motion to whoever was around to notice me. He frequently took me and other boys to Kennedy International Airport to watch the planes take off and land. He always tried to elevate me above my inferiority complex and fears. I did not completely know what it was that made me feel inferior to others. I didn't understand it.

Though Raymond had problems, he always found time for us guys, and we soaked it in like a sponge. When Raymond wasn't with us, he was riding that bike of his or swimming. He spoke with Steven, Butch and me about buying new bicycles with four speeds. Each week he took us to a bicycle store near Coney Island Amusement Park that had many bicycles. An Italian guy who was very pleasant with us owned the store. Raymond acted as if he were a friend with him, but Raymond wasn't a friend with him; he just had a respectful attitude and took care of business well. We paid money on three brand new blue four-speed bikes. My parents gave me money each week to pay down on my bike. After many weeks, we had our bikes, and it was a good feeling being one of three boys in Red Hook with four-speed bikes.

One day Raymond was fixing a boy's bike when I was trying to fix my front brake. I asked him for help, and he told me to wait. I acted out my frustration, grumbling and panting to myself, and Raymond called me a "bonehead" and asked me to wait. I was agitated and accidentally broke my brake cable in frustration trying to fix it. When Raymond realized what, I had done, he didn't get upset. He looked at me and said, "That's what you get for being a bonehead." I wanted to curse him out. He didn't help me that day, and I was angry. It was a day I will not forget, because Raymond taught me a lesson in patience. I was a member of the Drum and Bugle Corps, and Raymond taught me the basic rudiments of drumming. Though I wasn't as good as the other boys playing, I had a spot to play. He also tried to teach me how to fence, but I would get angry because I couldn't tag him with my foil. So I quickly gave it up without a fight, but never stopped admiring how graceful Raymond looked when he fenced. He took a group of us to Washington, D.C., including my friend Randy. Randy was my neighbor and I especially liked him because he made me laugh a lot. He enjoyed cracking jokes about almost anything. Raymond piled us into his Plymouth car that had push-button controls. We rode the New Jersey Turnpike to Delaware, then Baltimore, and into Washington, D.C. He even pushed that Plymouth to one hundred miles per hour.

I liked Washington, D.C. I marveled at the Lincoln Memorial and Washington Monument. My favorite site was the United States Capitol building, where we rode the underground train. When I returned home, everyone had an earful about my trip.

Raymond continued to do many things with my friends and me. My most exciting time with him in the Boy Scouts was when he took me to an old armory in Harlem, where he was responsible for the artillery room. I saw huge bullets and mortar shells. He even let me hold and play with a walked-talkie.

Bothering my Neighbors

I had a mean streak in me. When I felt things had gotten too orderly in our courtyard, I devised ways to disturb people without their ever knowing I was doing it. If my neighbors were sitting on the benches having a good time, laughing and discussing everyday life after dark, I would sneak into the building (which was six stories high), go up on the roof, and throw gravel onto them. They would jump up hollering and cursing about being hit with gravel. Someone would usually say, "Who the hell is throwing that gravel again?" I made a match launcher out of a thread spool with rubber bands. While sitting on my bed, I would set up my attack, then kneel at the window ledge where no one could see me, and take straight wooden matches and launch them against the red-brick building. The matches would burst into flames. People would be jumping. A few times I heard someone say, "That's that Buddy again," and I would burst with laughter. I never got tired of surprising my neighbors, but when I ran out of matches or my hands hurt from picking up so many rocks, I'd quit. This was my little secret, and I never let on to any grownup what I did to disturb them at night.

Chapter 5

Challenges

Yea the darkness hides not from thee; but the night shines
Like the day, the darkness and the light are both alike to thee.

Psalm 139:12

I tried to overcome my math problem in school and stop counting on my fingers, but I continued to struggle with it. I knew that I was as smart as anyone was in my class. It bothered me being thought of as stupid or dumb. In the fifth grade, it never mattered because it drew attention. Now I was tired of being looked down upon academically. I had to show my friends and Ronald that I was just as good as they were in school. Throughout my sixth grade, my performance was marginal and my writing and reading skills were below average; math was never mastered and I still didn't know the time's table. However, they promoted me to the seventh grade and sent me to Junior High School 142.

Junior High School 142 was not located in Red Hook projects. It was across a highway that separates Red Hook from an Italian neighborhood, in Carroll Gardens. Most of the homes in that area were brownstones. No Blacks or Hispanics were living there that I was aware of. Racial prejudice was definitely a part of the neighborhoods make up. The Baptist church that I attended was all Black, and it was in that neighborhood. We constantly had problems with some residents. A few times, I saw references to us as "niggers," telling us to get out of the neighborhood, written on the ground in front of our church. I recall a couple of times when they got more aggressive. They put a dead dog at the front gate. Another time a dead fish was placed on the steps. I didn't like going into that neighborhood even when I attended a church service, because of the way some people looked at me. I never looked at anyone straight in their face. I was too scared.

Camping

The summer of 1961, I went away to camp with the Boy Scouts. We went to Pauling, New York to a camp called Sanita Hills Boy Scout Camp. It was for three weeks; the longest camping trip we ever took. My friends, Butch, Sam, Clinton, Steven, and Philip went also. In the first few days at camp, Steven got hurt on his bicycle and had to go to the hospital. His parents came for him and took him home. Clinton got homesick after a few days and decided to call his parents to pick him up. I remember watching him look out of his father's car through the rear window. I was upset with him because he wouldn't stick it out like a tough Scout, and secondly because he was smiling, and really I wanted to go with him.

That trip started with a bang. First, a Scout, named Estrada, stomped a big bullfrog to death for no apparent reason except to watch its brown gut come out. Raymond was very upset. He didn't believe that it was necessary, and it was done in the cabin. A few days later a guy named Johnny found some baby rabbits in the woods and neither him, nor Raymond would let any of us play with them. Seeing all the wild animals was fascinating because Red Hook only had a few squirrels and some pigeons, and a few stray dogs here and there.

A mile-wide lake was in the center of the camp. Some older Scouts were going to do a mile swim, including our scoutmaster, Raymond. They told me from the beginning that they excluded me and had me take a swim test in order to get into a canoe or a rowboat. I took the test and passed.

One morning I got up early while most of the other Scouts were sleeping and walked around the camp, as I marveled at the beauty of the woods. We had our regular Boy Scouts' duties and tests for our merit badges. I didn't like going through all the details for the awards, but I did earn three little round colorful patches on my sash: the cooking, swimming, and hiking merit badges. Raymond encouraged me and looked forward to the day I would even become an Eagle Scout. One day Butch and I went down to the lake and saw some Scouts boating, and we threw rocks at them. The word got back to Raymond. He summoned us into the cabin. "What is the matter with you two guys?" Don't you know you could have hurt someone with those rocks?"

Butch said, "Yeah, thanks, Buddy, to your big ideas."

"Hey Butch," I said, "It wasn't only my idea."

Raymond said, "You two boneheads are going to do kitchen duty."

"We have to do duty for a whole week? Hey Raymond," I said, "That isn't fair."

"Was it fair when you guys decided to throw rocks?" he replied.

For a week, we did kitchen duty. We didn't do it without mouthing off. We had to wait until all the other Scouts went to the lake, before we could check out a canoe or rowboat.

The following week Raymond had to discipline me strongly. He was playing with me, put a big roach in a plastic bag, and dangled it in my face. I was afraid of insects, and he knew it. I cursed him out and said something bad about his mother. I don't know why I said anything about his mother, but he went into a rage and grabbed my T-shirt collar and got close to my face with his, and literally told me that he would waste me if I ever said anything about his mother again. I was frightened to death because Raymond never spoke to me that way. I knew I had pushed his panic button. He pushed me around a bit and pinned me against the sleep bunk, then he let me go. He told me to never say anything negative about his mother again. It was a day that I would never forget. I respected and loved Raymond. The most memorable thing about my camping trip was going to the lake alone with a fishing pole and some bread to catch fish. I stayed on the lake for hours. I enjoyed putting soggy bread on the hook. I would throw the line into the water and wait until the little round red, and white float went under. When a fish was hooked, I would become excited. Most of the times I caught small fish and threw them back into the lake.

When we arrived back in Red Hook, I went to the swimming pool to show off on the ten foot-high board and look at the girls in their bathing suits. Not much more happened that summer, but I was grateful to Raymond for taking me away from Red Hook in order to enjoy a different kind of life. I wished that I could have taken Ronald to camp and left him there with all the other animals. Ronald was still showing me his ugly face and teasing me about going into a dumb class. Ronald was intelligent, but that didn't give him the right to make me feel small. He was my nightmare in living color. He was an evil kid.

As usual, my parents bought brand new clothes for my sister and me to attend school. On the first day in seventh grade, I wore sharkskin pants, pointed-tip shoes and a knit sweater. I was not interested in entering one of the dumbest classes in the school, and I didn't want to go. When I arrived,

Ronald was in the schoolyard smiling at me. He didn't say a word, and he knew that I could read his mind. He was calling me stupid, with that smile. My courses were basic. They were not challenging, and I did my share of not paying attention in class. Although I liked science, I had difficulty remembering facts. Math wasn't much better than it was in the sixth grade because I was still counting on my fingers. After years of being harassed by Ronald, he convinced me that I was not intelligent. I felt foolish. I didn't know how to handle having low self-esteem, an inferiority complex and feeling unintelligent I could not boast of good grades in school, and it reinforced in me a belief that I was dumb. No one ever told me I was intelligent, so I had no reason to believe that I was. My defense against the negative feelings of Ronald was to plot to hurt him any way I could. It was a difficult time for me emotionally. It was the first time that I had to struggle with me; I felt like I was losing. I wanted to go somewhere and hide. On weekends, I got bored and left Red Hook, even if it were only for a couple of hours. Most times, I went to downtown Brooklyn, where the big stores were, in order to look in the electronic store windows at the walk-talkies and cameras. On occasion, I went to 42nd Street, and walked to 59th Street at Central Park, looking in store windows.

Hate and Murder

I didn't know that the United States was in racial turmoil. Blacks all over the country were demanding equal rights and protection of the law. Horrible crimes were committed against many black people in the South and in the North. Red Hook was in some ways a protective zone where I didn't have to worry about my life being threatened by hateful, racist people. I began listening to the news on TV and reading the newspapers. It was 1961; however, in 1955, on August 28, Emmett Till, a 14-year-old black boy from Chicago, Illinois, was murdered in Mississippi. People were shocked, knowing that the United States did not protect children from hate crimes. In 1960, John Fitzgerald Kennedy became president of the United States. Many Blacks thought that it would change the climate of racial prejudice and hatred in America. It didn't. It made things worse. The President had his hands loaded with the whole mess. He was expected to pass the Civil Rights Bill in order to help black people gain their rights in the United States. The First Civil Rights Bill to pass through Congress since 1875 occurred on August 29, 1957. It would be a challenge for Kennedy to convince Congress to pass another. People were suffering because of racism. The Passing of The Civil Rights Bill was critical. In some places in the South, people still didn't have the right to vote.

Martin Luther King, Jr. was putting the heat on President Kennedy to pass another Civil Rights Bill, and the President was dragging his feet. King, a pioneer of the civil rights movement, was caught in the midst of its early violence. His home was bombed on January 30, 1956 in Alabama. An organization called the White Citizens Council used its racial strong arm against him and his family for exercising their rights to protest injustice in America. In 1954, the Brown versus the Board of Education decision was passed, which overruled the "separate but equal" laws in school segregation. Only one school in Texas and two schools in Arkansas complied. In the rest of the South, not one classroom was racially mixed.

Daisy Bates, who was president of the NAACP in Little Rock, Arkansas, fought in the struggle to have integration fully started in the United States schools in the South. In her book, The Long Shadow of Little Rock, she recounts the night that a stone was thrown through her living room window and said, "I threw myself to the floor. The glass covered me. I reached for the rock lying in the middle of the floor. They tied a note to it. I cut the string and unfolded the soiled piece of paper. Scrawled in bold print were the words: "Stone this time, dynamite next." On September 23, 1957, nine black students called the "Little Rock Nine" gathered at Daisy Bates house in order to integrate Little Rock's Central High School. Shortly after, they notified Daisy's family that at 8:00 a.m., police would escort the nine students to school. Four Black journalists waited at the school. Someone had a brick in his hand, and he hit reporter Alex Wilson on the side of his head. Wilson was more than six feet tall and an ex-Marine, but he went down like a tree. Time magazine reported, "A cop stood on a car bumper to get a better view of the fighting."

The South had boycotts. Blacks were demanding what was their right to have, the same opportunities as any other United States citizen. Blacks were denied equal protection guaranteed under the United States Constitution by local laws. The right to vote became a part of the agenda.

If anyone had tried to hold a discussion with me on racism and Blacks in America, I would not have known where to start or end my views. Being a Black boy in Brooklyn, New York did not make me any less a target for racism, it just came in a concealed package. As for me, I was a Black boy growing up in a racist country. I didn't know that since racism existed that it would have a hold on me. As a Black person, I did not know how I fit within the scheme of things.

It was during the time in my life, when I was thirteen years old; I focused in on the race question. I hated that race and color permeated my life.

I had two black teachers who taught me; one was my band teacher, and the other one was my typing teacher.

The following year I told my mother that I wanted to be placed in a more demanding class. She went into the school and demanded that they give me courses that were more stimulating. They transferred me. I couldn't believe my mother pulled it off. I was in science class learning about jet engines, electricity, and animal kingdoms. My English teacher had us reading Walt Whitman, Robert Frost, poetry, and writing essays.

Most of the people in my class were smart. One guy named Douney sat next to me almost every day and counted down to the second when the period bell would ring. He was bright and played basketball well. I admired him because he was always pleasant to me and liked to laugh. He would enter a basketball game, calmly walk onto the court, and score high points, and it never seemed to go to his head.

I joined the school band and learned to play the clarinet. I didn't like playing the clarinet because it looked stupid to me. I only did it because I wanted to go home with an instrument. I really wanted to blow a trumpet, but they did not offer it to me, and they had no empty spots. My friend Herman played it, and I admired him.

My interest in education and learning became short-lived, and I did the least requirements. It wasn't because I didn't like school, I was bored. I was placed on the last clarinet row. Sometimes I would miss notes and just fake it. I did the same thing in typing class. We had to memorize the keys. I didn't. Each time the teacher told me not to look at the keys I did and never learned to type. I hated typing. The only enjoyable thing about my typing class was my teacher, who was a pretty woman. I loved when she came to my desk in order to help me because she smelled sweet and had attractive hands with red nail polish on her fingernails.

Slam-Dunk Time

I became a regular at the Police Athletic League Center and ironically; I felt very insecure being there, because every night while the guys played basketball, the girls were their greatest audience, and I didn't know how to play. These guys were working up sweats and sporting their jockstrap strings above their shorts, looking sexy and heroic. People cheered after hoops were shot with accuracy or someone slam-dunked a ball. Only a few guys could go that high to slam it in, and Downey was one. Guys like Clinton and Myra, who were brothers, who were also good-looking, were favorites. Lawrence Hannahan was the shortest one on the team, but he survived. Often people poked fun at his height, but it didn't seem to bother him.

I was still in the Boy Scouts, and I was hearing comments about tin soldiers (Boy Scouts). It didn't bother me until it became aggressive. I'd have on my uniform, and someone would yell out, "Look at the tin soldier." At first, I didn't understand what it meant, until they called me a punk a few times in relation to it. The Boy Scouts was considered in my neighborhood by a few Red Hook bad guys a "sissy" organization, full of punks.

I kept leaving Red Hook when I was bored or felt like I was missing something. I made a ritual of going to automobile and air shows. Airplanes and helicopters fascinated me. Once, I bet my friends Butch and Sam that I could beat them to Kennedy International Airport traveling by helicopter, and they would travel by the subway train. I had to catch the train from Red Hook to lower Manhattan, and then get into the helicopter at a heliport. I could fly in the helicopter because my parents gave me the money. My parents knew that I loved airplanes and helicopters. I beat them by one-half-hour. Flying in that helicopter was greater than beating them at the bet. I did things like that, and my friends dared not follow me. Ever since, I can remember, whenever my parents gave me, some rope to venture out of Red Hook, I pushed my limits. Sometimes I just went into a museum and would spend half a day there. If I had enough energy, and I usually did, I went to Central Park to visit the zoo.

I'm Not A Punk

I frequented the Police Athletic League. Hanging with Butch, Sam, and the Boy Scouts were a part of my activities. One night while at the Police Athletic League, a tough guy named Lacey, who was considered one of Red Hook's bad boys, kicked me. I was sitting on the gym floor watching a basketball game. He called me a punk and invited me to the boys' bathroom to fight. I hadn't fought anyone in at least two years, and I knew that he would beat me, but I said, "Let's go." As we were on our way out of the gym, a couple of his friends told him to forget it. He called me a "jive-punk," and walked away. I was thankful to his friends because I didn't believe I could beat Lacey. He was a good street fighter, and I never took well bleeding from my mouth or nose (I suffered nosebleeds when I was younger). I didn't want to lose any teeth and besides; it would hurt. Another guy named Willie grabbed me by the collar when I walked out of my building. While he tried to choke me to death, he asked me why I was messing with his woman. I told him that I wasn't, and his friends had to pull him off me. I was afraid of Willie because he was massive, had big muscles, and looked mean. I was grateful just to get away from him.

I could not understand why suddenly Red Hook's bad boys were troubling me, but they felt I was a punk tin soldier. So I figured I should change my image. I quit the Boy Scouts, went to my friends Butch and Sam, and told them I would not be hanging out with them anymore. Both stood motionless, looking at me. It wasn't that they were the source of my trouble with the Red Hook bad guys, but we clowned around a lot, and it drew too much attention. Butch said okay. That was it. The following morning, while I was going to school, Butch's Sister Gloria grabbed me by the collar and said, "Who the hell do you think you are?" "Do you think you're better than my brother?" I didn't say a word to her because she was much bigger than I was. From that day, on, Butch and Sam didn't speak with me or I with them. The decision to abandon my friends was difficult, but I didn't enjoy being thought of as silly anymore. Being a target for the Red Hook bad guy wasn't healthy.

My Sisters

My sister Janice was one of the craziest people whom I knew. She loved to laugh and joke. She could make some ugly faces and steal the hearts of even strangers around her. As my sister, however, she sometimes created confusion in my life. I'm not implying that I never gave her a reason in order to attack me, but sometimes she did it with a smile on her face. Out of all the people, I created hell with; I could unleash some wicked power on her, and I did it while loving her also.

When my mother was away at work, she would ask my sister Janice to cook for us. Janice had a favorite dish that she liked to fix; white potatoes, onions, and hot dogs. She would mix it together in a black frying pan, and some burned potatoes would stick to the bottom of it. She always made enough for us to eat. I would put ketchup all over mine until I hardly saw the stuff, and then thoroughly enjoy it. She made that potato mix often, and I developed an aversion to it. It was so bad that while it was cooking I got a slight headache. Nevertheless, what is a kid supposed to do when his sister says, "You better eat it, or else?" My sister Janice was special to me, and I loved her very much. She wasn't a perfect sister, and I was definitely a challenging brother.

Shelly

My sister Shelly never cared about much, except sitting around looking innocent. She was chubby and my father constantly spoke with my mother about her weight. My mother would mumble under her breath because she felt that he contributed to Shelly's heaviness. He constantly brought home sweets (chocolates) for us all, and he would parade the box before Shelly. She would behave shy and hesitate, knowing that my father would encourage her on until she took some. I watched my mother look seriously at him for pumping Shelly with candy. She knew that he would mention Shelly's weight in a negative way when he wanted to blame her for something.

I remember when Shelly was small; she sucked a baby bottle like it was going out of style. When she was about five years old, she was still sucking the thing. When she wasn't sucking it, she held it in her hand like a football. I think that she was afraid to put it down, thinking someone wanted to suck it or make a pass for it. Shelly was the only one in my house; I believed, who thought that I was a good boy. I always viewed her as being in need of my protection, maybe because she kept sucking that baby bottle.

I often fought with Janice, and sometimes they were punch, knock down, and get up fights. Once we were fighting over my not wanting to listen to her, and she beat me up. Doing it wasn't hard for her because she was muscular and much bigger than I was. Even when she walked, she looked strong because she bounced on her toes. I got angry because I couldn't win. Then it was snowing outside. I tied T-shirts around my feet and went out in the snow without a shirt on. I hollered and screamed at her from the ground level and refused to go upstairs; however, when my feet got cold enough, I did. I may have been stupid, but I wasn't crazy, even if my mother took me to a psychiatrist when she thought that I was.

I loved my two sisters. I was the only boy. My sister Janice got caught drinking alcohol in the girls' bathroom in school and got suspended for a few days. That was a big event in my house. It even overshadowed my stealing my father's money and my mother having taken me to a psychiatrist. I felt Janice was stupid for doing that, but especially for being caught. I was angry with her for her conduct, and I also felt sorry for her, because I knew that she was ashamed and hurt.

Shelly was still chubby and quiet. She remained the benign one in the house. My father was just as angry as ever. My mother was beginning to fight back the tears and raise her voice at him. As for me, it was long overdue. I saw her pick up many plates of food and put it into the garbage, which he threw against the wall. I never heard him say he loved her. I felt more for my mother's emotional state than I did for my fathers. Although I didn't think that he had his life under control, everyone was afraid of him, and I felt he could take care of himself.

Chapter 6
Raw Life

If I say, surely the darkness shall cover me:
even the night shall be light about me.

Psalm 139:11

When the school year ended, I believed that I accomplished something; I knew how to play a clarinet. I passed all of my courses, but I didn't learn to type.

That summer I met a beautiful girl at the Red Hook pool. She had long wavy hair and a soft complexion. I saw her sitting on the concrete deck. She was leaning back on her hands, and her legs were crossed. I saw her often in Red Hook. She was sitting with a couple of girls, and I walked over to her. "Hello. I'm Buddy." She ignored me. I sat in front of her, and she smiled. I didn't know what to say so I talked about how enjoyable the pool water was. I saw her a few times, and we started dating. She was a Jehovah's Witness, and I didn't know her mother was going to ask me to become one. She told me that her mother wouldn't allow me to date her, unless I converted from being a Baptist to Jehovah Witness. When I failed to convert, her mother made her end our relationship. I didn't feel too bad about it because I realized I only liked her for the way she looked.

The girls whom I was curious in didn't seem to be interested in me. My neighbor Patty was attractive, but she too had no interest in me. Once I tried to kiss her. She stuffed her mouth full of potato chips, and then she opened it for me to see the slimy yellow stuff. That cooled me out. Then,

Donna was another girl who I felt was pretty, but she was more interested in guys with athletic ability and intelligence.

Clowning Around

I had another year before completing junior high school. They promoted me to class 9-5, and it was loaded with challenges for me. My teacher was a Black man who taught the school band and orchestra. Butch was in my class, which was not one of the best situations for either of us. We were in competition together for attention and we both made fools of ourselves. To top it off, 9-5 was not considered one of the smarter classes. The students in my class were not considered to have many academic promises. I had not proven that I was smart enough to be in a more challenging class. A guy in my class read at the third-grade level. My reading score was sixth grade, and I needed at least a seventh-grade level in order to get a diploma at graduation.

A quiet Puerto Rican girl in my class named Rosa had my attention. I took an immediate liking to her. Rosa could have cared less about me, but I made sure that she noticed me by teasing her about how beautiful she was. Butch was in competition with me for her attention. I clowned around a lot with Butch, and it irritated my teacher. Once before going home, with my books weighing heavy in my arms, my teacher stopped me. "Why don't you stop being a clown?" he said. He had a frustrated look on his face, and I felt he was embarrassed, being a Black teacher, seeing how terribly most of us black kids behaved. His words stung me because I knew that he was right. I did not respect him. He had a weak streak in him. I really wanted him to tell the whole lot of us to shut up and sit before he beat all our behinds. He never did and he paid for it, because one-third of us aggravated him.

My most exciting class was English. My teacher was in love with poetry, and she demanded that we memorize at least two hundred lines of poetry. I loved the poem "Oh Captain, My Captain," by Walt Whitman. I learned my lines well. I always did my homework, but did the average in class. I tried to get higher grades, but it just didn't happen. The problem was I couldn't read well. I could repeat the words on the page, but my comprehension of the information was slow. I had to read one page over about three times in order to get all the information and even then; my test scores were average. It was frustrating, and it angered me. When the film "West Side Story" came out, I caught a bus and went to Ridgewood

51

in Brooklyn to see it. I sat in the movie house all alone, mesmerized by Natalie Wood, who was, playing Maria, a Puerto Rican. My fantasy with Hollywood started again, but this time; I was old enough to understand it was a plaything. "West Side Story" had such a great impact on me that I visited the site where they filmed it. The writing in the street, "Jets," the name of the white gang, was still there in dull yellow paint. Then, I found the name "Sharks," the name of the Puerto Rican gang. When I saw Rosa at school, I started singing a song from the movie to her. When Butch realized that I was getting Rosa's attention, he butted in and robbed me of time with her. My teacher saw me in Rosa's face often, and this irritated him because besides my disrespect for him, I was not respecting others with my harassment. A few times, I tried to follow Rosa home, but was distracted by my friends. I didn't want them to know that I really liked Rosa. One day Rosa approached me and told me not to follow her around the class, and she wanted me to leave her alone. Because she said it with a smile, I didn't take her seriously. I continued to sing love songs to her in class, and she just smiled. One day Rosa caught me following her home. The next day she told me that her parents were very strict and not to follow her. I stop following her home, but never stopped singing to her or loving her.

Betty

Betty was the second girlfriend whom I had. It was love at first sight. Betty had the prettiest teeth that I ever saw and a smile to go with it. She reminded me of Dionne Warwick, the singer. I had to watch out, for when she didn't have a smile, she could be vicious. I don't really know what attracted us because we were as different as peas and rice. Our relationship was fine for a few weeks, and then she broke off with me because she said I was too childish. We went back together until she was aggravated with me and called it quits. Each time she vowed never to date me. The third time around Betty decided to renew our relationship because I literally begged her, but it was on her terms. Betty believed that I was not serious about her, and she asked me to grow up. After my split with my friends, I thought that I had grown up, but she had a different opinion. She told me that the relationship was going to be done her way, and if I didn't like it, it was too bad. I never did appreciate her gross arrogance, and this time was no exception. Nevertheless, I liked Betty, so I let her have her way. One day-after school, I said something that she didn't like; she scratched my arm, and some of my skin was under her long beautiful fingernails. I told her that if she scratched me again, I would cut them off with scissors. A few days later, she did it another time, and I chased her home after school. While she was running up the stairs, I was at the bottom, and she accused me of looking underneath her dress.

The following day I asked a boy in my class to put a note in her violin case asking if I could see her legs again. My home room teacher, Mr. Harris, who believed that I acted like a clown, was also my band teacher. He intercepted the note and sent me to the guidance counselor, Mr. Fitzpatrick.

Mr. Fitzpatrick was a stern Irish man who spoke bluntly. He said what he meant. "Wilbert," he said, "what do you think this girl would feel knowing you wrote a note like this and put it in her music case?" If you do not stop your foolishness, you're never going to see high school."

That was it for me; no high school for messing with Betty or any girl was crazy. I decided from that point I would never clown in school again. As the school year was nearing an end, I was allowed an opportunity to bring my reading score up to seventh-grade level. Each day I had to stay after school and read, read, read, and then answer questions about what I read. I worked at it very hard, and increased my reading score to seventh grade. I was informed that if I graduated to high school, I would get a diploma.

Betty and I called it quits for all time, but still stayed friends. Being only friends was better for both of us.

During my last week of school, one afternoon, I was with Betty. We stayed late getting some of our few remains for the school year from our classrooms. As we walked across the street from the school, Betty went ahead of me, turned the corner, and was out of my sight. Three white men called me to them. At first, I hesitated and when they realized it, they got verbally aggressive. One guy said, "Aren't you the guy, who's been starting trouble around here?"

"Come on, let's pull him into the hallway," another said. One grabbed me by my arm while the others coaxed him on. I told them that if they wanted to mess with someone, I would get someone to mess with them. One of them took a bucket of dirty water from a car wash and tossed it on me. He told me to walk straight and don't say a word, or they would bust my head open. I was frightened.

I went to a gang member of the "Kovons" in Red Hook and told him that these three men messed me up. He said, "Man, if you were one of us, we'd fight for you, but you aren't one of us." Being Black, I felt like one of them, but they didn't consider me a part of their family. I found out later that those three men belonged to a gang of five brothers called the "Sumner Brothers." That was the second incident that happened during my life, which I believed, was racial.

Farewell

Graduation from junior high school was great. The graduation ceremony was in a movie theater in the Bay Ridge section of Brooklyn, not too far from 78th Street near 5th Avenue. The traditional graduation song almost made me cry. It was beautiful. The only award I got was for 100% attendance. I especially remember my friend Herman, who blew the trumpet in the school band with me. He looked so silly with his graduation hat on his head, tilted to the side. I will never forget the smile on his face.

Some of our parents decided to have a graduation dinner for us at the Police Athletic League Center. I remember how they arranged the food neatly on the tables. The record player was hooked up to large black speakers at the front of the room. The lights were dim, and we played 45-r.p.m. records. We were having a great time until one of Red Hook's deviant kids urinated at the open window where the food was. To this day, I forget what happened to the food on the table. We had to close the windows for the rest of the party. Closing the windows didn't disturb us. We continued the graduation party until late in the evening. I had a chance to dance with some girls who wouldn't give me the time of day during my three years at Junior High School 142. My mother had her first glance at watching me dance. When the party was over, I felt a bit sad. I knew that my life was moving in a different direction, and I was going to enter a new world. I hugged some of my classmates and bid them farewell, and told some; I would see them later.

Going South

I enjoyed my summer before high school. I went to Virginia with my friend Clinton with his brother, father and mother to visit his grandmother on her farm. The drive from New York seemed endless. It was 1963, and finding a place to rest in a motel was not easy for Blacks. We drove straight through, only stopping to get gas. We even parked on the Chesapeake Bay

Bridge to eat fried chicken, potato salad, and collard greens that Clinton's mother cooked.

Clinton was learning how to drive. His father allowed him to take the wheel, and he drove the car well. I sat in the back seat, envious of what was going on. I was thinking that my father could have done the same thing with me if he wanted. He still refused to learn to drive. He wasn't going to buy us a car, no matter how much money he had; and he wasn't cheap. Maybe it was the Polio, or he didn't believe that we needed one. Nevertheless, he wouldn't buy one.

I enjoyed staying on that farm eating fresh corn, collard greens, corn bread and fried chicken. We stayed in his grandmother's house. When I stood on the porch, I looked out and saw a huge field, and my heart was beating fast. I was excited, and I didn't know why. I believe it was my fascination with open space and nature. I thought, "You're going to have one of these one day." Clinton's grandmother looked just like his mother. She was pleasant to me and welcomed me into her beautiful home.

My mind shifted to Ronald. I was more than 300 miles from Brooklyn, New York where he was. I had my thoughts on a BB gun to shoot him. BB guns were illegal in New York City. I decided to break the law and finally finish him off after six full years of total harassment. He was still bothering me, and I wanted to light him up with a few pieces of metal. I went into a hardware store and purchased a high-powered CO_2 cartridge pistol that was semiautomatic. I tucked it into my luggage and checked it every day to see if it was still there.

When I arrived home, I secretly hid my gun away, in my closet. All I needed was the trouble maker, Ronald, to walk down the path of my line of fire.

That summer of 1963, I reflected in my life and how dissatisfied I was with myself. I realized how much precious time I had wasted in school, and I believed I did not learn anything. I was still counting on my fingers. I felt inferior to my peers. Giving up my friends Butch and Sam didn't help me to feel any better. I had no new friends at the time. Being Black was tough. Hollywood did not help. Knowing I was confused about my place throughout the world made me feel terrible. Everything my father said to me about racism, and racial prejudice had raised its ugly head. I was hurting.

No Where to Hide

Racial prejudice in America was at a high in 1962. The Federal District Court ordered the University of Mississippi to admit its first black student; James Meredith. Within the next three weeks, a riot broke out and some people died, while hosts of others were injured. Racial hatred was really brewing all over the country, and race caught black people in the middle.

It was August 28, 1963. I graduated from Junior High School 142. The civil rights movement was on the line. America had to deal with the complaints of Blacks who believed not enough was being done to protect them against hatred, bigotry and injustice. Martin Luther King Jr. led the March on Washington, D.C. It was one of the historical events to take place in America where Blacks and whites rallied for freedom and justice in America. I didn't fully understand how this event would shape my life. Nevertheless, the marches on Washington became a major event in my life, and I would join in the civil rights movement in America.

Choices

I had the choice of entering one of two high schools. Boys High School, or John Jay High School, and it was dangerous for Black students at John Jay High. A Black guy named Stanton was beaten badly at the school. He was admitted into the hospital. It was in my best interest to attend Boys' High School, which was predominantly Black. I didn't want to be there. I felt stigmatized going to school with mostly black students. I hated that my color became a major issue to others and me. I wanted to forget the color thing, and it refused to go away. My second challenge was surviving the train ride miles from Red Hook into a tough black neighborhood called "Bedford Stuyvesant." The school had two gangs: One from Red Hook, the "Kovons," and another from a housing project called the Marcy project, the "Buccaneers." Butch and Sam went to other schools that were trade schools. Philip went to Aviation High School, and Clinton went to Eli Whitney High School. Steven also entered Boys' High School and was placed at the annex building, which was a couple of miles from where I was. My first week at school was uneventful. The school had a reputation for fighting, but I didn't see any fighting. The school had a great athletic program; especially track, football and basketball. I could have cared less because I wasn't efficient at sports or sports-minded. Boys High's offered college-preparatory studies. I entered its academic program, and my first challenge was Algebra. It was like a foreign language to me. I failed every test that I took. I liked Art and hated American History with a passion because I didn't like memorizing all the dates of events in history. I enjoyed Biology but found it hard memorizing animal kingdoms and families, etc. The written tests were all challenging to me. When the first semester was over, I failed Algebra, and I did average work in my other courses.

Ronald was attending Boys High School. He still harassed me and called me stupid. It was very painful for me. Ronald was determined to hurt me. One day he embarrassed me in English class by challenging me on the word "bison," which I pronounced incorrect. Though it was a simple word, I had never seen it before. He laughed aloud at me and pronounced the word correctly. My struggle to pass basic Algebra, and difficulty pronouncing words correctly at high school-level made me feel terrible.

School became an issue, and I started studying as if it were the only thing left on earth to do. I stopped other activities, but I joined the high school glee club. I took Algebra again; and barely passed it. A guy in Red Hook named Lenny Malloy, who was a whiz in math, took a liking to me, and he offered to tutor me. I spent late hours in the Red Hook Public Library studying with Lenny. He was very patient and compassionate with me. When the problems were difficult for me to figure out and my face started to twist in frustration, Lenny would encourage me to calm down and think.

I got accustomed to being at Boys High and sported its T-shirt and shorts proudly. I even put its book covers on all of my books. Boys High School had available the academic courses, which I needed to be prepared for college. Though I was struggling through my courses, I was excited about taking them.

I saw Steven infrequently. He was taking a general course of study. I didn't understand why Steven took that road because I believed that he was much brighter than I was. I still admired Steven because I knew he was taking school seriously.

Anna

I didn't have any close friends. I didn't even have a girlfriend. I liked a girl who lived in my building; her name was Anna. She was a Puerto Rican, and she was almost as dark as I was. I admired her from the first day that she moved in. She had long brown hair, and she smiled a lot. She never said much to me. We were in the Drum and Bugle Corps together, and that's where I got close with her. After a competition event, we sat in the bus next to each other on the return trip home. Within a couple of weeks we were dating, and I liked her a lot.

Her mother was not happy about the relationship because I was a Black. I did not understand what her mother's problem was because her mother was just as black as I was. Once her mother referred to me by the Spanish word "negro," and had a terrible look upon her face when she said it. I knew that she had not read my birth certificate, so I wondered how she knew that they called me a "Negro" when I was born. I understood from her daughter that she was calling me "a Black." Anna afterward told me that her mother didn't want her around me. We continued to see each other without her mother knowing. Anna added excitement to my life on a social level, and she made me feel good.

My relationship with Anna ended because her mother separated us. That was another bittersweet relationship that ended in rejection.

My High School Heroes

My friend Alberta was smart, attractive and witty. She loved to laugh and crack jokes. She got tired of hearing me telling people how terrible I was doing in school. She took notice of the way I spoke about myself and couldn't stomach it anymore. One day she asked me to improve on my vocabulary and that, she would help me. She suggested a book for me to read, which had all these big words in it, and she spent many hours tutoring me. She told me that I needed to have greater confidence in myself and constantly badgered me about my low self-esteem. She also kept me laughing, while she joked. Her laughing and joking were healing for me.

Depression had become a norm with me because no matter how well I did in school; my grades were never better than my peers were, and Ronald continued to harass me.

I admired a guy named Raymond Frost. He was excelling academically and socially, and the girls liked him. Once a guy named Meredith was taunting him, teasing him about his deceased brother, a Harvard University student, who died in a boating accident. I went home with Raymond. He didn't say a word all the way. He put on his dirty sneakers, went back to that guy, and beat him down. Raymond took his time punching him in his face, but my true admiration for Raymond was his coolness and his "smarts" in school.

I also admired William Emerson, who was a whiz in Chemistry. I could not figure William out for he hardly ever studied and still got A's and B's on Chemistry tests. I was studying hard and struggling through Chemistry. While riding the subway train to school, William would go over some chemistry questions with me between stops. I liked William because he was serious and didn't take well to foolishness.

Ronald was still around and very intelligent. I even admired his gray matter, but he was still evil. Most of my peers were intelligent, and I never believed I belonged in their academic circle. I settled one issue in my mind. I would never be as smart as they would academically no matter how hard I tried.

My Friend Randy

Randy became my new friend. He was big for his age, but had muscles in the right places. He loved playing football. I could never understand how he played that brutal game without getting all beat up. Randy encouraged me because he was respectful of me even when he joked about me, and he was kind. Eric, his brother, was much younger than I was, and Randy was very affectionate with him. Their mother Norma was just as loving with both, and she was kind to me. Sometimes I sat and talked with her for hours and unloaded all my problems, and she patiently listened and responded to me. Randy, was the perfect son; very obedient to his mother. I liked being with him because he always had a good joke to crack or laugh, a lot like Alberta.

One day we decided to horseback ride in Central Park in mid-Manhattan. Neither of us had ever been on a horse's back before. Randy's horse was skittish and kept doing the "inner-city waltz" in the streets of Manhattan, and my horse seemed to know exactly where I wanted him to go. While we were crossing Eight Avenue in heavy traffic, Randy's horse threw him in front of a yellow taxi cab. I laughed so hard that I almost fell from my horse. To make Randy's life more complicated, the horse ran back to the stable blocks away. We finally did meet in Central Park and otherwise thoroughly enjoyed ourselves.

Randy's mother wouldn't let him hang out with the guys staying up late hours. She tried her best to help him stay out of trouble, and it worked. I never remember Randy getting into any kind of trouble. I didn't know anyone who didn't like him. Sometimes he would stand around the guys and just keep people laughing. He had a way of rewording a story about some Boy Scout experience or something that happened within the neighborhood. People would stop what they were talking about to listen to him. His mother had him in a Catholic school. I liked Randy and always will. I am grateful to his mother for her affection with me and for listening to my problems patiently. I also respect her for the way she raised Randy and Eric. She was a great mother to them, and I watched them respect her and give her love and affection.

Loving Mrs. Grudinsky

My home room teacher, Mrs. Grudinsky, continued to expose me and the guys in the singing group to all forms of music, and I became fond of her. She took us to Broadway plays and music concerts in mid-Manhattan, New York. I studied Beethoven, Bach, Aaron Copeland, and a host of others.

I fell in love with Mrs. Grudinsky. She may have reminded me of my fourth-grade teacher, Mrs. Aronawitz, with whom I was still in love; by the way, both were Jewish. A student told me that she was dating a Black man, and this indicated to me that she didn't have any hang-ups about Blacks. I fantasized being with her. I played up to her, but she never gave me any special attention above the other guys. I told my mother about her, and she cautioned me about my romantic thoughts. Once Mrs. Grudinsky invited the singing group to her house, and I went. This was the closest I ever got to her.

The All-City High School Chorus

The United States was engaged in the Vietnam War, and I started hearing about it in school, seeing it on television and reading about it in the newspapers. I had no idea what it was all about. We had a President, Kennedy, who had promised to help black people in America get their fair share of opportunities. He was young and full of energy, and the whole country seemed to like him. I marveled at the way he spoke and the things he said; especially about the New Frontier and reaching outer space. I became fascinated with rockets and astronauts.

Martin Luther King, Jr. didn't especially appreciate the fact that Kennedy was dragging his feet concerning passing a Civil Rights Bill.

60

Kennedy didn't feel it was the right time to push hard in that direction. Nevertheless, regardless of what was occurring on the high level with his administration and other areas of government in response to civil rights, I viewed the President as my hero and friend and felt intimacy in my acceptance of him.

On November 22, 1963, my friend and hero, President Kennedy was assassinated in Dallas, Texas while I was in the Boys' High School library learning to catalog books. When I heard the broadcast over the radio, I stood silent in one spot, not believing the report. Then I understood that black people in America had lost a vital player in the saga of racial prejudice and racism in my country. The man who federalized National Guard troops in Mississippi in order to ensure that James Meredith could enter the University of Mississippi safely on September 29, 1962, the same man who had met with civil rights leaders on June 20, 1963 about the March on Washington, was dead. He was gone forever. His death affected my life. I hurt because of his death.

After they buried John Fitzgerald Kennedy, I sent Jacqueline Kennedy a copy of Walt Whitman's poem, "Oh Captain, My Captain," which I had memorized in junior high school. I also sent letters to her in order to let her know that I cared deeply about her husband, and her loss. One evening while watching the news on TV, I heard a news reporter reciting "Oh Captain, My Captain" about the slain president. A few days later, I got a strange call. The person who called asked if I were Wilbert Williams Jr., and if I was a "Negro." I said, "Yes." The caller said okay, and hung up the telephone. I told my mother that I was sure someone from the White House called me. A few weeks later, I received a card from the White House with the slain president's wife's signature stamped on it. I expected her to write me in her handwriting, considering all the letters that I sent her. I guess that would have burdened her further in her sorrow, considering all the mail that she was receiving (and perhaps I was expecting too much).

Low Self-Image

I tried improving my social image. When my peers gave parties, I went, though I didn't know how to dance well. All I could do was stand on the floor, do the grind with a girl, and afterward pray that nobody saw my erection. Most of the time, I would sit in a chair or lean against a wall as I watched others display their dancing.

I tried basketball and ended up making a fool of myself. Raymond, Lawrence, Hannahan, William, Clinton and Myra played well, and I still admired their abilities on the basketball court. I was just as excited as the girls were watching them make baskets, and slam-dunk. The girls stood around cheering them on, and I wanted some of their attention. At the time, I didn't have a steady girlfriend, and I had not had any sexual relations with any girl. My friends knew it because I continued to talk about it. It wasn't that I was trying to impress anyone, but my firm religious belief had a profound influence on me.

Some of my peers had a good time laughing at me. So my chance to show my friends that I had something going for me was to enter my first basketball game in competition. They didn't even give me a basketball uniform like the other guys. When they put me in the game, I was shaking like a drunk, and my head was just as foggy. When they passed the ball to me, I shot it so hard at the rim that it passed the rim and shot cleanly over the backboard, and people roared in laughter. I felt like hiding. No one passed the ball to me again, and they pulled me from the game. When the guys played softball, I would sit around with the girls' watching. As for me, I was athletically inept, and this helped to destroy any confidence in which I could shine like the others. So I decided that my chance to excel was in academics, if I applied myself more. I knew that it would be difficult because even in scholastics, I lagged behind the others, but I was determined to excel in at least something.

Lydia

Lydia was the second girl after Anna to like me romantically. Lydia was Black and had West Indian roots, about which she never talked. One day I was at her apartment, and her mother showed me pictures when Lydia was younger and in show business. I never knew Lydia could dance professionally and understood that she was on "The Ed Sullivan Show." Lydia was kind to me. I enjoyed her company. The next fall I auditioned for the All-City High School Chorus in Manhattan, at Julia Richmond High School. Only the best voices were picked to represent New York's finest choir at Lincoln Center for The Performing Arts. They asked me to sing a portion of "Just a Song at Twilight." They rejected me. Mrs. Grudinsky told me not to worry about it and to try out again the following year. I wanted her to be proud of me, and I felt as if I failed her.

I was now doing well in Geometry, and I had an earth science course that I liked, but I still hated History. By the end of the semester, I did so well that I made the honor roll. My name was in big bold white letters on the Dean's list for six months. It had company in the names of Lenny Malloy, Raymond Frost, William Emerson, and Ronald. I felt proud to be at Boys High School, and the fact that I was on the honor roll gave me confidence in pursuing an academic course of study. Ronald was still in my life, and I still hated him even more than ever. I was frustrated because he wouldn't walk close enough to my bedroom window, so I could shoot him with my BB gun. Each time that he saw me, he would look at me and smile and say something insulting. I decided to forget him and concentrate on doing well in school. I felt that I could compete with him in my studies. I passed all my courses that year, but I was behind in math, so I had to go to summer school. I hated it, but fought the feeling and endured it. I soaked my peers of their knowledge, and focused on my goal to get an academic diploma that would allow me to attend a four-year college or a university. I realized that the key to success was remaining focused on my studies and goals, and not going to jail for "gorilla" Ronald. While most of my peers were concerned about being popular, I was studying my buns off.

During my third year in high school, I auditioned for the All-City High School Chorus again, and made it this time. I was proud of myself, and I knew that Mrs. Grudinsky would be happy. Each Saturday I caught the public train from Brooklyn to Manhattan and met hundreds of other students who sang very well. Every moment that I practiced added to myself-esteem. Sometimes some of us, while riding the train on our way home, would start singing the "Hallelujah Chorus." We knew that we were good because people took notice of us and encouraged us.

That year I became very religious and started taking my Bible to school in order to read it. When I took my test, I would pray to God to help me pass. A guy in my class named Kirk criticized me for doing so. He asked me if I really believed that God helped me to pass, and I told him yes. He laughed and said that he didn't think so. We constantly argued about God and His existence and presence in our lives, and I never stopped telling him that God was with me.

In the gym, we had a track suspended from the ceiling, and sometimes I would take my Bible up there and read it, all alone. That is where I argued and had my greatest discussions with God.

Racism Again

My history teacher planned a trip to Washington, D.C., and I waited anxiously for weeks to go. When we arrived outside the Washington hotel, some girls from the South occupied the hotel. Though there was space in the hotel, they would not let us check in. We had to check into an inferior quality hotel across the street until those girls checked out the following day. They told us that the management of the hotel refused us because they didn't want a bunch of Black guys in the same hotel with these white female students. That incident offended and hurt me. I tried to enjoy our trip after that, but it was hard. One day I got up early in the morning and took with me an 8mm movie camera, shooting almost every monument and flower garden in sight. I took a short walk behind the Capitol building and was shocked to see black people living in slums. I could not understand how they could be in the same district that legislated to improve the living conditions of all Americans. Here in the Capital state, Black people were living in poverty.

After my trip to Washington, D. C., I could not stomach my history teacher, because I believed he didn't protect us from those racist people in the hotel to which they refused us admittance. After I thought about his lack of protecting us, I felt that by him being Jewish he was probably considered no better than us and was just as vulnerable as we were to racism. After my involvement in the civil rights movement, I understood why they hated him as they did me. Jews were an integral part of the civil rights movement.

That summer I went to summer school in order to take History. I hated it just as much as I hated it during the school year. I suffered through the course and passed it. During my last year in high school, I concentrated on finishing my college-preparatory work. I had to take the New York State Regent's exams in all of my major academic courses, and the regent's exams were hard. I had to repeat Chemistry; I finally passed the second time. My life did not have much excitement, and I became very serious about myself concerning the world.

Death

I saw guys wasting away on drugs, and it scared me. My friend Tyrone got himself drunk, climbed the pool wall, and jumped into the 16-foot-deep pool at night. A guy named Michael saw him struggling to swim and when he went in after Tyrone, Tyrone bit him. Michael let him go, and Tyrone drowned himself. I was a pallbearer and helped to Carry Tyrone's casket with some of his other friends. Lawrence Hannahan was there and had beads of sweat pouring down his face, and he cried like a baby. I knew that Tyrone had deliberately wasted his life, and I was upset with him. I felt bad that many times I saw Tyrone on 42nd Street in Manhattan, standing on the corner looking like a bum. I never had the nerve to encourage him to go home. Many guys like Tyrone just got lost on their journeys. I knew that I didn't want to get lost like that and lose my life. It scared me, seeing the world around me so unstable. I felt that I was no longer in control of my little world, and I was anxiously trying to understand how to survive it.

I continued to socialize with friends, but I made studying my number-one objective. I studied anywhere I could. Sometimes I stopped off at the library and studied before going home from school. Often when I arrived home, it was dark. I was afraid and angry, and I didn't know why. I felt there were things that were not fair in the world being a Black. All the racial turmoil going on in the country didn't exactly encourage me to be patriotic. It happened in little steps, until I found myself thinking and talking just like my father. It wasn't that he, and I had exhausted the topic of Black and white relations in America. The situation of race in America seemed hopeless, and I gave up on America. I began to see and understand things that continued to affect black people. I wanted to leave the United States, even if for a moment, as if getting a burst of fresh air. I wanted everyone to see beyond my color and love me. I was looking for a color-blind world, and it wasn't there. I was confused, and that is what the aftermath of racial prejudice did to me, just as it had done to my father in Alabama and in New York, and many other black people. I was hurting inside, torn apart emotionally, and sometimes I felt like dying. I started writing poetry, and all of it spoke of my "Blackness" in relationship either to America, depression or religion.

My friend Hannahan graduated. He went to Vietnam to fight in the Vietnam conflict. He sent me a picture of himself dressed in Army rags with a monkey on his shoulder. I worried about Lawrence and wanted to go to Vietnam in order to help him when I graduated. I didn't know why the United States was in the war and didn't really care. All I was concerned about was my friend, Lawrence, whose life was in danger.

Graduating High School

When I graduated from high school, I had one of New York's most prestigious diplomas. It was an academic diploma and it signaled that I had completed college-preparatory work. Although I had achieved my goal, no four-year college accepted me for admission. I thought about going into the Army or Marines in order to fight for my country, but I didn't believe America was worth my dying. I guess I felt like my father about America. It had not proven to me that I was a part of its agenda. My friend Lawrence was still in Vietnam, and I worried about him. I wasn't admitted to a four-year college, and I felt terrible about it. This had proven to me that I wasn't as smart as my peers were.

Lenny got a scholarship to Princeton University. Alberta got a scholarship to New York University. Raymond was admitted to City College. William may have attended college, and Ronald was accepted into college. I believed most of my peers were moving on, and I couldn't even get off the ground. As I looked back on my four years in high school, I realized how tough it was for me, though I worked diligently. All of my work did pay off, even if I were the least academically gifted among my peers. I probably might have gotten into a four-year college, but I never thought about moving out of my parents' house, and definitely didn't want to leave New York City. The colleges I applied to were in New York State.

I filled out an application from New York City Community College, which was a two-year school. They accepted me into the night college program. I was guaranteed admission to their full-time program during the day if I maintained a 3.0 grade-point average in Trigonometry, Anthropology and Western Civilization. I buried myself in these courses and thoroughly enjoyed Anthropology.

I got a job working in May's Department Store in downtown Brooklyn. Though I made $60 per week working a full forty hours, I didn't feel good about working there. The only job, which they had for me was wrapping packages at the checkout counter with an elderly woman named Mary. I didn't see anybody with any supervisor role working at the store who was a Black. One Black man stood out in my mind every day, and he operated the elevator. He just seemed to do it out of habit and had no feeling concerning it. He was very polite to people, and no one seemed to care much about what he did, but taking them where they demanded to go. I never experienced his being grumpy or hostile. He sang to himself and ran the elevator as if it belonged to him. I felt as if I had no business there, and I saw my father and myself in that man. He was the first black man (besides my father) whom I felt intimate with, though I only said hello to him daily. He represented what my father and I was running from, losing ourselves in this world. When I left that store, I went straight to school by walking the streets of downtown Brooklyn to Cadman Plaza near the Brooklyn Bridge. After the first semester, I got my 3.0 grade-point average and was admitted into day College.

My Friend Clinton

My friend Clinton attended the same college, and we hooked up in the cafeteria many afternoons. Some students stayed in the cafeteria all day instead of going to classes and still got their grant and loan money until they were expelled. It was such a waste. They created the Affirmative Action program in Congress to help minority students gain a headway in jobs and vocations, which then excluded many minorities. All we had to do was go to school and pass our courses. At this point, Affirmative Action had not benefited me because I was in night school paying my way through college without the assistance of Affirmative Action. I was paying for my tuition with my job (May's Department Store) money. I didn't understand why these Black and Puerto Rican students were acting like some fools. It was hard enough just being a Black trying to make it, and they were wasting an excellent opportunity to be educated. I couldn't afford to be stupid.

Clinton introduced me to two young women in the cafeteria one afternoon. They found out I sang, and they invited me to sing with them with a guy named Earnest on a Saturday morning radio show. Each Saturday we got together and sang. I shared with them my struggle to get into day College and how hard I had to study in order to get decent grades. On one of our radio programs, Bonnie sang, "You'll Never Walk Alone," and dedicated it to me. When she sang it, I almost cried. I knew that I was not walking alone, God was with me.

I hated my job at the department store. A woman was angry with me because I wouldn't give her a shopping bag. My boss told me not to give anyone a shopping bag, unless they had at least three small packages, and she didn't have three. She told me that if I were so smart, I wouldn't be packing bags in a department store. I felt small, and I wanted to hide because she did it in front of the public. I was determined from that point on that I wouldn't settle for anything less than getting a Bachelor's Degree from college. I became fond of a Black woman who worked there with me, named Helena. She was much older than I was. I teased her a lot, and she was well aware that I liked her romantically. Many of my working hours in May's Department Store were spent looking at her.

Black Power

Stokely Carmichael, a Black West Indian from Trinidad, coined the phrase "Black Power." I didn't care where he was from and, like many Blacks; I caught on to the phrase quickly. He was an early member of the Black Panther Party. I didn't care much for them because I believed that they were militant. I didn't know that their main objective was to protect our communities and help black people help themselves through force. They were too militant for me. I, however, was at a point in my life where I felt I needed to say something about my African roots and myself.

My burden, being a Black and having to face the fact that black people were not treated fairly, encouraged me to be bold. My Blackness would evidently not go away. I decided to sport an Afro, Dashiki, and a Black Power button. It made me feel more confident because I was expressing to America that I didn't care about how they felt about me. I didn't care if people didn't like what I was doing because they were becoming less important to me; at least, that is what I convinced myself. One day, Helena, whom I sought attention from, asked me why I had on the Black Power button. I told her, "It's because I'm tired of the system." She didn't know what to say to me, and I walked away.

When I was over the anxiety of wearing my Black Power button, I tried building confidence with young women. I saw a dark-skinned Puerto Rican woman in the department store cafeteria. She was sitting alone eating dinner. I spoke to her politely and said, "Hello." She ignored me. I thought that she did not hear me, and I spoke to her again. She still didn't answer me. The third time I spoke to her; she acted like I wasn't there. I simply said to her, "I'm only trying to be friendly; I'm not trying to get fresh." She never looked at me. I was embarrassed. I felt terrible. I was invisible at that moment again.

Day College

After admittance into a day school, I quit my job in order to study full-time and applied for loans to pay the tuition. I felt very proud of myself;

having achieved what others thought was important. Not that I didn't feel that getting good grades were foremost. It never really proved anything to me; I didn't already know that I could do well at anything at which I tried hard.

All the young women at school were a distraction to me. I still had no one special in my life; at least not of the opposite sex, because Lydia and I were no longer in touch.

My Grandmother

I'm sure when my Grandmother Queen Victoria Smith was my mother's age, she looked just like her. I don't know who thought of her name, but I liked it. My grandmother spoke her mind. She once said to my mother, "La Verne, one day that boy of yours is going to make you cry." She was right because I almost drove my mother crazy. I heard my grandmother say often that I was terrible. I respected and loved my grandmother. She was my mother's mother, and she cared about all of us.

I remember the times that we went to her house on Pacific Street in Brooklyn. She lived in an old musty damp, dirty wooden three-story building. She didn't live there because she couldn't get out of that place. The fact that it was her rented place made it special. The whole neighborhood once was Jewish until the Blacks moved in. The hallway smelled of urine. When I walked up the stairs, I was afraid to hold on to the stair railing because it shook and made noise as if it would fall apart. The stairs squeaked as I walked up. It was a nasty building. My grandmother's apartment was clean, but hundreds of cockroaches were running all around. Cockroaches took over the building and allowed the tenants to live there. Sometimes one would crawl over me, and I felt sick. My appetite was usually shot after that, and I tried not to eat anything. It was an ordeal if I had to go into the bathroom because cockroaches would run up the walls and jump off. I almost never closed the door. Everybody in the apartment knew when someone used the toilet because it made tons of noise while the water tumbled from the wooden box above your head. I couldn't wait to get out of there.

My grandmother was always hospitable. She liked to serve us what we wanted. I would sit on the old couch and try to eat whatever she gave me, although sometimes I had to go downstairs and buy something from one of the local stores. I would dash down the staircase to the street because the hall was dark. I never remembered any light in that hallway. I always had to purchase food from a Jewish person. That didn't bother me. The only thing that I knew about Jews was Jesus Christ was one, and some Jews whom I bought things from looked like Jesus. Though I loved my grandmother, I couldn't wait to leave her apartment. Each time that I went there, I wanted to spend less time. Those cockroaches worked on my mind.

My grandmother had diabetes mellitus. She became ill, and my aunt Doris took her into her house on President Street in Brooklyn. Convincing my grandmother that it wasn't in her best interest to stay on Pacific Street wasn't easy for my aunt and my mother. My grandmother was defiant. They forced her against her will. It was the best thing for her. My aunt Doris took good care of her. After a couple of years, my aunt Doris needed a break so my mother took my grandmother, Queen Victoria Smith, into our apartment.

My grandmother developed a condition where she needed to clear her throat of excessive mucous. Each time she did; I felt sick. I knew my grandmother was ill. She had a big lump on her neck, and I looked at it every day, hoping that it would go away. The last time that I heard my grandmother tell my mother that I was going to make her cry one day, was in our apartment. She was sitting around our dining room table. "La Verne," she said, "that boy is going to make you cry one day, and you just wait and see." My grandmother continued to be right, because while I was growing up, my mother was pulling her hair out over me.

My mother took care of my grandmother for years, until my grandmother got so sick that my mother couldn't help her. She reluctantly put her in a nursing home. I visited my grandmother there often. She was never without us, because we all respected and loved her enough not to abandon her. She got sicker and remained in a coma for weeks at Long Island College Hospital. I felt that if I were a doctor, I could help her get well. I didn't feel the doctors did all that they could for her. I'm sure that they tried to keep her alive, but I believe that I would have tried harder. So I decided at this point in my life to become a medical doctor.

I was so hurt about her illness that I went into Visitation Catholic Church near Coffee Park. I put holy water on my face, lit a candle, and asked God to spare her. Within a few days, she died. I received the news about her death while I was in Calvary Baptist Church preparing to march with the choir down the aisle. A neighbor whispered it to me. I burst into tears and marched down the church aisle singing, "We Have Come This Far by Faith Leaning on the Lord."

I will always love my grandmother and know that she loved me. Each time she told my mother that I was going to make my mother cry, she only spoke the truth. She tried even in her old age to prepare my mother for challenges in life. Queen Victoria Smith had no idea that her death would seal in me a hunger that would never cease; namely, to become a physician.

The Existence of God

Philosophy at New York City Community College was challenging, and I spent a great deal of time studying. It dealt with life on terms with which I could identify. Almost everything in life seemed to me to be abstract, and nothing was for sure; not even God. My philosophy teacher was an ex-bishop in the Anglican Church, and he challenged us on the existence of God. My religious belief was that God surely existed, but I found the arguments compelling to deal with. I would take some of this knowledge home with me and toss it around, and my mother would listen to me as if I were crazy. Noticing the reaction of my family hearing, this new stuff was fun.

Talking About Sex

After leaving my job at May's Department Store, my former attachment to Helena was long past. At times, I visited her just to say hello, and she received me well. I still believed that she was attractive.

I was attracted to a beautiful black woman in New York City Community College, and it took me many weeks to say anything to her. When I finally did, we started talking about sex before marriage. I told her that I didn't believe in it. She looked at me angrily and said, "You're either crazy or a liar," and walked away from me. We never spoke again. It was a confusing part of my life, and I didn't know where the acceptable level to approach females was. I felt stupid in revealing that information to her, and it cost me. At that moment, I never wanted to talk with a woman again.

Gwen and Her Church

I became very unhappy in my life and buried myself into my schoolwork. Philosophy continued to challenge me, and I became critical of every aspect in my life and my surroundings. I wanted a female friend; someone whom I could talk to and confide in. I started talking to a young woman named Gwen in my Philosophy class. She was plain looking, a bit on the heavy side, and refused to wear makeup because she was an Orthodox Pentecostal. She invited me to her church in Queens, and I accepted. Her father was the pastor, and her mother helped him. She had a sister who looked like her twin.

I sat in that little storefront of a church and sank myself into the music and the praying. I was so vulnerable; hurting emotionally and feeling rejected that I just wanted to feel good about something, anything. Suddenly, I started shaking and calling Jesus. I knew that this was what her parents expected from a boy who wanted to be a friend to their Christian daughter, so I fell right into the mold. When I thought that, they had seen enough of my struggle with the Lord I gave up the fight and settled into my seat. I could tell that they were happy that I allowed God to bless me. Gwen and her sister sang a song; we prayed some more, and I went home. I knew my behavior during the service was not for real. When I saw all that Pentecostal energy going forth, I knew if I didn't join in they would single me out as needing salvation. I would not be able to see Gwen again.

I saw Gwen almost daily in school, and we decided to date. I took her to Red Hook in order to meet my mother and friends. I could tell no one was very excited about her, and I think that it was her plainness. Ironically, it was one thing that attracted me to her. She was a challenge to me, but I cared for her. She had my respect, and I was cautious in how I behaved around her. Once I took her to Prospect Park in Brooklyn and sat on a bench with her, doing little to nothing, but holding her hand. My relationship with Gwen didn't last long because she claimed that I was depending on her emotionally. Though she could not explain to me what it meant or how it affected her feelings for me. She decided to end the relationship.

Depression

School was running neck and neck with my love life, and my grades were below a C average. I was dropped from the day school. That was another turning point in my life because I had no idea where I was going educationally or what I could do with my life. I was depressed again and was writing poetry about everything I could think of; especially those things to which I was sensitive. I wrote about my loneliness as a young Black man and how it was destroying me. Vietnam was still affecting my life and my friend Lawrence was soon to come home. Two other boys I knew who lived in Red Hook projects had died in Vietnam, Pop and Samuel. I felt so bad that I decided to play "taps" on the bugle each evening for a few nights.

I was feeling guilty that I wasn't in the war. Church was as the church was, singing in the choir, hearing the preacher sermonize, and praying. I really enjoyed being there every Sunday, but it had become a way of life for me, and it was definitely a routine. I was even beginning to challenge its importance in my life.

I was very active within the church. I attended every Sunday morning and most evenings. I sang in the choir, prayed during morning service, and read Scripture from the Holy Bible. I didn't like Sunday school except the times that I could debate the Scripture. Sometimes a discussion would break out beyond the prepared lesson, and we wouldn't finish the study. I believed the Scriptures to the letter except where it says, "Servants, obey your masters in the Lord." I believed that every Black person in America had a problem understanding what it means for us, in particular. I was nineteen years old.

Our Pastor Died

Our pastor, Reverend Enoch B. Scott, died in a car accident, our church was devastated. We loved Reverend Scott. He was strict and didn't take to foolishness. He founded the church in 1954 and started having church gathering in a basement dwelling in Red Hook projects. The church moved from Red Hook projects to 120-4th Place, not too far from the project. My mother was one of the original members. They purchased a building that had old stained-glass windows and had an apartment on the third-floor level.

Assassinations

It seemed like the whole country was going mad. Assassinations were taking place. My first reaction to President John Fitzgerald Kennedy's assassination on November 22, 1963 was shock and dismay. When Malcolm X was shot on February 22, 1965, I was confused because black people killed him.

I watched my mother sit in front of the television and cry during Malcolm's televised funeral. I was more shocked over her tears for Malcolm

73

than I was over his death, because I had no idea that she even cared for Malcolm.

Martin Luther King, Jr. was murdered in Memphis, Tennessee during the sanitation garbage workers' strikes. King was at the forefront of the civil rights movement.

When they assassinated Martin Luther King, Jr., on April 4, 1968, I knew that the world stopped spinning for most people. I was frightened because I believed people would never find their way to freedom without him. When Robert Francis Kennedy was shot in June 1968, my emotions from assassinations almost stood still. I was saturated with it. I wondered, why was America going mad?

The Poor People's Campaign

In June 1968, I decided to get involved in the civil rights movement. I packed a knapsack and told my parents that I was going to the poor people's campaign in Washington, D.C.

When I told my parents, I was leaving, they didn't have much to say to me except to give me some money and tell me to be careful. I flew to the nation's capital and caught a taxi to the Washington Monument mall, where thousands of people were living in little shanty houses in the mud. As I was walking through the camp, my sneakers were sinking into the mud, and it was touching the bottom of my pants. A woman who couldn't have been more than twenty-five years old approached me and asked if I needed a place to stay. She took me to a wooden shanty where I met a guy who was friendly. I stayed with them for a few days.

David Ralph Abernathy, Jessie Jackson, Andrew Young and many civil rights activists were there. We were all waiting for the big day when we had a chance to voice our concerns to the United States government. They planned a March to the Lincoln Memorial. King's wife, Coretta Scott King, was going to be there to speak from the steps of the monument. The first night I was there, the Black Stone Rangers, a gang from Chicago, and a rival gang from California was at each other's throats. They were shooting guns and fighting, and some people got hurt. I was frightened. This went on for two nights of my stay.

I met many people, took pictures and spent time talking to people of other nationalities. People from varied fields were there in order to speak for the poor and the oppressed people throughout the nation. On the day of the rally at the Lincoln Memorial, there were thousands of people. I had my 35-millimeter camera strapped across my left shoulder, which was customary for me. I loved taking pictures. I followed the press past the security guard to the top of the monument and sat at the feet of Coretta Scott King and her children. I snapped as many close pictures of her as I wanted to and no one said a word to me. She was beautiful. News reporters were all around. Newsweek magazine was there with a host of other magazine companies. Newsweek magazine got a picture of me while I was attentively with others listening to a speech, and put it on the front cover of their magazine.

I saw Dr. King's brother there and walked by him often. He would, within a short period, drown in his swimming pool. I enjoyed listening to Jessie Jackson. Andrew Young and Ralph David Abernathy aroused the crowd in our camp. I knew that I had embarked on something historical and great. I was happy with myself for having the courage to do what I thought benefited me the greatest during this time in my life. My mother, spoke to me about famous black leaders, shared with me what she believed would benefit me. My father shared with me the story of the renowned George Washington Carver, and how he made hundreds of different products from the lowly peanut. It was one of the few things that my father never hesitated to share with me. It was as if George Washington Carver were his relative. I guess in many ways all black people are relatives, one way or another. I caught a flight back to New York and buried the experience of that historic moment in my life and in my heart. I will never forget it.

Disappointments

My mother shared with me some of her emotions and thoughts. Two things she told me: "If they don't want to teach you anything in school, just sit there and listen while they teach the other students." Second, "the proof is in the pudding." She told me that truth would never change no matter how it looks. After a few months, the members of the church decided that they needed to find a new pastor because the congregation believed that we needed a Shepherd full-time. Having pastors come to preach was not the congregation's desire. They invited few pastors, but one guy they really liked. A man named Yarber, who had charisma and could preach, was invited. He had a beautiful wife and a daughter. We didn't know that he was a lying thief and would ultimately take twenty-five thousand dollars of our money for his own use. He even had the guts to send his German shepherd dog to obedience school with it. I remember when he first spoke. The people were falling out (getting touched by the Holy Spirit), and clapping their hands and saying "hallelujah" to almost every word that came out of his mouth. He talked a lot about Jesus Christ, and that's what the people needed to hear to confirm that he was sent from God. It didn't take me long to catch on to him when I did, he knew it. He would ride some teenagers in his car coming from a preaching engagement and allow them to smoke cigarettes. He even smoked it, and to do that in our church was considered a sin. He at no time spoke on that one topic. He also never spoke on stealing other people's hard-earned money. Once I went to his apartment on the third floor of the church, he stayed there when he wasn't at his beautiful private home in Queens, New York. Most of the church members lived in the project while he was robbing us blind and living in luxury in a better neighborhood. When I went to the apartment, he came to the door with no shirt on, bare feet, and smoking a cigarette. I was shocked. When I informed my mother, she told me to mind my own business. We had a church business meeting, and I went and raised some issues concerning the teenagers in the church. He asked me to put it to rest. I continued to press him, and he asked me to leave. I said, "No." He told the members if I didn't leave; he would not continue the meeting. My sister Janice looked at me and said, "Buddy; you're always starting trouble." My mother was sitting next to me, and she asked me to leave. I told her, "No." She begged me, and I would not leave. Yarber told me that he was leaving the church auditorium, and if I was there when he came back there was going to be trouble. When he returned, I was still telling my mother that I wasn't going anywhere. Yarber looked at me in frustration. That lying stealing preacher closed out the meeting, and most people were furious with me. They should have been enraged with themselves for not standing up to the crook. We planned to approach him that Wednesday. The Monday before, he came into the church when no one was there and took with him preaching robes worth thousands of dollars.

Chapter 7

Lorraine

I will praise thee: for I am fearfully and wonderfully made:
Marvelous are thy works; and that my soul knoweth right well.

Psalm139: 14

Lorraine was like no other girl I had ever met. She was meticulous about caring for her body. Sometimes she washed and changed outfits two or three times a day. I met her at Calvary Baptist Church; she was fourteen years-old, and I was eighteen. I never thought of her romantically because she was younger than me. I treated her as if she were my little sister. She was pretty, witty, smart, and lovable. Lorraine had a charm that enticed me and a smile that warmed my heart, both of which ultimately turned cold. If looks were all that mattered in a romantic relationship, ours would have been near-perfect. She had a golden-brown complexion and long brown hair that passed her shoulders. I loved the way she styled her hair. Each style said something about her attitude. When she wore the French roll, she looked dignified and kept her head high. When she dragged her hair to her mid-forehead in a bang, she looked like a school kid. Sometimes she let it dangle to her shoulders, and she looked sexy. Lorraine could be versatile in appearance and manners.

Lorraine and I spent a great deal of time with each other, and ultimately; it was to our detriment. I'm not saying that we didn't have a good time with each other; much, to the contrary, we had some good times. I believe that the first time that I closed mouth kissed her was at the Red Hook pool;

she was sixteen. One day she was like my little sister and the next day she was my girlfriend. I fell in love with her.

Many people liked Lorraine. She was outgoing and friendly. She had three sisters and a brother, and they were very pleasant. Her mother was a faithful member at the Calvary Baptist Church, which we attended, and she loved her children, like most mothers. Lorraine and I were officially dating, and we did not ask our parents what they thought about it. We had our relationship in our hands. They tried steering our relationship and sometimes suggested that we not be with each other often and share time with other people, but we did not listen. Everything that happened to us was our fault. We were responsible for everything that happened. Both of our parents loved us dearly and showed it even in the midst of the tragedy to come. On holidays, our church had many outings, and Lorraine and I often went. I especially remember trips to amusement parks, state parks, and the Danbury, Connecticut State Fair. On one of our trips to the Danbury State Fair, Lorraine and I flew in a small aircraft. She was nervous with the distance between her and the ground; she was afraid of heights. In spite of her fear of flying, she followed me.

She did anything that she could to please me. I enjoyed all the trips to other states; church picnics, and special activities, which the church planned. Lorraine liked our pastor, because he gave her the attention that she wanted. It was important for people to know that the pastor liked them. He was a person whom they thought was sent from God to show us the good Christian way (but I never believed God sent him). Lorraine never had anything ill to say about him, even when he stole our money. I believe that Lorraine needed a father figure because her biological father was dead. She wanted someone who she could confide in and who would love her. We spent considerable time talking-to each other about life, our families, and our relationship. Our parents were concerned because they felt that we were spending too much time together. They warned us about it and encouraged us to seek other friends. It was not that they wanted us to forget each other, but they wanted us to include other people in our lives. Once, Lorraine and I were arguing because I wanted to spend time with Alberta. Alberta's brother, Barry and Lorraine were close. When Lorraine felt Alberta was a threat to her, she would greet Barry with a kiss on his lips. Barry did not mind because that is how I saw him greet most females. I got upset with both each time it occurred, but I never said anything to him. I liked Barry, and he was always pleasant to me. He liked teasing me about being a virgin. I spoke with Lorraine about kissing him on his mouth. She told me since I had a special relationship with Alberta; she would have the same with Barry. My relationship with Lorraine was showing signs of strain from the beginning.

Long Island College Hospital

I was dismissed from day College for poor academic performance. I went to Long Island College Hospital and applied for a job. The only job available was working as a corpsman in the operating room. I had to clean the rooms after each operation with a mop and disinfectant. After my first day, I knew that I could not stay there.

My boss was a tough old woman who told me that I had to work on the weekend, including Sunday. It was my Sabbath. It was the day my father gave me hell for thinking about riding my bike or going into the movie theater. They did not allow me to play marbles on that day; I was not going to work Sunday for anyone. When I told her that I could not work Sunday, she told me that Jesus Christ healed on the Sabbath Day, and it was all right for me to work. I thought; I was not Jesus Christ, and I am not working Sunday. I cleaned the operating room floors for about two days and could not take it. The job was way beneath being able to challenge me. It was a dead-end job, and not for an aspiring student. An employee told me that medical records needed a person in their department. When I spoke with the supervisor at the department, I told her that I was a college student, and they took me in.

The medical records section was loaded with some Black women. One woman, in particular, took a liking to me, Helena. She was the second woman named Helena that came into my life and made a great impact on me.

Helena was from the West Indies, and she was proud of her roots. I liked her a lot. She smiled most of the day, cracked jokes, and always had something pleasant or encouraging to say to me. She teased me about how good-looking she thought I was. Helena looked out for me and helped me around the medical records department. She was pleased that I was in college and told me often, "You're smart, and if you study hard you're going to do well." She constantly encouraged me to move ahead in life and get all I could scholastically.

I did not like the medical records system. I could never find a chart without a hassle; no matter how often the women helped me, there were too many color codes to read. My job was pulling medical records for the outpatient clinic. I was up and down the elevator and stairs with records all day long. I met a West Indian named Steven Welch from Barbados. Steven was a friendly guy, who did all he could in order to make me feel comfortable. We became friends, and he helped me out in the clinic. He warned me about being entangled in the gossip and showed me how to get around.

My Friend Paul

Paul worked in the financial-aid department at the hospital as a supervisor. It was not until later when Paul became an important part of my life. He was the person whom I learned to trust then. He cared about having a relationship with me. His wife was very pleasant to me, and she was beautiful, and they had two children; a boy and a girl.

A coworker in medical records told me that Paul needed someone to work in his department, and I was tired of medical records, with all the color charts. When I applied for the position, Paul took me. He told me later, "I did not hire you for your looks or your color; I hired you because I liked you from our first meeting."

My working attire went from a neat pair of pants, shirt and tie to a suit. They had me looking like a lawyer or a banker. Many clients in the hospital thought that I was a doctor when I walked into their room, until I asked them for money that they owed. My job was collecting unpaid bills from family members, and they gave me the authority to collect it any way I could. Once I walked into a patient's room, and a relative said, "The doctor's here."

I said, "Oh, I am not the doctor." The family member put a sour look on his face when I told him I was there in order to collect an unpaid bill. For the most part, I didn't like collecting money from people in the hospital. I felt that they were burdened enough with their illness and did not need the added pressure, but the hospital hired me for that purpose. I did the job well.

I had the opportunity to help many needy people and put them on medical assistance. This was the highlight of the job, besides working with Paul.

Tumbling Walls

I enrolled in New York City Community College's night school program. They told me I could not get back into college during the day, unless I obtained a B average. It was embarrassing telling my mother and father what happened. They encouraged me to push against the odds. I studied hard and spent many weekends at the Brooklyn Public Library.

Lorraine Again

My relationship with Lorraine was not getting any better. We were fighting most of the time. Our parents were seeing our frustration and depression. Lorraine's mother told me that she never had me picked out for her daughter, and my mother told me to give up Lorraine if we could not get along. We did not listen to our parents, and we paid for it. Once we got physical with each other, and the twisted romance took a more dangerous turn downward. Although Lorraine and I loved each other, we were tolerating and enduring each other painfully. I don't know why we put up with each other; maybe we did because we allowed ourselves to think that we couldn't make it without each other. We would not break up, and we did not stop arguing and fighting. I had a booklet of poetry that she typed for me. It contained a bunch of poems about being a black boy in America, racism, and Vietnam. She took an interest in my hobbies and liked helping me.

I went to my friend Raymond for some answers, but I was not ready for his answer. "Buddy, just break up with Lorraine; it is obvious you two cannot get along, and you guys cannot agree." I wanted Raymond to pamper me and tell me that it would all work out, but he knew differently. So did many people who knew us. We doomed our relationship, and we needed to break up.

At work, I talked to Paul about our problem. He spoke with me gently, but firmly. "Buddy, you have to let her go. Look at you, it's destroying you, and it is destroying her also." His suggestion to leave Lorraine was difficult for me. I loved her, and I didn't want to do it.

I worked hard in school and at work. The more people thought that I was a doctor at Long Island College Hospital; the closer I became to believe that I could become one. I did not see one black doctor in the hospital; most of them were foreign-born and foreign-trained. I wondered where all the Black doctors were. I had never touched a Black doctor's hand.

So that role model was out the window. Though I did not see one black doctor in the hospital, I did know about one; Dr. Evans, at Kings County Hospital (where I was born). My cousin Sarah told me what a wonderful and intelligent doctor he was. I believed that she tried to encourage me to look at medicine as a vocation. She never told me that she thought that I should think about becoming a doctor, but she never stopped talking about Dr. Evans.

A Freaking White Guy

My relationship with Paul was growing, and he showed himself trustworthy. I confided in him, and we became close friends. He continued to talk to me about my life, and anything that he felt would help me see the world as it is. He even talked to me about some attitudes that he had as a man and told me that I would understand better, when I got older. I believed that he loved me and did not care about my race or color. "Buddy," he said, "I'm a freaking white guy and there is no reason that you should trust or believe me. Nevertheless, I think that you're an honest, respectable guy." Paul was not just a freaking white guy. He was a great guy and a decent person that cared about people. He was not only my boss; he was special, and he was my friend.

Looking for Love

I was doing well in school and though my relationship with Lorraine was still challenging, we were going through one of our better periods, and our relationship became more intimate. We thought that it would bring us closer to each other, but it only served to put a wedge between us. We did not know what love was and never found out; at least not with each other. After our intimacy, our relationship became bittersweet and even worsened, and we were fighting almost every week. I do not know what had us holding on to each other.

I believe Lorraine, and I was convinced that we loved each other. We could not figure out what was wrong, and we did not think anyone else knew. That was one of our biggest mistakes. Many people saw our relationship and to them; we twisted it, and they did not hesitate to say it. If we loved each other, we were not mature enough to allow our love to keep us together or protect each other.

I was a few months away from graduation from New York City Community College. My job was going well. Lorraine was accepted into Hampton Institute, in Hampton, Virginia. I told her if she went, I would not guarantee our relationship lasting. I wanted to be honest with her. She was disappointed with me and decided not to go. I'm not sure why I told her that, because it was one of the worst mistakes that I ever made in my life. I think that I was afraid of being abandoned like Beverly and Richard abandoned me when I was younger, and like losing relationships with Mrs. Aronawitz and Mrs. Grudinsky. I had no right to complicate Lorraine's life any more than it already was. A friend of hers promised never to speak to me again if I did that to Lorraine. I didn't change my mind. I did not want Lorraine to leave me. So I told her that I might not be there for her if she left me in Red Hook.

The Seduction of Love

Lorraine and I created hell on earth for each other. I don't know how badly she really wanted to go to Hampton Institute. "She should have left me standing in Red Hook; looking anyway I chose to look." "It was her life." Our biggest problem was that we didn't know when to let loose and free each other of the agony.

The world has not changed about people messing up each other's lives. Most young people think that they understand what love is, and how to conduct their lives based on their false ideas of it, and it ruins lives. Lorraine and I were no different. She was depressed and I thought she was suicidal, but she was crying out for help. There were other conflicts in her life other than me, and although, she tried to hurt herself other times by taking pills, I never thought that she would really try to kill herself. I think that she was crying out for attention. She wanted to tell the world that she was in pain. I didn't understand her agony and didn't know that she needed to be heard. My thoughts were that she was confused and depressed, and I didn't know how to help her. Compassion and protection were very much a part of my relationship with Lorraine because I believed I loved her.

God, Not Lorraine

I graduated from New York City Community College with an Associate of Arts Degree and had a wonderful graduation at Cadman Plaza near the

Brooklyn Bridge. My family was very proud of me. I was accepted into Brooklyn College and decided to major in Chemistry.

Lorraine graduated from high school, decided not to go to Hampton Institute. She enrolled at Staten Island Community College instead. All was going well, so I thought. After her first week at school, she was very excited. I called her on the telephone late one evening, and we had a casual conversation. We were discussing how great school was, and she exchanged some hostile words with her mother about telling me the family business. We were not discussing any family business. Lorraine never resumed her conversation with me. The phone was silent. I dialed her phone number a few times, and no one answered. I told my mother that I had to go to Lorraine's house and dashed out the door. As I ran down the street, a member from our church named Reggie informed me that someone jumped out of a window from five stories high. I ran faster. "Oh God," I said, "I hope it's not Lorraine."

I thought of the times that she told me that she would kill herself when our relationship was on the rocks. When she took some pills and fell over in Coffee Park across the street from her house, I believed that she was serious, and she was crying out for help again. When I arrived at her apartment building, Lorraine was lying in the grass, flexed, looking up, saying, "Let me wake up, let me wake up." I didn't know what to say. Her mother didn't address me, and I didn't address her. A friend of mine named Reverend Charles Hall was there, and he tried to console all of us. When I arrived at the hospital, Reverend Hall approached me and said, "I spoke with the doctor, and he said she may never walk again." In that instant Lorraine changed the course of her life forever. I stood with Reverend Hall, and I didn't want to believe what he had told me.

A news reporter approached me and asked what happened. I told him that I didn't know. He asked me if I thought that it was her mother. I told him that it was possible, but I really didn't know. The following day they broadcast on the radio that I implicated her mother. I tried to defend my statement, but it was too late. I should never have said a word to anyone. I had no proof for what I said. I was wrong for saying it. To this day, I am sorry for the words that I said to the reporter.

My life took a sharp downward turn, and I was bewildered, shocked and hurt. I couldn't understand why Lorraine believed that life wasn't worth living. That morning I went to the hospital, Reverend Yarber and her mother were there. Her mother told me that it was my fault for running around with women. I told her mother that I was nowhere around when

Lorraine did what she did, and it was not my fault. We argued, and Yarber broke us up.

When Lorraine came from the emergency spinal surgery, I didn't recognize her. Her face was swollen like a balloon. She was motionless, and I felt terrible. I left the hospital and went to school. At work, I told Paul what occurred, and he was hurt and disappointed with me. He did not say, "I told you so." He tried the best he could to console me; I devoted my energy to seeing Lorraine at Kings County Hospital, and whatever energy was left for studying. I was wiped out.

Majoring in Chemistry challenged my mental capacity. The textbook was thick, and they gave me multiple chapters each night to read. I couldn't understand the mathematical portion of the course. I could not do the equations to measure moles, millimoles and Avogadro's numbers. It was all confusing. Between Chemistry, my other courses, and Lorraine's tragedy, I didn't know which direction to put more energy in. I went to the college bookstore and bought some cards. I had a book with delightful sayings and wrote one on a card each day for her. I visited her in the hospital practically every day. Her mother and I didn't have anything to say to each other. I tried to visit Lorraine when her mother wasn't there. Most of the time, I sat with Lorraine and tried to encourage her emotionally. As the weeks passed, Lorraine was recovering. Her doctors were pleased with her ability to push onto recovery. When she could sit up, I stayed with her for longer periods. Sometimes we argued about whose fault it was that she was paralyzed from her waist down. When she got upset with me, she told me if it were not for me, she wouldn't be paralyzed. Each time she said it, it tore my heart in pieces. I felt responsible. Lorraine wanted me to feel guilty, but I did not know it. I don't blame her for feeling her paralysis was my fault. She had some problems and challenges, and I was not helping her with any of them. I didn't make her life any easier. I'm sorry I never heard her cry for help. If she had told me, she needed help, I'm sure I would have tried to help her. This is a good example of how some young people believe that they make the best choices for their lives, and they don't. They mess their lives up.

My parents believed that I was taking on Lorraine's misfortune. They sat with me and tried to help me recover from my guilt. My father asked a friend of his, whom he called a doctor, to speak with me. I went to my father's barbershop, and a neatly dressed middle-age man was waiting for me. I didn't know what kind of doctor he was, or even if he was a doctor at all. All I knew was that my father trusted him to talk some sense into me. He was very gentle and polite. He simply told me what happened to

Lorraine was not my fault, and she was programmed before she met me to hurt herself. He said no one could make another person do what Lorraine did. I did not agree with him. I believed that I had to be responsible in some way.

Leaving Home

I told my parents that I was leaving home and going to my aunt Doris's house on President Street to live. I believed that they didn't understand my hurt concerning Lorraine's suicide attempt. They were hurt that I did not want to live with them anymore, and they knew that they did nothing to hurt me. I knew that they loved me very much. That is why I believe they let me go. When I left, I was not in a good mood. I kissed my mother and may have shaken my father's hand. I forget saying farewell to my sisters. I did not see my mother or my father shed a tear, but I know that I broke their hearts.

I thought that it was going to be great living with my aunt. She gave me a little room in the front of the house to live in. My uncle Billy, who was my aunt's brother, stayed in the same room when he lived there. Many of his books were still in the room. I felt lonely for my parents the first night, but I was determined to show them that I made the right decision.

My aunt let me settle in, and then gave me a hard time. To make matters worse, I bought a Great Dane puppy, for $250.00, in order to keep me company that had markings like a tiger and called her "Amani," which means peace in Swahili. My dog did waste in my aunt's kitchen by a back room where I kept her at night. Aunt Doris awakened me many nights and said, "Buddy, get up and go in that kitchen and get that dog shit off the floor your dog made." She would say, "Buddy, go take out the garbage." When she told me to take out the garbage, there was either snow outside, or it was freezing weather. She was showing me that I was not wise to leave "her sisters" apartment, and move into her house. Between her scolding me, Lorraine blaming me for her paralysis, failing chemistry and a couple of my other courses, and the dog-dung, I was tumbling like a weak wall.

My aunt wanted me to start making good decisions about my life. She loved me and proved it. I remember when I graduated from junior high school; she bought a motorized airplane that operated on gas for me. I never told her that I wanted it, but I had wanted one for a long time. She didn't give me much money, although I believe that she had enough to give some of it away. My aunt was determined to teach me some lessons concerning tough living.

Lorraine's mother and I continued to have contentions. I tried not to be at the hospital when her mother was there. The fights did not end between Lorraine and me. It was a sign to me that Lorraine was getting physically and mentally better, though she still could not walk. Each time I looked at Lorraine; I felt that if I were a doctor, I could help her. I could do more for her than what her doctors were doing. I got into a big fantasy thing about helping her to walk again.

One evening I went to the hospital, and Lorraine asked me to tell her mother to leave us alone and not interfere in our relationship. When her mother arrived, I sat quietly for about one-half-hour. I told her mother that I wanted her not to interfere in our lives. Her mother was furious, and we started fighting verbally in the hospital; making lots of noise. The nurse told us to quiet down or leave. We continued to argue, and the nurse threw us out. I had no idea how her mother must have felt when I told her not to interfere. Her daughter was paralyzed and she felt it was my fault, and I was asking her to get out of Lorraine's life. I do not think that Lorraine really had any idea what she had asked me to do, nor did I. Her mother had every right to protect her, and I should have respected that. I was the intruder. The next night when I visited Lorraine, she told me that I had no right to speak to her mother the way I did. I said, "What way?"

She responded, "The way you talked to her wasn't right." I was confused, not knowing what Lorraine wanted from me. I believe that Lorraine was confused, and she was using me like a puppet on a string, and I was doing the "jig" for her.

Leray's Tactic

My cousin Leray with her piercing eyes was at her mother's house. My aunt went through her usual and told me to take the dog's shit out of the house. I got upset. My life was just a mess. Leray, who never minced words, said, "What the hell is wrong with you? Do you think you're the only person who has problems? You better get your life together. You want to be a doctor, but you aren't going to be any doctor. Doctors are born, not made, and you don't have what it takes." She spoke her mind to me, took a big bite, and opened me up. I started to cry. She verbally tore me to pieces. I left the house that morning depressed. Before going to college, I went to the hospital and told Lorraine what happened, and she tried to console me.

One moment Lorraine didn't want me to leave her and the next moment; she was beating me emotionally.

Every Chemistry test I took I failed, I was failing Calculus. A young West Indian woman in my class who befriended me tried to help me through the calculations, but it didn't do any good. I did not understand the stuff. My brain was in reverse, I was failing college. Each time I got an F on my Chemistry test; I knew I was moving further away from medicine. I said to myself, "How are you to become a doctor when you cannot pass chemistry."

My cousin Leray's comment to me kept surfacing in my mind. I wanted to believe she was wrong, but the facts stated otherwise. When the semester was over, I failed Chemistry; and other courses.

My relationship with Lorraine cooled, we were not fighting as much. When we did, however, Lorraine reminded me that her tragedy of paralysis was my fault. It hurt when Lorraine blamed me for her tragedy. They scheduled her to leave the hospital in a couple of months, she was receiving physical therapy, but still could not walk. I was praying and believing that she would suddenly walk. Nevertheless, I lost hope and believed that she would never walk again. I felt terrible and I wanted to be absent from her life, but I could not. I cared too much about her.

In 1969, at Brooklyn College, I changed my major from Chemistry to Biology. I could not continue chemistry as a major because I failed the subject. A student could not keep a major in a subject that he failed. I took chemistry the second time, while the school was in political turmoil. Many colleges and universities were protesting the Vietnam War and unfair government policies. The Vietnam War was winding down, and the civil rights movement was heading in a new direction without Martin Luther King, Jr. The Jesus movement, the flower children, and the Hari-Khrisna religions were going strong. Brooklyn College had its share of the mass confusion. I wanted to move ahead educationally. I believed my life was staggering. In my Chemistry class, they gave us the chance to take an exam. If I passed, it would satisfy the first half of Inorganic Chemistry. We were more than halfway through the course. I took the exam and failed. I could not believe that I failed Inorganic Chemistry twice.

Lorraine came out of the hospital with leg braces, crutches and a wheelchair. Her mother and I had enough sense not to fight openly anymore. I knew that she had the right to help her daughter anyway she wanted. I was just feeling so guilty. Lorraine was not helping me feel otherwise; she was still blaming me.

Professor Harmon Finston

Professor Harmon Finston at Brooklyn College was a lifeline for me. He taught Quantitative and Qualitative Chemistry. I went to his office and told him that I did not understand Chemistry and failed it twice. He told me that he was aware of my difficulty and promised to help me. He asked a young Jewish professor to tutor me after-school hours.

Up to this point, I never spoke with Professor Finston. I did not think that any of the professors cared if I passed Chemistry. Something was special about him, for he was a fine human being of quality (like Paul Garguilo, my old boss at Long Island College Hospital).

Professor Finston was soft-spoken and calm and liked to talk to me. I told him about my growing up in Red Hook and my difficulty in school. He listened to me and told me that he would help me. He made sure that my tutor was available to help me any time I needed.

I decided to leave my aunt's house and go back home, and I believe my aunt was glad to see me go. She taught me a good lesson. Don't jump out of the frying pan into the fire. My aunt Doris tried her best to show me that life is full of choices, and I could make as many wrong choices as I pleased. I would understand her role later in my life. I would understand why Leray said to me that doctors are born and not made. I continued to go to church and was very involved in the programs. I was working with the young people there, and they saw some of my struggles. What they did not see, I shared with them. At the end of the college semester I finally passed Chemistry. Professor Finston, my tutor, and I were very happy. It was at this juncture that I became determined to become a doctor no matter what. Academically I had not done well; I had a long journey before me. I knew in my heart that I would be a good doctor who cared about people, who would love them. I started telling various people that I was a premedical student majoring in Biology; though I failed Botany, which was in my major. They then dropped me from the Biology Department, I was without any major.

Lorraine was going through her trials with her paralysis. She kept saying that she did not feel like a whole woman. She was about eighteen years old, and I tried to convince her that she was. I carried her in my arms where we went. Sometimes people thought that we were joking around; especially when I carried her into the movie theater. She told me that people were looking at us, and she was self-conscious about it. I took her many places in my Volkswagen Bug that I purchased with part of my school loans. I packed her wheelchair in the back seat. I even took her with me to upstate New York that winter when I went hunting and let her shoot my high-powered rifle. I tried hard to help her, but it was useless. I had mixed feelings. I was trying to convince myself that her paralysis was not my fault, but Lorraine was convinced that it was. I was doing a job on myself, and I did not realize it.

My parents were bearing my mistakes and tolerating my dog. Amani, a Great Dane. Our project apartment seemed smaller with her in it. My mother didn't like dogs, but she did more than tolerate Amani. I believed that she actually liked her. She even walked her for me. Sometimes I had Amani packed in my multicolored polka-dot Volkswagen with Lorraine and her wheelchair. We were a sight.

Harvard University

Michael Mc Cloud was a premedical student at Brooklyn College. He told me about a summer program for minority students; he was in at Harvard University. Harvard was interested in helping minorities get into medical school. They gave housing and offered two science courses and a hospital rotation. If a student passed the courses and got a decent evaluation from the hospital, Harvard University gave a recommendation to any medical school in the United States. It was all free, sponsored by the federal government. He completed the program and did well. He suggested that I apply for the program. I knew that I wasn't Harvard University material, and I didn't take him seriously. He gave me the address, and I applied. Within a few weeks, they accepted me. Harvard accepted ninety students from all over the United States. I could not believe that I was one of them. I told Lorraine that I was going to Harvard, and she did not want me to go. I told her that I had to go because it was my chance to show that I could become a doctor. My parents were excited and many who knew me were shocked that I was going to Harvard University. When I went to the airport in order to catch the flight to Boston, Massachusetts, Lorraine was in her wheelchair with my parents and me. When it was time for me to board the aircraft, she started to cry, and I felt terrible. I told her everything would be OK. I kissed her. I kissed and hugged my mother and father and walked swiftly away. I needed a break from Lorraine. It was crazy trying to please her and trying to convince myself that she, and her mother were not right about her tragedy being my fault. I guess I had some nerve going to Harvard and leaving her in Red Hook projects. I did not want her to do the same thing to me as two years prior, but it was time for me to care for myself.

Harvard and Eleanor

When I arrived at Harvard University and saw the historic campus and the huge courtyard, I thought, how was I ever able to convince anyone to select me for the health careers program for ten weeks? I thought it had to be God helping me.

The following day I went to the orientation meeting and met the other students. I met a fast New York-type guy. He was from the Bronx, named Chris. He was checking out some women from the South. He told me that they were interested in meeting some men. He asked me to go with him to one of their dorm rooms to meet them. He said that they were waiting for us. When we arrived about five young women were in the room. They giggled when we walked in. Chris said, "What's happening, how you all doing?"

One young woman was a spokesperson and responded, "How you all doing?"

I didn't say anything. I was shy, and the leader of the pack picked me out. Soon someone dared another to take their clothes off . . . The leader said, "If the guys do it first, then we will do it."

Chris said, "Go on, Buddy, take off your clothes."

One young woman said, "We won't look; we'll turn the lights off, but let us blindfold you first." They turned off the lights, and I took my clothes off down to my underwear and one of them turned the lights on. They all burst into laughter. Before I took the blindfold off, I knew what they had done. I scrambled for my pants and shirt, and they screamed in laughter.

One young woman was sitting with a half-smile on her face, looking at the floor. When I looked at her, we made eye contact. She didn't poke fun at me like the other women. When the commotion cooled down, I went and sat by her and introduced myself formally. "Hello," I said, "My name is Buddy."

"My name is Eleanor," she responded. I told her where I was from, and she said she was from Rome, Georgia. She told me she was finishing her last year of college in education. Eleanor impressed me that she was so young and was going to be a teacher. Chris was having a ball with the women, and I focused on Eleanor. When the evening was ending, I asked Eleanor if I could see her again. She told me, "Yes."

The next day I was on cloud nine. I saw Chris, and he told me what a wild time he had with the women. "Man, that one you were talking to look really good. I noticed you spent much time with her." He cracked jokes about how funny some women acted, and we parted. The next day I was studying Cell Biology and Organic Chemistry, I was scheduled to be at the Boston Lying-in Women's Hospital. The first time I ever saw a baby born was there. It blew my mind, and the slimy baby fascinated me when it came. That woman's vagina opened like the Holland Tunnel, and the baby came like a Mack truck. A guy by the name of James from North Carolina was with me, and his eyes were bugging out. From that, instant I said to myself, "If this is medicine, I want it."

When I saw Eleanor, my heart beat fast, and I did not know what to say to her. Eleanor looked at me and did not say a word. I greeted her and we walked the campus, talking about how crazy the previous night was. When she talked to me about my taking off my clothes, she told me it was an old trick. We laughed about it. After that walk with Eleanor, I thought about her often.

That evening Lorraine called me. I don't know where she got my dorm phone number, but she tracked me down to the public phone in the hallway, like a Federal Bureau of Investigation agent. From that time, on, Lorraine burdened my mind. One evening she called me, and I got depressed and went to see Eleanor. I told Eleanor about Lorraine. I stood in the middle of the floor and wept. Eleanor put her arms around me and held me tight. She told me that it would all work out, and I would be fine. She helped me forget my guilt for a few moments and free my mind and heart from Lorraine's misfortune. I will never forget how I felt in her arms: while she held me, I felt safe. I was now in love with Eleanor from that night on. When Lorraine called me, I told her about Eleanor. She was furious with me and blamed me again for her paralysis. After that conversation, I didn't feel bad because I was not alone. I had Eleanor.

I studied hard at Harvard and when I had a break from it, I took long walks with Eleanor along the Charles River. We sat most of the time on a bench. She told me about her boyfriend in Georgia named Poncho, whom she was not sure she still wanted. They were having problems, and she felt their separation was healthy. We talked about our lives. I did most of the talking, and she always listened. Eleanor knew my whole-life story because I told it all.

Five weeks passed, and the program was half over. Eleanor had three more weeks at Harvard, and I didn't want her to leave me there. I knew that I was going to miss her tremendously. Conversations with Lorraine were ongoing, and each time we spoke; we fought. Lorraine gave me an ultimatum. She told me to leave Eleanor in Boston when I came home. I told her that Eleanor was coming with me. Eleanor had a sister in the Bronx who she wanted to see. I planned to take Eleanor with me to Red Hook. Lorraine told me if I did, our relationship would end. Eleanor came with me and Lorraine "griped with rage." I didn't let Lorraine shake me up because Eleanor helped me by giving me emotional support. She was almost holding me up.

When I took Eleanor to Red Hook projects, she wore pink hot pants, and they were tight. I don't think that my mother appreciated the way she was dressed, but as usual, my mother was pleasant. A neighbor in my building who was from Georgia said, "you have a Georgia peach; she is beautiful."

After I took Eleanor to her sister's house, I visited Lorraine, and she was mad as a wounded rattlesnake, spitting venom. She told me to get rid of Eleanor like one would get rid of a sick dog with mange, and if I did not, our relationship was finally over. I called her bluff; I went back to Boston in a few days and wrapped my arms around Eleanor. I believed that I loved Eleanor, and I knew after I returned to Harvard University, I would separate myself further from Lorraine. I was feeling guilty, sick, and tired of her pulling me down. I didn't know what love was until I met Eleanor. For the first time in my life, I was intimate with someone who I believed loved me. I cherished Eleanor's affection. She made me feel like a man. When Eleanor left for Rome, Georgia, I felt like my strength left with her. I told her that I would never forget her and would go to Georgia to see her. I made love to her the night before, gave her hugs and kisses and said, "I'll see you later." My last two weeks at Harvard were trying. I kept thinking about Eleanor, and Lorraine kept calling me. Chris was fooling around with a new set of women, trying to encourage me to join him, but I refused. I wanted to be faithful to Eleanor. A young woman from New York tried to start a romance with me, and I turned her down. Chris thought I was crazy. He told me no woman was worth turning down another.

After the ten weeks were completed, I passed Cell Biology with a C+ and Organic Chemistry, I with a B. I was proud of myself. I enjoyed the hospital rotation and was positive that I wanted to be a doctor.

My parents gave me some money to spend at Harvard, and I had some left at the end of the program. I used some of it to go to Rome, Georgia and visited Eleanor before returning to New York. She picked me up at the airport in her Karmann-Ghia. We drove 90 miles to her home in the country from Atlanta (for the first time in my life; I saw and tasted a yellow watermelon). I met Eleanor's mother and father, and they were kind to me. They prepared a room for me to stay in. I had a wonderful time with Eleanor. She told me that she might want to keep her relationship with her boyfriend Poncho because things got better between them. I never believed that she would pick him over me. I thought that she loved me. I made love to her before I left for New York. I gave her a ring that Lorraine bought for me and kissed her. I told her that I loved her. She didn't respond. I then realized that she was not sure what direction her life would take concerning Poncho or me.

It's All Your Fault

I was back in New York and feeling guilty because Lorraine was blaming me for her paralysis. Lorraine was upset and I couldn't blame her, but she didn't own me. We didn't discuss my affair with Eleanor at length. Lorraine was deciding what direction; she wanted her life to take. After a few days, we were corresponding regularly by mail. She decided that she wanted us together again.

I received a package from Eleanor, and it had the ring in it. She gave me a "Dear John" letter. She told me that she renewed her relationship with Poncho, and our romance was over. She apologized to me for leading me on. After I received her letter, I lost contact with her. I did not want to believe that Eleanor didn't want me. As much as I loved her, I didn't write her back. I told Lorraine that my relationship with Eleanor was over and Lorraine and I started dating again. I felt sorry for Lorraine, and at the same time confronted with the reality of her paralysis. She reminded me that it was my fault that she could not walk. We were not getting along. I was carrying her in my arms when we went out. When we went to church, I carried her down the aisle. Once, a sister in the church approached me and said, "Buddy, I'm proud of you, you're still with Lorraine, and treating her well." That sister had no idea the burden Lorraine added to my life. I was convinced that if I left Lorraine, I would be considered the villain. I did not feel I could leave Lorraine under the pressure. I was struggling in school and still failing courses but getting some Ds in others. I now wanted to be a doctor more than ever. Michael was accepted into medical school. When he broke the news to me, I was happy for him, but also jealous that I was far from medical school.

I was taking Comparative Anatomy. My professor was British, and he was tough. I was failing his course. We were dissecting the nurse shark, exposing the twelve cranial nerves. I liked the lab portion, but hated the written test. He said that his course would separate the men from the boys because he taught the course on the same level as Downstate Medical School's course. He told the students if we couldn't pass his course we most likely couldn't get into medical school. He discouraged and frightened me. I had to be a doctor, whether I passed his course or not. At the close of the semester, I failed Comparative Anatomy.

The only courses in which I did well were English courses. I did not particularly like English, but it was a subject with which I felt comfortable. I had an excess of thirty credits in English. Nevertheless, it was not English that I needed for medical school it was science.

Professor Finston was still encouraging me. Beside him, the only other professor who encouraged me was Professor Williams. Professor Williams was another super guy who taught in the Chemistry Department. He was the professor who spoke positively to me about my goal to become a doctor. I admired him. He and Professor Finston encouraged me. Professor Finston told me if I didn't make it into medical school, not to give up reaching goals.

"Wilbert," he said, "wherever you reach on the ladder of success you're climbing, don't jump off. If you do not make medical school, continue your journey upward." I appreciated him for his words. I loved Professor Finston, and he made a big difference in my life.

Dr. Dillard was the only Black Chemistry professor whom the school had. When he was a student in the 1950s, he received a full scholarship to a prestigious college in Virginia to be a major in Chemistry. When the college realized he was Black, they rejected him. Racism wounded him, and he suffered the trauma of it at the hands of the establishment. He was still talking about it. In return, he committed himself not only to the field of Chemistry, but also to Black students. I believe that he understood the emotional strain on us being blacks. Brooklyn College was a challenging college. I heard Dr. Dillard was tutoring the Black student's after-school hours and was doing it with old exams. One week before the course exam, he gave a similar exam to the students that had the same type of questions on it. Midway through Chemistry-II, I went to a few sessions. At the end of the semester, I passed Chemistry-II. Dr. Dillard became my instant hero, and I respected him even more highly. I saw him on campus walking very dignified with his gray hair and broad shoulders. I wondered what it had cost him to be at Brooklyn College; the price he paid being an intelligent and educated black man in America. Dr. Dillard would become another pillar of hope for me.

Family

My family knew that I wanted to be a doctor, and none of them discouraged me for they believed that I could make it. Things were well at home. My sister Shelly was married, and she got a job working at Long Island College Hospital.

My sister Janice had four children, and she was going through some trials with her husband Randy. She was not happy. Janice continued to laugh and crack jokes, but her problems at no time seemed to get her down to the point where she could not function. I knew her problems were serious, and I was furious with her husband who; I think, never did right by her. My mother helped him when he came from North Carolina in the winter with only a thin coat without buttons. He got a job in the bubblegum factory making Bazooka bubble-gum. My mother gave him an application from the US Post Office, and encouraged him to apply. The Post Office hired him. He was involved in a stolen car ring based in New Jersey, and served jail time. My sister suffered through his ordeal, and I believe it broke her down.

My Life

My life rotated around Lorraine, school, church, and family. I was doing terribly in school, paying for Lorraine's paralysis, crying at the altar in church. My life was a wreck. I wanted out of the emotional stress. I didn't think that there would ever be an end to my misery, and I didn't know what to do.

In the summer of 1971, I enrolled in Long Island University to take Organic Chemistry-II. Lorraine was enrolled there. She transferred from Staten Island Community College. They had a special program for the physically disabled. She had a small apartment, which the school provided for her. It was across the street from the university. I visited her often, and our relationship continued. Organic Chemistry-II was very difficult. The professor taught it on an accelerated level, and I wasn't able to understand the molecular structures. I had four weeks to study and pass it. Sadly, at the end of four weeks I failed. Lorraine went to the professor who taught the course and asked him to pass me. I had no idea she did that. Instead of failing me, he gave me an incomplete in the course. The incomplete saved my grade-point average from dropping further. In spite of Lorraine's pain, she cared about my future. I was beginning to believe that I would never become a doctor. I wondered if Leray was right after all, "doctors are born, not made."

The Medical College Admission Test

I took the medical college admission test without completing all the premedical requirements. Physics I & II were not completed. My Chemistry sequence was not complete. I repeated Comparative Anatomy and received a D, and I got a D in Botany. My grade average was having a cardiac arrest, 2.1 and dropping. I needed at least a 3.0 grade-point average to get into medical school. They organized a Black science student organization on campus. One Black student recommended that I attend. I never went to the meetings, and each time he saw me; he let me know that I needed to get involved.

The Stanley Kaplan course, a prep course for the medical college admission test was available. It cost $100 per student. They gave it each year throughout the United States. The Black science students at Brooklyn College believed it was another competitive edge for students. Ten Black students each contributed $10. The plan was to take the course and make photocopies for the rest of us.

Orlando, one of the Black science students, approached me and told me I was making a mistake not getting involved with the organization. He was bright, and I admired him. I never officially joined the Black science student's organization, and I suffered because of it. I took the medical college admission test and failed. The Black students, who accepted the prep course and studied, passed. My chances of getting into medical school were slim from the start and failing the test put me even further behind, but it was partly my own fault. I was too preoccupied with believing that I was not smart enough to pass the test.

Crying at the Altar

When I went to church, I fell on my knees and cried before the altar. I wanted to be a doctor, and I was distraught. I didn't understand why I couldn't achieve excellent grades like most of my peers? What was wrong with my brain? My parents were still encouraging me. My mother told me to hold on, and my father told me that I would make it. At times, believing them was difficult because it seemed a useless journey even to me.

My relationship with Lorraine was as stormy as ever, and we were going down for the third count. I tried everything I knew to please her. When things didn't go the way, she wanted them to go, she put her paralysis before me. I felt trapped. I kept telling myself that God created me free, but I could not free myself from anything; especially Lorraine. I felt helpless and cried out to God to rescue me. I read the Holy Bible every day. I read the Book of Psalms; the same way I did when I was lonely in Boys High School.

New Friends

John and Valerie became my new friends in college. We liked each other from the start. We had lunch together often at Brooklyn College. I liked John and Valerie because they were my sincere friends. We could discuss anything. John knew about my relationship with Lorraine even before our friendship because he lived in Red Hook projects. I never said much to John in Red Hook because I felt he was a tough guy who bullied people in the project. I was wrong. John was gentle if you didn't try to take advantage of him. Even then, he would be civil. Valerie was calm and considerate. When I talked with her, she relaxed and listened to me, never taking her eyes off mine. I believe Valerie was in touch with herself. She was good for John because he was more carefree. He had Red Hook in him (like me), and it showed in his actions and mannerisms. Sometimes John and I would crack jokes and laugh, and if Valerie saw a way to join us, she would.

Trying Romance Again

The young women at Brooklyn College, for the most part, were pleasant. I wasn't attracted to anyone, in particular. Two young women liked me romantically. Both were from the West Indies, Camille and June. They were very feminine and gentle. I dated them at different times. I tried romancing June, but it didn't work. I didn't like her romantically. Camille cared for me, but she wasn't my type, whatever that was. Lorraine's image was always in my mind, though I wanted to forget her. I allowed her to enslave me, and I had become her prisoner. In spite of how I felt; I still saw Lorraine as much as I could. I took her out in my red, blue, and silver polka-dot Volkswagen bug. Sometimes my Great Dane dog, Amani, was in the back seat, blowing smelly hot air on us. Lorraine liked Amani. Wherever Lorraine and I went, I carried Lorraine in my arms, although she had learned to walk with leg braces and crutches. She complained about not feeling like a woman. I tried to help her feel otherwise. We were still making a mess of each other's lives.

An Exodus of Black Power

In the fall of 1971, there were few Black science students at Brooklyn College. One young woman, Deidra, after not doing well in the sciences, quit college. A guy I knew, who wanted to be a doctor, literally packed his duffel bag, quit college, and went to Africa. Some Black students were victims of the system in more than one way. It caused many exoduses from college. It was like an "exodus of Black minds." If it was not racial prejudice, racism, or apathy for Blacks by the system, it was what racist America did to our people as a whole. Slavery was long gone. However, the system that operated it was alive.

Michael and Orlando were successful educationally and made it through the system, and were accepted into medical school. They did not become statistics and failures. They danced to the tune, went through the fire, and survived.

I finally studied the Kaplan prep course notes that Orlando gave me, and took the medical college admission test over. My score was 50% better, though the score was below the national average. I did my very best and there was no more to give. I decided to reapply to medical school.

Applying to Medical School

I applied to medical school before completing Organic Chemistry-II and Physics II. I had a D in Physics, and decided not to take it over. Physics was hard and painful on my brain. The math part of it drained me. I hated it.

When I took the medical college admission test, it didn't seem hard, it was just long. My score was very low. I had the Harvard University recommendation. I did well in the minority health career's summer program, but my grades at Brooklyn College were horrible and the medical college admission test confirmed my weakness in science.

I went to Professor Finston, and he spoke with me plain. "Wilbert," he said, "how am I going to give you a recommendation to medical school with your grades? The only thing I can tell the schools is you are a hard worker. If you had greater opportunities educationally, you would probably be one of the best students around. Wilbert, I told you before, if you don't make it into medical school, do not give up. "At this point, you should not stop on the ladder keep climbing." I respected Prof. Finston for honesty. He was right, and I knew it.

I went to the Comparative Anatomy teacher. I had a D in his course. He almost laughed at me when I told him that I was applying to medical school. "Wilbert," he voiced, "how can I give you a recommendation when you only attained a D in my course? I do not think that you are medical school material. I am sorry. I cannot write you a recommendation." I went to my Botany professor, and he told me the same thing, but he didn't have a smirk on his face.

I went to Professor Dillard and asked him to write a recommendation for me, and he agreed. He asked me how many schools, and I told him about thirty, which turned out to be forty. I waited patiently in the fall of 1970 to hear from the medical schools. Rejection letters started coming back to me after a couple of months.

The Lowest Score in the Whole Country

"Downstate Medical School and Stony Brook Medical School" requested interviews. At Downstate, Dr. Green interviewed me. He told me that he was sure I was a nice guy, and he believed I could make it through medical school. He said that I needed to show it by getting some A's and B's on my college transcript in the sciences. "Wilbert," he said, "I am sure you got the lowest score in the whole country on the medical college admission test." I was shocked when he told me that. He did not apologize for saying it, and I swallowed it. What he said to me became a part of my low self-image. He told me if I attained what he suggested; he would personally handle my application favorably the following year. I rode the Long Island Railroad two hours to reach Stony Brook Medical School. It was a new school, and they were accepting only twenty-four students in their first-year class. I waited patiently for hours to get an interview. When they finally called me into the interviewer's office, the interviewer continued to tell me that their school interviewed all Black students. After looking at my record, he had no idea why someone asked me for an interview. He said, "Many bright students are applying to medical school and some of them are engineers, and I doubt if you're going to get in." I sat there wondering, "Then why ask me out here, to tell me I am not good enough?" I was mad. I got a car ride back to Brooklyn and was upset all the way home.

Rejections from schools were pouring into my mailbox. Downstate medical School and Stony Brook rejected me. All forty schools rejected my applications. I felt terrible. I broke down and cried in church, and no one really knew I was crying because I was afraid I would never become a doctor.

Attending Two Colleges

That spring semester I enrolled at New York City Community College's night school while I still attended Brooklyn College. I didn't let either school know what I was doing, because it was not allowed. I was determined to get the A's and B's Dr. Green talked to me about, even if he was lying.

I took Microbiology, Physics II, and Organic Chemistry-II. I worked hard at these courses. At Brooklyn College, I took a course called "History of the English Language." It had one exam at the end, and I thought it was going to be easy. I failed the course. It set me behind six months in college. I changed my major to English in order to get out of Brooklyn College, because I had more than thirty credits in it. At that point, I didn't care what my major was. I needed a Bachelor's Degree. Medical schools preferred candidates to have a Bachelor's Degree in anything, and that is what I was going to give them. I bought a ten-speed bike, rode it to Community College at night, and took the subway train to Brooklyn College during the day.

Chapter 8

Romancing Iris

For thou hast possessed my reins:
Thou hast covered me in my mother's womb.

Psalm 139:13

My life was at a strain, and I was in and out of depression. I rode my ten-speed bike to pass the time and think about my future. The only relief I had from my troubles was sharing my life with a girl named Barbara, who attended the same church that I did. We were not romantically involved. We were friends. We shared many conversations about Christianity, God, and man. We enjoyed talking and spending time together. Barbara was pleasant. We were involved in the youth group at Calvary Baptist Church.

When I was not with Lorraine, at church, or studying, I rode my bike to pass the time. One day I was riding through the project, and I saw Barbara. I stopped to talk to her, and Iris passed. She was beautiful. Iris's light brown hair was long over her shoulders. She was wearing blue jeans, sandals and a tank top blouse. I looked away from her for a moment, continuing to speak with Barbara. Suddenly, Iris yelled, "Hi." When I turned in her direction, she was waving her hand in the air looking at me. She had a smile on her face that could have taken the heart of any young man. I wasn't sure that she was talking to me, so I tried to ignore her. Iris's friend, Minerva, was looking out of a window. Minerva yelled to Iris. She said something to her that I thought was about me, and they laughed. These two girls were talking to each other. Iris's hand was still up in the air waving at me, and I said to me, "No, she's not trying to get my attention." As quickly as she appeared, she was gone. I found out from her friend that her name was Iris.

Iris lived in Red Hook projects, and I saw her often, but never said anything to her because I was older than she was. Nevertheless, now she was grown up and beautiful. I remembered her as a little girl with bushy eyebrows and bright eyes. Once I was with my dog Amani. She walked by and asked me to move my dog, so she could pass. I told her Amani would not hurt her. That was the closest I ever remember being near her.

After my conversation with Barbara, I got on my bike and tried to find Iris. I still had this thing about "West Side Story" and Natalie Wood playing the role of a Puerto Rican. The song "Maria" was playing in my soul. I thought of "West Side Story" as I did in the ninth grade. Nevertheless, Iris was more beautiful than Natalie Wood or Rosa. I found Iris by the Red Hook swimming pool sitting on a bench with her cousin Rosaria, who was her same age and her cousin Adelita. My heart was pounding while I slowly stopped my bike in front of her. She looked at me with a smile, but was silent. "Hello," I said, "My name is Buddy." When I asked her what, her name was, she said, "Iris." She introduced me to her cousin. The next words I heard come out of her mouth were, "Aren't you the guy whom Lorraine jumped out of the window over?" I wasn't surprised she asked me, but I was shocked that she had the nerve to ask it as if she believed it to be true. I got on the defensive and told her that is not the way it was. I was straddling my bike making conversation with her, feeling like I was defending myself. I resented the position; she put me in, and she appeared to enjoy the whole fiasco, watching me squirm like an earthworm. While I spoke with her, Adelita fell on her knee and cut it on the concrete. I jumped at the chance to offer limited medical experience. Iris took her home, and I followed. I walked into her apartment as if I lived there, which was not like me. Iris had enticed me, and I liked what I saw. I was looking for her up and down as if I had no control of my senses.

When the door closed behind me, the first face, I saw was her father, Zacharias. He stood motionless and stared at me. I focused on his frown, then his strong-looking body, and started quivering. Commotion in the house over Adelita's cut gave me some air time. Her father gave attention to Adelita, and then glanced at me. I tried not looking at him. I said to me, "You better say something or attention will focus on why you are here." While Iris was explaining what took place, Iris's mother, Doris, was looking at the cut. She was short, just like my mother, and I immediately related to her because of it. She looked at me and smiled. I figured; let me play a junior doctor. After all, I did apply to medical school, even if I got forty rejections. It was a small cut, and I knew it would be OK. Her father looked at me and did not say one word. Iris's mother, Mrs. Santiago, got some antiseptic, and I cleaned and bandaged the wound. "There," I said. "She'll be OK." I talked after that until people in the house looked weary. I believed they had enough of me for one exciting day, and I left. I told Iris I would see her around.

A couple of days passed and her cousin Rosaria encouraged her to seek me out so I could take them to Coney Island Amusement Park for a good time. Nevertheless, I had to work. Her cousin must have figured that I had money to throw away.

I had a job working in Larsen's Bakery while I was attending college, which was the neighborhood bakery in the project. They baked the pastry and bread during the day, and I washed the dirty baking pans at night and early in the morning. During the day, the aroma of Larsen filled the air blowing west of it. Walking by and smelling the air made one want to go in. Some people went in, even if they had no money, to get a bigger smothering of the aroma. Often I went in with a few cents in my pocket and walked out empty-handed with nothing to eat because I didn't have enough money. I had the privilege of not only cleaning the baking pans with all the remaining pastry left on the bottom; I was also eating as much as I could find in boxes, while working on Fridays from 7:30 p.m. until 5:00 a.m. at $40 per night. I put baking pans on the conveyor belt and took them off all night. I would sit on a stool and listen to preachers like Reverend Ike and Reverend Shambock on the radio stations. Sometimes I was so mad at Rev. Ike with his get-rich-quick pious schemes. I felt like smashing the little cheap radio that I heard him on (which is not the one I stole when I was eleven years old). Rev. Ike would tell people to send him some money, and God would bless them with a Cadillac Automobile, as God did for him. His favorite line was, "Ain't no pie in the sky; the pie is right here loved ones." He begged for money so much that it made me emotionally ill. Rev. Ike needed a whipping for telling all those lies that he told to people. I took it personally. Rev. Shambock was a bit wild with all his hollering, but he was more believable. I enjoyed listening to him. I was extremely religious at the time, and I let people know it.

When Iris finally caught up to me, she told me that her friend Minerva thought that I was fine looking. Minerva told her, "Honey, if you don't want him, I'll take him." Minerva was kind to me, but too aggressive and loud, although the few times I was in her company, I enjoyed it.

A Stupid Mistake

Lorraine was still a factor in my life, and she found out through her sister that I was seeing "a Puerto Rican girl who looked white." Lorraine was very blunt; she told me that I had better stop seeing Iris, or she would end our relationship. I continued to see Iris, and Iris did not know I was still dating Lorraine. I liked Iris a lot. I was still feeling guilty about Lorraine's paralysis. She continued to tell me that she didn't feel like a woman and blamed me for her being crippled. She practiced her usual serious game on me, and I was still her prisoner. That is the only reason I made a stupid mistake by continuing to trust her.

I introduced Iris to my family. My mother liked her from the start. My sister Janice was a bit laid-back, wondering why I had to date a Puerto Rican girl. Shelly, as usual, was noncommittal verbally. I believed that she liked Iris. My father was silent on the issue until he realized I was serious about Iris. "Buddy," he said, "why can't you find a Black girl to date? There are plenty of them out there."

I responded, "I like Iris." He never said another word to me about it.

Iris's father was not happy about our relationship either. He told me our cultures were different. Her mother liked me and kept feeding me rice, beans, steak, and plenty of milk, and that spoke enough about how, she felt about me. Iris's sister was going through her rough teen years and was having her own problems. Running away; she could have cared less about me. Her younger brother Tibbs was cool with me. He was dating a girl named Nancy with who he loved. Iris's little baby brother Pito was too busy having Mrs. Santiago do his homework and eating avocados at the dining room table. I watched that boy put away avocados like they were becoming extinct. Our relatives, overall, were quiet about our romance. One in her family and one in mine voiced their negative concerns about our relationship. To my knowledge, everyone else in the families was either accepting or tolerating our being together.

I was doing well at New York City Community College. I finally enjoyed Physics and Microbiology and tolerated Organic Chemistry. I even took an English course called Chaucer at Brooklyn College, it was tough. I underestimated that course. I didn't think that I would do well, but surprisingly, I got a B.

Lorraine finally decided that there was nothing she could do to separate me from Iris. She told me I could be with Iris if I told her what went on between us. I fell for it, completely. I foolishly told my mother and Iris I was no longer with Lorraine.

Mr. Santiago Protecting Iris

Iris and I had some great times together. Each time I wanted to take her out during the evening; I had to ask her father. It was an ordeal I had to go through, but I respected Mr. Santiago's concern for his daughter. I tried waiting until there was no one in the living room before asking to take her out. Iris tried to clear the conversation zone when I arrived. He never gave me a hard time; I believe that he knew that I was afraid of him. He could put a look on his face, and gas would bubble in my stomach. I wanted his daughter, and I was willing to do the jig to get her.

I usually took her to Manhattan, New York to see a movie. After the picture, we walked a lot and when we got tired of that, we found a restaurant to eat. Once I took her to a Hawaiian restaurant. She enjoyed it, and I felt good showing her a great time. I remember when I went to the bathroom; there was a guy in there who tried to wipe my hands with a towel. I wasn't used to going to fancy places, and I didn't know what was on his mind. I left him standing where I met him and walked out. When I told Iris about it, she laughed. Iris saw her first play with me and my family, "Your Arms Are Too Short to Box with God." It was a memorable evening. I wanted my family to accept her, and I wanted her to like them, and it was happening.

Sometimes I took Iris to Coney Island Amusement Park in my sister Janice's blue car. I needed some money and sold mine for $300. My sister did not even know that the car was gone because I would just take it while she was in her house. It wasn't like stealing, but it was as if it was revenge for her telling me to steal my father's money, then saying she did not. Taking her car was also a payback for her beating me up. I liked eating the fries at Nathan's restaurant. On our way home, we would stop the car under the Verrazano Narrows Bridge in Brooklyn, to tell each other how much we cared about our relationship. We liked doing that, and we did it often.

My most memorable time with Iris was when I went to a lake with her family in Pennsylvania. She wore a two-piece bathing suit that I didn't appreciate because it was too revealing. We played as little school kids splashing water on each other in the lake and laughing a lot.

I tried to expose Iris to my family as much as possible, and I spent a great deal of time in her house relating to her family. I sported a Puerto Rican flag on my army jacket. It helped me feel a sense of oneness to Puerto Ricans and loyalty.

Iris showed me how special she was when I needed to study. Once we were sitting on the bench in front of her apartment, and I told her that I needed to study. She told me to go do it. I felt good about it because it showed me that she cared about my future. I called her on the telephone to find out if she was upset with me, if that was the reason she told me to go home to study. She said that she was not upset and only wanted me to do what I needed to do.

I was elected for a community spot on the Red Hook Board and was asked to go to New Orleans, Louisiana to a conference. Iris, who helped me pack my clothes, was very special from the early days of our relationship. These are the invaluable things that people never knew about her. Her gentleness and her strength were often hidden from outsiders because the things, she did for me were special to her, and she did them privately.

Racism on a Grand Scale

New Orleans was a "trip" never to forget, because the American fiber of racial discrimination was there, and it affected me deeply. New Orleans was one of the main historical centers for jazz music, and Black people were at the forefront of it. I didn't realize it, but I was in the state of Louisiana, which was known for its deep racial prejudice. I went to a massage parlor. I found it in the Yellow Pages. When I arrived at the parlor, a middle-aged white woman told me, in a Southern drawl, "We don't have any Black girls in this place. An older-looking black woman sat in a chair looking at me. I imagined her saying, "Don't you understand you are not wanted here?" At first, I thought that I didn't hear this lady correctly. Then she said it to me again, "I said, we don't have any Black girls." I understood. I needed to get out of her establishment. I never wanted to go to New Orleans again. I felt degraded. I disrespected myself.

When I was in New Orleans, I met a person named Stoney, who worked as a health center Administrator. He told me that he would help me get into medical school. Stoney lived in the Bronx, New York. The health center was in Valhalla, New York; a few miles from where he lived.

He invited me to his house in order to take me to the health center where I met some key people who were connected to New York Medical College. Iris did not agree. She believed that he had other motives, but I met him anyway. When I arrived at Stoney's house, he was happily waiting for me. He delayed our leaving his house in order to talk to me about going with him to California, where he claimed he had a beautiful house. He told me that he would take me to Europe, and I would not have to spend a cent. He asked me to think about it. He tried to arouse me sexually by talking about dick sizes and having sex. I told him that I was not into that. He came close to me and did some funny motions with his tongue. He made me mad, I was sorry that I went to his house. He kept trying to get at me, I aggressively retreated from him. I guess he got tired, and we left for Valhalla, New York. While we were in the car, he had calmed down outwardly. When we arrived at the health center, he introduced me to some people, but I had no idea if they had any influence in order to help me. I got tired of hanging out with him and wanted to go home. Stoney tried to keep me with him, as long as he could. On the way back to his apartment he kept looking at me, rolling his eyes and sticking out his tongue. As for me, his being gay was his business, but I wanted nothing to do with it.

When I arrived home, I was glad to see Iris. I missed her terribly. We saw each other as often as we could, she encouraged me to study and do well in college.

The Final Blow

Lorraine became a bad habit. Nothing was going right between us; she brought the worst out in me, and it was dangerous for both of us. Iris wanted me to be hers and only hers. I was lying to Iris big time and failing her.

One evening I was coming home from a youth meeting in the church, and Barbara was with me. It was an unusual foggy evening. I held Barbara's hand while walking her home and Iris saw us. She knew that I was friendly with Barbara, but it upset her to see me holding another girl's hand. I did not understand it at the time, but Iris had a righteous jealousy for me because I expressed my love to her. Iris broke up with me after she could not convince me that my relationship with Barbara was not right. Lorraine called Iris and told her that I looked sad in church. She was hoping that she would create a disturbance and keep Iris and me apart for all time.

Iris and I kept in touch, and we resolved the issue concerning Barbara and got back together. One night I was supposed to meet Iris at 9:00 p.m. after youth meeting. Lorraine called Iris, harassing her. Iris told her that we were together again. Lorraine got upset and came to the church in a taxicab. She knew that I was going to meet Iris. After the youth meeting was over, she asked me to take her home. The next-day Iris was at my apartment. Lorraine called about seven times. I told Lorraine that I was busy and couldn't speak with her. On the last call, I didn't hang up the telephone. Iris asked me why Lorraine was calling me if we were no longer together. I told her that I didn't know, that I didn't want Lorraine and she was annoying me. Lorraine heard the conversation. That evening she called Iris and told her that I was lying to her, that I was seeing her and another woman. Iris didn't believe her until Lorraine told her intimate things about us. Lorraine told Iris no matter how much I messed around with her; I would eventually come back to Lorraine. Iris was shocked. She confronted me. She asked me if I were still with Lorraine and did I convey information to Lorraine about us. I told her yes, and I was sorry. I told Iris that I felt trapped, held like a prisoner, I could not free myself. I told her that I would leave Lorraine. Iris was extremely distraught and hurt that I deceived her. I didn't have a good answer for her. It wasn't really Lorraine, who held me imprisoned. My own weakness and inability held me captive. I was determined that I would not take any more guilt that Lorraine was ramming down my throat. Iris loved me and was willing to give me another chance.

One Monday evening during a youth meeting at the church, Lorraine had someone drop her off and leave her. After the meeting, she asked me to take her home. After taking her to her apartment, she said, "I know Iris was waiting for you tonight." I told her, Iris was none of her business and it was over between us. I took the ring that she gave me, threw it on the floor, and crushed it with my shoe heel. I told her to give me back everything that I ever gave her, including the engagement ring, which I gave her years before. She told me no. I walked out of her apartment, got on the elevator, and she followed me in her wheelchair. We argued to the ground floor level. She followed me to the parking lot. I got in my sister's car, and she rolled her wheelchair in front of it, while she dared me to run her over. I got out of the car and pushed her to the side of it, and she rolled in front of it again. I got out a second time and rolled her away from it. She maneuvered it again in front of my car. I got out of the car a third time and smacked her face. A person was looking from his apartment window and yelled at me, "Hey, stop beating on that woman in that wheelchair." I jumped into the car, and sped away. That was the end to my relationship with Lorraine. I went to Iris's apartment and told her what happened. I felt terrible smacking Lorraine, but I was finally free from her.

Moving On

At the close of the college semester, I passed Microbiology and Organic Chemistry-II with B's and even got an A in Physics-II. I passed my English courses, getting two B's and a C, and was proud of myself. I had proven that I could get good grades, even if I had to work very hard in order to get them.

I still wanted to be a doctor. I was obsessed with it. I knew that if I became a doctor, I would do my best to be an excellent one. I told Iris that I was continuing my journey to medical school, and reapplied. We spent time together, and some of it was writing postcards to schools for applications.

Reapplying to Medical School

I decided this time to apply to forty-one medical schools, including some foreign. I went to the Italian consulate in Manhattan, New York. When I walked into the consulate, I felt nervous not being Italian and being a Black, asking for an application to attend medical school in Italy. An Italian woman sat behind a wooden table looking very stern. I told her that I was there in order to get an application to medical school in Italy. She stared at me for a moment. I waited patiently for her to give me the documents. I was suspicious that she wondered if I spoke Italian, and who did I think I was trying to get into an Italian medical school. I went to the British, French, and Canadian consulates and requested their documents in order to apply to their schools. Iris was very considerate of my desire to be a doctor, and she never doubted for a moment that I would make it. She spent much energy convincing me that I would get in.

Graduation Again

I graduated on June 12, 1972 from Brooklyn College with a Bachelor of Arts Degree in English. I did not believe that I knew any more English than I did after leaving high school. My parents and Iris were very proud of me. I looked back over the six years that I had spent in college, knowing it should have only taken me four. I knew that I paid a price for sticking it out, and I paid the price in full with my sweat, tears, and prayers. My relationship with Iris was going well, we were reading the Holy Bible together, and thinking about our future. I wanted to be admitted to medical school before we discussed marriage. After I applied for medical school a second time, I worried as I waited for the responses. They started coming in within thirty days. I did not think that any medical school would accept me.

Tired of My Journey

I enrolled at Richmond College in Staten Island and took Black Study, Art and English courses. As I rode the Staten Island Ferry from lower Manhattan to Staten Island, I reflected on history and how it affected Black people. Often as I passed the Statue of Liberty in New York Harbor, I thought about black people's journey, how they arrived on slave ships to America. I wondered, was there any justice in America? Could Black people make it in a country that practiced racial discrimination and bigotry? Does the symbol of the Statue of Liberty mean the same for me as for other Americans? These questions were before me daily. I felt as though the fire and fumes covered me, as I imagined how the fire and fumes were in ancient Babylon before its destruction. I was very tired with my journey.

PART II

Kindling Flames

I put myself in the midst of this highly charged atmosphere

Chapter 9
Albany Medical College

If I ascend up into heaven, thou art there:
If I make my bed in hell, behold, thou art there.

Psalm 139:8

Affirmative Action was in full motion. Albany Medical College in upstate New York was looking for qualified Black applicants to interview for their freshman class. Previously, they did not accept any Black students in three years. The college was private, with stiff requirements. A student in my class asked me if I applied to Albany Medical School, and I told him that I wasn't sure. "You better look into it," he said, "because I hear they want black students badly." They had rejected me the previous year, but I sent a second application for admission.

Two weeks after my conversation with him, I received a letter in the mail asking for an interview. I wasn't optimistic about the interview because I didn't think that it would be any better than the previous year's interviews at Downstate and Stony Brook Medical Schools.

I took a three-and-one-half-hour trip on a New York Trailway's bus to Albany, New York. I had plenty of time in order to think. I thought of how desperately I wanted to become a doctor. I would do almost anything in order to be accepted into medical school and was mentally exhausted. If I had any energy left, I would need it for the interviews.

When I arrived in Albany, I quickly caught a taxi to the medical center. I was dressed in a wool suit, and I carried my leather briefcase, which gave me a sense of security. I walked into the main lobby, and didn't see any Black people. I thought, "Surely there must be some around."

A woman approached me and asked if I needed any help. When I identified myself, she welcomed me to the medical college. She was very friendly and smiled the time that I was with her. She told me that two doctors, a Psychiatrist and a Pharmacologist, would interview me. The Psychiatrist, Dr. Bell, to my surprise was Black. He told me that I was granted an interview because the admissions committee was amazed that I had the nerve to apply to their school twice after being rejected. They wondered why with my marginal grades, I believed that I would ever be admitted to their medical school.

Dr. Bell said some professors believed that with my determination and their help, I might become a fine doctor. He said that the only problem in the interview would be with the Pharmacologist, Dr. Reynolds. "Wilbert," he said, "he doesn't believe that you'll make it through this medical school, and he's serious; you will have to win him to your side." Dr. Bell told me that I didn't have to worry about his interview. I thanked him for his frankness and anxiously awaited my interview with Dr. Reynolds.

When Dr. Reynolds came into the room, I was ready to speak to him with confidence. After asking me a few questions, he politely said, "I don't think you can make it through this medical school."

I said, "Yes, I can."

He replied, "I don't think so."

I became aggressive with him. I said, "Hey, man, I can make it through this school." He told me that I would have a very difficult time, and he would recommend that I not be admitted to the college. I guess my grades were enough to convince him that he could judge me on paper.

I traveled back to Brooklyn with mixed emotions about being accepted to Albany Medical College. I didn't think that I had a chance of getting in.

My family was very supportive. My father kept telling me that something would come through. Iris continued to encourage and support me. She waited patiently, while I waited impatiently, for an answer from Albany Medical College. My studies at Richmond College became a burden. I didn't want to be there, and I didn't want to hang out on the street either, because I wasn't working.

Admittance to Medical School

After an anxious two weeks, I received a letter from the medical college, accepting me. I couldn't believe it. I called the Admissions Office and asked the receptionist if they had made a mistake.

"Are you Wilbert Williams, Jr.?"

I said, "Yes."

"Then we have the right person. It's no mistake." When I told my parents that I was admitted to medical school, they were very excited because they knew how much it meant to me. I went to Iris's house and told them the good news. Everyone was happy, and I still couldn't believe it. I quit college because I was tired of undergraduate school, and my brain was saturated. I applied for a job at Long Island College Hospital to work in the outpatient clinic department where I would pull and deliver medical records. Paul Garguilo, who was my boss when I worked there before, was still there, and would still be a friend to me.

Getting Married

Iris and I decided to get married. We told our parents about our decision, they were not happy. They wanted time to prepare a wedding for us, but we believed that there was too much confusion surrounding us. We had a few days in order to prepare for the wedding, and it created its own confusion. Mr. Santiago was grieving over losing his first daughter, and my father informed me that there would be plenty of pretty girls in medical school. Our mothers didn't say anything negative. Our wedding was small at Calvary Baptist Church in Red Hook. There weren't many people there, but our families were represented, along with a few friends. We had our honeymoon at Howard Johnson in Manhattan, and it was Iris's first time in a hotel. Within a few days, our honeymoon was over, and I was back at work, and Iris was being a new homemaker.

We found a small apartment in an Italian neighborhood in Brooklyn's Carol Garden section, a few blocks from my job. It was a dreary place with black ceilings and dark painted walls. The only window in the living room looked at an adjacent red brick wall of the next building, where there was an alleyway. We repainted the apartment and settled into our new home.

While I worked, Iris stayed home. She had a little dog-named "Mudley," that didn't seem to like me. I constantly complained about her dog. My dog Amani was with us. In addition, the longer I complained, the more the dog didn't like me. One day while I was at work, the dog ran into the street and got hit by a car. When I got home, Iris was crying, I cried with her. It was our first tragedy in our brand-new family.

My job was challenging because I didn't like pulling medical records and going up and down in the elevator and occasionally running up the stairs when charts were needed. It was, however, bringing in needed income, and I needed to be responsible; especially as a married man.

I often walked to and from work, which was about seven city blocks. When I was working, I could sit in a little room and read a Gross Anatomy text. I went to the store across the street from the hospital and bought a $6 stethoscope and a $10 blood pressure cuff.

The admissions committee at the school believed that I, and the other incoming black students, would benefit from a special orientation program for minority students. They planned for us to take Physiology and Biochemistry for three weeks before the entering freshman class.

I didn't work very hard at the hospital. Many of the people who knew me when I was in college were happy that I decided to work at the hospital before going to medical school.

One time I was walking home from the hospital through an Italian neighborhood, which was a few blocks away. A little boy stood in front of me and called me a "nigger." I looked straight in his eyes, and he looked at me and walked away. My heart broke. I felt that he was too young to understand what it meant to call someone a "nigger." Either he heard that word in his neighborhood or someone encouraged him to say it. I went home and told Iris that a little Italian boy called me a "nigger." We didn't discuss it, but for a long time I never stopped hurting over it.

I missed my family and wanted to see them. Iris was upset about it. I wasn't prepared for this side of marriage, and I became angry. I didn't understand how important my relationship with her was. She was a good wife, constantly trying to please me. I was too immature to accept her.

We had the opportunity to save some money. Raymond's mother, Angelina Scott, was dying of cancer and was in the hospital. She offered her apartment rent-free to Iris and me. We took it. Iris didn't want to go back to Red Hook, but she knew that it would save us money. We stayed there until I started school.

I Love My Wife

Eleanor came into my life again. She called my mother's house and asked for me. She was visiting her sister in the Bronx. I was not over her from my days at Harvard, but my marriage to Iris meant a great deal to me now, for I loved Iris. I called Eleanor and arranged to meet her at Flushing Meadow Park in Queens, New York. When I saw her, I was surprised with myself because I was excited to see her. I had not seen her in more than two years. I took a blanket from the trunk of my car to sit on. I spread it over a small patch of green grass, and we sat. I kept enough distance from her in order to relay the message that things were no longer the same between us. We talked about Harvard, and the good time that we had. She looked at me in a way, which I understood that I could have her, but Iris kept flashing in my mind. There was nothing left for Eleanor that was romantic or intimate to me and there was no way that I would give into her. I talked to her about her boyfriend, Poncho. She told me that they decided to break off their relationship for all time. I asked her what happened between us, and she told me that she thought that she felt more for Poncho. I reminded her that I was married and couldn't get involved with her. She moved closer to me, and I believe that she wanted me to kiss her, but I didn't. I was proud of myself that day because I did the right thing for once and remained true to myself and faithful to Iris. When we parted, I told her to take care of herself.

I never saw Eleanor again.

Going to Medical School

A few days before August, I quit my job at the hospital to go to Albany. On the day, we were leaving Brooklyn for Albany; I had a mixed bag of feelings. On one hand, I wanted to start medical school as soon as possible, but emotionally I was tied to my family. Leaving them would be difficult regardless, but medical school was the road that I had to take.

Iris was ready to go in our old Ford Torino, which was painted with blue enamel paint, and had bald tires. We brought it a few months prior. After loading our car with the few things, we had and after saying good-bye to our families, we headed for upstate New York for a three-and-one-half-hour ride. I kept thinking about medical school and how long and tedious my journey had been, and still couldn't believe that I was really going to become a medical student. I envisioned myself with white clothes and with a stethoscope around my neck, and with books stuffed in my coat pockets. I mentally saw my parents smiling at me, full of pride.

Driving up the New York State Thruway, I thought about my journey from Red Hook projects to medical school. I worked very hard to walk into the ivory hall of that institution. I didn't know what was awaiting me. When we were two miles from the exit to downtown Albany, the radiator was steaming and the car slowed. I prayed that the car wouldn't shut off until we reached 566 Madison Avenue, where the one-bedroom apartment, we were renting was. I didn't know it, but we would spend the next five years in Albany, New York, instead of four, and it would be the most academically trying years that I would ever experience. When we reached the block where the apartment was, our Ford "buggy" just stopped running. I rolled the car down the inclined street in neutral and parked it in an open area in front of our window.

There is a beautiful park called Washington Park across the street from the apartment, and it would become one of my places to steal away to. I loved it. Iris was excited about being in Albany, and I was excited about becoming a medical student, but I quickly put medical school behind me, for the moment, and was worrying about my car. After we settled in our new apartment, I went outside to start the car and the engine wouldn't turn over. We went to bed early that evening because I was due in medical school the following day.

Black Peas in a Pot of White Rice

I got up early the next morning and anxiously went to the medical center. I met three black students. We were scheduled for a special orientation at the medical school. The admissions committee believed that our educational backgrounds were weak, and we would benefit by studying Biochemistry and Physiology before the incoming freshman class.

Jimmy Stevenson was the first black student who I met. He graduated from Brooklyn College, but I had never seen him on campus. He told me that there were two other students coming. Sure enough, within a few minutes I saw two black guys come into the main lobby looking lost. When we realized that we were searching for each other, we started laughing. We joked about being four peas in a pot of white rice. One student, Oswald Hayes, who was from Brooklyn via the island of Jamaica, said, "Well, they got four 'niggers' in this school. Here come the 'niggers.'" None of us said a word; we chuckled. Harrison Lenoir was the quiet one. He was a graduate from Howard University who was the only one of us who had a master's degree; his was an advanced degree in science. His father was a dentist in Los Angeles, California.

There were three professors scheduled to meet us on our first day. Dr. Procitor, a professor of Pharmacology, greeted us and ushered us up to the third floor for a talk. He greeted us warmly, and I liked him from the start. He told us that he was going to be our mentor. He spoke with us about the Affirmative Action program and stated that we were able to get into the school because of it. He made it clear that we were also picked on our personal qualities and ambition, but compared to most of the students in our incoming class we were probably in for a rough ride. He then took us to various department heads and introduced us to them. Dr. Procitor told us that Physiology and Biochemistry were the two courses, which most students found the hardest, and that's where the first point of separation began as far as who would probably make it through medical school.

Dr. Beeler, the Biochemistry professor, who we met, told us that his course, along with Physiology, would separate the men from the boys. "My course is a difficult course, and I teach it quickly so you better be ready to keep up with me. Steroid Chemistry is a lot to know, and I'm going to move rapidly." He wasn't joking.

Professor Grumboch taught physiology. He taught the electro physiology portion of the regular course during the year. I wouldn't understand a thing that he would speak about in electrophysiology, during and after the orientation to medical school. The final professor who we met that day was Professor Edmunds. He taught the Anatomies and started us out in cell anatomy and the electron microscope.

All of these professors treated us well and were very polite. Professor Grumbock would speak to us with a half-smile, as if he knew something about our future, which we didn't know.

Beginning the Nightmare

The first couple of days with these professors were very challenging to me. The other Black students appeared confident in their abilities to do well.

When we had our first physiology lecture, I sat in my seat as I listened and watched Professor Grumbock draw the electrochemical potential wave and did not understand any of it. After class, he lit a cigarette, walked slowly in front of the room, smiled, and asked us if we understood the material. I didn't understand a thing and was very confused. I didn't know why because I had read the textbook. After Dr. Grumbock asked us a few questions, he realized that I was confused with the material and said, "What is it you don't understand, Williams?"

"None of it," I answered.

"I can't go over all of it again; tell me what specifically is bothering you?"

"All of it," I said.

While he dragged and puffed on his cigarette, he looked frustrated and drew that square, which represents a human cell and the sodium and potassium ions and started making all kinds of lines with the chalk again, and I was confused even more. "Do you understand it now?" he said.

"No," I responded.

He went over it two more times, and I still didn't get it. He told me to go home and read it again. Oswald, Jimmy and Harrison didn't say a word to me about what happened in class. I kept saying, "I don't understand that stuff." I had my usual mental block and was again behind my classmates.

Biochemistry was more interesting than Physiology, but Dr. Beeler talked as fast as a person in an air-traffic control tower. He moved through Steroid Chemistry as if he were reading his Social Security number. He wouldn't stop scribbling with that chalk while he bounced up and down like a basketball. Steroid Chemistry was coming out of my nose. I literally felt sick after that lecture, but it was just another day for Dr. Beeler. After the lecture, he asked us a bunch of questions. "What do you guys like to do after hours? You know you guys are not going to be able to dress the way you did before coming here, because you are in medical school now with other priorities. The social life is going to be a bit difficult for you guys." We didn't understand where he was coming from and left the classroom baffled.

We set our minds on our next lecture, with Dr. Edmunds. I liked Dr. Edmunds because he was straight with us. He told us that he was going to talk about Cell Biology, and if we had any questions, he would be glad to answer them. He started asking us about the human cell and seeing if we understood high school-level biology and abruptly stopped. "Hey, what am I going over this stuff with you guys for, you know this stuff. How would you guys like to do some things with the electron microscope?"

We jumped at the chance. I saw some things under that scope which I had never seen in my life, and I was fascinated. After the session, we all walked out of his lab feeling charged up.

Oswald said, "Now I could dig that. What do these guys think? We're some high-school students or something?"

Iris had a new job in the medical college library and was doing fine. She made some friends quickly and was enjoying it. I was missing my family in Red Hook and wanted the security of being there. I needed to grow up and understand that what I had embarked on was a serious decision to get a piece of America's apple pie; namely, medicine, and that it was going to be a tough part of my journey.

I needed to muster up strength and endurance because it was going to get hot. Physiology continued to be challenging, and I still didn't understand anything Professor Grumbock taught. It was very frustrating.

Biochemistry was also challenging, but at least I could understand the material. When the orientation was over, I was convinced that I was in for a rough journey. Iris was encouraging me through my period of low self-esteem and struggle. I was blessed that Iris was with me.

The First Official Day

The first official day of medical school was like standing in a soup line. Everyone was running around like chickens with their head's cut off. Confusion was everywhere. We were standing in threes in the hallway, waiting to have our mug shots taken (as if we were criminals). I felt like I was in undergraduate school again. Some things don't change.

A few days after the "official" orientation to medical school had cooled down; people began thinking seriously about studying. The scheduled courses for that semester were Physiology, Biochemistry and Psychiatry. Three courses seemed very little, yet I had no idea until the first week was over, just how much material would be covered that semester.

I studied hard from the first day. I didn't put down my books for almost anything except to sleep. Occasionally, I tried to study and watch TV, but that game ended after the first few tries. Most nights, Iris would go to bed without me. It was difficult for her to stay up while I was studying, even though she tried many times. I felt abandoned when she would go to bed, but I never said anything. Most times, she watched the TV with an earphone to keep from disturbing me.

When the weekend arrived, I was so geared up that I couldn't stop studying. The weekend just seemed like extra study days. I studied every weekend and didn't tire easily. My energy came from two endless sources, fear and God.

The First Test

Our initial examination was scheduled to be at the end of the first four weeks. I was trying to study in advance, but it was nearly impossible to do that. I had a lot to read, and the material was becoming more difficult to understand. Every time I thought that I was ahead, there was always some new material that took extra time to study. The night before my Physiology exam, I stayed up until early the following morning and tried to put the last pieces together. The exam was "open book," and we were allowed to bring with us any material we wanted. I walked into the lecture hall with five physiology books, which Iris helped me carry to school.

When I arrived, some of my classmates were already there, talking about Physiology as if it were the most important thing in the world. I disliked jam sessions like that; they always made me more nervous. As I sat waiting for the professor to bring the examination, my body felt as though it were falling apart. I felt as if something heavy was weighing on my chest, and my heart would beat right through it. When the professor arrived at my row and handed me the test, it felt like a book. When I started writing my name, my hand wouldn't stop shaking.

At first sight of the questions, I realized that no books were going to help me. The questions did not require direct answers. I had to think them out. All reasoning escaped me. The fear of failure filled every part in my body because I believed that I didn't understand the material. I could not hold my pen steady. At certain moments, I felt like crying. I started speaking to myself aloud, while grabbing at my head and pants. When the exam was over, I picked up my books and left the hall.

That afternoon, the Biochemistry exam was scheduled. I ate lunch and sat around, praying that the following exam would not be anything like Physiology.

I went to the lecture hall just about the same time the exam was starting. The professor was handing out the papers. I made up my mind that I wasn't going to let what happened on the Physiology exam happen on Biochemistry. I tried to remain calm while turning the exam pages. I saw matching questions on the last page and began to complete them. I answered seven out of ten. I did the entire exam from the back working my way to the front, which was the wrong way to take the exam. The exam was designed to aid the student in answering the following questions by working from the front page, though I actually felt confident that I had a good chance of passing.

The next few days I walked around extremely worried. I sat in class impatiently, and wondered if today were the day, that they would return the grades. I had diarrhea after each lecture. Finally, the day arrived. The announcement was made that the exam papers were in the Physiology and Biochemistry lab rooms. Everyone started running to the exam rooms. When I reached the lab, people were pushing and grabbing for their exam papers. They were in alphabetical order on two large tables, and like a dummy, I looked on the wrong table for mine. My hands shook. I ran around to the other side of the table, but still didn't see my paper. I saw handwriting that looked like mine. It was! It was my exam paper. I went for it like a lunatic. With my paper in hand, I headed for a nearby corner. I began to pray. There was a big "U" written on my exam paper, "U" for unsatisfactory. I glanced at the crowd of students still at the tables; a few of them were jumping with joy because they passed. I overheard other students talking about how they almost got "excellent" on their exams. I felt embarrassed.

I went to the library where Iris was working and told her about it. She tried to console me, but I felt too low to be picked up. She knew what it meant to me to fail. That evening I was depressed. Nothing else mattered more to me than knowing that I had failed the exam.

A few days later, there was an announcement that the Physiology examinations were in the lab room waiting to be picked up. I spotted my paper and picked it up. I was stunned by another failing grade and almost passed out. My body felt as though something was draining it. I couldn't believe that this was happening to me. I was convinced that nothing could help me. I imagined my dream to become a doctor vanishing away.

Iris tried desperately to encourage me. She said that God would not allow failure to win out over His plan for me to become a doctor. She realized that my faith was the key. Every chance she had to reinforce my faith in God; she did.

I studied and concentrated on those areas, which were the most difficult to understand. I tried to relax, but it was difficult. Two failures in the most important subjects in the first year of medical school were enough to cause anyone to have a nervous breakdown.

"Buddy, You Should Have Known Better"

I went to Professor Grumbock and asked him what he thought about my being in medical school. "Do you want my honest opinion?" he asked.

I said, "Yes." He looked at me with a smile on his face and said, "I think you're not cut out for medical school; you need to go into the paramedical field." My heart felt like it would stop. I just looked at him, and then I tilted my head to the floor. I left him standing in the classroom puffing on a cigarette. I went straight down to the emergency room and asked to see a Psychiatrist. I broke down and cried in the emergency room. My dream to become a doctor seemed so far away and impossible with my poor grades.

I called Steve Goodman, who befriended me. Steve was in the sophomore class. I trusted him. He and his wife were friendly, and they accepted us like family.

The first time that I ever water-skied was with his father's boat in Lake George Resort near the Adirondack Mountains. I used to go hunting there for deer and bear. Steve wasn't home, but his wife said that she would let him know that I called. I was still crying, and she sensed it. She asked me where was I and was it an emergency. I told her that it was an emergency, and I was in the Albany Medical Hospital emergency room.

When I got home, I told Iris what occurred. She consoled me and said, "Buddy, what did you expect him to tell you, asking him a question like that, you should have known better? You know how he feels about you being in medical school."

I was so depressed that I eventually went to sleep in order to try to forget what Dr. Grumbock told me. I thought about my cousin Leray's words to me that "doctors are born and not made," and I wasn't going to become any doctor, when I was living in my Aunt Doris's house. The words were still haunting me. I was wondering again if she was right.

The following morning Iris told me that Steve came to the house after I fell asleep. He told her that he would catch up with me, and he did. I told him what happened, and he got upset. He asked me if I felt Grumbock had anything against me. I told him I wasn't sure. That week some of the upper-class students held a meeting in the student lounge and asked me to attend. In the meeting, I was asked why I thought Professor Grumbock was always calling on me to answer questions. I told them I did not know. Steve said, "Well, you won't have to deal with him much longer, because his portion of the course is almost over." The meeting was positive, at least to the point that the students understood that one black student was discouraged and hurt and needed some help coping with the courses.

Steve decided to help me with electrophysiology, and I was glad to accept his help. I did get frustrated at times trying to understand the stuff.

I found the energy and courage to continue to face Professor Grumbock. I didn't stop studying hard, and I read the material repeatedly in order to absorb it.

When I took the second physiology exam, I tried being positive. I was convinced that I could pass the test, and I did. I remember the feeling, which I had when I found out that I had passed. I was now convinced that I could do the work. The Biochemistry exam did not yield the same return; I had failed and was extremely disappointed. I knew at this point that I would probably fail the course. It was a setback to think that I would fail the course after having worked so hard. I went through countless measures in order to study for the final exams. I visited every faculty member I knew who would sincerely encourage me. It was plain that some of them had given up on me. In fact, some didn't have any hope to begin with. I studied for long hours, burning the light into the morning, hardly speaking much to Iris. This was it; the last chance to pass Physiology and Biochemistry during the regular school year. I took the Biochemistry exam with confidence. Though it was difficult, I believed that I had passed. The Physiology exam was no joke. The exam was 230 multiple-choice questions, to be completed in three hours. This was cutting it a bit close, and by the time I finished it, I knew that I had failed. When the exam was over, I was so upset that I took my exam and stuffed it in my pants. I wasn't going to turn in that item of shame. My plan was to let them wonder what happened to the exam and get a retest. I walked the halls for about ten minutes with the exam in my pants. I couldn't decide what to do with it. I finally decided to turn it in. I walked into the Physiology room. While the professors were sorting through the exam papers, I slipped mine on the table. Professor Grumbock was there. I looked at him, and said, "He must be right; I'm not cut out for medical school." I stood there to notice their reaction when they saw this wrinkled paper. No one questioned my being there. Someone noticed it and summoned me. Of course, I was there instantly. A professor asked me to sit and transfer my answers to another sheet, one that was not wrinkled. Later, that day, I went to see the chairperson. I told him what I was going to do with the answer sheet. I think he must have believed I was foolish to tell him that. As I talked, I explained to him what medical school meant to me. Tears rolled down my face; I couldn't hold them back. I broke into an uncontrollable cry. He asked me to calm down. I'll never forget that moment. I was very disturbed. He suggested that I go on my Christmas vacation and not worry about the exam. He said that there was nothing I could do about what had happened. Of course, he was right.

When we arrived in Brooklyn, I tried to hide my worry from the families. I wanted to go back to Albany for my grades; at the same time, I wanted to remain in Brooklyn to rest and spend time with my family. When Iris and I finally did return to Albany, the report still had not been returned. It was agony waiting for it. One day I went to the Mailroom, and there it was visible through the little peep window; it was folded nicely. I was shaking while I opened the mailbox door. A feeling of despair came over me when I saw a "failure" in both Biochemistry and Physiology. As I walked through the halls, I wondered what I would do with my life. How could I ever live, knowing that I would never achieve my goal or fulfill the dream to be a doctor? Worst of all, Iris was going through all of this with me, sharing every ounce of my pain, while having her own. My frustration in school and failing during those past months didn't make my life easy at all, and I fell along the way.

I tried forgetting about my problems in school and the problems at home and being frustrated with Iris when I felt that she didn't understand what I was going through. It wasn't that Iris didn't understand what I was going through. She knew that in order to help me that she had to be truthful with me and tell me what she believed concerning my attitude. I was going through the fire of my journey. My problems at home were, not wanting to face the fact that Iris was right in everything that she told me. Iris loved me and treated me like a royal king, and if it was not for her love for me, I would have not made it through my first few months in medical school.

I enjoyed the open woods, and sometimes I went to the railroad track and hunted squirrel and rabbits. Most of the time I came home with a squirrel, skinned it, and hung the skin on my wall. I guess in some ways I was working some of my frustration out by being in the woods and killing animals.

The first half of the year finally ended. Our grades were sent to the registrar's office. Two failures were sent for me in Physiology and Biochemistry, while I did receive a passing grade in Psychiatry. For the time being, these troublesome two courses were over.

The second semester included Gross Anatomy, Histology, Neuroanatomy, and the remainder of Psychiatry. I couldn't wait for the courses to begin. This was my second chance to prove myself. The Black students wanted me to work with them in Gross Anatomy. There were four students to a cadaver, and they wanted me to be the fourth student. I didn't want to study with them, and I expressed it. I didn't want them to feel as if they helped me in any way during the first semester. They never offered me any help in Biochemistry or Physiology. Harrison was the only one to encourage me. He told me many times not to worry about what some of the professors thought about me. He knew what he knew, and no one was going to tell him otherwise. I believed that Oswald and Jimmy only cared about themselves, and all of Oswald's talk about being black brothers and sticking together was not true. They kept pestering me about being the fourth student working on the cadaver, and I gave in. I spoke with Iris about it. Before I did, I already had an idea what she would say. She told me not to do it, and against her advice, I said yes to them. Iris warned me that I would find myself in the same situation as before.

Finding Friends

I liked Histology. It was an interesting course, and I discovered I was good at recognizing differences between tissue specimens. One day a thin woman named Judy was walking around the lab helping students. She was taking a special interest in helping the students understand the material. When she approached my table and talked to the other students around me, I listened to her. I didn't feel she would show the same interest in me. As she passed by me, I spoke to her. I told her my life story and don't know what got into me. Everything was pouring out as if I were just waiting for her to come along. She was attentive and didn't interrupt me. I asked if she would be willing to help me with the Histology lab portion of the course during her spare time. She told me that it was no problem, and she would like to. She arranged some off school-hour studying with me. The next day, the Chairman of the Anatomy department, Dr. Cowden, who was a Southerner, came over to me in the lab and introduced himself. He said that while he was talking to one of his staff members (Judy), it was made known to him that I asked for special help in Histology. I told him that I was in scholastic trouble; on probation, and I needed the help. He wanted to know more about my situation. I told him that I didn't think the people in the Physiology and Biochemistry departments cared much about my success in medical school, and as far as I was concerned, few other people cared. He replied that he was concerned and realized the school accepted me in order to obtain federal monies, and they didn't really care if I made it or not. He told me that many schools in the United States were involved in the same practice because they had been pressured into accepting minority students against their will. He believed it was an explanation for their attitude. He stated that the college didn't know how to deal with minority students, and no medical school had the right to accept students without the willingness to help them through the program. In his opinion, the school had made a commitment and had refused to live up to it. He said the school would not purposely try to fail me but, on the other hand, would not fight too hard to keep me either. He assured me even though many people did not care if I sank or swam, he wasn't one of them. He was happy that I had asked for help, and offered his services to me. After having that conversation with him, I became concerned because I wasn't sure if Dr. Cowden was being honest with me or was just collecting information. I didn't know if I could trust him. Another exam was scheduled. Whenever I thought, I needed help; I went to Judy, who was Dr. Cowden's assistant in the Histology lab. She went over the material with me. Although she was busy sometimes, she would stop whatever she was doing in order to help me. These sessions were very rewarding, and I learned a lot from her. She showed me some memory tricks to identify certain information on the Histology slides. On the day of the exam, I was definitely confident. When I walked into the exam room, Dr. Cowden and Judy looked at me and smiled. I knew at that moment; I found friends. The exam was set up in a musical-chair fashion with 68 slides. When the bell rang to begin the test, I quickly looked into the microscope. I knew the answer at first glance. The exam went smoothly. The written exam took more time, but I was pleased with it. The following week the exam was returned. I passed both exams with good grades.

As usual, my grades went to every faculty member who asked for it. Faculty members outside of the Anatomy department knew my grades without my telling.

The Gross Anatomy exam was coming up soon. Iris helped me with learning the bones, muscles and nerves. She would ask me to tell her what nerves worked certain muscles and the attachment of muscles to bones. I would go to school early in the morning before the nine o'clock lecture, and study the cadaver. Sometimes, one of the Black students would see me there, and it raised their suspicion about my trying to get ahead of them. During the lab sessions, we hacked away at the cadaver. We had a male who was 76 years old, who died of cardiovascular disease. It was a bit difficult at first to deal with a dead body that smelled to me like cooked barbecue spare ribs. I had dreams at night that I was eating it, and it tasted very sweet. I asked our Anatomy Professor if he knew what human meat taste like. He told me he personally didn't, but a friend of his had to eat some in Africa among some cannibals, and he told him that it tasted like any other kind of meat except a little tough. Sometimes I would clown around, like when I was in Junior High School 142. One day I pulled the intestine from the abdomen of our cadaver, hooked it up to the water faucet, and turned it on. I waited until the water came to the end, and laughed about it. After a couple of weeks, I developed respect for the cadaver. I understood it was a privilege to learn from it, and it once was a human being. I came to thank God for it and even talked to it when no one was around but me.

Iris came to the lab often and watched me as I cut the corpse and ate my lunch. It made her stomach turn. On the day of the exam, I went to the cafeteria to get some food in order to calm my stomach (I was now getting diarrhea every time I took an exam). The test was easy; except for some relationship questions, which would even have confused a surgeon. The following week, we were informed that the exams were in the Histology lab. I ran as fast as I could to the lab. When I got there, the papers were spread over the table in alphabetical order. Two grades were on the exams; one for the lab and the other for the written exam. I did very well on the lab but not so well on the written. My overall grade was a solid "Pass." I was not, however, satisfied.

Passing

I eventually passed histology with a good grade. The struggle of working hard had paid off, and I realized the true value of the friendship of Dr. Cowden and Judy. I knew for sure at that point I could make it through medical school.

Iris was very happy concerning my performance. It made me feel good to know that my wife was with me "100 percent."

Pharmacology was also a course that gave me trouble. It required an integration of Biochemistry and Physiology. I failed the first pharmacology exam. I don't think it was the material; I couldn't get my conceptual thinking together. When it came time for the second exam, I was more prepared and passed it. I also passed the final exam, with a marginal grade.

It was during the Pharmacology course that I worked out my differences with the Black students. I told them I didn't think they cared about me. I told Jimmy I didn't like him because he was always bragging about how he was going to "ace" some exam. Oswald voiced his concern and said, "If you don't want to study with us anymore, it's OK." I told him that wasn't the situation with me. I believed that they only cared about themselves.

Neuroanatomy was the course that was supposed to separate the men from the boys. One exam was scheduled and if a student failed it, he would fail the course. I didn't appreciate having one exam because it took me some time to get used to the style of each course. I remembered what happened to me at Brooklyn College with that History of the English Language course, and how I failed the one and only exam they gave, and spent six additional months in school because of it.

I approached a South American medical doctor, who did not have a license to practice medicine in the U.S., who was helping in the Neuroanatomy lab. I asked him to tutor me, and he agreed. He met me twice a week through the course, and he didn't charge me anything. If I didn't understand the material to his satisfaction, he would stop the session and tell me to go home and study. Oswald found out that I was getting help from him, and I believe he was jealous. He approached me and asked if I was getting help in the course, and I told him yes. This was the last time Oswald spoke with me about studying with the Black students. I was glad to be rid of him. My tutorial sessions helped me tremendously, and I passed the course.

I passed Pharmacology and received no failures that half of the year in any subjects. The pace was now beginning to slow. The time was approaching for me to concentrate on taking the Biochemistry and Physiology reviews; these results would determine if I would graduate to the second-year class.

The medical college had a policy that gave students the opportunity to retake a subject or two when they failed, in order to be retested. The promotion's committee believed that one subject should not cause a student to be left back, if he or she could accomplish a pass grade. What bothered me about the review policy was that 100% on the final exam would not have given me enough margins to pass the course; my grade was too low. The maximum percentage that could be received from the Biochemistry review was 25% on the makeup test. I believed; they were sending me through the motions.

Conspiracy in the Working

I spoke with the Chairman of the Histology department, about the possibility of repeating the school year. He told me that he didn't believe I needed to repeat the year because two white girls in the class didn't do much better than me, and they were graduating to the second-year class. He said, "It definitely appears to be a conspiracy against you." He promised that he would do everything in his power to help me get to the second year. He asked for time to investigate the matter. When I saw him the next day, he told me the Physiology people simply felt that I didn't know enough Physiology in order to go to the second year. The Chairman of Biochemistry was sticking to his guns as long as I had a failure in Physiology. He told the Chairman of the Histology department if I had passed Physiology, I would have been given the passing grade. I was furious. The two departments wanted a guarantee that I would be repeating the entire school year, so they both failed me.

The Chairman of the promotion's committee confessed it all to me. "Wilbert," he said, "If the promotion's committee had received one failure for you, they would have requested the faculty to give you a reexamination." He told me that his hands were tied. When I reminded him of the conversation, which I had with him about the matter of passing earlier during the year, and how difficult I felt it would be because my grade was so low. He told me that the school reflected society and that society unfortunately was racist.

I went to the Dean of the medical college about my case. He said that he couldn't figure out what was wrong with the Biochemistry Chairman. The Dean then told me that he would tell me something in confidence.

He said that three faculty heads from the Physiology and Biochemistry departments came to him after two months into the academic year. They requested that two other students and I be thrown out of the school because we obviously were not medical school material. He told them not to ask for that because we had paid tuition for a full year. He was not about to throw anyone out. "I told them that we took you for a year, and we were going to keep you for a year. After that they would decide," he said, looking straight at me. I told Dr. Cowden what the Dean told me, and he assured me that he would talk to a few people. Dr. Cowden asked the Dean to help me graduate to the second-year class. He told the Dean that he believed a conspiracy was in the works, and the Dean told him not to use words like that in his office. According to Dr. Cowden, he and the Dean cursed each other. The Dean then told him he would talk to some of the faculty members and was sure they would swing the decision in my favor. It was becoming a matter of who would persuade whom to allow me to enter the second-year class. The Biochemistry department took a vote to decide if I would pass or fail. The vote was taken, and one person voted in my favor to pass the course. The promotion's committee voted and decided that I would be better off repeating the academic school year. Dr. Cowden and Judy, his assistant, were the only ones in the school who had tried to help me at this point that I knew of.

He recounted a meeting, which he had with the Chairman of Physiology. They sat around a table during a conference with the executive faculty committee and literally cursed each other out concerning my situation. Dr. Cowden made it clear to me that though he was a Southerner and didn't particularly love Blacks, there was something about me that encouraged him to fight for me. He regretted there was nothing more he could do to help me pass Biochemistry and Physiology. I was out of energy to deal with these powerful people.

I thanked Dr. Cowden for his courage in helping me. Even though he was from the South, from where my father was born and from which my father left, Dr. Cowden proved to be a friend to me in the midst of kindling flames. I may have been the first black person in his life whom he cared about. He summed up his relationship with me by saying, "I never did what I'm doing for you with any person, but there is something about you, and it makes me want to fight like hell. What they're doing to you is wrong."

It was possible that I may have been paying for my statements about some of the professors, for I had referred to them as racists when I was taking Biochemistry and Physiology. What I said got around the school, but I didn't care, because some of them were racists.

You Can Leave Medical School Now

I was sent a letter from the promotion's committee. It simply stated that I could choose not to return to school, go on a decelerated academic program (take fewer courses than the rest of the students), or repeat the entire school year. I was not going to quit medical school, to go back to Red Hook or move to another place. I wanted to be a doctor, not a failure. I decided to repeat the entire school year.

Harrison, whose car I washed, and who gave me Mary Jane candy during lecture class, was terminated from medical school because he failed every subject. The day he left, he was still saying nobody was going to tell him what he knew. Oswald and Jimmy did well so they were promoted, to the second year, and I was to repeat.

Iris was mentally tired, and I felt bad for her. She was by my side during the entire ordeal; never for a moment visibly shaken. Her wisdom and strength were unbelievable.

Trying to Relax

The summer of 1974 was trying. I was upset about repeating the entire year, but resigned myself to it. Iris and I decided to go camping. We bought camping equipment and went to a lake called Thompson Lake, near the Helderberg Mountains. When we got there, I was the only black person. At first, it didn't bother me, but as we walked around the camp, I felt intimidated. No one said anything to us. It was just the stare. There was a beautiful lake on the side of the camp where I went fishing in the morning before Iris got up. I didn't catch anything worth talking about. I relaxed, throwing the line in and watching the little red and white float move up and down in the green water; then, dip under, as I was pulled by a small fish. I wondered where all the Black people were; didn't they know about Thompson Lake?

We enjoyed our camping trip and vowed to do it often. It helped me to forget some things I needed to forget.

I tried not going to the medical school, because I felt rejected and humiliated. Iris was trying to keep me balanced; she consoled me, while I sulked. I knew that there were trying days ahead. I was on a long journey that would challenge every fiber in my being.

Iris told me God hadn't left me alone to fend for myself, but at that time, I believed He did. I had never thought I would charge God for my troubles, but I felt He left me alone in the kindling flames of this life. It really wasn't my intention to put Him in the background when I failed, but I was afraid. His promises were enough to keep me going. Iris knew this, and that is why she constantly talked to me about God. "Buddy," she would say, "God is not going to leave you alone. He is going to fulfill His promise to you."

God and Religion

We went to a Baptist church in Albany. It was a huge concrete structure. When we walked into the main sanctuary, Sunday school was in progress. Rev. Roland was teaching, and he was on the topic of tobacco companies' sales, profits, and employees. He stated that if the tobacco business were halted, there would be many people out of work and that was justification to support it. He wasn't condoning smoking. He was just concerned about its effect on the economy. I differed with him and verbally stated so publicly. Eyes and ears were attentive while I spoke. Rev. Roland and I started arguing. Iris and I vowed not to return to the church.

We tried other churches in Albany, and none satisfied us. We were invited to a church function by someone who knew we were Christians. We met Mother Smith. Mother Smith attended a church called Refreshing Springs Church of God and Christ. She was full of energy. She grabbed our hands and asked Iris and me to attend her church in Schenectady. It was only fifteen miles from Albany. As she talked to us, I saw her face tense when she spoke about God. I believed she had the kind of heart that cared for people. We told her we would visit.

The following Sunday we went to Refreshing Springs Church of God and Christ. They were meeting in a small building. The service was charged with fast music, speaking in tongues, and seasoned throughout with bursts of Hallelujah. An elegant well-dressed woman sat on the left side in front of the church. She held her head high, praising God. We came to know her as Sister Georgetta Dix. Sister Dix was beautiful and had a heart for people. And if a person believed they didn't need God, she knew differently. She was strong spiritually and a lighthouse in the community. People knew and loved Sister Georgetta Dix. Her husband, Rev. Eugene Dix, who passed away, founded refreshing Springs Church. Sister Dix was still in love with him and didn't hesitate to tell it. She took an immediate liking to us, and the feeling was mutual. The service was high-spirited, as most Pentecostal services are. I don't remember who was speaking that day, but the message was dynamic.

They Loved Gospel Music

We met a couple named Michael and Margie Owens, and they had two children. Michael was outspoken, being very positive about his ability to keep my attention with his gift of speaking. His wife Margie was a bit reserved, but nice and introduced herself to Iris; then, to me. They invited us to their home, and we accepted the invitation. That Sunday afternoon we went to their house in Albany. Margie fed us her famous fried chicken with vegetables and plenty to drink. I found out later that there was always plenty of Kool-Aid to drink because Michael had a large glass all the time. I enjoyed Michael's company and admired Margie.

Our going to Refreshing Springs was to become an integral part of our lives. We met a Puerto Rican couple named Ephraim and Yoli Donez, who were from New York City. Ephraim was college-educated, working with a community health center called Carver Health Center. Ephraim was bright and reserved. Yoli was the typical homemaker, taking care of their daughter and being a wife to Ephraim. They were a happy couple. We saw them for the first time when they came to Refreshing Springs Church. They sat in the back of the church in the middle section. I noticed Ephraim moving his head from side to side, back and forth while the music was playing and the song, "I'm Going All the Way with the Lord" was being sung. He had that Puerto Rican rhythm. When the music stopped, he stopped with it, but I noticed a smile on his face. Yoli sat next to him trying to control the children, not appearing to enjoy the service very much. Sister Dix stood in the front, as near to the middle as possible with a microphone saying, "This is the little church in the heart of the city, with the people of the city in its heart." She said this every Sunday morning after the choir marched down the aisle (Michael and Margie were in the choir).

Running Out

Refreshing Springs Church moved from the little building to a massive church edifice with stained-glass windows. I remember our first time in the building. A white minister gave the keys to Refreshing Springs Church. It was the last time his congregation would be worshiping in the sanctuary. Apparently, the neighborhood had changed in ethnic makeup so people began to move out of the neighborhood. The pastor delivered a strong message to the congregations. As if he were speaking from a megaphone he said, "I hope and pray that at some time we can find ourselves worshiping in the same house of God." He and his members bid the building and the new congregation farewell, and the service was terminated.

God's Shadow Over Me

After church, Michael, Margie, Ephraim, Yoli, Iris, and I huddled together and we all became friends. This friendship was a part of God's protective shadow over me. We spent a lot of time together, and many of my great moments were with them.

Medical school was still a major issue ahead of me. Even though I had to repeat the school year, and had resigned myself to it, it was a burden upon Iris's and my shoulders. I didn't tell my new friends about my plight. I didn't want them to think I was not good enough to be in the prestigious private medical college that was highly praised in the tri-city area of Troy, Schenectady, and Albany. The hospital with which the school was connected took care of people as far away as 75 miles. I had put myself in the midst of this highly charged atmosphere, and was frightened to death of being a failure.

Washington, D.C.

Before the summer of 1974 ended, I took Iris to Washington, D.C. We got in our old Ford Torino (with the bald tires) and traveled more than 350 miles one-way. We stopped in New York City to visit our families. I didn't tell them I had to repeat the year. I didn't want them to think I wouldn't become a doctor.

When we got to Washington, we checked into the Howard Johnson's Hotel and had a ball. The only damper on our vacation was Iris's almost drowning in the swimming pool. I forgot she couldn't swim, and I threw her in on the deep side. She was going down for the third time before I rescued her. The remainder of our vacation was great.

I was upset about repeating the school year. I deliberately arrived at school two days late. I was notified by the registrar's office that they had called my mother to find out if I was going to return to school. They did not tell my parents that I had to repeat the year.

Repeating the School Year

When the summer ended, I returned to studying Physiology and Biochemistry. The Chairman of the promotion's committee told me that it would be my choice to repeat the subjects I passed, but the school would not force me to take them. I didn't want to take Psychiatry, Gross

Anatomy, Histology, Neuroanatomy, Biostatistics and Epidemiology again. The committee allowed me to sit in with the second-year class, if I had the time. I opted to sit in the Hematology course. I found it interesting and not as difficult to understand as Physiology. Some of the faculty members were upset that I was given these options, but apparently there was nothing they could do. I studied a lot and prayed to God to help me . . .

I passed my Physiology and Biochemistry exams. One of the Physiology professors told me not to have a false sense of security because some students who do well on the initial test may do terribly on the second, if they don't study as hard. He didn't have to tell me anything about studying, because I knew I had to read those textbooks for longer hours than my classmates did.

Four new black students were in my class. Richard and Loretta were both from New York; Richard via the island of Jamaica in the West Indies, and Loretta from Brooklyn. Both were having a stormy time with Biochemistry and Physiology. Loretta kept to herself, but Richard and I became friends. His wife, Barbara, was studying to be a nurse, and they had two children in Jamaica living with Richard's mother. Barbara was a Christian and Richard had not committed himself to any religion as far as I knew. I tutored Richard in Biochemistry and Physiology toward the end of the course. Loretta did some crying over her struggles. I could relate to them well. Both knew I was repeating the year.

Frustration

I went to the railroad tracks to hunt when I had the time. Although I saw many rabbits run past me, I wasn't quick enough to shoot one. Sometimes I sat on a log or a rock thinking about my future. I thought about Red Hook many times. My heart and soul were in Red Hook projects. I often thought about the people with whom I grew up and who were still living there. Some of them got involved in drugs, and they were literally losing their lives. I wanted to help them and there was nothing that I could do. I had my own problems. My marriage to Iris wasn't going well. We did argue sometimes about my wanting to go to Brooklyn each time holidays came and even on some weekends. Iris wanted to spend time with me because she hardly had any quality time. I was either studying or we were in church, or she was working.

Fried Chicken and Friends

When we got the chance, we had dinner at Michael and Margie's house. Margie would feed us her famous fried chicken, and we enjoyed it. After eating, we lounged around their house "teasing" Michael. He was a bit heavy, and would sit at the table and eat his heart out; fill a big beverage glass, fill it again. Margie would sit at the table and shake her head. It was all fun for us, and Michael never got offended; he just enjoyed the food.

On occasion, Iris and I went to Ephraim and Yoli's apartment and had lunch or dinner with them on Sunday afternoons. Ephraim was particular about many things, and he encouraged me to be more disciplined. He would even go so far as to polish the soles of his shoes. The first time I saw him do it; I didn't believe he was serious.

I thought that he was joking. When I saw the serious look on his face, I was shocked. Another time we went to the Price Chopper Supermarket, where he opened a carton of eggs and touched and rolled over each one to make sure that they were not cracked. I openly laughed at my friend, and he laughed with me. I loved Ephraim because he truly cared about my family and me. He had a beautiful heart. Michael, in contrast, loved my family and me also, but I had to work on our friendship. Ephraim and Michael's wives were super, and I admired them both.

Golden Friends

We met some new friends who attended Refreshing Springs Church, John and Doris Belton. They loved us from the beginning without effort. He was the Principal at an inner-city school in Schenectady, and she worked for the state government. They lived comfortably in a modest house in a beautiful neighborhood. He was cool, calm, and assertive. He and his wife always projected a positive image, and they were my cherished older friends. I respected and loved them dearly, and they were to take a very important role in the health of my marriage.

I continued to pass all my tests in Physiology and Biochemistry. School was going great, and my relationship with Iris was good. One time a professor approached me and said, "Wilbert, it's nice to see you here; I'm glad you are not bitter because you have to repeat the year."

I looked at him and said, "Thank you." I didn't have the time to be bitter.

.

Overcoming the System

I enjoyed our Christmas holidays and New Year also. I passed Biochemistry and Physiology. I did it! I overcame the system again: the system that was not created for me to succeed, the system that hurt my father, the system which my mother tolerated while she cleaned houses. The system that reminds most black people that we are not accepted fully as Americans.

Chapter 10

Roads

Thou has beset me behind and before,
And laid thine hand on me.

Psalm 139:5

During the summer of 1975, I worked with Dr. Marjorie Smith in East Berne, New York. I worked in her doctor's office on a farm in the Helderberg Mountains in the country. I enjoyed going into the country and especially liked the Helderberg Mountains because the area was so beautiful. I always looked for deer crossing the road or peeping from the edge of the woods. Dr. Smith's office was about twenty-five miles from Albany. She was an excellent doctor who took care of mostly country folks in the surrounding area. I was a little apprehensive about going there because I had not been around country folks. When I called Dr. Smith about the position, I told her I was a Black medical student and wanted to know if I could work with her that summer in her office. "I don't care what color you are," she said and told me that she would have an answer for me in a few weeks.

When I called her a few weeks later, she agreed to have me in her office. I felt foolish thinking that my color was the most important credential I had. The preceptorship offered $600 for two months, and we certainly needed it to supplement our weekly income of $115 from Iris's job.

Dr. Smith was friendly, to the point, and open with me. She would not guarantee me that there would not be any racial problems, but she assured me she was on my side. She told me she just wanted things to work well. I visited her office before the preceptorship to see how the patients would react to me. When I got to the farm, I saw a bunch of cows and a big barn where they milked them. Dr. Smith was practicing in her home; there on the farm. She started out in a trailer and built around it. It had a beautiful fireplace and wood logs were stacked to each side of it. It was my kind of setting. I loved animals, and one of my boyhood dreams was to one day live on a farm. She introduced me to her husband, Harry Garry. He was a big guy with a gentle disposition, I was told by Dr. Smith that he didn't like seeing interracial couples. He at no time said anything to me about it. Harry was always nice to me, and if he had a "hang-up" about seeing interracial couples, it did not appear to affect our relationship. He treated me as if I were his son.

From the first day, I was seeing patients. I was well received. When I told Dr. Smith how her patients treated me, she said, "That's because my patients know I wouldn't put them in bad hands, they trust me."

I enjoyed watching Dr. Smith take care of her patients. She was very attentive to their needs, and I learned a lot. She told me that she was sure things would work well and looked forward to seeing me in a few weeks. I was to commute to her office daily from Albany, which was about twenty-five miles away. When the time arrived for me to work in her office, I was excited. My first official day went well, and Dr. Smith was supportive. I was shy with her patients and kept thinking someone was going to refuse my care because of my color. Harry was encouraging and he kept talking to me all day, wanting to know if things were going OK. Harry ran the dairy farm they lived on. Their three children, a girl and two boys, helped him with the farm chores. I liked seeing them interact. We ate dinner at noon each day and while at the dinner table, there was a friendly bickering between them. It was strange for me to think of eating in the afternoon and calling it dinner. Dr. Smith told me that we needed our biggest and best meal at noon because that's when most people expend the greatest energy. It made a lot of sense to me. I never saw so much meat and milk on one table at one time. With all the cows around, we had plenty of meat and milk daily. I got along well with her children, and I believe they enjoyed having me with them.

As the preceptorship continued, Dr. Smith gave me more responsibility in the office. There were a few people who wanted to see her, and I understood why, because she was both loving and considerate, and they trusted her. Some people drove many miles to see her, and it was disappointing for them to be taken care of by another health provider. I made many home visits with her to care for elderly people. We also visited a nursing home weekly. She hugged her patients, held their hands, and let them know that she cared. We had an emergency call one day. A man was pinned under his tractor. He was riding it on an incline, and it turned over. When we arrived, he was trapped under the tractor, in pain, but he wouldn't accept any pain medication. She stayed until he was freed and taken by ambulance to Albany Medical Center Hospital. I only had one experience in Dr. Smith's office that shook me. She asked me to see a little boy who was with his mother, whom I had treated before. On this particular visit, his mother stood attentively watching me. When his father came into the exam room, he looked at me with piercing eyes. As I talked to him and his wife, his facial expression stayed fixed on me. I started playing with his son, and he became upset, and I left the room. I'm not sure if this incident was racially directed at me, but I never had any other negative encounters, which I thought was because of my color.

Most of the patients expressed to Dr. Smith, that they liked me very much. She enjoyed telling me things like that because she knew I needed to hear them. She told me that she knew I had come a long way from Red Hook projects in Brooklyn to Albany Medical College, and that I had the opportunity to be an asset to many people in poor communities.

Dr. Smith was a good doctor and my friend. She never failed to try to encourage me. We talked a lot about racism, and the system. She listened to me and consoled me when she felt it was appropriate. I learned a great deal about preconceived reactions and stereotyping people. For the most part, the people whom I thought would react adversely to me did just the opposite. It was my first experience in building my confidence as a future doctor. I will always remember and love Dr. Marjorie Smith and Harry Garry, her husband.

Where Have We Gone?

I began seeing racism as a permanent fixture in America. I was seeing first-hand how it affected people. There were two black doctors on the staff at Albany Medical College Hospital; Dr. All's, a radiologist and nephrologists, Dr. Hinds. Neither of them was involved in any committed way to help us to alleviate any ills that we suffered emotionally as far as I know. I went to Dr. All's, and she told me to work harder. Dr. Hinds had a position at the veteran's hospital, and he never sat with the Black students to see how we were doing. Dr. Robinson was a Black physician that spoke with us about seeking his help if we had any problems, and I at no time did. I don't know why. I think it was being caught up in trying to do all that I could to stay afloat. I was distracted many times by fear. It was my loss. I saw him one day at the school, and I told him I had to repeat the year, and he reminded me that he offered support to me.

A Southern Gentleman

Dr. Cowden was a Southern gentleman. I remembered his words to me, telling me he was from the Deep South, and Blacks were the least of all people he thought he would defend. I believe he was hurting inside for me. He understood the injustice and hypocrisy in which the school was involved, taking federal money for each Black student; then not caring if they sank or swam. I remember how upset he was, blaming the system for giving Blacks a hard time. He sounded off in front of me and said, "It's a shame, Wilbert; this country hasn't moved beyond this. I don't have any special liking for Blacks, but you've been handed a dirty deal and it upsets me."

He told me there were some people who were out to force me to repeat the year, and there was nothing that he could do about it. I saw the hurt in his eyes. He was a man of integrity who followed his convictions, and I respected him. It was the first time any person told me, that he wasn't fond of Blacks.

I was very critical concerning racism and bigotry. I didn't hold my tongue. It cost me a lot. Iris kept telling me to shut my mouth and concentrate on learning. She called me a rebel. She was suffering my pain. When I was hurt, she was the only one I could go to for comfort. I knew that she loved me.

Sticking With Me

Iris protected me. She understood that I was in fear of not becoming a doctor. She constantly spoke to me about God's love for me, and that God would not leave me in my quest to become a doctor. I did not realize how difficult it was for Iris to see me struggling. We were enduring the journey together. She never failed to stay close by me.

The Precious Hand of God

Church and religion became a greater part of our lives. We went to church a lot. On Sunday, mornings, I could release some of the hurt, anger and frustration I had pinned up inside. It was at Refreshing Springs Church of God and Christ in Schenectady that I could release myself to God. The people at the church had no idea what we were struggling with. I held these things even from my friends. They were like a shield from the blistering heat that we were in. That's why I saw them as the shadow of God in my life. They had no idea what role they played in their relationship to me.

Elder Mac Daniel

Our pastor, Lovell Mc Daniel, whom we referred to as "Elder Mac," was precious to me. He was raised in Brooklyn, New York. He had the gift of oratory and held me spellbound every time he spoke. He had a way of unfolding the Scriptures from the pulpit to the pews in such a way that people drew near to God and sought to know more about Him. Elder Mac wasn't your typical Pentecostal minister, and I once heard a member in the congregation refer to him as such. He didn't throw a bunch of Bible passages at you sprinkled with flowery words from the pulpit. He spoke to the souls of the people, and they received him well. Sometimes he would sit with me and talk about non-spiritual matters. I believe he understood as a man first, then as a minister that I needed his attention. I spoke with him about many things, but never about my pain at school. He gave me the impression that he thought the world of me. I listened to him sermonize many times, and he never failed to have a positive message. When Elder Mac wasn't at church, the congregation shrank. Elder Mac lived in Waterbury, Connecticut with his beautiful wife and three children (who were adorable). They weren't angel children, but respectful of their parents and the members of the congregation. His wife carried herself with dignity.

He drove for more than two hours from Waterbury, Connecticut to Schenectady twice per week to minister. We didn't have a permanent pastor, and the people wanted Elder Mac to fill the position. He was torn between being established in Connecticut and uprooting to Schenectady, New York. It was a big decision for him and his family, and he never made the move. He did look at homes, but still stayed in Waterbury. I don't know what his reasons were for not moving, but he did tell me it wasn't as easy as some people felt for him to move. He spent a considerable amount of time in Schenectady. He didn't do a half job ministering to us or the people in Waterbury from what I heard. He spent many counseling hours speaking to the souls of people.

Mrs. Mc Daniel was always polite with me and smiled often when I spoke with her. I could tell she was being tried by fire. Some people looked down at Sister Mc Daniel and spoke ill of her, and she knew it. Her husband was feeding the flock and giving his life for it in many ways. She watched it and endured it.

False Security

I made a new friend at Refreshing Springs Church, Richard. Richard was a fascinating guy, who was an ex-pimp and ex-drug dealer. I loved to hear him give his testimony. When it was time in church for people to get up and tell the congregation what God has done for them, up popped Richard. He'd say, "I want to thank my Lord and Savior Jesus Christ for what He took me from. He truly has saved my soul. I used to be 'everything,' you name it. That's what I used to be, you-all don't know what I used to be, but I know. I ran me some women. I was a devil, and the Lord rescued me from the streets. I'm going to try to serve the Lord for the rest of my life. You all pray for me." If one kept his eyes on him, one might catch him doing a Holy Shuffle (dance in the Spirit). Richard would get "amen" and "hallelujahs" resounding off the chandeliers. Richard had a limp, so his legs and hands were not well coordinated. As he put it, he was so full of hell when he was pimping and drugging it up, God had to stop him by allowing him to be in a car accident. He was laid up in the hospital for months and nearly died. He credits his survival to his Lord and Savior Jesus Christ. I liked Richard. He represented hope to me. I was proud of Richard because he had a heart for people and was very active with ex-drug addicts and alcoholics.

Richard once told me if he had known me when he was pimping, he would have had me take care of his women, and I would have made lots of money. I will always thank Richard for his testimony and his honesty (and for offering me a job, even if it was too late).

God's Love

John and Doris Belton were two very special people to us, and many other people. We affectionately called John "Brother Belton" and Doris, "Sister Belton." We never referred to them without these distinctions. They loved us like family, and we loved them the same way. When we had marital problems, they were always willing to help us. They never got involved in our business, unless we invited them to. They lived in a beautiful house, not far from the city line of Schenectady.

I was encouraged by the way; they took care of their belongings. They had a nice motor home in their driveway and a little portable swimming pool for their daughter Jane. One time we were at church and after the service, I saw Brother Belton with a motorcycle helmet in his hand. He told me to look across the street from the church. He bought a motorcycle. At first, I didn't believe it was his until he put the key in the ignition. He gave me a ride, and it was great. Brother Belton was unpredictable, and I'm sure that's one of the reasons I liked him. Sister Belton was as sweet as anyone could be. I never saw her angry, and she was loving and kind to people.

When Iris and I were having financial problems, Brother and Sister Belton came to our house and prayed with us. We didn't have any food to offer them. Brother Belton pulled me to the side and asked me if I needed any money. He had no idea we didn't have any food or drink for them. I told him we were all right. He gave me two ten-dollar bills and told me to pay him back whenever I could, and if I couldn't, it was fine.

I know by experience that Brother and Sister Belton were beacons of light for many people, and if it was not for their openness, a few people would have had more problems than they already had.

Sex and Medicine

My second year in medical school took off like a rocket. The first course was Hematology. I understood the material because it made sense, and the professor made a world of difference. Professor Tartaglia, who was a medical doctor, taught the course, and he made it interesting. Other required courses were Community Medicine, Microbiology, Human Reproduction, and Introduction to Medicine. Albany Medical College was a bit aggressive in teaching us sexual human reproduction.

A guy in my class had a Ph.D. in sexology from Johns Hopkins University. He helped in the course construction. He told me he had a basement full of pornographic material from his study. Some of the material was included in the course. The college wanted to desensitize the students sexually before we took Obstetrics and Gynecology. They put a notice in the classified section of the newspaper asking women who had a number of deliveries to apply for pelvic examinations by the medical students. Three women were picked.

Our first desensitization session was in the auditorium where we had our lectures. We sat with popcorn waiting for the cinema "The Devil and Mrs. Jones" to start. We were wild during the movie. For a so-called pornographic movie, I wasn't impressed. We didn't know it, but the heavy porno material was to follow in the next couple of weeks. They showed us hard porno where women were having sex with animals and posing with their sex organs, men and women having hard-core sex, and gay sex. In one session, they showed us a Masters and Johnson film where a woman was hooked up to wires and diagnostic devices, which included measuring her vaginal, clitoral and vital signs to self-masturbation. I had a hard time watching that one. We also had a lecture where they had a transvestite in the audience, and he was sitting next to me, looking and smelling very much like a woman. When they introduced him and he got up and spoke, I was shocked. I didn't recognize "he" was a man with a sex-change operation. The whole course was freaky, and I know it didn't desensitize me. For the culmination of the course, we had to do pelvic examinations on the women who responded to the article in the newspaper. When it was my turn, the nurse said to me, "Don't worry, we only watch your hands." Some of the students had erections. I was not desensitized. I didn't enjoy Microbiology. It took me back to undergraduate school. At one point, I was having difficulty with it. The professor pulled me to the side and asked me if I wanted to repeat the year again. I looked at him as if he were a crazy fool, because I wasn't doing that badly in his course. At the end of the semester, I passed my courses, including Microbiology.

The Rat Race

It was a rat race in medical school. If one couldn't keep up with the pack, he or she was lost in a separate world. One girl in my class was having emotional problems. The promotion's committee allowed her, to take a year leave of absence from school. In contrast, the only Asian student in our class was also having emotional problems. They promised him if he saw a Psychiatrist and took a leave of absence for six months he could come back to school. He went to Manhattan, New York's Chinatown and stayed with his family. We never saw him again. We heard he tried to return, but failed to be re-enrolled. During the next semester, I continued to study hard, and I passed all my courses. I was scheduled to graduate to the third-year class.

Not Enough to Eat

Sometimes we didn't have meat to eat or milk to drink so I went down to the train tracks to shoot squirrels, but this time for food. I would put the smelly thing in a pot of boiling water and Iris, and I painfully ate it. One time Iris's parents came up from Brooklyn and caught us boiling one in a pot. Her mother Doris said, "What is that smell?" I tried to hide it, but it was too late. When we told them what it was, they commanded we get rid of it. They broke out with a cardboard box that had steak, plantains, and vegetables in it. They were great and were always willing to help us. We just never let them know what we were going through. My family also had no idea we were at welfare status either.

Food Stamps

My grants and loans ran out. I didn't have money to complete school or even buy food. We went to the food stamp office, applied for food stamps. For $12, we could purchase $114 worth of food. Every two weeks I went to the bank around the corner from our apartment and exchanged the coupon for stamps. One time I believed the teller mistreated me because she spoke rough verbally with me, so I told her off. I called the bank manager. He told me that he heard me tell her off and there was nothing for him to say to her. I stormed out of the bank, upset.

Black Students

Jimmy was the first of the black medical students who I met in the school lobby; His father was in the military and Jimmy was stationed with him all around the world. Jimmy's exposure to the outside world was greater than any of ours, and I believed that made him more open to all people. I liked him at first because he wasn't a threat to me. Later, however, I disliked him because I believed he at no time saw me. He never spoke to me about the challenges I faced at the medical college, and he knew I was struggling.

Oswald was a character. He was the "bold black man" from New York City via the island of Jamaica, West Indies. He liked to use the "nigger word" like it was conventional and acceptable anywhere. He did, however, not use it in the presence of white people. Oswald was cold and calculating. He said if all the "niggers" had to go back to Africa one day, he was going to Jamaica because he was a Jamaican, a true "Island Man." He let the rest of us know from the beginning that he wasn't one of us. I was the first one to be blinded by Oswald's talk. Iris told me not to take Oswald seriously. Although I didn't think Oswald was a great human being; he was what he was because he like many other black people was a victim of the American system. Harrison was an honorable human being full of energy. He didn't care if you were black or white. He spoke his heart with kindness. He was a lot of fun and if anything, taught me how to eat Mary Jane candies in lecture class and kept me asking him for more. Harrison saw me. He understood my pain, and tried to console me. "Buddy," he would say, "don't let these people shake you up. All they want to do is get you upset so you can flunk out; that's all they want. I know what I know and can't anybody tell me differently."

Harrison knew what the good comfortable life was like. His father was a dentist in California. Harrison had a Master's Degree from Howard University. He was driving a new Buick Le Mans. Sometimes he would pay me to wash it. I would wash that car and wish that I had one as nice. Harrison never talked down to me about any of the Black students. He talked about Black people need to stick together, and that was our problem. Harrison didn't care what the professors thought about him. He was a lover boy. Sometimes he would sit in lecture class with a beautiful girl from Washington, D.C., and some of the professors would be checking him out. When he was kicked out of school, Professor Cowden told me personally, "We're going to throw this guy Harrison the hell out of this school. He thinks everything is roses around here, bringing all these women to class. That guy failed every course he took, he didn't pass one. He's on his way out of here."

I should have had something to say to Professor Cowden about what I thought about my friend, but I didn't. Maybe I didn't because I was also shackled in my mind and didn't have the strength or courage to tell Professor Cowden not to talk about him the way he did.

Harrison was intelligent and could have done well. I don't think his heart was in becoming a doctor.

When I think about Black people, I see us clothed in someone else's garments. I see us still very much in slavery. I know it is a game, which has been played on us to believe we have to do some kind of shuffle to survive. We don't have to shuffle for anyone, and if we do, it's been our choice, and we'll pay for it. Life is full of choices, and some of them are very tough. We can survive as people in America, and if we have to dance in fire, we will.

Dr. J.T. Henderson, a Black Doctor

That summer I worked with Dr. J.T. Henderson in Schenectady, New York. He was a Black family doctor. It was a wonderful experience. He was by far one of the most compassionate doctors whom I had ever met. His practice was interracial. All the patients who spoke to me were thoroughly happy with him and respected him very much. To my surprise, Black people who were not his patients spoke of him negatively. They had various reasons for not going to him, and it made no sense to me. Sometimes Black people are critical of their own kind because of their ignorance and preconceived ideas that if a person is Black and professional, he or she can't be as competent as a white person. Black people have been successful in every field of life and have proven their ability to excel. Society has done a hell of a mind game on us. I believe most people who knew Dr. Henderson took pride in him. He was an excellent physician and a kind man. Some, however, were jealous because he had achieved an academic level, which they, as Blacks, had not. My experience working with him was contrary to anything, which I heard.

He constantly tried to build up my low self-esteem. He was a graduate of Fisk University and later Howard University Medical School. He knew medicine well and enjoyed the interaction with his patients. I was in awe of him. He was the first black doctor with whom I had the opportunity to rub shoulders; just being with him boosted myself-worth.

Dr. Henderson spoke with me often about my outlook on racial issues. He believed that one's respect for oneself was the ultimate in success. He didn't let what people believed about him surface in his interaction and relationship with them. He told me that one time a woman was referred to him. When she walked in his office asking to see Dr. Henderson, he told her he was Dr. Henderson. She told him that she was looking for another Doctor Henderson. He assured her that he was the only Dr. Henderson in Schenectady, New York. She told him she made a mistake and walked out.

He told me the story with such coolness and ease. He even had a smile on his face. He said he wasn't concerned about people's reactions to him as a Black doctor because he saw himself as a doctor first. I watched his ability to heal the sick, and he did that very well.

My direct involvement with patients in his office was restricted; I did a lot of listening and watching. Many times, I sat in his office and read. It was different from the preceptorship I had with Dr. Marjorie Smith. I don't know why he didn't give me more hands-on with his patients, and I thought about it a lot.

Each day at 12:00 noon, we had lunch, which for him was usually peanut butter and jelly sandwiches, Coca-Cola, and ice cream. This was really the most enjoyable part of my day, watching him put away what I called the "bomb." After lunch, he would insist that I go upstairs and lay down in the bed. He didn't care if I fell asleep. He just wanted me resting in the bed. While in the bed, I read a book or waited for the time to pass.

When Dr. Henderson relaxed, it was usually talking with his beautiful wife. They had a good relationship. She called him "Hon" and he would call her "Babe." He told me a couple of times that he loved his wife very much, and she was one of the best things that ever happened to him.

She would often speak gently with me about my career and assured me that things would turn out well, no matter how they appeared, and to remain strong and confident. I adored the way she balanced her time at home doing what needed to be done and enjoying it. I felt very close to her.

Most of the time we saw routine day-to-day medical problems like sore throats, bronchitis, urinary tract infections, hypertension, and diabetes. A couple of times a week a drug detail sales clerk came into the office.

One day a woman came into the office complaining of a headache. Before Dr. Henderson could check her blood pressure, she made a high-pitched scream, grabbed her head, and fell on the floor. I wasn't sure what happened, but Dr. Henderson knew right away that she suffered a ruptured blood vessel in her brain. He called the ambulance, and they took her to the hospital. When I saw her in the hospital the following day, her face was swollen, and she was connected to a respirator. Tubes were going into her and coming out everywhere. The machines were making their customary sounds. I believed that she didn't have a chance to live. Dr. Henderson told me that her condition was poor, and the likelihood that she would live was slim. I felt sorry for her. One day she was standing in Dr. Henderson's exam room and the next day she was fighting for her life in the hospital. Dr.

Henderson visited her each day until she stopped breathing on her own. One day while sitting in Dr. Henderson's office reading a book, Iris called me. I knew that something was wrong. She spoke to me with shallowness, as if she couldn't tell me what was on her mind. Then she told me the bad news. "Buddy, you didn't pass your national board exam." It hit me like a ton of bricks. She started to cry and apologized for opening my letter. She felt terrible about the disappointment I was feeling. We both knew that I needed to pass the exam to start the process of getting a license to practice medicine after medical school. Once again, Iris was sharing my pain.

I asked Dr. Henderson if I could go home. I explained to him that I had failed the national board exam and just couldn't work the rest of the day. He told me not to take it too hard because I had another chance to pass it. I spent the evening with Iris and remained depressed. She tried to console me, but I was too stuck in self-pity.

What I took away with me from the preceptorship with Dr. Henderson was priceless. He gave me a gift; himself. I understood that I needed balance in my life. However, more than that, I needed self-confidence. I realized that Blacks were competitors in the field of medicine. It established a basis of Black pride for me. When the preceptorship was over, Dr. Henderson and his wife invited us to dinner. It was a happy parting. I gained an enormous amount of respect for him and loved his wife. In her own way, and probably not even realizing it, she comforted me many times by just listening and speaking gently with me concerning my life. Her relationship with Dr. Henderson gave me a first-hand look at why Dr. Henderson was content. He and his wife were in love. I will never forget their warmth and the love they shared with me.

Chapter 11

Moving On

If I take the wings of the morning and dwell in the uttermost
Parts of the sea; even there shall thy hand lead me,
And thy right hand shall hold me.

Psalm 139:9, 10

The snow and cold of the winter months in Albany took a heavy toll on Iris, because she was pregnant with our first child. I remember many times walking to school with her early in the morning. She had to be at work about the same time I had to start class. We had to stop on the way, so she could catch her breath. Our hands would be freezing, and I would switch my books from arm to arm while trying to keep Iris from falling on the ice. She braved the winter months and hardly complained of the weather. Sometimes it was so cold a few feet from the house we couldn't go any further; we'd turn our back to the wind and just stand there.

Shoshanna

Iris was close to term. We were excited that our baby would be coming soon. I thought it would be easy to be pregnant and to deliver a baby. It was Friday evening after Iris arrived from work; she was having contractions. After having contractions for several hours, I thought it would be best to take her to the hospital. They kept Iris all night and into the morning. They said that she was not ready and sent her home. We waited at home. That Monday her water broke. I collected some of the amniotic fluid in a bottle and proudly walked into the hospital with it. They registered her, put her in the bed, and she was in labor, huffing and puffing about how she wanted more water from the nurse. Labor was difficult. She was in labor for twenty-three-hours. I went to the student lounge, and the delivery staff was paging me. The baby was descending through the birth canal. When I arrived in the delivery room, Iris was on the delivery table.

I rushed into the change room and put on the operating room clothes. I dashed into the delivery room, and there she was with her legs aimed at the ceiling, trying to deliver our child. The doctor was making everyone laugh.

"Pu-ha, pu-ha," he said in Spanish, he was telling Iris to "push." He knew my wife spoke English, so he must have been trying to learn Spanish. He told her that the baby was not coming, and if she didn't push, he was going to get the forceps, clamp the baby's head and pull the baby out. Still nothing was coming, so he proved he wasn't joking.

"Nurse," he said, "get my forceps." The nurse brought in something wrapped like a baby. "Put-ha, pu-ha," he screamed. His tone was one of jest, but he meant business. He pulled what looked like huge spoons out of the towel wrap. "Pu-ha, pu-ha, I'm going to use these forceps."

I looked at Iris and said, "You better push, or he'll use the forceps."

"Pu-ha, pu-ha," he commanded once more.

Like magic, out came this baby girl. A site that I was not prepared for. This was my first experience at being a father. I was very emotional. She was very pale. She had a head full of straight black hair. She opened one eye only. That made me nervous. By the third day, I spoke, to the pediatrician about her only opening one eye. Sure enough she tricked me. She opened the eye she kept closed and closed the other.

Iris was on the table, but half in another world. I told her the baby had ten toes and ten fingers and didn't tell her at the time that it scared me. I gave her a kiss, patted her on the head and left, carrying the baby to the transfer nursery. The nurses were asking me about a name for the baby. Iris and I had not really agreed on a name, so this was my opportunity to plug my choice for a name without any interference. "Shoshanna," I said.

"What?" the nurse asked.

"Shoshanna," I repeated. Shoshanna is a Hebrew name which means "lily" or "rose." Then, there was the question of "How do you spell it?"

When Iris recovered, naturally she had some complaints. I did two things that she didn't like. First, I left her twice, once before going into the delivery room and again just after the delivery. The second and perhaps the most important thing was that I named our baby without any further input from her. Iris had a name, "Anandi" which means joy. Nevertheless, "Shoshanna" was her name.

We enjoyed the presence of our daughter. She was an active child. She loved to watch "Big Bird" on Sesame Street and other educational shows. She loved playing games, puzzles, jumping, running, climbing and chasing daddy. She didn't like playing with dolls.

My financial aid was exhausted. As a result, I applied for a Public Health Scholarship. Within a few weeks, I was notified that the money was granted. I was very happy because I didn't want Iris to return to work. We both wanted her to stay home with Shoshanna. The scholarship paid for my tuition in full, which was $6,400, and we were given $750 tax-free to live on every month. She quit her job and became a full-time mother.

Chapter 12
The Hospital

Thine eyes did see my substance, yet being imperfect; and in
Thy book all my members were written, which in continuance
Were fashioned, when as yet there was none of them.

Psalm139:16

I believed Psychiatry was a wasted discipline in medicine. I saw people with
mental problems being spaced out on medications, which didn't seem to
help them. I didn't like Psychiatry because I rarely saw people get well.

"Ron" was my first psychiatric patient. He came into our unit via
the emergency room, handcuffed by the police. Ron lived on a farm and
spent much of his time reading. He read 'The Late Great Planet Earth'
and proclaimed to be John the Baptist and Jesus Christ. His mother told
me after he read the book; he locked himself in his room, refusing to talk
to anyone.

Then the following day he started praying for her, trying to cast demons
out of her. He prayed with such zeal that he leaped at her and grabbed
at her head; later, ran away. When the police found him, he was lying in
chicken manure from the barn, saying he was John the Baptist. I was asked
to care for him after the Chief Psychiatrist, Dr. Conner, injected him with
a high dose of Thorazine. He was diagnosed as having had a psychotic
episode. After spending some time with Ron, I believed there was more to
his experience than just a crazy episode. As the week passed, he continued
to confirm his experience, though he had trouble speaking because of being

drugged. He told me it was not fair to drug him, but when they found him, he was in a crazy state and needed to be calmed.

When the medication began to wear off, he started preaching to and counseling other patients concerning their problems. After a few days, he was writing poetry about all the staff members. It was very sensible and precise writing. His poetry became so popular that Dr. Conner wanted to read it. When Ron was better, he helped other patients relax. He could relate to them.

He was diagnosed with manic-depressive illness. I wasn't sure that's what he had. Instead of contradicting the diagnosis, I suggested to Dr. Conner that he might consider decreasing or stopping Ron's medication of Thorazine. Dr. Conner yelled at me and asked me if I wanted to throw Ron out of the hospital. I was stunned. I told him that my intent was to make things better. I realized that I had challenged Dr. Conner's authority, and it had offended him. Dr. Conner said nothing to me for the next few days. He simply ignored me. I was left with almost total responsibility for Ron.

I went to Dr. Clement, the only Black Psychiatrist on staff. I told him what happened, and that I believed there was no-good reason for the Chief to tell me off in public. It was a learning experience, and it was the Psychiatrist's responsibility to teach me the correct way. He assured me that he was very surprised and would speak with Dr. Conner.

After giving the matter further thought, I went back to Dr. Clement and suggested that he not say anything to Dr. Conner. I informed him that things were better, and the Chief invited me to do rounds with him. Unfortunately, it was too late; Dr. Clement already spoke to the Chief.

Ron proved that he wasn't a threat to himself or anyone else and was sent home on psychotropic medication. I wondered if we helped Ron and if what we did would last long enough for him to do something positive with his life. I hoped that he would remember my concern for him.

Dolores, another patient, was too much to believe. She came through the emergency room with a delusion that was out of this world. Dr. Conner asked me to accompany him immediately to the emergency room. A middle-aged woman lay on a stretcher; she was very emotionally disturbed. She was shaking and talking to herself. Dolores's hair was wild, and her mouth was dry. I asked the Chief what was wrong with her.

He said, "She's crazy."

I said, "What?"

He said, "She's crazy."

She told us, in a fast pace, that she was standing on the corner at night, and some men captured and raped her; then, put razor blades in her vagina. I questioned her repeatedly about her story, and she never changed it. Dr. Conner assigned her to me. That evening, I had a captive audience with Iris telling her about Dolores.

A couple of days later, Debra, another patient, was brought in by the police. She was violent and talking like Donald Duck. She was quite muscular for a woman. Dr. Rosenberg asked me to see her. He was a Psychiatrist to whom I was assigned. When I walked into the room, Debra told me not to come any closer, or she would break my face. She warned me about three times and stated that she wasn't kidding. She was so violent I couldn't stay with her. I walked out while telling her I would see her the next day. She said, "No, you won't."

The following day I walked boldly into her room and said, "Hello." She told me to keep my distance and don't touch her. I moved slowly in her direction, challenging her until she told me to stop where I was standing.

I told her I was from New York City, and she said, "so what?" She asked me how I could relate to her. I told her I grew up around people who used drugs, and she cursed me out. I told her that I cared about her. After three days, she was calm and let me near her. She told me that she was part Native American Indian. She also said her father abused her because of that she didn't want anything to do with men. She told me that she would speak with me if she could trust me. I assured her that she could.

When Dr. Conner went to see her, she wouldn't cooperate. She told him that she would only speak with me. He approached me and asked that I acquire information from her and then give it to him. I gave Debra my word, and I silently refused his request. Debra told me that she was gay and asked me to swear not to tell anyone. When Dr. Conner realized he was getting nowhere with her, he turned her case completely over to me to manage. He suggested that I select her care. I had full power to do with her what I believed would benefit her greatest.

In the meantime, Dolores was still complaining of razor blades in her vagina. She was given Thorazine, but it didn't help her depression. Dr. Conner decided to give her shock treatment. This was the first time I had ever seen electricity applied to a human being. I watched in horror as she stiffened up while the electricity rushed through her body. The little stick with gauze wrapped around it that was placed in her mouth had her teeth prints on it. It served to protect her from a sliced tongue and broken teeth, which would have occurred without it. They then placed her on a stretcher and rolled her out of the shock room, and she appeared dead.

The following day she was up walking around, smiling and cooperative. That was a bit of Psychiatry I had seen, which appeared to have a clear benefit. Debra told me that she needed eyeglasses because her vision was blurred. She said that she would not cooperate with me any further unless she got eyeglasses. I asked Dr. Rosenberg if I could take her downtown to get a pair of eyeglasses. He told me that I could, if I had a note from the Optometrist stating that she had glasses to pick up. I told him that she would get it. She wasn't able to get the note, but I took her anyway, without telling Dr. Rosenberg. After she got her glasses, she was more confident that I was her friend. The Psychiatrist continued to probe her for information, but she still would not cooperate with him. Dr. Rosenberg told Dr. Conner what I did in taking her downtown. Dr. Rosenberg told me that I did not have permission to do what I did. From that point in my relationship with him, Dr. Conner, as well as with Dr. Rosenberg, was destroyed.

Though I was busy taking care of two patients, I was assigned to a third one, Sarah. She was a heroin addict. She was young and pretty. When I went to see her, she was very friendly. She motioned for me to sit on her bed. She told me that she was on drugs and needed to kick the habit. She didn't believe that she belonged in the hospital; in spite of the fact that she was suicidal. I went to see her every day and sometimes-on weekends.

Dr. Rosenberg had a meeting with me and questioned my motives for visiting her so often. Then he told me that I didn't know how to speak very well. He said, "When you say 'asked,' it sounds like "axed," and people will think you don't know how to speak."

I was very confused and did not understand what his motives were. I didn't understand why the way I spoke made any difference to him. He may have thought I wanted to get in Sarah's panty. One thing I knew for sure, I was very embarrassed and felt he was upset with me for having visited Sarah so often; after all, she was, pretty and female. When I left his office, I was very angry. I had my hands full and was burdened on Psychiatry. At first, treating patients was exciting and rewarding, but now I was dealing with my emotions toward these professors. Dr. Clement, the only black psychiatrist on staff, also had his own problems. I was told he had a nervous breakdown, and used to take patients, whom he was treating to his house. It was too much for him to bear.

I was assigned a fourth patient, Mary. Mary was depressed because her children were taken from her. She wasn't able to cope because of family problems that extended a generation back to her father, who had molested her. Ironically, she needed to forgive herself for being molested, and then forgive him. I spent a lot of time trying to show her that she would recover from depression and be well enough to care for her children, and it worked. She left the Psychiatric Ward and did get her children back.

Debra could see better and was enjoying her new glasses and found a friend in me in whom she could trust. She cried the day she left the hospital, and she couldn't stop hugging me. I also felt like crying that day, but I was too worn out to shed a tear. All of my patients gave me a great sense of satisfaction in knowing that they appreciated me as a person and thought well of my care. The person I felt the saddest about was Dolores, because she was still convinced that she had razor blades in her vagina. I suggested to Dr. Conner to perform a mock operation in order to pretend to take the razor blades from her vagina, but was put down about the suggestion. He didn't believe it was a good idea, and I believed he was closed-minded. Dr. Rosenberg and Dr. Conner probably believed that I belonged in the Psychiatric Ward as a patient. Maybe I did belong there, but if I did, we all needed some level of psychiatric care. I realize that I had no right to challenge my superiors who were trying to teach me psychiatry, and I apologize for my behavior. If I had to do it over again perhaps I would do things differently.

During the last week of the Psychiatric rotation, we were asked to attend a meeting with a couple of Psychiatrists in order to discuss our rotation in Psychiatry. The professors sat with us in a small room where we were huddled in a circle. The Psychiatrists asked us questions of a psychiatric nature. They didn't want any feedback on the rotation and wanted to test our knowledge of psychiatry. Three other students and I were upset. There were only four of us doing the rotation. I personally believe that Dr. Conner and Dr. Rosenberg wanted to take me down a peg or two because of my independent attitude. I sat with them and practically ignored their questions. After the session was over, we realized that it was an oral exam. We were told at the beginning of the rotation that there would not be an exam. The other students soon cooled off, but it wasn't as easy for me, I remained upset. The following day we were given a multiple-choice exam. I passed the exam with a good grade. I didn't attend the last day because I had a scheduled appointment with the Associate Dean. I left a note with Dr. Conner before leaving the previous day. A few weeks later, the grades were returned. I wasn't allowed to have my grade from the Psychiatry Office; it was in the Dean's office. After speaking with the Dean, I learned that a special letter had been prepared, which stated that I had no respect for authority, no relationship with my patients, and didn't get along with my peers, and staff. I was given a grade of passing, but that wasn't all. They wrote that they had reservations about my being in postgraduate training in their department. I spoke with one Associate Dean. I also spoke with the doctor, who had written the letter. I was angry that the Psychiatrists downplayed even the positive things that happened with my patients while, I was doing the rotation.

I was glad the Psychiatry rotation was over, and I knew for sure I didn't want to be a psychiatrist.

Medicine

I looked forward to being in the Coronary Care Unit for one month at the Albany Medical Center Hospital. I was on general rounds one morning when I heard on the public address system that a patient was having a cardiac arrest. We stopped what we were doing and ran to the patient's bedside. When we arrived, as usual half of the hospital staff was there. My medical preceptor grabbed the paddles to the cardiac machine and put them on the patient's chest to get the heart beating properly with an electric shock. I was standing near the EKG monitor with the paper readout in my hand. It was a policy of mine to get involved as much as possible because sometimes nurses would ask people who were standing around idle to leave. I looked at the EKG strip while the doctors were trying to revive the patient. His heart was beating forty beats per minute. This was too low to sustain his life. My preceptor asked the Neurologist what he wanted to do. The Neurologist replied, "Nothing." I was astonished, for I couldn't believe what I was hearing. There we were, appearing to revive a man in cardiac arrest with a brain tumor. They were actually saying, "Let him die."

The family was waiting outside the patient's room, believing that we were doing everything in our power to save their loved one who was dying. The doctors stood there and looked at each other for about forty-five seconds, doing nothing. They were waiting for the patient's heart to stop beating, but it didn't. Staff started moving out of the room while the patient's heart continued to show forty beats per minute on the EKG machine. It was crazy. They were just letting him die. The thing that disturbed me was their dishonesty, convincing the relatives; they were doing their best to revive their family member. Someone was preparing a great lie to tell them, and I wasn't going to be part of it. I asked the intern if he thought what we did was right. "If it were my father with brain cancer dying in the hospital, I wouldn't want him to live," he responded reflexively. I then understood exactly why he said what he did, but I felt bad for the family.

We were supposed to save lives, not give them up. I knew we weren't gods, but the attitudes were so cold. I kept wondering, "What if that were my father, would I have wanted him alive with brain cancer?" It almost seemed a blessing to many in that room when he died. Physicians are trained not to waste energy and time to revive terminally ill patients. The rationale is that it is neither beneficial nor cost-effective to the patient or the family. I didn't like what I believed were some of the cold and inhumane aspects of my chosen profession.

Pediatrics

I didn't like Pediatrics. The children made too much fuss. No medical values, which I had learned in adult medicine, seemed to apply with children. There were many new things to learn. I decided to do the Pediatric rotation in a small hospital in Albany. It was a very friendly place, and it made taking care of children a bit more pleasant. I was with two doctors in training on Pediatrics. Dr. Degnan was the attending doctor responsible for us. He asked me to follow children with medical problems of interest, which appealed to me. My first patient was a boy named Kevin, who was about twelve years old who had muscle weakness and partial paralysis due to an unknown cause. He had a history of streptococcal sore throat for one-and-a-half weeks. He was prescribed penicillin by his local family physician; however, his symptoms did not subside. He was left with severe muscle pain and weakness. He had a staggering type of walk, slowed speech and a fine tremor in his hands. I was asked to follow his case. After doing the history and physical examination, I came to the initial conclusion that his streptococcal sore throat must have been somehow related to his present state. I presented my findings to the attending physician, Dr. Degnan. He quickly dismissed them. He said that there was no relationship between the two and to forget any such theory, and don't try to "write another textbook." He suggested that I practiced documented medicine and not try to invent any. The following day, a group of physicians discussed the case, and they were confused. They had no idea what had happened to

Kevin. Some believed that his inability to walk without staggering was due to his extreme weakness and fatigue. Others believed that there was possibly something taking place in his brain and spinal column. They really didn't know whose guess was the right one. No one wanted to take into account his streptococcal sore throat. They wouldn't even mention it, but it still seemed to me to be the most obvious cause. I wanted his throat infection to be high on our list of causes. Dr. Degnan again asked me to drop the whole idea. The investigation continued for days. We did manage to agree on one thing; he had a muscle illness of unknown cause. Everyone imaginable was in on the case. The various opinions concerning Kevin prevented a proper early evaluation of his case. Some wanted to perform a muscle biopsy. One doctor was bitterly against it. All the time Kevin was getting sicker. The attending physician believed that the interns were too aggressive. I was checking Kevin during the day and sometimes at night. He was so weak and sore in his muscles that he had to be fed. A Physical Therapist was working with him every day. I became a friend to him. Many times, I was asked by the staff to encourage Kevin to cooperate with them. He was, after all, a bit stubborn. On one occasion, the Physiotherapist wanted me to be there during the sessions to help in encouraging Kevin to work harder. Kevin responded to me. Though he was responding, he was not really getting any better. I was asked to present Kevin's case at a Friday morning conference. That week Dr. Degnan agreed to have a muscle biopsy done. It took days before the procedure was performed. I carried the biopsy to another hospital to have it read by one of the best Neurologists in the northeast, Dr. Hansen, a female Neurologist, and gave the biopsy to her secretary. After two weeks the report was finally returned, the biopsy was not suggestive of any known muscle disease. The muscle specimen was a normal piece of thigh muscle. I was asked to present the case that Friday to the staff. Dr. Degnan who was the pediatric attending physician supervising me was there and other important faculty members. I presented the case just as it was worked up without findings and the opposing opinions. I researched the subject of a muscle weakness and streptococcal sore throat and found no connection. I gathered the pertinent clinical and laboratory findings and presented the information. Halfway through the talk, Dr. Degnan stopped me and said, "You're running out of time, windup your presentation." I needed more time, and I told them that I had more to say, but could not do so because of time. After the presentation, Dr. Degnan told me that I messed up the talk. He said it was not educational and that no one learned anything from it. When I returned to the ward, the interns wanted to know how the presentation went. I told them that the attending doctor didn't like it. They were surprised and didn't understand what had gone wrong. They told me that my outline was great. When I told them how I presented the case, they said, "That's how we worked it up. "I ended the conversation because I didn't want anyone to overreact or relay it back to Dr. Degnan. After rounds that afternoon, Dr. Degnan approached me and told me that what I shared was disappointing. He didn't appreciate me sharing the controversy concerning the case. I didn't say anything to him. I continued to take care of Kevin, and he still wasn't getting any better, so the house staff made the decision to send him to New York City to be seen by a Neurologist. A few months later, I learned the doctors at that New York hospital also concluded that Kevin's muscle problems were due to his streptococcal sore throat. After the Pediatric rotation ended, we had an oral exam. I didn't do very well, but I wasn't worried because I had done my work and was given good recommendations from the staff. The following week I received a note in my mailbox asking to see Dr. Degnan. He told me after my presentation, he wanted to give me a failing grade in the course. I knew he had no grounds to fail me. He gave me two reasons why I received only a "Pass" grade instead of a better grade; namely, that the oral exam was not up to standard, and there was my "poor performance" in the outpatient clinic. Otherwise, he said I would have received a decent grade. I asked him if my presentation influenced his decision to give me a mere passing grade instead of a grade of "good." "To be perfectly honest, it probably did," he replied. I was upset with him because the presentation was not supposed to decide a part of the final grade. He was upset because I had discovered the truth concerning the case, while he and his colleagues looked bad. They didn't know what was wrong with the patient, and I didn't find any need to hide it. The case was interesting, and that was the way I presented it. My intent was not to injure anyone. I made an appointment to see the Associate Dean, who was the Chairman of Pediatrics and who taught me in the clinic. When I saw him, he acted as if he had no idea why I was there. He told me he gave me the grade I deserved. In his opinion, my performance in the pediatric outpatient clinic was inferior to that of the other students. I asked him to reveal to me by name which of the patients I cared for in an inferior manner. He got defensive and said, "I don't carry names of patients in my pockets." He did remember one patient whom I had seen, and he believed I didn't know what was going on with the case. When I asked him to help me, remember the patient, he was speaking of, he got upset. He told me that there was no way he could recall the incident any more than that. We argued for about ten minutes. His final words were that I had not performed as well as the other students, and that was his opinion. I then went to the Associate Dean and explained to him what happened in Pediatrics. He promised to summon the people involved to settle the matter. I knew I was on a merry-go-round again with my professors and that bothered me. It was my fault for failing to understand that the system did not operate the way I wanted. There were a few other things to deal with besides the grade. The Chairman of Pediatrics told me that the interns had informed him that they had to look over my shoulder to make sure I didn't do anything wrong. I didn't believe it, because the interns gave me good evaluations. When I spoke with one of the interns, he said it was a lie, and that "looking over my shoulder" was something suggested by Dr. Degnan. The intern believed that Dr. Degnan twisted the truth. The intern did not appreciate what had been said about him and volunteered to call the Chairman who taught me in the clinic. He maintained that he wouldn't have said anything like that; especially after giving me a good evaluation. He informed me that the other doctor with him gave me a decent evaluation. I received an excellent evaluation from the Neonatologist, who was a pediatrician. I thanked the intern for his frankness and decided to let the case rest. At least now, I knew what the deal was.

I began to question my attitude and the way I did things because it disturbed my superiors. I questioned whether I was the problem.

I was critical of the profession and my performance.

Obstetrics and Gynecology

When I started Obstetrics and Gynecology, I found myself lacking the energy needed. Iris believed that I was a rebel trying to fight every cause I believed was unfair. She was tired of my rebelling. Iris asked, "When are you going to learn that you cannot do well in school if you are on a crusade?"

She reminded me that I wasn't in school to fight, but to learn. She was sick and tired of seeing me suffer for it, for not heeding her warnings. I knew that she was right, but I just couldn't see sacrificing all of my values to please people who knew little about me. I wondered if I could benefit, in the end, if I continued my apparent rebellious behavior. I was tired of some people trying to bring me down, such as the professors who gave me bad grades just because they didn't like my attitude. I decided to keep my mouth shut to see if my academic and social life would change any.

I took Obstetrics and Gynecology at a hospital in Schenectady, about fifteen miles from Albany. All the residents there were foreign trained and were very friendly. They made me feel very comfortable and relaxed. They took an interest in me, as soon as they met me, and I appreciated that. I was encouraged by the fact that I got along with nearly everyone there. I hope that, nothing would come up to rock the boat.

There was a lot of work to be done on the ward. The Operating Room was constantly booked with cases, and it was all very exhausting at times. We were on call every third night, and when we were on call naturally, we didn't get much sleep.

Abortions

Each day we had from three to five abortions to perform. I had previously vowed that I would never do one, for it was against my religious beliefs. I spoke with my minister and family about it, and their general attitude was that I should participate for now because, unfortunately, it was a part of my training. No one was advocating it, and the hospital staff stated that it would be okay if I refused. I did some heavy thinking about the abortions on the ward, and decided that it would be in my best interest to help the other physicians. A couple of doctors told me that I didn't have to help them. I, however, decided not to trust that advice. I didn't want any attending physicians questioning my willingness to help. The following day, I started doing abortions. In abortions, we used a device that operated like a vacuum cleaner. The patients were pre-medicated before the procedure. Then, the instrument was placed into the uterine cavity, and the fetus was destroyed by the suction. We had one case with miscalculated gestation. While suctioning the cavity, the fetus' spine broke away from the body and wouldn't pass through the suction catheter. The doctor had to pick it off and push it through. He looked at me with a sick face. It was a horrible sight. Everyone in the room was visibly shaken. I realized something. I was involved in murder with consent; unfortunately, not the consent of the murdered.

Within two weeks, I was actually doing abortions myself. I knew it was wrong, and it disturbed me to know that I'd gotten accustomed to murdering so easily. Perhaps it was most disturbing because the murdered never spoke. I paid a terrible price to join the fan club of my colleagues. I lost myself-respect and dignity, and some of my value system had crumbled.

After the rotation was over, I received my grade of "good." Not only had it been a successful rotation academically, but socially also, because the staff liked me. At the end of the third year, I was pleased with my performance in medical school. At least, I completed the year without any failures. This helped to compensate for the indifferent attitudes of some physicians. Many times, it seemed like a chore for them to share their wealth of knowledge with me. I am sure at times I did not help my professors to be kind or friendly to me.

I eventually told my family what had happened in the first year, the one I repeated, and kept secret from them. The secret couldn't be kept any longer because four years had passed, and according to the calendar, I was due to graduate. I was ready to tell them anyway. They seemed to understand and weren't upset with me for it. It was just another bridge crossed.

Chapter 13
Hanging Out

The earth is the Lord's, and the fullness of it,
the world and they who dwell in it.

Psalm 24:1

When I wasn't studying or in church, I spent time with my friends. Being with them was my chance to be free of stress and have fun. It made me feel good. Sometimes I got in touch with Eddie. Eddie worked in the college Physiology lab. I liked Eddie because he helped me forget about school. Ironically, his working in the college encouraged him to try to forget about anything connected to it. He liked hunting and we often talked about hunting together. We did go hunting one time, and it was freezing, but I enjoyed being in the woods. Sometimes I stopped at Eddie's house to talk with him and his wife. His wife liked talking about all kinds of stuff, and I liked her. She was a beautician. She and Eddie spent quality time with their children at ball games and other activities. I respected both and enjoyed their company. Eddie had completed a number of years of college and once wanted to enter medical school. On occasion, we talked about racism and how it affects people, and I felt he was bruised by it, like most people in America. Whenever I visit Albany, I always try to contact Eddie because he was true to me when I was in school.

Ephraim was another hangout; a partner of mine. I tried to contact him as much as I could because in many ways he was my idol of a cool guy. He understood the racism game played on us, but acted as if it didn't exist when he had to take care of serious business. One time I told him

I started writing an autobiography, and he said, "Hey, bro, I don't advise you to do that. It's going to make trouble for you."

Ephraim was a man who fought for what he believed, but he had a particular cool style in doing it, not letting his opponent know his moves. In many ways, I have wanted to be like him.

Paul was another guy I enjoyed being with. I don't know where he is today. He wanted to be a doctor, but didn't get into a U.S. medical school. He was accepted at a school in Tampico, Mexico. In some ways, I feel I let him down because he had money problems when he was there, and asked me for help, and I couldn't. It wasn't because I didn't want to, for I was having money problems myself. Paul trusted and believed in me. Paul was a student at the State University of New York, at Albany. He had a Bachelor of Science degree and all the premedical requirements. He was working full-time at a job at which he was determined to stay. I encouraged him to apply to Albany Medical College, which he did and was turned down. Paul and I spent many hours talking about racism and how it affected people. I loved Paul very much, and I still hurt that I didn't come through for him.

I probably spent more time with Michael than I did with any of my other hangout friends. I liked Michael because he kept me on my toes with everything. He was always asking me questions about some situations either of us was in. He seemed to be the most inquisitive about my future career as a doctor. I believed at times that he was fascinated to have a friend who was going to become a medical doctor. He made me feel extra special. "Hey, man," he would say, "I'm really proud of you making it, and I want you to believe that. If I had done what I was supposed to do in school, my situation would be better."

Michael worked for General Electric, and he never believed they did right by him, and I agree. Michael was proud of his job because he understood that in spite of his feelings about not applying himself in school, he had come a long way. His job paid fairly well, and he purchased a house at a young age. I think Mike's problem was that he hated depending on anyone for the next day's subsistence. Mike was really the independent type that had just not found the right break to start his business. I saw the possibility of work independence in Mike, and I saw him in his own business.

Michael was very close with his parents. They were nearing retirement, and he was concerned that he wasn't doing enough for them. I often told him to remember, honor, and cherish his parents because it was right, and they were all he would ever have for parents. I spent hangout time with Brother Belton also. The fact that he was older than I was never made any difference to either of us. I looked at him as I did the other guys because he was energetic, full of surprises and enjoyed having fun. Most of my hangout time with him was in his house, and Iris was usually with me at these times. Sister Belton was always there and willing to share with Iris and me. I had many memorable times with him and most of them were quiet times talking about life and God.

If I had to say which one of my hangout, friends I enjoyed being with the most, I just wouldn't try. They all were very special to me and still are.

Chapter 14
Medical College Admissions Committee

How precious are the thoughts unto me,
O God! How great is the sum of them!

Psalm 139:17

During my fourth year in medical school, a Minority Affairs Committee was formed. We had six Black medical students in the college out of 500-plus students. The medical college still accepted a small number of Black students. They claimed that there were few minorities that applied and those who did apply were not promising. I believed that one sure way of getting African Americans into the mainstream of the system was to get on the Admissions Committee. A number of students were running for the available positions. No seat, however, was designated as a minority seat. The student Minority Affairs Committee asked me to run for the position. I never imagined ever doing anything like that in medical school. I had been a controversial figure and didn't imagine anyone would want me on the Admissions Committee, because it meant working closely with the faculty without prejudice. I agreed to run anyway.

On Election Day, we gathered in the auditorium lecture hall. The students were all excited, waiting for the chance to elect their friends. Apparently, I wasn't in such good favor, because all the candidates had been required to write a letter explaining why we wanted a seat on the committee. I wrote about the minorities and their situation and mentioned the class as a whole. I think I overemphasize my minority pitch. A few believed my letter was too strong and prejudicial. I had the letter rewritten by a couple of classmates, but I remained strong on the minority issues. On the day of the voting, students were tense, because naturally, they had their favorites to win. The result ended in a tie. When they voted again, some of the students who had voted for me the first time changed their minds and didn't vote for me. Even the black students didn't vote for me, apparently because, one told me; they felt I had no chance of winning. It was just another time that we failed to stick together. I lost the election.

The Minority Affairs Committee had a meeting and decided to ask that a minority seat on the Admissions Committee be filled. We made a lot of noise and were finally allocated the seat. It was planned for me to have it automatically, but they voted on the candidates anyway, thus making it democratic. This was an important move for me. I saw it as an excellent opportunity to pull some people over the wall who might not otherwise have been admitted to medical school. My role on the committee was equal to all other students. I was to screen and interview minority as well as non-minority candidates. I took home applicants' folders and sat with Iris to screen them. Iris would be my second opinion and my "checks & balances." If I didn't like a candidate without looking through the folder, she would say something to me that usually caught my attention. I remember one applicant whose father was a judge in California. He tried to use his influence to get his son an interview. The judge had spoken with a friend of his, who knew the Chairman of a large department in a New York City hospital. The Chairman, in response, wrote a letter to someone in the medical college asking for a return favor. It angered me. It was obvious that his son was an outstanding student. I didn't understand why he felt the need to get a favor returned on behalf of his son because his son had excellent grades. I immediately handed the letter to Iris. I told her that I would not consider the applicant for an interview. I thought about the less fortunate who had no one to speak for him or her. I wanted so much to be fair, but it was difficult to do so while at the same time dealing with the way the system worked by feeding itself.

There were times when committee members didn't know where I was coming from. They couldn't predict what kind of attitude I would have at any given meeting.

The students whom we interviewed on Friday were voted for on the following Tuesday. Each person who interviewed students was required to present or plead his case to the entire Admissions Committee. Sometimes, during these meetings, I wanted to respond to certain issues but did not do so for fear that, the subject of race would arise, and I might be accused of giving a motivated interview and possibly be discredited. Many times, I held my peace and sat quietly.

A situation arose once with a Black student whom I had interviewed, who had decent grades and average medical college admissions test scores. One of the committee members from the Microbiology department questioned the student's ability getting through school. This student was better than most minority applicants we had interviewed up to that point. It was evident to me that the student had the qualities needed and did have a good chance of getting through medical school. This wasn't the first time this had happened. "Why is it that we evaluate black candidates with such negative feelings?" I asked. It was a while before anyone answered me. When someone finally spoke up, he said that black students, regardless of their educational background, didn't seem to achieve as well as the average student. Before I could say anything, another committee member added, "Minority students just have a difficult time dealing socially."

I told them I believed it was unfair that black candidates with good solid grades were evaluated poorly. The moderator of the meeting put a halt to the conversation, and we continued our presentation of cases.

Whenever I spoke what was on my mind, I always left the meeting feeling as if I had said something wrong, and usually I did.

I enjoyed the interviewing on Friday afternoons. I tried to tailor every interview according to students' first comments to me. After they had their say, I knew what questions to ask. I tried not to give a pressured interview, since the interview was a very crucial part of the selection process. In addition, I remembered my own interview and didn't want to subject anyone to what I had gone through. We had been given guidelines concerning which questions to ask, but were given liberty to ask our own questions also. I would ask the white students if they thought it was wrong that so many Black people voted for President Carter in spite of his Southern background. I would question them about their feelings on minorities in medical school. The Blacks didn't escape my piercing questions either. I asked them if they were anti-Semitic and what they thought about the attitudes of whites toward minorities in the medical profession. I remember one black student, whom I questioned about the movie "Roots." He told me that he didn't have the time to see the television version, but that he had the book at home, although he hadn't read it. I was upset with him and asked why he hadn't read the book. He informed me that he just hadn't. At that point, the interview was over. I knew I couldn't give this candidate, Black or not, a positive evaluation. As I look back on my decision concerning this student and reading "Roots," I don't think I would do differently. Something about him appeared to me to be phony. I believe he was apathetic about his own people. I was personally offended over his passive decision not to share the Black experience through one of the most historic epic stories of our times, "Roots." This attitude did not match his blown-up outward rhetoric about Blacks. Another interviewer asked him the identical question about "Roots," and got the duplicate response.

If a candidate was honest during the interview and didn't try to pull the wool over my eyes, I considered him or her. I was looking for people who were willing to admit their weak points as well as their strong points. I met a few people like this; when I did, I was quite impressed. Sometimes, I felt as though I had unfairly judged an applicant, and it bothered me for days. As I looked at credentials on Tuesday morning, before the meeting began, my doubts surfaced. I was not sure if my approach in evaluating candidates for medical school was correct. I may have exhibited the same kind of discrimination that, I objected to so much. In spite of my doubts, I ultimately generally felt comfortable with my judgments.

I advised a few college students whom I knew to apply to the medical school. Their credentials were not usually as good as the average candidates, but they demonstrated the ability to achieve scholastically. I was very optimistic about getting them at least an interview.

The Assistant Dean offered to let me help him screen all the minority applicants. He wanted me to question his decision on anyone. I took full advantage of that opportunity. I convinced him to reconsider about five applicants, two of whom I knew, Paul and Cheryl. I wanted to interview one of them, but I knew that it would not have been fair. I asked one of the committee members, named Barry, to interview one. I asked him to interview Cheryl. He agreed and assured me that he would ask another interviewer to give her the second interview. I made it clear to him that I wasn't trying to put him on the spot, but I believed he was the best person I could have approached about the matter. The student's interview was Friday, and I had no worries about it. I coached her on some ways to sharpen her interview. I saw the Assistant Dean in the college. He told me that he wasn't sure she could get through school at that point in her life. He suggested that she would be wise to attend graduate school, take a few courses, and reapply the following year. That night I called Cheryl and explained what had taken place so far. She said that she didn't know what had happened at the interview that made him feel so negative about her, because she believed he was positive during the entire interview. The following Tuesday morning at the medical center, we discussed the students. The Associate Dean said that he had interviewed her and liked her. He was willing to give her a chance until he found out how the other interviewer had evaluated her. I turned to an interviewer on my left and told him that I knew the applicant personally and deliberately did not interview her for that reason. He wanted me to mention this to everyone at the meeting, in case they might reconsider her. I couldn't, for I had selected her application in the Assistant Dean's office. I failed to be impartial in my selection, and it was a clear conflict of interest. At this point, my action was no different than the father who wanted his son to be given a favor to enter school. I was sitting on the edge of my seat, halfway between speaking up and walking out. I thought that any public admission that I knew Cheryl might bring on unfavorable reactions. The interviewer next to me kept speaking to me in a low tone, asking me to speak up. I couldn't. I wouldn't even look at him. One person raised an issue about the split decision between the Associate Dean and Barry. He asked why another applicant was considered more favorably than Cheryl, the previous applicant having been white with no better grades. This opened up a new assortment of problems and people became defensive concerning their decisions. One group believed that race was not the point. The point was there were two groups, which were evaluating similar credentials in distinctive ways.

One group believed the credentials presented were terrible and not acceptable, and the other group didn't. The entire situation had me boiling. As far as I could tell, it appeared to be racial and very few people were ready to deal with that.

After the long meeting, I picked up my coat and departed without saying a word to anyone. I dreaded the thought of telling Cheryl what had happened. This difference in the opinion was to shape her future goals. When I spoke with her that evening, she broke down and cried. I felt terrible. Being zealous to get a fair interview may have hurt her. She cried so much I couldn't even speak with her over the telephone, so I told her that I would be over to pick her up. I explained the situation to Iris and immediately left the house. When I returned to the apartment with Cheryl, we sat in our living room that evening and talked until we both felt better. After that experience, I understood how the system worked and how I could be an integral part of it.

I lost contact with Cheryl. Paul was also turned down. I became friends with a young black man named Simon, who was a janitor mopping floors at the medical center. He had a college degree from The State University at New York. He wanted to be a doctor, but according to the system, didn't meet the mark to be accepted into medical school. Simon and I had many discussions concerning black people. That brother believed in himself, applied to Albany Medical College, and was accepted. He's a doctor today, and I'm very proud of him.

Pregnancy and Finances

Financially, Iris and I were in trouble again. Iris was pregnant with our second child. We spent our Public Health Scholarship money. I had received a check every month for $750, tax-free, not realizing that some of it had to be saved for the summer months. The checks were only to come for the school year of nine months. We had no summer income in sight. We took the remaining few dollars we had and paid our current bills. After doing that, we had $375 for the entire three months ahead. I knew something would work out, but I just didn't know how or what. I kept telling Iris that everything would be fine. As the weeks passed, the money dwindled rapidly. Often I was worried, but I didn't tell Iris.

I inquired about a preceptorship. There was an opening in a small town in the county, outside of Albany. The position was offered by Dr. Gifford a family physician. The preceptorship didn't have much educational value. The doctor refused to let me help in doing anything of importance. In fact, whenever a female patient was to be seen, he would make sure she was all covered up, as if I wanted to peek at her private parts. Whenever a woman had to have a pelvic exam or be checked for any problem, he would make some excuse for me to take a tea or coffee break (and I drank neither). It never seemed to bother him about his actions, and I felt terrible. Dr. Gifford was impatient with most of his clients. He also appeared not to be professionally honest. I watched him examine ears with an otoscope from one foot away (most people in medicine know you have to stick the thing in the ear). Well, I never saw him do it the correct way. He would tell them that their ears were fine. He looked in the eyes in the same manner.

Dr. Gifford complained about having to do histories and physicals on children and college students. He used the excuses that most of them were well and cut short the exam. He never complained, when he took their money after doing a sloppy job. Every time a patient complained of a headache; he would give them Valium and blame the headache on their nerves. If a patient complained of an upset stomach, he would blame it on their nerves and give them Lomotil medicine. Dr. Gifford never completely examined any patients while I was there. New patients were no exception. I guess I did learn one thing from him, and that is, I didn't want to be like him, ever. The last day of the summer preceptorship, I barely said good-bye to him. I didn't tell him I had a good experience because it was terrible.

I spent some of that summer fishing with my friends Ephraim and Paul in Schenectady on the Mohawk River. I bought a yellow inflatable raft that I purchased with some of our income tax money. We had a great time with it. We fished on a little island until we got tired. Ephraim took me back to land and returned for Paul. On the way, back the water got rough and Paul fell out of the raft. I laughed so hard my side was hurting. Ephraim almost fell out of the boat himself. Sometimes it was hard to get Ephraim to laugh, but this time it was no problem. Paul didn't get hurt; just a little wet. We all laughed about it.

I went fishing on the Mohawk River many times, and it helped me deal with some of my stress.

Doing My Job

After my summer preceptorship with Dr. Gifford, I applied for a job at a local hospital, St. Clare's Hospital. I did histories and physical exams. I spoke with the Medical Director, and he hired me. It paid $15 per hour plus meals and a place to sleep. I rarely slept there because I didn't want to leave Iris alone at home with Shoshanna. I worked twice a week for six hours each day. The income kept my family afloat. I liked that little hospital, and in addition working there would help us pay bills.

The Last Miles

During my last miles in medical school, I began to feel like a doctor. I wore a clean white jacket every day. One morning I was awakened at 3:00 a.m. I had to see a patient with excessive weight loss, fever and generalized pain. When I arrived at the patient's bedside, I took one look at her and knew she was very sick. I tried to draw blood from her, but her veins were hidden and small. When I stuck her with the needle, she cried like a child. I stopped and told the nurses that I couldn't draw it. After taking her history, I learned that she had lymphoma, diabetes and a peril-rectal abscess. I ordered the necessary medications, lab tests and went back to bed. I awakened in the morning to do hospital rounds, which started at 8:00 a.m. I presented the patient to the staff. They listened as my voice shook from anxiety. I stumbled through the presentation, but I managed to finish with the staff smiling. I spent the rest of the morning and afternoon speaking with the patients.

My patient with lymphoma wasn't doing well. She was going to die, and she knew it. She displayed a lot of courage and never stopped hoping. Sometimes, I would enter her room while she was asleep. I would stand at her bedside and just look at her. Knowing that this life, which existed, would soon be no more, I had to come to grips with life's mortal finality. She finally left the hospital only to return later and die. It affected me deeply.

The Matching Program

The time arrived for me to decide where I would do my postgraduate training after medical school. I needed to decide what field of medicine I would enter. I picked Family Medicine. Iris didn't want to leave Albany because she came to love it. It was a safe place for her away from Brooklyn. She told me she would go to another place to live but not Brooklyn and definitely not Red Hook. I understood how she felt, but I had made a promise to some people in Red Hook that I would practice medicine there one day. The decision-making process involved the matching program where one tried to match up with an internship and residency program. Upcoming new doctors applied to various hospitals by way of selection and interview. There was no guarantee that I would be placed. It was more a matter of God's grace and chance. Early in the school year, I went to Brooklyn for one month with my family in order to do a preceptorship in a Family Practice program. I liked the program, and the Director of the program informed me that he wanted me to practice there. I was told to put that Family Practice program first if I felt the same way. When the match came through, I matched with the Family Practice residency in Brooklyn, just as I wanted.

Acting Internship in Surgery

I began an acting internship in surgery at St. Peter's hospital in Albany. I regretted it later. I tried to get out of doing it, but the schedule was already made up. I hadn't enjoyed surgery in my third year and knew it was going to be a drag. They wanted me to be on call every other night, and I really didn't want to. My second week in surgery convinced me that I might never survive in a surgical residency. The chief resident assigned me with a surgeon who gave most of the students a hard time.

Once during a lymphoma staging, he was annoyed. I was holding a retractor in order to keep a patient's abdomen open, so he could stage her cancer. The procedure was long, and my fingers were hurting. He shouted at me, "Wake up. You're not in any pet shop with puppies." That wasn't so bad, but then he smacked my hands. I told the chief resident that I wasn't working with that surgeon again. On another case that same surgeon needed a student to work with him, but I refused when they asked me. He was not going to have a second chance to smack my hands.

The most challenging time in my fourth year surgical rotation was when I was in the veterans' hospital and had to give a presentation on lung cancer. I thought I was prepared, and all the residents were rooting for me. Halfway through my talk, a highly respected surgeon yelled, "Why doesn't he sit the hell down; he doesn't know what the hell he's talking about." The resident doctors were shocked and believed his remarks were not called for. I did sit, but not before, I finished my talk.

I was given an excellent grade in surgery, and I am not sure why. I will admit that I was rigid in my attitude and behavior, and I spoke my mind. I really think things went okay because I exhibited the same attitude that they had; say what you have to, do what you have to, and keep on going.

Taina

Iris gave birth to our second daughter, Taina, born March 12, 1978. She weighed 7lbs and 9oz. The name comes from the Taino Indians. I was sure she would be beautiful. Taina was an excellent baby. Iris says, she was the best baby in terms of behavior and attitude. She was a very calm child. She slept well, ate properly. She set the pace for the others; she wanted her bed by 7:30 pm. Taina was a quiet child. She was happy playing with a baby doll by herself. As she grew older, she questioned everything (why) was the favorite word. She would argue about everything. She was a great debater.

Finishing Up

The remainder of the fourth year was pretty much routine. I had taken a number of other rotations like Cardiology, Neurology, and Urology and I hated them all. I did well. Some people on the faculty reassured me that they knew I would be a good physician. Not all of my stands for or against certain matters were appreciated, but I made my point known. I gained the respect of many people.

During my last few weeks in school, a professor of Epidemiology and Biostatistics approached me. He said, "Wilbert, the only problems some of us are concerned about with you is, will you ever get a license to practice medicine after graduation?" His statement stunned and hurt me, and I thought seriously whether he was right. Nevertheless, I was leaving that institution to enter another situation just as challenging.

Racism

I never thought a bunch of bigoted, hateful people who amounted to a mob of cowards would threaten to kill me and my family for trying to rent a nice apartment on a tree-lined street in Brooklyn, in a Norwegian and Irish-American neighborhood. It was the harshest experience that I ever had concerning race. It started when my future Family Practice Director at The Lutheran Medical Center Hospital in Brooklyn promised me a nice apartment on a tree-lined street a few months before I graduated from medical school. He asked me to contact his real estate agent, who was selling his house. When we arrived at the agency, we were told that most property owners really didn't want children, and that we should visit other rental agencies.

They didn't know we had visited a number of agencies that only showed us roach infested apartments. Iris and I visited them again, and insisted that they show us something descent. The agent took us to two places. One was an attractive apartment in a six-family complex that was still being built on 78th Street in Bay Ridge, Brooklyn. Another was on Staten Island, a cheap apartment in an otherwise well-kept building. He tried to convince us to take the latter, yet the Bay Ridge apartment was really, what we liked, and we told him so.

He called us the next day and told us the Bay Ridge apartment would not be ready in time for us to move in because of a building permit that was needed.

After returning to Albany, I asked my friend Richard, who was due to graduate with me, to accompany me to the real estate office and pose as my lawyer, and he agreed. The following week Richard put on a suit, and both of us headed back down to Brooklyn to the real estate office. When the real estate sales agent saw us, he quickly summoned us to his desk. Richard and I sat before him as fake client and attorney. Richard never verbally stated that he was a lawyer, but his mannerism spoke otherwise. Richard sat silently with his hand on his chin, he was cool. The agent looked frightened. The agent told me that he still didn't have anything available for my family, but he would continue to search. When we left the office, Richard and I looked at each other and started smiling. "Did you see how scared that guy looked?" I said. "Yeah," Richard said, "he got the message." I thought that we were on top of the problem. After my return to Albany, I prepared for the last few miles of medical school. The Swift Real Estate office was still playing games with me.

Chapter 15
Graduation and Racism

Search me O God, and know my heart:
Try me, and know my thoughts.

Psalm 139:23

It was May 25, 1978. My friends and relatives in New York were excited. A host of people came to my graduation from Brooklyn. They came to see me through the graduation ceremony. It was a great day in my life, and many in my family were there to share that moment with me.

Brother and Sister Belton drove me in their motor home to Saratoga Springs, New York, where the graduation ceremony was being held. As usual, they treated Iris, and I like royalty.

Elder Mc Daniel was there, as well as many people from Refreshing Springs Church, including Sister Dix, my friends Michael and Margie, and Ephraim and Yoli. Dr. J.T. Henderson and his wife were there. They gave me a brand-new Littman stethoscope. I was happy that they all were there because they were a part of my life. I called them God's shadow over me.

The graduation ceremony was great and, as usual, too long for those graduating. When my name was called to receive my large old-fashioned medical degree certificate, I swiftly walked onto the stage. When the Chairman of Anatomy shook my right hand and handed me my degree he asked, "What are you doing here?" I looked in his eyes and laughed. I was told later that I was screaming on the stage. My journey was over. I achieve my goal to be a doctor. I finally made it, in spite of the fire I had walked through and some I had created.

Refreshing Springs Church had a celebration for me. Iris said I grinned the entire time. When it was all over, I knew for sure that Iris and I were victorious. I was grateful to God and the people who encouraged me. During this time, Iris and I did not agree where we were going to live while I did my internship and residency in Family Medicine. She told me that if I decided to make Brooklyn, New York the location for our new home, she would not be pleased. I didn't think she really meant it, but she was serious. Iris made it clear that whatever went wrong in New York City with us would be my fault, and I should not forget it.

Racism on a Grand Scale

I called the Human Rights Commission in Manhattan, New York. I was told to put a deposit on the apartment. The situation spiraled afterwards. Mr. Swift, the agency owner, tried to steer us to other apartments in rundown neighborhoods, and tried to give us our deposit back several times. My friend Raymond spoke with Mr. Swift. They attended the same church. He told me that Mr. Swift was pressured by some of the Norwegians and Irish-Americans in the neighborhood. They threatened to mess up the apartment building and kill my family if he rented to us. They even threatened the builder's daughter. They told him, "If those "niggers" get the apartment, we're going to rape your daughter." Her bra and panty size was quoted on the telephone to the builder. He became hysterical, and as a result sent her to Norway. Mr. Swift received threats that they would blow up his real estate office. Someone from the neighborhood went inside the establishment and spit on a sales agent. Mr. Swift claimed that he didn't feel the way the people did who lived in the neighborhood, and he was more concerned for my family than for his business. I didn't believe him. He was a part of the racial discrimination being practiced against us. The people who were threatening us, he says, were threatening to burn down his business. I was angry with the Swift Real-estate Company in the Bay Ridge section of Brooklyn and its owner, Mr. Swift, for allowing members of his company to be racist, while he claimed to be a Christian. He deceived me. They had a real estate agent take me to two unfit dwellings. They tried to get me to rent one. Mr. Swift and his friend invited me on a fishing trip along the shore of Staten Island, New York, one evening. They took me out in their boat, and then stopped it. They frightened me. I thought that they were going to throw me overboard. When they took me ashore, it was, by then, already dark. They drove me to an isolated street on Second Avenue in Brooklyn. Mr. Swift threatened me. He yelled in an uncontrollable rage, saying repeatedly, "You better not take that apartment." His saliva sprinkled my face. He wouldn't let me out of his car until I said, "OK, I won't take it." "When I got out of that car, I thanked God for my life. I was angry and scared. I told Iris what happened, and she begged me to forget about the apartment. She said that we could find another apartment in a neighborhood where people didn't care about color and race. After she spoke with me, I understood her fear because I was again frightened for my family and myself. The thing that kept tearing at me was that not even at this point in my life was I protected from racism. I had never felt so low and broken in all of my life. My Family Practice Director urged me to walk away from the situation. The Human Rights agent told me that we should not give in to the apartment residents' pressures. He believed that they were just bluffing with their threats to the builder, the agency and my family. Iris was strong throughout the ordeal, up to that point. However, after the personal threats to our family, and a brick was thrown through the balcony sliding glass door, we thought that we should back off and live in a safer place. I just couldn't, bring myself to back down so soon. I believed my manhood was at stake. The situation got worse. The builder refused to complete the apartment, even though we had all the paperwork to move in we couldn't do so. All the tenants in the building had moved in, even though they applied to rent after we did. Both of our families urged us to forget it all, but I was stubborn. The Human Rights Commission gave the builder and real estate agency until July 15 to have the apartment ready. July 15 arrived. I was still determined to have that apartment. I met the Human Rights officer and together; along with police escorts, we went to the apartment on 78th Street. There was a good-sized crowd of people outside the apartment building. There were two police officers with the Human Rights agent and me. One of the officers had a gun strapped to his lower leg. When I got out of the car, a man standing across the street grabbed his groin and shook it at me; an exercise in mental castration. The Human Rights agent asked the builder if the apartment was ready, and the builder replied, "No. I'm not going to get killed." The Human Rights agent asked him to show us the apartment. He didn't want to. However, the agent insisted. While we stood there talking, a woman named Mrs. O'Keefe approached us, threatening the builder right before our eyes. We tried to ignore her, but by this time, more people had gathered around. As we walked up the stairs to the apartment, I believed someone was going to shoot me; I was scared. Inside, the apartment fixtures were unconnected.

Wires were hanging from the ceiling, and the floor and walls were not finished. The brick that was thrown through the dining-room window was still there, on the floor next to the broken glass. At that moment, I knew that I couldn't bring my family around these people. They were willing to kill us. After viewing the condition of the apartment, the Human Rights officer asked the builder when he could have it prepared. "I won't." The builder replied. "If you want it ready, I'll give you the money and you can fix it yourself. They're going to kill me." When he said that, I became engulfed with fear. I finally told the Human Rights officer that Iris and I no longer wanted the apartment. He was disappointed. We settled the matter at the Human Rights office. Iris and I were given an apology and $700. I requested the money in personal checks from Mr. Swift and Mr. Hansen to show my children one day, and they gave me the checks. I felt less than a man that day. I was depressed. I believed that my medical degree and all the respect that comes with it were enough to make some people treat me as a human being. Not even my nice car and my intern clothes would change the racist attitudes of many. I was deeply wounded, and once again; I was angry with America. A person who worked at the hospital where I worked heard about our plight and found an apartment for us, ironically it was in an Italian neighborhood, in the Bensenhurst section of Brooklyn.

My Mother, Laverne Williams.

My Father, Wilbert Williams, Sr.

Left to right: My sister Janice, acting crazy, as usual. My usual calm self, and my sister Shelly.

I was handsome when I was 8 years old.

Graduation from Boy's High School, 1966.

Contemplating my life's journey at 25 years old.

Graduation from Medical School, Left to Right:
Iris' mother, Doris Shoshanna, Me, Iris Taina, and
Iris' father, Zacharias.

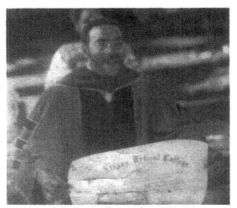

*I couldn't believe I finally had the Medical Degree
diploma in my hand!*

*My pastor - and friend, Elder McDaniel, as usual,
supporting and encouraging me at Graduation from
Albany Medical College.*

*Iris and I on our
wedding day. She was
19 years of age and I
was 24.*

*Iris and I, with our new family. Left to right:
Saladine, Shoshanna, and Taina.*

My new Piper aircraft, my "Cocoon," tied with a red ribbon at the former Alexander Hamilton Airport, St. Croix, U.S.V.I.

Awaiting a flight in our new Piper aircraft are my wife Iris & daughter Cilicia.

Hurricane Hugo destroyed my "cocoon" and my escape from the stress, and gave me even more stress

*Cilicia, our daughter, enjoying
something sweet.*

*Daughter Ariana with her very
enticing smile.*

*Daughters Shoshanna and Taina   enjoying
a vacation.*

Son Saladine studying diligently in the Good Hope School library.
Photo-Vaughn

Jamal, really getting with it on vacation

Wilbert, smiling, as usual — he is from St. Croix, not Washington, D.C.

*Oh, happy days!
Iris and myself
on vacation.*

*My lovely and loving
wife, Iris with a
Valentine Day Rose.*

*Ready to go to the office
after visiting Pelican Cove
on St. Croix*

Photo-Vaughn

195

My Grandmother Maggie, my Father's mother, who lived In Alabama.

My Aunt Queen as a young girl, my Father's sister-in law

My Aunt Doris, my Mother's sister from Brooklyn, who taught me many lessons, including cleaning up after my dog (see my book Dancing in Fire).

Left to Right: Back - Felisha, Oscar, Orlando, Louis Jr., Jackie, Myra; 3rd Row - Angie, Katie, Elmira; 2nd Row - Anginetta, Shayla, Patrick; 1st Row - Aunt Queen.

Uncle Louis, my Father's Brother, in graduation regalia.

My cousin Louis, Jr, son of Uncle Louis.

197

Hurricane Hugo devastation to our home on St. Croix, when we all suffered trauma — including our horse.

Our family smiling through it all, even though traumatized at our Hurricane Hugo destroyed home

PART III

Lost

Professional or not, I had to protect my family and myself

Chapter 16
Lutheran Medical Center

Though, I walk through the valley of the shadow of death,
I will fear no evil, for You are with me.
Your rod and Your staff, they comfort me.

Psalm 23:4

When I first saw Lutheran Medical Center, I was shocked. I remembered it as an old rundown factory. I passed it many times while going to Coney Island and heading to Staten Island across the Verrazano Narrows Bridge. It connects Bay Ridge, Brooklyn with Staten Island, New York, where Iris and I used to park and tell each other how much, we were in love.

The buildings surrounding the hospital were old and falling apart. Many Puerto Ricans lived in the neighborhood. The area looked nicer when I was growing up. However, as usual, the people ran like hell when they realized some darker people wanted housing as decent as theirs. When they left the neighborhood, so did the quality of services; the sanitation and police departments, and the public school system. The Family Practice residency program was on the other side of a highway called the Belt Parkway, which separated the rundown area from the more kept up area. The Hispanics occupied the houses on the rundown side. The other side had some Hispanics mixed with whites, and their homes looked better than the ones surrounding Lutheran Medical Center.

The Family Practice clinic was in a three-story brownstone building. I had an office in the rear of the building; it faced an ally. The center was comfortable, but I didn't like it. I felt as if I was in prison. Steel bars were on the windows, and a special buzzer system was used in order to get in. There were four black doctors in the program; one white, and one Filipino. They never had that many Black doctors at one time. We had a number of females on staff making sure the clinic functioned well. Mickie was a Puerto Rican, and she was the head receptionist. Wanda was Black and she was one of three nurses. We had two white nurses and two Hispanic female aides who worked with us. As for ethnic diversity, I felt the Family Practice program was balanced for the population of people that we took care of. Our boss, Dr. Fanta, was an older man who was very dedicated to the program, which was the first Family Practice program in New York City.

Early during my internship in the Family Practice program, I was assigned to the Cardiac Ward at Lutheran Medical Center. I didn't enjoy working with patients who had heart diseases; one minute they were fine, the next minute they were dead.

Most of my patients there had emphysema or heart failure. Cardiology was not one of my favorite areas. Much of my time was spent reading electrocardiograms with the resident and deciding how much medicine to give, and I hated electrocardiograms because they teased my brain.

One night, I had first call. I checked each station, and made sure that no problems were missed before going to bed. A couple of nurses approached me and suggested that I not leave. They thought that a patient was about to have a cardiac arrest. My adrenaline shot up so fast; I immediately became anxious. The nurses started to laugh. I quickly recalled the protocol for instructions during a cardiac arrest, which I'd never fully researched. I paced the floor, hoping that the patient would take a turn for the better. A nurse in the patient's room calmly stated that the patient just coded (heart stop beating). In a hurried frenzy, I tried everything that I could think of in order to revive this dying man. By the time the other doctors arrived, the patient was dead. The nurses encouraged me not to be too concerned because the patient wasn't expected to live anyway.

From then on, cardiac arrest became an everyday occurrence for me. I actually waited daily; I expected to hear the code alarm. I had a weird high as I ran to a code the feeling that I may save a person's life took over. I would run through the hospital; as a crazy fool, and live out my fantasy. There comes a time in every conscientious doctor's life when the realization of just how crucial he or she is to the sick and dying really sinks in. This realization came to me during those first five months of my internship. Three patients died during those months when I was on call; not only had I watched them die, but through what I believed was my own foolish behavior or neglect, I apparently helped in one such death, and it affected me deeply.

I was on call. I neglected to take the blood of a patient in pulmonary edema for blood gases (checking the amount of oxygen in the blood) before she went to sleep. She was dying the following morning when the nurses called me. I called for a code 66, which is for cardiac arrest, but the patient died before the other doctors could reach her. I remember that time quite vividly because I walked the third-floor corridor crying. I promised myself that no other patients would ever die because of what I thought was my neglect. Another time, I was in the emergency room, and a patient came in with a similar pulmonary edema from which three of my other patients died. As soon as I saw her, I knew what the problem was. I immediately ordered the nurses to give her lasix and digoxin. I ordered a chest x-ray and summoned the resident. When the resident arrived, I informed him that the patient came into the emergency room looking as if she was dying with pulmonary edema. She was fine; she sat up in the bed in a matter of thirty minutes. She was sitting there comfortably, smiling. The senior resident examined the chest x-ray and told me that he did not like the fact that I treated the patient for a pulmonary edema without consulting him first.

I wasn't going to take the chance of the patient dying in order to stroke his ego or wait for him to be a hero. I wasn't concerned about his feeling or his ego. All I knew was that this patient was dying, and she was now alive and doing well. I made another promise to myself that no patient of mine would die due to procrastination.

We started attending Calvary Baptist Church after our return to New York. The church wasn't exciting to me anymore. I knew that there was something missing, but I didn't know what. Calvary Baptist Church became a way of life with me. It was traditional to go there. It still had something to offer people, but my life was so much in conflict that I needed more. Therefore, it was my fault and no one else's that I had separated myself from God, and it wasn't Calvary Baptist Church's fault or Iris's.

I spent time with Shoshanna and Taina, but it wasn't a lot of time. I loved them dearly. When I wasn't with them, I was in the hospital on call or at the Family Practice program late into the evening. Iris was alone many times.

Chapter 17

Emergency Room

Do not I hate them, O Lord, that hate thee?
And am not I grieved with those that rise up against thee?

Psalm 139:21

The emergency room was both an ordeal and a learning experience. I enjoyed working there because I had always enjoyed emergency medicine. The challenge of a problem with a patient every half-hour or so kept my interest high. That first day I must have treated two head wounds, a few fractures, vaginitis, cervicitis, multiple upper respiratory illnesses, pulmonary edema, myocardial infarction, and one patient with cardiac arrest. Each day was as busy as the one before. Before long, though, I ran into some problems, some of which were engineered by several nurses. I found that I lacked the tact and humility that were apparently needed in order to deal with these problems. Some of the nurses were treating patients before I gave the okay. They were trying to help, but sometimes it was at a risk to the patients. Intravenous lines were being inserted on cardiac patients without doctors being informed. Aspirin suppositories were being inserted into children's rectums without regard to an allergy, which is a known complication if the child has nasal polyps and asthma. Consultations were being ordered without the doctors being notified, even though it was the doctor's responsibility to decide what was necessary. I knew these things were improper, but I let them go on for a few days.

Finally, I approached one of the nurses and told her what was happening wasn't proper, and I didn't want her to use these procedures with my patients. We got into an argument, and she asked me if I threatened her. I didn't consider what I had said a threat, but I told her if that's the way she took it, then I guess it was.

The following day, the word was out that I had overstepped my bounds in dealing with the nurses. Many doctors feel that to get a nurse on your bad side is the ultimate in stupidity. Well, I wasn't concerned about that. Some of the doctors informed me of some of the things that they were hearing. "I don't know what you did," one doctor said to me, "but the word is out to 'get' you." I wasn't surprised, and I knew that this was only the beginning of my struggle to practice good medicine regardless of the consequences. Shortly after this, a young boy of about fourteen years of age was admitted to the emergency room for a head wound. I immediately ordered a skull series with appropriate laboratory data and evaluated the case as a possible concussion. His blood pressure was 150/90, which was clearly too high for him. I requested that he be observed for any changes in vital signs, such as blood pressure and pulse, and asked a few nurses to notify me if anything happened. I had written a note that if the child was okay within a few hours, then he was to be sent home and requested to return to the outpatient clinic in five days. It was very busy that day, but before I went home, I informed the oncoming physician of the child's status. The following morning the Director of Family Practice, Dr. Fanta, asked to see me in his office. With the emergency-room sheet on his desk, he accused me of being medically incompetent and told me that the hospital was not in need of any publicity, as it already had a number of cases pending against it. I tried to explain to him, to no avail, that some of the nurses were out to get me. Apparently, before I went home, the nurses neglected to inform me that the boy's blood pressure was still elevated. After I left the hospital, someone on the nursing staff decided to call a neurological consultant (a specialist for the brain and spinal cord), after which the child was admitted to the hospital. The conflict between the nurses and me continued. Some of them accused me of doing too many pelvic exams. The nurses alleged that every time a young, pretty female came into the emergency room, I wanted to put a speculum into her. When I asked the nurses for medication and other things for patients, they sometimes tried to embarrass me by saying loudly, "Wait a minute! I'm busy; I only have two hands." As a result, patients whom I saw in the emergency room were often neglected and forced to wait unnecessarily long. Most of the time, I, would get the items that I needed for the patients. People sat in the emergency room suffering from seizures and asthma attacks, waiting until some nurse believed that they were sick enough to be brought in the treatment area. Sometimes workers would approach me about patients (usually Hispanic) whom they thought were being treated unfairly by the nurses, and I was expected to do something. One time a young man came in with blood on his T-shirt, and was made to wait on a chair inside the reception area. A Puerto Rican aide approached me saying, "Hey, Doc. You've got to see this guy." A nurse looked at him and said, "He just has a little blood on his T-shirt." When I spoke to the aide, however, she told me that the patient had been stabbed in the back. Oftentimes, incidents occurred when a nurse's judgment was incorrect, and no doctor was notified. It seemed to be such an indifferent, apathetic way of dealing with the sick and dying.

Ethnic Bias

Minority groups suffered the most in the emergency room. Biased comments were often made by a few of the nurses about Hispanics or Jews. Many of the Hispanic people were harassed publicly. I heard a nurse state that all Hispanics say, "No speak English." Although I've heard Italians and a few Scandinavians speak in their native languages, I never saw them being treated as poorly. Some of the nurses there appeared to have it out for particular ethnic groups. They rarely mentioned anything about Black people because there weren't many being seen in our emergency room.

A Black security guard acted just like an "Uncle Tom" whenever something was said about Blacks. He would laugh and joke with these same nurses. Many times, they even made racial slurs about him, and he would just laugh. I believed that he needed a long swift whipping. I despised him for doing the 'slave camp shuffle' for those bigots.

Some police officers weren't much better than the bigoted nurses were. I was once suturing a man's head, and a police officer punched him in the face. I left the treatment room to tell the head nurse about it, but she only said, "Williams, don't get involved." I couldn't believe what she was saying. I was tired of what was happening. Frustration was mounting because I believed that the patients were suffering, while the medical staff closed their eyes, made money and went home.

The racism prejudice that existed in the emergency room was blatant, and I never heard anyone say anything about it.

Racist Liars

On New Year's Eve night, my tolerance was at its lowest. A patient came to the emergency room after having had a seizure. An aide came to me because she believed that the patient had been waiting a long time. She told me that no nurse had seen the patient, even though he had been processed. No vital signs were taken, and the patient was sitting in the waiting room feeling very sickly. I asked the aid to bring the patient in. After taking initial lab work on him, I requested a nurse to take him to the intensive care area. When another nurse heard that I wanted the patient transferred, she cursed me aloud. I asked the nurse who was transporting the patient to insert an intravenous line with a dextrose solution in his arm. The patient was left alone in the intensive care hold unit for about an hour, after which time the nurse checked on him and came running out, yelling that the man was having a seizure. I instructed her to get 10 mg of Valium and give him 5mg of it. When I went into the intensive care area, there was no IV line to put the medication in. She did not follow my previous orders. The patient convulsed, making it impossible to establish an IV line. After the seizure, I asked, the nurse to order an emergency chest x-ray.

I told a few of the staff that I wanted something done about the inhumanity to the patients. Their advice was for me not to disturb the waters, because I could get hurt. They were concerned about my losing the internship residency program and not being able to work in any other hospital due to being "blacklisted." I told everyone that I would go to outside sources if I didn't get any positive results at the medical center. I was prepared to expose the emergency-room situation to the community; I was willing to call the Daily News.

When I mentioned these things to a couple of emergency-room administrators, one told me that if I did that, one would have to go, either the hospital or I, and it would be me, even if I were right. He told me that the hospital had to survive. They were not going to let me destroy it.

I then approached the Family Practice residents. When I told them what was happening, they were reluctant to get involved. Most of them believed and agreed with the allegations against the emergency room nurse, but decided to not do anything. I told them that there had to be a time during their lives when they would have to deal with problems of this sort, which affected the patients and physicians alike. If we believed in competent medical care, this was our time to defend it. I made it clear to them that I didn't think that they cared, but with or without them, I was going to do what was necessary.

The Family Practice Psychologist, Dr. Sheldon, was present and asked the other residents if they were going to let me bear this burden alone. One resident made the suggestion to have a letter written by the residents in Family Practice, in order to state their support for me. They all agreed, though some of the residents appeared worried and hesitant about this position.

A meeting was arranged with the general house staff, who believed some of the issues were questionable and didn't want to get involved at the time. They wanted more time to think through the issues, but I thought we didn't have that kind of time.

Meanwhile, a meeting was arranged with a couple of head nurses of the emergency room and the emergency-room administrators. My original outline for the meeting was dismissed because it was thought to be too personal. Some of the residents got together and wrote up a new agenda. They also asked me to sit back and say very little, because I was too emotionally involved. They were to give me cues for when to expound on a particular point during the discussion. In their opinion, this would be more effective and would not readily turn people off. I didn't agree with the new setup, but I went along with it.

We gathered for the meeting in a portion of the hospital designated by the emergency-room administrators. When the nurses came into the room they would not look at me. When the meeting began, I thought that the issues were going to be dealt with effectively. The meeting turned out to be a disaster. The Family Practice Director, who was in command of the emergency room, was very uncomfortable. He did not want this meeting held. He sat in his chair, protecting his emergency-room staff.

When I realized what was happening, I refused to hold my peace any longer. I challenged a statement made by one of the emergency-room nurses. She said no patient had ever waited in our emergency room for hours without anyone knowing that they were ill, and that patients were not doubted as to the seriousness of their complaints. I refuted her statement; I cited a couple of my own patients who had waited unnecessarily long, and a few patients, thought to be constant pesters who were left to wait in the waiting room. I told them the nurses were not telling the truth.

At that point, Dr. Fanta made a motion to end the meeting. I was furious. I walked out.

The situation seemed to be a total loss. People were suffering in the community. I knew that before there could be healing; the system would have to heal itself. This was part of the problem that seemed impossible to resolve.

After the meeting, I was ready to do anything in order to get results. I thought about calling the "Eyewitness News."

Some people approached me that day; they wanted to know why I walked out of the meeting, but they were already out of my mind. I didn't want to have anything to do with them. They were not involved in any cause, which I was fighting for, and I did not need them. I had it with Lutheran Medical Center that day; I didn't trust the opinions of anyone. I only trusted how I felt.

In a few days, I went to see the emergency-room administrators in order to express my displeasure over the meeting. I told them that the people of the community had only us to fight for their rights in the hospital in order to assure them of proper medical care. The administrators said that they were concerned, but my cause wasn't clearly stated. They also questioned whether I stood to make any secondary gain in this matter. I informed them that I personally was looking for no gain. I only wanted to do something positive for the patients. One of the administrators, a Puerto Rican, assured me that if I went to the community and exposed these problems, even he would be forced to side at the hospital. They may have been his people, but from where I sat he didn't seem to care what happened to them, as long as he kept his job. I was told by an administrator, if I pushed them, they would push me. I went three times to see the administrators, and each time they told me that they would do their best to improve things.

For weeks, I continued thinking about contacting the Daily News and informing the community. I did speak with some community people, but it didn't go very far.

Burn Out

After all the energy, I used to stand up against those racist's nurses, I was exhausted and disappointed. I was burning out, but didn't realize it. I knew that there was some way to handle the fight against this inhumanity, and I was determined to find the answer.

As the weeks passed, I began to feel isolated and alone. In my efforts, I didn't want to be bothered with anyone. I tried using my energy to think.

I wanted to crack the system wide open and to use it for the benefit of the people.

The World on Fire

I wouldn't talk to anyone for weeks at a time. I believed that there was no use in it. Some people wanted to know if I had a problem. They questioned my sitting alone in the cafeteria, and why I didn't visit the nurses' station anymore.

I tried not to reveal anything to them, but sometimes it didn't work. Usually they would tell me to take care of my family and myself and leave the problems of the hospital to the hospital. Their attitudes just pushed me further away from them. I'm sure that they meant well, but there was work to be done. I stayed alone.

My home life was intense because I had many problems thinking about the hospital garbage and how some people were treated there. I was engulfed in a raging fire, and if I was in the fire, what were the people in, those who were less fortunate than me? I couldn't stand seeing people hurt. I kept thinking about my roots and how I came out of Red Hook, and I was supposed to make a positive difference in people's lives. It was a burden that at times was terribly difficult to bear, but I had to bear it. I made promises to myself, and to God that I would stand for what I believed was right rather than walk away from what I believed was wrong. I saw the world on fire, and it was consuming masses of people.

I Want to Quit

There were days when I got up and told Iris that I didn't want to go to work. I was sure that I didn't want to be a doctor anymore. This was the first time that I considered leaving medicine. I don't think that she took me seriously.

The months following the emergency-room experience showed me the reality of trying to fight every cause sometimes without guidance from God. I was burned out. I was mentally and physically exhausted. I was no good to my patients, my family, or myself. Not only did I have problems with the emergency room, but I had a problem with me. The conflict with the nurses in the emergency room expanded. I wanted to resolve the problem in the emergency room, not fight with nurses. Even when, however, I held my peace, the trouble continued.

Bigotry

"Cathy," the head nurse in the emergency room, made a statement about not wanting any more black doctors to work in the emergency room. I was told that she made the statement because of me. She knew that I was onto her bigotry and prejudice. She was the main nurse involved in the ethnic remarks against Hispanics and Jews. When I sat with the hospital staff at the conference table meeting, Cathy was there. One evening she was in the emergency room supervising. I was on call in the hospital. Someone called me on the telephone and said, "Hey, Williams, come on down to the emergency room." I was upset that I was referred to that way (I was Dr. Williams, not hey, Williams). When I got to the emergency room, Cathy was attending to my patient. When she saw me, she stopped taking care of him and walked out of the treatment room. She wouldn't even tell the patient's status to me. This happened on a number of other occasions.

When someone mentioned my name, she would go into a rage, and display her disgust for me. No one could say anything to her about me without her making a scene. Sometimes, I was stopped in the hospital, only to be told how Cathy hated my guts.

Cathy converted a few other nurses with her hatred and bigotry for me. Those nurses, however, were more conservative. Occasionally, they would make themselves scarce when I needed them, or they would speak to me in a nasty tone of voice, and a few times; I was just plainly ignored. Nurses with whom I had a good relationship previously changed their attitude and behavior toward me. I felt terrible about it.

The situation grew. I began to loathe going to the emergency room. The atmosphere was such that I couldn't relax, and it interfered with patient care.

Cathy was the leader of the pack for one entire year; she succeeded in making my work hell. I have to give it to her. She was an expert at calculating and practicing hatred and bigotry in the midst of minorities, and she had a good show going on in the emergency.

Family Support

I didn't spend much time at my parents' apartment in Red Hook. When I had some free time, I called my mother and spoke with her. It was hard not unloading my problems on her. She often listened to me with patience and would tell me to calm down and relax. She understood my energy, being my mother. There were few things that changed about me over the years. She knew that I was a fighter and wouldn't quit until the battle was over. She vividly remembered my early days at Calvary Baptist Church. I fought spiritual wars with Rev. Yarber and anyone else who dared to challenge me. She always encouraged me to release my weapons of warfare and move on. She hated conflict and had enough wisdom to know when to quit, but I didn't have enough wisdom to listen to her.

I didn't regret fighting battles. I only wished that there were none to fight, and that I had the wisdom to know how to fight battles. I was never able to convince anyone who knew me that I was not looking for fights to pick. My father was his usual self, as he encouraged me to do my best. He told me to stand up for what I believed in, but he didn't like all the confusion, which I got into. I learned to respect my father's opinion because he held his ground on issues. He had a soft heart for people, and one of his strong points was standing up for them if he believed that they were wronged. I also respected my father for his constant counseling of me; particularly, his concern for me not to be too hard-on people. In spite of his pain from being paralyzed, he shared the pain of others. I know that his, being Black and living in Alabama, challenged his human fiber, and he survived. He loved people in spite of it all. Even when he talked about some people, being crackers and full of racial hatred, I did not believe he hated anyone. He was hurt as a result of being oppressed because of his color and race. He never stopped telling me how the people in Chesson, Alabama ran the Black doctor out of town for taking care of a white woman. My father was proud of me and all he really wanted for me was to be successful. Being an extension of him would help me stand tall and move on.

My sisters were going through their own problems on a marital and social level. I tried not to burden them with my problems. Sometimes it was too much to bear, and I used them as a sounding board. They listened to me and were upset that I was going through problems.

My aunt Doris was pleased that I was a physician. She would call me on the telephone and ask me all kinds of questions. She helped me through the heat that I was in by just believing in me. She hated the fact that I was always fighting the establishment. She didn't see any need for those kinds of battles for me. As far as she was concerned, I had made it, and I needed to enjoy it.

A Trip South

In the summer of 1979, our friends, Michael and Margie, who still lived in Albany, New York, decided to take a trip to Vero Beach, Florida; they invited Iris and me. Neither of us ever was to Florida. We did not see Michael and Margie for a long time. We were in need of a break. We made a small bed in the back of our little Datsun 610 and headed for the sunshine state of Florida. Iris and I took turns driving. We were to meet Michael and Margie in Vero Beach.

Iris was pregnant with our son (Saladin). She was more than halfway through the pregnancy. We drove for 23 hours, alternating drivers. Shoshanna and Taina were comfortable as they slept on the makeshift bed, which we made for them. The trying part of the trip was driving that distance with the broken air conditioner in our car. It was working well before we left New York; then, it broke down and we were baking in it once we crossed "South of the Border."

When we got to Vero Beach, we were both relieved and tired. The children slept most of the way. We stayed with Margie's mother. Margie's sisters were there. Michael and Margie went to someone else's house to stay because her mother's house was too small. It was so hot and humid in Florida that I couldn't breathe well. Iris was braving the heat. Even being pregnant, she did better than I did with the weather. We took the children to Disney World in Orlando. We tried to enjoy it, but it was too hot, and we couldn't relax. We didn't enjoy Vero Beach very much. We did go to a family gathering where people were very nice to us. Iris wanted to do more in Florida than just sit around. We decided to drive to Miami, Florida. It took us about two hours and thirty minutes. I just wanted to see what Miami looked like. After we got there, we stopped at a gift store, purchased some items, and drove back to Vero Beach. Iris was miserable, hot, and not enjoying how we were spending our so-called vacation.

One day Michael asked me to go with him in order to get fresh-squeezed orange juice. We got big glasses of orange juice for twenty-five cents. After we downed a few, we talked for a while, and then went to the car. A carload of white people drove by us and called Michael "a big black nigger." I looked at Michael in shock, and Michael said, "That's the way them crackers are." That was my first experience of racial prejudice in the state of Florida. I was deeply hurt that they said that to my friend. I could see the hurt in his eyes, and he appeared helpless. That ruined my Florida trip, and I would never heal of its stain. I developed a fear in

Florida because I felt out of my northern element. I knew that there was racial prejudice in the North, but for some reason, I felt more protected. In the South, I envisioned mobs of white people stringing me up to a tree as my father told me that they did in Chesson, Alabama. Alabama was not far from Florida, which made Florida more threatening to me. On our return to New York, Iris became sick and started to vomit and have abdominal pains. We had to stop on the roadside in the state of Virginia. Michael had a cold, apathetic attitude about our misfortune. He didn't want to wait and help us. Gas was rationed according to odd-and even-number license plates, and we were driving on the day when Michael could get gas, but it was about 11:30 p.m., and he was afraid he would be stuck without being able to get fuel. He decided to leave us on the roadside with Iris sick and our two small children. As a friend, Michael made the wrong decision. It hurt us very much, and it only sealed our Florida trip with more disappointment. I loved Michael, and I wasn't going to let what happened to ruin our friendship. Iris and I were both glad to leave Florida.

Chapter 18
Second-Year Residency

I hate them with perfect hatred:
I count them mine enemies.

Psalm 139:22

I was well into my second-year residency, and even though Iris was encouraging me, and my family stood by me, myself-esteem was low. My life was falling apart at the seams. I was fighting the establishment. I was depressed and I didn't want to go to work, ever again.

French Fries and Prejudice

One day, I went to the cafeteria and heard a food clerk harassing two Puerto Ricans. She told them not to speak Spanish because English was the language of this country. I told her that she had no right to say that to them. They were Americans, and Spanish should be the second language of the country. That was the end of that situation, or so I thought.

For the next three months, the food clerk placed very small portions of food on my plate. On the other hand, she would load up the plate of the person in front of me. She maintained a condescending and cold attitude.

One evening when I was on call, she and I were arguing over potato fries, which she refused to, serve me. The nurse in front of me asked for fries. The clerk told her to come back later; she would keep the fries on the side for her. She planned to let the nurse pick up the fries on the way out

215

of the back door. When I asked for the same, she said, "Why don't you ask the cashier?"

I called her a racist. She told me not to use that word with her. The following week, I was told that the cafeteria clerk reported me to the hospital administrators. She accused me of harassment. The administrators evidently took her word. They never called me for clarification, but sent a notice to my Family Practice Director about my behavior.

They Used My Services

That same week, I was asked to see a prominent woman who had political ties with a hospital administrator. She had a severe nosebleed. She wasn't even my patient, but a hospital official requested my service personally, and called me at home. I had never seen her before, and she wasn't a patient in the Family Practice program. She was in the emergency room for a time, and then admitted to the hospital. She had no personal physician, and for that moment, I was it. I treated her by burning the blood vessels in her nose with silver nitrate, and the bleeding stopped. One night while I was home, a nurse called me and informed me that the patient was bleeding again from the nose. I asked her to get silver nitrate sticks to stop the nosebleed and told her that I was on my way in. When I arrived, the patient was sitting in bed bleeding. She told me that she had been calling the nurses' station, but no one responded. She was very anxious. The nurse who called me on the phone was giving evening reports before preparing to go home.

When I approached the nurse, she told me that she couldn't find any silver nitrate sticks, and if I still wanted them, that I could go get them myself. She wasn't offensive about it; however, she was indifferent. I lost my cool and yelled at her. A nurse standing nearby told her to get the silver nitrate sticks for me. She took her time; in fact, I never got those sticks from her.

Someone suggested that I direct the aid to the emergency room in order to get the sticks. The aide came back with one stick to cauterize the patient's nose. I sent her back for two more.

When I questioned the aide as to why she brought one stick, she said that the emergency-room head nurse was very mean. The nurse told her to go get her own silver nitrate sticks and not to return because they had a couple left.

I knew that they had more than just a couple because I was in the emergency-room earlier that day and saw an entire tube full. I asked the aid why the nurse had been angry with her, and she told me that she didn't know. I went down to the emergency room with the aide, took the required silver nitrate sticks and left six in the tube.

The nurse grabbed me and asked, "Who are you?" "I'm Doctor Williams. You said that there were only a couple of silver nitrate sticks. You lied and was rude to this aid for no reason. I needed more silver nitrate sticks than you gave her, and I have a patient bleeding upstairs." I left the emergency room yelling at the nurse, who was boldly yelling back.

The following day, I was reported to the emergency-room head nurse for harassment. Things just continued to happen. It was a crazy time, and the incidents were building up.

Cathy was still on the rampage.

Fire and Brimstone

I looked for a way out of all the hellfire and brimstone, which I faced at Lutheran Medical Center and medicine in general. I was involved in church again; I tried to help the young people. They looked up to me. They knew that I worked very hard in order to become a doctor, and I believe it encouraged them to continue to respect me.

I was spinning my wheels at Calvary Baptist Church. For all the years, I attended there. I didn't see much of a change concerning the young people. Some of them were married, and others had joined the church looking for someone to guide and lead them spiritually. My life wasn't where it should have been, but I had spent many years at the church. I knew that I loved them dearly, and I offered what I had to give at the time; unselfish love. The reality of my life's situation was that I needed to change some of my ways. I was depressed and in no shape to help anyone, but I tried. I encouraged Iris to go with me to the pastor's house. She told me it wouldn't do any good, and the pastor would not receive my suggestions well. Against her advice, I went. It was a terrible meeting. I told the pastor that the teenagers needed better guidance, and he listened until he couldn't take it anymore. He wanted to know who I thought I was coming to him, telling him what the youth needed. He politely told me that I couldn't speak for the young people in his church. I left his house in frustration and realized again the wisdom of my wife's advice. After that meeting with the pastor, I started a street film ministry called the "Agape Film Ministry."

I showed religious films in neighborhoods. I showed "The Cross and the Switchblade" by David Wilkinson, not knowing I would experience God in a deeper way through it.

A Continual Source of Pain

My life at Lutheran Medical Center Hospital and the Family Practice program was a continual source of pain. I had an emergency pediatric case one evening, and someone telephoned me, saying, "Williams; you better come down here to the emergency room." By this time, I was fed up with all this "one-minute personal, the next minute impersonal" stuff.

"Why are they calling me by my last name?" I wondered to myself. "I'm Dr. Williams, not Hey Williams or Williams." They don't have that kind of right.

I didn't know who called me. I quickly went to the emergency room. When I arrived, there was a hydrocephalic baby having seizures. Instead of devoting my full attention to the baby, I tried to find out who called me.

The nurse taking care of the baby wanted me to help her suction the baby and give oxygen. My senior resident was on the telephone, trying to contact the patient's doctor, so I stood at the patient's stretcher and helped in giving the oxygen.

After checking with two nurses, who told me that they hadn't called me, I saw Cathy and asked her if she had called me. She said arrogantly, "No, I didn't call you." I had it with her insolence. This had been going on for a year. I told her that I knew it was she, and she started to walk away. I told her that she was a racist, and that she made racist statements about Hispanics, Jews, and Blacks. I assured her that she wasn't fooling anyone by laughing with the Puerto Ricans and talking about them like dirt behind their backs.

I let her know that others and I knew she was a racist, against not only Hispanics, but Jews and Blacks also. She denied it and said that I was acting like a crazy man. (I am sure she was somewhat right because I was very angry.) I also told her that she hadn't treated my patients or me professionally. I reminded her, of how she, for one entire year, never gave me information about my private patients, for whom she was the primary care nurse.

Cathy phoned the administrator and said, "There is a man down here who calls himself a doctor. I think he has gone crazy. You'd better call King's County Hospital Psychiatric Ward to take him to the crazy section of that hospital." Then, she walked into one of the treatment rooms. As I followed her, we continued to argue, and she repeatedly called me insane.

When the administrator and two nursing supervisors arrived, they tried to calm me down. They wanted to know what happened and didn't seem to be surprised about my complaint. They advised me to document my complaint if I could.

The following day, I put in a formal complaint to the nursing supervisor; it pertained to the year-long vendetta against me.

A few days later, my chief resident in Family Practice informed me that Cathy was suing me for assault on her person. He told me that she was accusing me of bodily handling of her in the treatment room, that I threw her up against the wall and threatened her life. The hospital and the nurses union, which would supply her with a lawyer in order to pursue the assault charge against me, backed her. Not only, that, but she had a witness to verify that I had attacked her.

The chief resident thought it looked very bad for me, and he, along with others, suggested that I disregard the whole thing. I told him that I wouldn't. "You'd better," he said, "because you're going to lose. She has a witness against you. Do you understand what that means? Think about your family and your career."

I told him that I didn't care about the career. He told me that the hospital was ready to back Cathy, and if they had to, they'd destroy me. "You don't even have a license to practice medicine," he continued. "How will you live? Let it go." I told him that I would not.

I couldn't believe that Cathy was telling an outright lie. I never threatened her or put my hands on her person. I at no time even made a gesture to harm her.

White Power

The emergency-room administrator immediately terminated my being inside the emergency room. Up to this time, the hospital administrators did not summon me or anyone else for verification and proof of the charges. They took Cathy's word for what had happened and then took action against me. They came to her aid immediately. There I was, their salaried doctor, with an assault charge against me, without any hearing or any spoken word to me.

All this news came by way of the chief resident in the Family Practice program. My Family Practice Director, Dr. Fanta, sent all words of "condolence" by a Carrier doctor.

After a couple of days, the chief resident came back to me and asked me to think about letting the matter go. The hospital now wanted to suspend me from the staff, and the administrators asked the Family Practice Director to get rid of me. He told me that my boss let them know that he wouldn't do that. Things were mounting against me.

The chief resident informed me that Cathy was threatening to sue the aide whom I sent into the emergency room in order to get the silver nitrate sticks. The nurse who grabbed me when I took the silver nitrate sticks was saying that I assaulted her also.

The chief resident warned me that if they fired me, I would be in a fix, and probably no one would hire me in the United States.

Within a day or two, I was called into my director's office. He and his staff were there, along with the chief resident. The director politely invited me to sit. They started discussing the serious implications of the matter. My director said that it was the consensus that I see someone who could help me with my problem; a Psychiatrist. He went on to say; it was his responsibility to me in order to make certain I received the kind of help I needed.

I stopped him immediately and asked, "Whose opinion is this?"

"This is the conclusion that we all came to," he replied.

I asked again, "Who?"

"We," he answered.

"How can you come to that conclusion when you know nothing about what's going on?" I pressed. I told him that if they wanted me to see a Psychiatrist, all of us should see a psychiatrist.

"How can we help you?" he asked.

I said he could not help me, but maybe they could help some of the residents who had similar problems. I told him that it wasn't my problem, but it was our problem. The Director told me that they couldn't help me if I didn't cooperate.

"Good," I responded, "Because I'm not going to see any Psychiatrist." I knew what that meant.

When the meeting was over, they must have thought that I was one crazy doctor. The chief resident continued to speak with me. He told me that the hospital was ready and anxious to fire me.

I was told that my decision to walk away from the emergency-room incident would probably be one of the most important decisions in my life I'd ever have to make. The administrator wanted the matter resolved. He asked me if he arranged a meeting between Cathy and me, would I come. I kept thinking about Iris and our family and the decision I had to make. At that moment, I knew I had to "take the rap." At that point, professional or not, I had to protect my family and myself." I told the administrator that Cathy was lying. "Yes," he said, "I know she is lying. What do you expect her to do? You forced her by putting her job in jeopardy, and this was her way out."

When the meeting was called, Cathy lied so much that she made no sense. I called her a liar, before the administrator. She asked me if I had a tape recorder to prove it. I told her that I could prove her a liar by way of another nurse.

"Well, did she record any conversations?" she asked.

When I asked how I assaulted her, she started stumbling in her speech and fabricating her story. The emergency-room administrator asked her to consider my family. She told him that she would drop the action to take me into court. It was a dirty situation, but it was over.

Saladine

Iris had our third child, Saladine Joachim, born December 7, 1979. He was our first son. He weighed 7 lbs. and 6 oz. He had a very masculine look. I decided to name him after a medical resident whom I worked with. Saladine was an Arab warrior. His middle name Joachim is a Hebrew name.

He was the first boy with two sisters and so whatever the girls were doing he wanted to do. He was the little man. I would say to him Saladine, I am going to work, take care of your mother, and that he did. He was our serious child but at the same time loved to clown around.

Trying Times

The hospital backed Cathy all the way, while at no time considering the truth of the entire ordeal. They did not question me as to my complaints. They never followed up the assault charge with the witness. They wanted to settle the matter anyway they could, and they did, at the expense of my respect and integrity. I felt castrated by the whole system.

My attitude changed. I convinced myself that I didn't care about anyone or anything except my family. This was my lowest point during the residency program. Patients were dying, and I wouldn't blink an eyelid. I lost something valuable.

When I took care of patients in the emergency room and the wards, I cared very little. Many times, I would be impatient and in a hurry. A nurse took notice of my behavior talked to me. She told me that the good, caring Doctor Williams had died, and she wanted him back. I explained to her why he was never going to surface again, and that he cared less about the patients' problems, and the hospital's as well.

This wasn't the only time that I sounded off. People were surprised and shocked. They couldn't understand how I had allowed myself to become so hard.

One of the Family Practice doctors came into my office and tried to talk some sense into me. He told me to stop crying like a baby and put my efforts back into being a good doctor. I argued with him, and soon we were throwing ammunition about each other's medical competency. It all ended in a cursing match with nothing being accomplished except many nasty things having been said.

Not all these incompetence accusations were helping matters, especially when I was told that the hospital was ready to defend itself against my charges of their incompetence. They wanted me to shut up for good. The medical incompetence game was their backlash against me.

Patients were suffering under my care. I knew that I wasn't treating them well. All the continued frustration and depression had me fixed on destruction. Unless I changed my attitude, I was doomed and didn't know it. Cardiac arrest calls were being made in the hospital, and I took my time getting there. I rushed some of my patients out of the office at times. I was refusing to see difficult patients.

One day a patient of mine died, but I just didn't care. At that moment, I realized that I was dying from within. Whatever had sustained me in the past had been shut out. My relationship with God and man was at low ebb. God was shelved away in a dark corner of my mind. I was literally lost in anger and depression, and it was destroying me. It was not what Cathy had done or said, not the administrators, nor the hospital staff, but my own anger was killing me.

God and Me

Ever since I could remember, as far back as age five, my parents kept us in the church. They knew that the church would be vitally important to our survival. I was accustomed to forgetting God one moment and crying out to Him the next. Through it all, I knew that God's mercy was abundant and great, that He really loved my family and me, but now all that church going, twenty-five years' worth, didn't seem to be enough to unshackle me. I was in desperate need of spiritual healing. It was my only hope. I knew that God's mercy and love were still there, even though I had not felt it. I prayed, but I couldn't be healed. My wounds were wide open for the world to see.

One day I was singing some spiritual songs in the operating room when I was doing Gynecology, and this guy Nefty, an operating room technician, heard me. He asked me if I was a Christian. With inward hesitancy, I said, "Yes." I wondered if he knew anything about my attitude and behavior. I didn't want this Christian Brother to think that I was a hypocrite. We started talking, and he asked me to attend his church, Brooklyn Tabernacle. I accepted his invitation, but didn't show up.

When I would see him, he would tell me how beautiful the services were. Each time I felt bad because I told him that I was going to come. I wasn't completely out of the church, but I might as well have been.

One evening I suggested to iris, and a friend that we attend Nefty's church. During the service, the feeling that came over me was a calm excitement. It was a while before I began to heal. There was a big job yet to be done in my life, however; there was this stubborn kind of depression inside of me. As I continued to attend that church, I saw my ugliness.

I saw that I was badly in need of healing, and most important, that God could do it. Soon my home life improved. Iris was feeling better because I was more relaxed. The children greeted me each day at the door with kisses. I was still concerned about the injustices I saw in the hospital, but somehow I knew God would fix it all.

Where Is St. Croix?

One day I received a call from the Public Health Service. They told me that a doctor had visited their office from the United States Virgin Islands. The Virgin Islands was in need of a doctor. The Public Health Services asked me if I would consider practicing medicine in St. Croix or St. Thomas. I asked, "Where is St. Croix? I never heard of it, but I do know where St. Thomas is." The woman laughed. I told her that I wouldn't mind checking it out.

After speaking with her, I couldn't believe that I was being given the opportunity to practice in the Caribbean. Iris was shocked. We both agreed to accept at least the interview process. When we told our families about it, they weren't too excited because of the distance it would take us from them.

The Public Health Service sent us to both Caribbean islands, and we decided on St. Croix because it had more space and looked just as beautiful. We had a great time playing in the warm Caribbean Sea while there was snow in New York. We accepted the opportunity to work and live on the beautiful island; we believed that it was God's will.

MD Degree and Licensing

Though I had a medical degree, I didn't have a license to practice medicine. I started studying seven months before the New York exam. I studied everywhere and anytime, in the bathroom; in the car, I would even take the stuff to church. Iris would ask, "Where are you going with that?" I told her if I had a chance to study, I would study anywhere. I took the exam at Pratt Institute in Brooklyn. It consisted of sixteen hundred questions covering almost every aspect of medicine, including basic science. After the first day of exams, people were excited as they talked about how difficult it was. I didn't think so, but that was no guarantee of my passing that day. On each of the three exam days, I had a headache at the same time of the day. Sixteen hundred questions, six-and-a-half hours per day for three days, made me ill. I was glad along with thousands of others, to be rid of that test.

I told Iris I didn't think the exam was difficult, and I thought I had passed. She told me she knew I had. I tried to dissuade her a little, but she had enough confidence for both of us.

Three months passed, and I hadn't received my grade. A few people had taken the test out of state and had passed the exam. I became more anxiety-ridden. I knew that God was still with me, but here again was my shaky attitude.

Two more weeks passed with no grade. I was getting the news that a couple of people failed. Even a couple of people from New York had their grades. I called the New York State Licensing Bureau. They informed me that I had to wait along with everyone else in New York for the grade, and that it would be sent out the following week. All that week I was asking Iris about the mail. Sometimes, I would get upset because she didn't answer me fast enough.

Oh God, I Passed

One day that week, I was in my landlord's apartment taking care of his daughters injured arm. On the way out, I asked if they had any mail for me. His wife said, "No, not today, Doctor." Something caught my eye on the China cabinet. It was a large white envelope. I asked her if that was my mail.

"Oh yes, that must be your mail," she replied.

I quickly grabbed it and went out the door. As I stood motionless after the door closed behind me, I said a prayer and opened the envelope. I looked, slowly, for some numbers, not really wanting to pull the paper completely out of the envelope. I passed the exam. It was a great moment of my life.

Moonlighting Madness

The residency program in Family Practice was nearing its end. This meant that I would be finished with my formal post medical training.

I made a two-year commitment to work with the federal government in St. Croix, U.S. Virgin Islands.

We had no money, and there was no way that I could foresee any extra money coming in on which to live. Iris was beginning to worry about our lack of money. We were buried in bad investments and $20,000 worth of loans that needed to be repaid. I kept saying to Iris not to worry, God would provide all we needed financially and otherwise. That didn't prevent her from letting me know that we still had no money.

My New York medical license arrived in the mail. I knew that the license was my answer. Even though I was not supposed to moonlight while a resident, many third-year residents did so. That was no reason for me to break the rules, but I did.

I applied for a job with a medical supplies company. I made house calls all over New York City. After working there for a couple of months, I applied for a job with a health center in Red Hook. In a short while, I had three jobs. I worked almost twenty-four hours a day, six days a week, and sometimes-on Sunday. The money began to roll in.

Now Iris was complaining that she wasn't seeing me enough. I told her that she couldn't have her cake and eat it too. The more money I made, the harder I worked. My goal was to make $25,000 in a few months.

Making house calls in New York was a trying experience. Many of the people whom I treated were elderly. Some were living independently. Many things I encountered broke my heart. What I saw reinforced in me disapproval for abandoning the elderly. Often before leaving, I would pray for a patient. I met people who were in Hitler's concentration camps. Occasionally, they would freely speak about it. I wanted to find out in detail what some of them went through. I couldn't believe that I was speaking with people who were hated, and some with all family members killed and still enduring life's hardships. Sometimes people would point to some memorable picture or plaque on the wall. I enjoyed looking at old photos, and I often encouraged them to pull out more for me to see.

My driver, John, who was a minister, would look at me seriously. Sometimes, he would even say, "Let's go, Doc. We have more people to see." The driver had to walk out the door in order for me to realize that he was serious about leaving me; there running my mouth.

Many times, we had three or five calls to make. On some of those occasions, I was called early in the morning to see someone who really didn't need medical attention. They just wanted someone to talk to. It was frustrating, and I got angry, only to be hurt by my own anger.

John spoke with me many times about my life. He told me that he was concerned about me. We talked about everything from illegal drugs to sex, church, God, and the whole universe. John would tell me, "Doc, there isn't any justice in this world." He told me that many times, and I did not know how right he was. John really cared about me, as a brother would have. Some of the house calls were in tough areas of New York, such as Harlem, Bedford Stuyvesant, and East New York areas. Winos, drug addicts, and prostitutes roamed the streets and hallways. It was only the grace of God that kept us from being harmed. Often I prayed that God would get us in and out with our clothes still on our backs. Sometimes John and I would look at each other and shake our heads. It was a bad scene and dangerous.

Harlem on My Mind

One of my worst experiences was in Harlem about two o'clock in the morning. We were called to see a man who was ill with a chest infection. The morning was cold and icy, and we drove to Harlem in John's Ford Grenada. The windows were cracked so he could get some air while he smoked his mini slim cigars. The smoke made me sick. I was half with my nose pinned to the window and half wanting to tell him off. However, it was his car, and he could do what he liked in it.

After about forty minutes, we arrived in Harlem at a tenement building ten stories high, with rough-looking teens in the hallway, and no operating elevator. The driver and I debated whether it was wise to ascend the stairs. There wasn't much to debate; the call had to be answered.

As we were going up those stairs, I kept saying to myself, "Do you realize, Doc, there is no safe way out of here if someone comes behind you?" Every window next to the stairwell was open. A person could trip and fall out of the window or easily be thrown out. When we reached the top, we were out of breath. I thanked God nothing happened.

Promises to Keep

At times, the health center would call Iris, so she could inform me to show up for work. Sometimes, I had to refuse because of conflicts in time with the residency program. Usually, I worked something out. Often I didn't go to a rotation or would leave the operating room and go to the health center.

I wanted desperately to give some service to Red Hook projects. I had made a promise that I would return to the neighborhood in order to help out. I never realized it was going to be for money. I envisioned some volunteer work. The people were delighted to have me. I wanted to do a good job, and I worked hard and confidently. Being in Family Medicine made me somewhat popular. I could work various clinics.

One day I even tried running the surgery clinic. When the surgeon arrived, he just smiled and told me to continue doing what I was doing. Almost every Saturday, when they had no Obstetrician/Gynecologist, I filled in.

I was making $180 per day. My other job, making house calls, earned me $1,500 per week. With the residency giving $620 every two weeks, I was in the money. Almost all the money went in the bank.

Leaving Family Practice

In some ways, it was hard for me to leave the Family Practice program because I was fond of some people there. My last day while I was cleaning out my desk, I wondered how I ever survived the ordeal of being there. Mickie, the receptionist, constantly spoke kindly to me and respected me as a person and a physician. I respected her for her honesty and sincerity. She told me that day that she loved me, and she wanted me to remember it. When she said it, I paused and took serious notice of her, and she had tears in her eyes. She hugged and kissed me. Wanda, the nurse called me to her side. She encouraged me many times. She told me that she always cared about me and was with me when I was going through hell in the Family Practice program and at Lutheran Medical Center. I thanked her for caring about me. She told me to continue to be strong. The two aides, whom I harassed terribly, hugged and squeezed me that day. I believe all of these precious people experienced some of my pain and in their own way hurt for me. When I walked out of the center, I realized that chapter in my life was closed.

I Needed a Change

Our departure for St. Croix was nearing. I signed a two-year contract with the United States Department of Public Health as a way of paying back my student loan. The residency program was to finish soon, and I had just about reached my goal of $25,000. I purchased a new 1981 Toyota Celica for Iris and a motorcycle for myself, and we still had cash in the bank.

Even though I was making a lot of money, I wanted desperately to leave New York. I realized my life wasn't what it should have been. I thought to leave New York was one way out of a painful situation. Iris was definitely ready to leave.

The morning we were to leave for St. Croix was warm and quiet. My family was up early, as we hurried the last belongings to the car.

I took a few moments to reflect upon Red Hook projects. I wanted to help with the many problems that plagued the people who lived there. I used so much time dealing with Lutheran Medical Center's challenges that I lost touch with my dreams. Those racist people on 78th Street, who threatened our family, didn't help my focus either. The wrong turns I made on my own hurt my wife in ways I didn't fully understand. I loved Iris as I loved no one, but I was too immature in order to deal with it. I was responsible for the choices, which I made. I thought about Iris, and my three children, and how they deserved more than what I had given them. Many painful thoughts and memories flowed through me.

When we reached the airport, I didn't want to see anyone cry, but I knew it was inevitable. My niece, Nina, was going to St. Croix because she had some disciplinary problems. As we waited to board the jet, Iris's mother and father began to cry. Shoshanna was crying, and then Iris started. I didn't know what awaited us in St. Croix, but I believed it would give us a fresh start. While we walked the ramp to board the aircraft, I noticed Iris crying and my heart broke. I felt like crying.

A Pillow of Cloud and Warmth of Fire

As we were sitting in the aircraft waiting for takeoff, I thought about the Israelites, when Moses bought them out of Pharaoh's house in Egypt. As they crossed the wilderness, God protected them at night by fire in order to keep them warm, and protected them during the day with a pillow of cloud from the blistering heat of the dessert. I believed that God would protect us as he protected them.

PART IV

Shouting at the Rain

And the princes, governors, and captains, and the king's counselors, being gathered together, saw these men, upon whose bodies the fire had no power, nor was a hair of their head singed; neither was their coats changed, nor had the smell of fire passed on them.

Daniel 3:27

Chapter 19
Shouting at the Rain

Surely goodness, mercy, and unfailing love
shall follow me all the days of my life,
and through the length of my days
the house of the Lord shall be my dwelling place.

Psalm 23:6

As the jumbo jet soared through the air at 35,000 feet, I wondered what awaited us on the beautiful island of St. Croix. When we reached the huge island of Puerto Rico, I thought of the many Puerto Ricans, whom I had met through the years. I thought also of Rosa, Ana, Hector, and the Puerto Ricans; I grew up with. As I was thinking, the pilot announced for passengers to fasten their seat belts for landing in St. Croix. I looked at Iris, and she was happy. The tears dried up a few hours before, and she was smiling. I was happy for her.

I looked down and saw the beautiful multicolored water, and the bright beige sand. I was excited. When we landed, Iris and I looked at each other, knowing that we were on our own. We had no family within driving distance to go to if we wanted as in the past, and we had God to depend on. As I walked down the steps from the aircraft, the air felt clean and refreshing to my lungs. We were met by the landlady, who seemed very glad to see us. We got our luggage together, packed them into her car, and headed for our new home in a section on the island called Estate Whim. As we drove a couple of miles, I saw horses running wild on the roadside, chickens, goats, and sheep all over the place. I saw palm trees, just like the ones I saw in my dreams. We entered a dirt road that ran alongside a gas station. We looked at each other. We saw abandoned cars off the road, and a couple of the homes, which looked shabby. We expected to see something similar for ourselves. Suddenly, a pretty green house with flowers and two huge fruit trees came into view. The house was fenced in with a beautiful yard, and it would become our home for the next two years.

The Nazarene Church

During my first week at work, a patient invited us to her Church. We continued to attend. One evening I showed the "The Cross and the Switchblade," It was at that point that I truly surrendered my heart to God.

As the months passed, Iris didn't say anything to me about my change. Even though she said nothing, I didn't doubt the change. One day we were talking about spiritual matters, and she mentioned that she had noticed a change in me. I was encouraged. Of all the people throughout my life, Iris had to see something, for she had suffered the most.

Ellenville, New York

I left Brooklyn and went up to Ellenville, New York, to the conference. It was icy cold. My little frail, underweight body had lost its fat pads in St. Croix, and I was freezing. The medical conference went well, and I visited Michael, Margie, Ephraim, and Yoli in upstate New York (which was like being in Alaska in mid-winter). It was a joy seeing my friends, but I was glad to leave the cold. I became anxious and wanted to return to St. Croix. The 86 to 90 degrees daily spoiled me. I wanted to see Iris and the children.

When I returned to St. Croix, Iris met me at the airport. It was a good feeling seeing her and the children fresh in the island sun.

Those months following my conversion were trying. I wanted so desperately to live for God. I felt closer to Iris and the children; it was no longer a struggle to be happy. Every day seemed to be brighter and better than the day before. I carried my Bible daily. Frequent meditations in my medical office were common. From moment to moment, I sought God's direction for my life. A Christian brother asked me to go with him to a Full Gospel Businessmen's Fellowship meeting. After a couple of sessions, I decided to become a member. It was an exciting experience. I thought that I would never come down from my spiritual high, but I also saw that life's problems were still there.

I wanted to witness to people about God's love for them. I asked God to show me the needs among the people of St. Croix, their spiritual and physical needs. I asked Him from my own comfortable little world.

I had a horse called "Hope" and he was stolen. When I found him miles away from where I lived, I knew who had him.

I went into his house. He was a 17-year-old. He denied stealing the horse. After speaking to him about stealing, I took a New Testament Bible and a Christian tract out of my backpack. I told him that God loved him very much. He gave me his attention. I told him that God had something special for him. As we talked, we both began to cry. I embraced him and told him that God had forgiven him.

When I left that juvenile's house, I knew that God's power had shown itself. The experience helped me to forgive him. I prayed that evening that God would always intervene in crises in my life. I was confident and had faith that He would. My life was very busy as far as medicine was concerned, but every chance; I had to share my new life with someone I did.

The health center was busy. I was seeing about twenty-five patients per day, plus walk-in patients.

Exams Again

My first year for the government was nearing an end, and everything worked out well. I helped many people and was liked by most. One more year remained for me to complete my two-year stretch with the Public Health Service. The government of the Virgin Islands would not accept my New York State license, so I sat in the exam a second time. The first time I took it in New York, I studied for seven months. I was now on the second time around and into my fourth month of studying. It was a drag, and I definitely didn't want to do it. I knew, however, if I didn't, and wanted to practice in St. Croix privately, I couldn't. I asked God to see me through my exam-taking days again.

As usual, when I sat for an exam, I took my Bible and had fellowship with God in song and prayer. I sat for three days in St. Thomas and attempted to answer sixteen hundred questions. I was given one-and-a-half hours for lunch and two fifteen-minute breaks. On the third and final day, I had a headache.

I waited two months for my grade to return and when it arrived, I passed. I thanked God for His faithfulness to me.

I wondered after I passed the New York State and the Virgin Islands Boards what Dr. Carol at Albany Medical College would say to me having questioned if I would ever get a license to practice medicine.

I took the family on a trip to New York. We needed the change. We had talked about taking my father out of the nursing home where he had been for almost one year. I just couldn't stand the thought of leaving him there any longer.

When we arrived in New York, the first thing, we realized was that few things had changed. I thought of the great opportunity, which God had given me to escape the concrete jungle.

We had a nice time in New York. When we neared our last week, I reflected on the previous three weeks and made an assessment on my attitude and behavior. I believe God was pleased.

Loving My Father

My father was in a nursing home, and I wanted him out. I prayed to God to give me the answer. I didn't want the decision to be mine. I discussed it with Iris, and she believed God might have been speaking to us. I wanted a positive verification from her, but she was careful in her opinion. I believed that God wanted me to take my father out of the nursing home, and I continued to seek His approval.

Everything pointed to my compassion and love for my one and only earthly father. I loved my father dearly and needed to take him out of that situation. He became mentally unstable and aggressive. My mother couldn't take care of him, and her dreaded alternative was to place him in a nursing home.

Our last day in New York, I was happy and excited to leave. It was like being released from bondage. With all of my love for New York, it became an intolerable place after a few weeks. I guess being away in a different and perhaps favorable, more relaxed environment like St. Croix spoiled me.

We headed for the nursing home and got my father. We arrived at Kennedy Airport late, loaded down with many boxes, bags and packages. The baggage attendant suggested that in order to save expenses, I transfer some items to a plastic bag, which he would give me. This took time, but after that was taken care of, off we went to the loading gate.

I pushed my father in a wheelchair. Iris and our four children came next, followed by a host of packages. There were many people outside the gate ready to board the jet.

The ticket attendant, after telling me that we were late, gave us our boarding passes, and we all boarded the plane.

Suddenly, a flight attendant walked over to me and asked if I would kindly follow her to discuss a seating problem. As I exited the plane and went through the gate door, the jet door closed. The check-in desk clerk told me that I couldn't fly to St. Croix on that flight. I was shocked. They sent me to Pan American Airline to catch a connecting flight to Miami; then to St. Croix. The flight wasn't scheduled to leave in three hours. I had breakfast, read the newspaper for a half-hour and boarded the jet. I sat on that plane for three hours, and the plane never left because they couldn't close the cargo door. I was told to speak with the Pan American attendant; however, he told me to wait until my turn because he was busy. By this time, there was no way I was going to St. Croix that day. I went back to American Airlines, and the check-in attendant told me that I couldn't fly to St. Croix, unless I gave them $100 for a reissued ticket, and then I could fly the following day. I was shocked. It was now 4:30 p.m., and I was frustrated and exhausted. I told the ticket agent that I didn't have the money. He sent me to the information desk.

The information desk employee told me that she couldn't do anything about it. She advised me to speak with the manager.

The manager was busy. I told him I had a serious problem, he said, "I have others before you. I'll be right back."

When he finally returned, I explained the situation to him. He typed something into the computer. A few seconds later, he told me that I was late and had to pay the additional $100 fare. I explained to him that I was already on the original plane. "You were late," he repeated. I put my ticket before him, and he pushed it back to me. I told him that I wanted to return home to St. Croix where my wife and children had already arrived. He informed me that he couldn't help me.

I wanted to punch him in his face. Instead, I grabbed the telephone and pulled it off the wall. Then, I took some documents off the counter and threw them across the terminal floor. I told him to call the police, and that's exactly what he did.

My father-in-law had just arrived at the airport a few moments before my episode because I called him and told him that I was stuck at Kennedy Airport. Just in time, he arrived because he said a man was about to hit me from behind, but he stopped him. The police arrived, handcuffed me, and took me to the police station at the airport. A police sergeant there asked me what happened.

When I started explaining to him what happened, I broke down with tears. I felt humiliated, lost and afraid.

There my father-in-law was, standing outside trying to speak sense to the police. I prayed at his table many times. He was fully aware of my church-going, and he knew I was trying to live for God. After all the praying, witnessing to people about God and my new life as a born-again Christian, here I was in handcuffs. I was no better than any criminal was. I reacted violently and had broken the law.

I finally told the sergeant that I was a doctor in Uncle Sam's military. He was shocked. "You're a doctor," he exclaimed.

"Yes," I replied, "a Lieutenant in the Public Health Service."

He asked for ID. After looking at my service card, he demanded that they remove the handcuffs. "You're a doctor in Uncle Sam's Army, and you don't know how to control yourself?" he admonished me.

My father-in-law was by then outside the room; he threatened to sue the airlines. The sergeant excused himself from the room. When he reentered, he asked, "If we send you to St. Croix, will you promise not to give us any more trouble?"

"Yes, sir," I answered.

My father-in-law then took me back to the terminal. Laughing, he said, "I don't believe what you did." He told me that he understood, but he couldn't believe I went crazy like I did. The manager that said that he couldn't help me went inside the airline terminal and came back with a first-class ticket for the next day. He apologized and asked me to fly in style to St. Croix. I thanked him and apologized. My father-in-law told me later, that he laughed all the way back to Red Hook projects. That night I prayed and asked God to forgive me. My father was a burden on Iris and me. He was not mentally alert, and when we took him from the nursing home, he was taking medication for his intermittent psychosis. The medication worked in keeping him calm, but it also slowed him mentally. To make matters worse, my father could not control his bowels. I was constantly cleaning after him. Often he didn't want to take a bath. Iris frequently complained about his odor. She had her hands full with the children, my needs as well as her own. It was difficult for her. We continually asked God for strength. Sometimes, I would get upset with my father and threaten to put him back in the nursing home. I knew I could never do that. I believed

I at least owed this to my father. I wanted to take care of him in his old age. He had always cared for me, and never really denied me anything. After five months on St. Croix, when he felt better, we agreed to send him back to New York where he would live with my mother. Though I passed my test to practice medicine in St. Croix, it took ten months before I received my license. I was even given an oral exam a couple of months after passing it. I threatened to sue the Virgin Islands government. When it did come, I was grateful. I believe it was an administrative problem.

Wilbert

On February 9, 1981, our fourth child and second son was born just two days before my birthday. He was 8 lbs. and 9 oz . . . . He was named Wilbert III in honor of my father. He was our first born on St. Croix. He was a handsome, strong looking baby. Iris delivered Wilbert without any complications. We were very happy. We would have to keep a close eye on him while we were at amusement parks. He loved to explore and would often walk away on his own and get lost. He was a curious child. He would take toys apart. When you asked him why he did that he would say, "I want to see how it works."

Chapter 20
Red Monday

I cried unto the lord with my voice:
With my voice unto the Lord did I make my supplication.

Psalm 142:1

It was a Monday morning. In April 1982, I call it "Red Monday," the day I almost lost my life to a physician who was a paranoid schizophrenic and no longer took his medication to remain sane. The Frederiksted Health Center was busy. The waiting room was filled with people, and the medical staff was already immersed in work. I was sitting in my office speaking with two aides about our schedule during the day. While sitting outside my office, the head nurse summoned me, because I was the chief medical officer. I was often asked to handle administrative problems, which affected the health center. As I entered her office, I noticed that she looked upset. She was concerned about one of the doctors who was working that morning and asked me to investigate his behavior. In her opinion, he had been acting strangely for a few days, and today she noticed that he was wearing dark sunglasses indoors. Her main concern, however, was that the Doctor prescribed birth control pills to a patient without examining her. I reviewed the patient's chart, and realized that the head nurse had a reason to be alarmed. I decided to look in on the doctor and found him speaking with a patient. I politely interrupted him, and he did not respond to me. I continued to speak to him, and he still ignored me. I put my hand on his large shoulder, and he finally replied that he was "okay." I asked how his weekend was. He responded, "It was okay." I never did ask him about the patient.

After I returned to my office, two aides came to speak with me. Suddenly, the doctor barged in and started cursing at me. Yelling at the top of his voice, he said, "If you ever put your hands on me again, I'm going to kill you." I was totally taken by surprise and so were the aides, who instinctively ran from my office. When he finished telling me what he would do to me, he left the room.

I was taken aback by his threats; I remained seated on a stool as I gathered my thoughts. Then, the doctor came back into my office a second time; he repeated his threats to kill me. This time, however, he came at me; he grabbed my neck, and pulled a scalpel from his left coat pocket. When I saw that the plastic sheath was removed from the new scalpel, I knew that he was serious. I caught his hand holding the knife and began to wrestle with him.

During the struggle, thoughts of my family flashed before my mind. I called out to God.

Somehow, I got loose from his hold and ran from the room. I held the door handle to keep him from getting out. I knew that would only work for a short while. He was a strong, big-framed guy, much bigger than I was.

I yelled to the head nurse to leave the building. When I saw her run out, I let the door handle loose and started to run. I could feel him just behind me. After escaping from the building, I found myself surrounded by a crowd of people.

Realizing that the doctor could leave the building from the rear exit, I quickly asked a large man to hold the front door. While the doctor was pacing the floor, shouting and gesturing with his hands, he would get me, I ran to the back of the building in order to hold the door. With all the strength that I could muster, I held the back door closed. He pushed against the door three times, and it opened. When our eyes made contact, I gestured to him that I was willing to give up. He continued to chase me. I ran through the adjacent clinic and shouted that a doctor was trying to kill me. When I saw that he was gaining ground on me, I ran faster, out through the main entrance and into the street. I saw two police officers approaching, so I ran up to them and shouted that the doctor was trying to kill me. Instead of helping me, one police officer put his nightstick on my back and said, "You get over there." I told him that I was "Dr. Williams," but my street attire was not convincing to him. The doctor was dressed in a white lab coat. He continued to pursue me, and the police officers did not keep him from approaching me. At face distance, he was still shouting his threats. When I realized that the police officers were not protecting me, I called them crazy. At this point, one police officer lost control and cursed me. He placed a nightstick forcibly on my neck, while the other held my hands behind my back. I was thrown upon the back of the police car.

When I was pulled off and taken to the rear door to the police car, a nurse approached the officers and told them that they had the wrong man. One of the police officers pushed her with his arm. She approached him again, warning, "I want you to remember that I told you, you had the wrong man." People were shouting and trying to get the police officers to realize their mistake. During this time, the doctor was not apprehended. I was pushed roughly into the back of the patrol car, and I hit my head on the door molding. In the process, my glasses fell from my face.

I saw the doctor open the door of a four-wheel drive police Bronco, and he sat unhindered. As I was being driven to the police station, the officer wanted to know why I didn't tell him that I was a doctor. "I did," I responded. When we arrived at the station house, the officers took our statements. The doctor was still threatening to harm me. By that time, the Medical Director of the hospital and the Hospital Administrator arrived. My immediate supervisor was there also. After we gave our statements, they released him after assault and battery on me, and attempted murder. When I was advised that I could leave, one of the police officers told me that no arrest had taken place.

Iris arrived, crying. When she saw that I was okay, she calmed down. Some of the health-care workers were telling me to sue the government. All I wanted to do was go back to the health center to take care of my patients. Iris was advised to take me home. For the next few days, Iris and I tried to understand and deal with what had happened. I couldn't understand why the Virgin Islands government had put the patients' lives in danger by hiring a doctor who apparently was mentally ill. The circumstances of my own life being in danger troubled me. The thought of what my family would have gone through if I were killed, plagued me. I wanted some answers pertaining to the commitment of the Virgin Islands Department of Health.

Various stories began to funnel in my direction.

Some people believed that I harassed the doctor by pursuing the course of conversation, which pertained to his weekend. My immediate supervisor was saying that I was the doctor's boss. The Medical Director in the hospital assumed that the doctor's mental health was fully disclosed to me. I didn't know that the doctor was using psychotropic medication, and he was a diagnosed paranoid schizophrenic.

These statements were not true. My body hurt. I was depressed. My neck was hurting from the doctor's hold on me. Iris noticed my mood and attitude changing; I was very nervous and short-tempered with people. She told me that I changed, and she didn't like it. I noticed none of these psychological changes, although I knew I was preoccupied with what happened.

When I went back to work, many people were concerned and sympathetic. A number of them were offended and angry about what happened to me.

I wondered what I would do if the doctor returned to the health center. He never retracted his threat and had not been charged with attempted assault. He was loose in the streets within two hours after the incident. Even though no charges were filed against him, he did lose his job because of his violent behavior.

One day he returned to the health center, at which time the head nurse came to my office to advise me. I was stunned by the fact that he had threatened my life and was still coming into the clinic.

I decided to sue the government. I called a lawyer, who had previously helped to win a settlement for a patient of mine. After asking me to think seriously about challenging the Virgin Islands government, he agreed to take the case.

I received both praise and criticism from some people for what I was about to do. I was a Christian suing the government of the Virgin Islands and a few of my medical colleagues. It was not considered ethical among physicians to sue each other. I knew, however, that my obligation went beyond any loyalty to the profession. I was also told that if I sued the VI government, I could not work for them.

Seeing a Psychiatrist

My attorney requested that I see a Psychiatrist; he believed that it was probably needed in order to help the case. He suggested that perhaps some things needed addressing by a counselor. I agreed. After my first visit with the psychiatrist, he recommended that I return. He believed that I needed to talk out a few things. After the second visit, he asked for a third visit with Iris present.

By this time, I had second thoughts about continuing visits with him. I didn't think that I needed a Psychiatrist, but he believed that I was under extreme pressure and needed to rest. He told Iris that he was very concerned about me and suggested a trip to New York. It wasn't what I believed I needed, but Iris agreed with the Psychiatrist's recommendation that I rest.

My next visit to the Psychiatrist was trying. I told him that he would be asked to testify concerning my mental trauma, which pertained to the assault by the doctor. He became furious. He shouted that he was not going to get involved in court proceedings. I told Iris it was obvious that he was protecting the system. I decided to stop the sessions with him.

Jamal

On March 21, 1983, Iris had our fifth child, third son. He was a beautiful baby boy. Iris was convinced during the pregnancy that the baby would be a girl. She had a girl's name in mind. Much to her surprise it was a boy. I looked at the baby and said, "He looks like a Jamal." So, that is the name I chose. Jamal is an Arabic name. It means handsome. Jamal looked different from the rest of the children. His hair was blond and curly. I would often say to him, "Blondie where you come from." He was a happy loving child. Each morning he would say, "Good morning mommy. I love you." Jamal loved stuff animals. Every time we went to the Department store; he wanted a stuffed animal. Iris says, "He was a good baby."

Chapter 21

Private Practice

I cried unto thee, O Lord: I said,
Thou art my refuge
And my portion in the land of the living.

Psalm 142:5

I was one month away from signing my termination papers with the US Public Health Service. I was scheduled to open my private office.

A few days before starting private practice, however, a couple of head doctors called me into a meeting. In short, I was told of my need to work for the VI government Department of Health. The medical director at the hospital informed me that if I did not work in the government, he did not think I could make it financially with a family. Another doctor accused me of not practicing medicine "up to standard." He said that I didn't know how to read an EKG or take care of certain acute-care patients. He stated that he had to stop another physician from encouraging a family to sue me for the death of a cancer victim. A third doctor in the same meeting told me if I sued the government, I could forget about employment with them. When I left that meeting, my confidence was shaken.

I was going through a lot of stress.

My First Medical Office

After I received my license to practice medicine in the Virgin Islands, Iris and I opened our private office, which we had been preparing for about three months. We rented the bottom level in a house near the waterfront on Strand Street in the town of Frederiksted. It was a beautiful spot, and ideal for the practice of medicine.

We rented the space for $500.00 per month, and called the new practice "Agape Medical Clinic," 'Agape' meaning "God's perfect and unconditional love." Iris was my receptionist, and she handled typing and financial matters. She performed her job skillfully, even though she never received direct payment. Everything seemed to go properly. Patients were booking appointments every day, and we were full. People were walking into the clinic for on-the-spot care. There were occasions when we even handled emergencies.

During my first month in private practice, I made $12,000. We worked days and weeks and sometimes spent twelve hours at the office.

I talked about God, gave out Bibles, and prayed for patients. We were blessed financially; the Agape Medical Clinic was on its way.

Our lives were stable, and we were satisfied with our business. We knew that we had done the right thing by staying in St. Croix and opening a medical office. I could have gone back to the States, but it wouldn't have been what was wise for us. St. Croix offered what we needed in terms of peace and an environment to raise our children.

One day while we were in our office, Yoli from Schenectady called us, and told us that Elder Mac died. We were devastated, and for a few moments didn't believe it. He was traveling down the highway coming from a church function, and he crashed. The first thing I thought about was his wife and children. How was sister Mac Daniel going to make it without her beloved husband? Then, I thought about his wonderful sermons and how they made me feel great and there was never one that I didn't enjoy.

Refreshing Springs Church lost a good man. He was not only a Christian, but also someone who understood better than most Christians, that there was a lot more to life than calling Jesus' name as if He is a household detergent that cleans all of our dirty laundries.

I was going to miss Elder Mac Daniel very much. I looked at Iris, and she had tears flowing down her checks. I knew that she felt devastated, but neither one of us could bring him back. All I had left of him were his great sermons, his love for me, and a role model as a pastor, and I would never have one like him again.

Williams vs. the Government of the Virgin Islands

My lawsuit against the government of the Virgin Islands and the two police officers were set in motion. My attorney was not afraid to deal with the Department of Health and Public Safety of the Virgin Islands. After much soul-searching and some criticism, I decided to sue the system that had promised to protect me and the people of the Virgin Islands, but failed.

After a few months, our case was called to the District Court of the Virgin Islands. Seven women and one man were selected for the jury. The doctors involved included the Medical Director of the hospital, the Assistant Commissioner of Health, and the medical Director of the Frederiksted Health Center. I was suing them for negligence on behalf of the Virgin Islands Government Health Department for hiring a physician with a history of mental illness and endangering my life, and police brutality. The trial lasted three days. The attorney for the VI government tried to discredit me and show that my character was questionable. She tried many arguments, pointing to my psychiatric visits, and making of $12,000 in my first month of private practice, practicing medicine without a license, and stating that I was one of the most aggressive doctors ever to work at the Frederiksted Health Center. When the trial reached its third day, I was confident that our case was well stated. There was no doubt on my mind that the jury was aware of the tactics of the government's lawyer.

The Judge made a statement on the final day for the trial, he mentioned how the defendants tried to make me look bad for three days, but he wasn't going to let them do that.

After the jury gave their verdict, we were awarded $137,000.00 in damages. I was not surprised concerning the VI government's verdict and the verdicts against the police officers. I was satisfied by the results.

Chapter 22
Suffering

You prepare a table before me in the presence of my enemies.
You anoint my head with oil; my cup runs over.

Psalm 23:5

I knew that the stress of the trial was not good for Iris. Though she was stronger than I was, she disliked public confrontation. She was pregnant again. She was soon to lose the baby and would be sad for a number of weeks.

Iris and I tried to get back to our daily duties of practicing medicine and raising a family. We were evicted from our home; the landlady wanted us to move so she might remodel the house. She raised our rent in order to encourage us to vacate the premises.

We looked for a new house to live in, but we quickly realized that we didn't have enough money to purchase a house. We decided to start building one on a seven-and-one-half-acre piece of property; we purchased. We had about $6,000 in the bank, so we asked one of the men of the church, which we were attending to build the house for us.

It was time for us to make our first attempt at owning a home. We worked very diligently; we put in long hours in the office. As we made money, we paid the builder.

In a few months, we were encouraged by our landlady to move out quickly. Therefore, we decided to move into our new home before it was completed.

For two weeks, we lived without any water or electricity. There were multiple inconveniences, such as no indoor plumbing and no refrigerator.

I was accused of not thinking about my family in my decision to move in prior to the completion of the house. It didn't make much sense to me to see so many people doing the very same thing on St. Croix; doing well in the end, while I played the big professional, and refusing to sacrifice. Our goal was to be in our own home, and we accomplished that.

After a few weeks, we had a well dug and electricity was hooked up, and the house was more comfortable. God provided the house we began to live in.

The medical practice continued to flourish. God was bringing in people who needed our services. We tried hard to provide the competent care that people needed so badly in St. Croix.

In so many ways, the quality of medical care in the islands left much to be desired. There were constant complaints concerning the lack of proper diagnosis by some physicians, the prescribing of medications that do not help, and lack of compassion and competence. Many of these allegations from patients were damaging and did not help the general fear that locals and especially newcomers to the island had concerning malpractice.

Iris and I made a conscious effort to alleviate many of these feelings. Some of the allegations were true.

No matter what our effort was, some people were still not convinced.

Many were traveling to Puerto Rico for what they thought was quality care. I have to admit that the doctors in Puerto Rico are better equipped with modern facilities, which help them deal with the misgivings among the people. My opinion, however, is that some of those doctors in Puerto Rico were taking advantage of the fear that many patients from St. Croix exhibited.

I had to deal with the notion of some people that because I was practicing medicine in St. Croix, I could not really be that good as a doctor. Sometimes people would come to me for medical care and then ask for a letter to go to Puerto Rico. It was hard to work within that framework.

To add to our troubles, my victorious lawsuit against the government gave me a terrible reputation among the doctors who still worked in the government.

Although many people preferred and wanted private services, the government had created a monopoly on medical services. I was making far more money taking care of people at my office during the morning hours than the doctors who worked in the government all day. When those doctors arrived at their private practices in the afternoon, half of my workday was over.

I worked long hours in our office, made house calls and delivered babies. Many evenings, Iris and I went home exhausted. After arriving home, the telephone was constantly busy with patients calling. Sometimes, they would come into my house while I was resting. Sunday was hardly a rest day. I thank God, though, that Iris and I had enough strength in order to endure it.

Helping Others

I was in my office taking care of a full load of patients and an attorney phoned my office and said, "Hey Doc; we got this guy who was hurt by a doctor at the St. Croix Hospital. We can't find any doctor with a private license on St. Croix and a stateside license to testify for him, would you be willing to help this guy? We know you challenged the government, and you're still here. So what do you say?"

He explained to me that the man was married with three children and with a borderline IQ. The man had lost the use of his right hand, which he stated was because he was brought into the St. Croix Hospital Emergency Room, psychotic and handcuffed. The handcuffs were on for a number of hours before they were removed. He was then placed in a confined jacket and laid upon his stomach for about five hours. His hands became swollen, and no doctor examined him for five days. Because of that, he had to have two operations on his hand, both of which were not successful. He was a construction worker and could no longer work.

Three doctors from the St. Croix Hospital were apparently involved, and they were being sued. The attorney wanted me to testify on behalf of the patient and against those three doctors for neglect. I agreed. Although I sat in court all day, I never did testify.

The patient won his case and was awarded $85,000. This did not improve my image with doctors in the hospital. I knew, however, I had done the right thing. My business was helping people; not the system.

Chapter 23
Daddy Died

The earth is the Lord's
And the fullness thereof;
The world, and they that dwell therein.

Psalm 24:1

My father was sick for quite a while and all the family understood that his condition was guarded, but what we did not know was how near to death he was. His kidneys failed; high blood pressure destroyed his heart and blood vessels. Sugar diabetes followed, and to top it all he suffered a number of heart attacks and a couple of strokes.

I visited him for the last time in the Veterans Hospital at Fort Hamilton in Brooklyn. When I walked into his room, he was in a stupor, and I don't even know if he remembers me being there. My mother and my sisters were there. One of them asked me what I thought about his state, and I responded that it didn't look good. That was the best answer I could muster up, as I stood across the room with all of them and my dying father. After all, I was supposed to have an answer that would be satisfying since I was a doctor. I knew my mother was hurting deep inside her soul; I could see it in her face. She looked at me and shrugged her shoulders, and I felt helpless. I touched my father's hand and in my heart, I was telling him that I loved him dearly. He meant the world to me, and I never told him. I did tell him when I believed that he was receptive that I loved him, and he at no time rejected me when I did. So many things had occurred between us when I became a young man. We argued about God, man, heaven, earth, and hell. He never changed his position on these issues as far as I knew, and he believed 100 percent that he was on the side of right. The conflict rose when I thought that I was on the side of right. We butted horns like old rams until one of us got tired, or my mother told me to shut up. I think that we did it for the exercise of manhood between father and son. Sometimes the debates were so heated; the veins in my father's neck were bulging while his forehead wrinkled, and his eyes fixed on me. My mother worried that he would have a stroke or a heart attack, and she hated the arguments between us. I stood before my father; I believed that he loved me and forgave me for every stupid play on words, which I had with him because I was a college graduate. I never tried to make him look small. I'm sure he thought that I did at times, but he had no-good reason to feel small in my presence. He was more intelligent than I was, had a better memory, was much wiser, and was a strong man. I was no match for him even with my few pieces of paper from school.

I looked at him with intensity, as I tried to convince myself that he would make it through his ill health journey one more time, and I convinced myself that he would. I kissed my father on his cheek and told him that I would see him later. I told my mother his condition was more serious than I thought before we left his room.

When I went back to St. Croix, I was glad to see Iris. I told her about my father and all she could do was listen because there was nothing either of us could do but pray, and we did.

One early morning while I was in a deep sleep, my sister Janice called me. "Buddy," she said, "Daddy died." I do remember saying "Okay," hanging up the telephone and going back to sleep.

After waking up later that morning, the reality of my father's death hit me. I did not cry or speak much to Iris about it. I knew that there was a purpose in his death as in his life. I prepared myself to meet the family in New York City.

My father requested that I give his eulogy. Iris and the children stayed in St. Croix while I traveled to New York. While en route, I was constantly recalling the strength, which my father exhibited, even during his illness. As I watched the clouds from the jumbo jet window, I was at peace. I was glad to see my family. Everyone was holding together well. When I went into the church that evening in order to view his body, my friend Philip was there along with some other people whom I had not seen in a long time. Their presence helped to comfort me.

When I approached the casket, my father looked at peace. After I touched his hand, I fell apart. This was the man who raised me. He had given so much to me, and I loved him dearly. I broke down and cried.

The day at the funeral was challenging to all of us. When it was time to give his eulogy, I sang the hymn, "At the Cross." The eulogy wasn't long. I tried to sprinkle it with humor and yet capture the reality of my father's life. I wanted the sensitivity of my father to shine through.

I told the crowd that my father didn't take nonsense, but he loved people. I told them of the time that I watched my father hold a dead puppy of mine with tears in his eyes. I told them of the times he beat me for misbehaving and how he always told me he was sorry. They laughed and cried when I finished. I saw people shaking their heads in approval of what I said. Later, we buried my father on Long Island at the Veterans Cemetery. On that cold November day, my mother received his American flag with honor. It was over. My father's body finally was put to rest, and he would no longer suffer the cares of life . . .

Chapter 24
Hospital Admissions Privilege

A man that beareth false witness
against his neighbor
is a maul and a sword, and a sharp arrow.

Proverbs 25:18

My relationship with my colleagues and the hospital got worse. Though I did not work in the hospital, I did have admitting "privileges." I frequented the hospital if one of my patients needed to be admitted. The Chairman of Medicine, Dr. Evangelista wouldn't even speak to me. Each time I was in his presence; he ignored me. If I asked him, a question or addressed him, he would never give me eye contact, he would walk away from me speaking some words to the air. I continued to speak to him. He once complained to the Hospital Medical Director, that I should not be allowed to dress the way I did with dungarees and sneakers. The director asked me to try to dress better when visiting the hospital, because it was thought that I had no respect for rules.

Medical Discrimination

Adult medicine kept me very busy. A few of my patients were quite sick and needed frequent admissions to the hospital. I enjoyed the challenge of helping them get well, and 98 percent of them did get well. Another doctor admitted one of my extremely ill patients. He had a rare liver tumor, and I missed it. It was a tumor, which is often seen in Africa, but rarely in the

USA. The doctor who diagnosed it held animosities against me. I never found out what her problem was with me. She suggested to Dr. Evangelista that the family sue me.

Within a few weeks, my patient died. I had a difficult time holding my head up when I entered the hospital, because I believed that she spoke ill of me to other physicians.

After his funeral, I visited his wife in their home. They lived in a wooden shack that was kept very neat and clean. I watched her children playing in the living room (I thought of my own children and wondered how they would react if I had died). His wife was very hospitable with me. When I left her house, I felt terrible.

The "Rectangular" Table

The Medical Director's secretary at the Hospital called me and requested a meeting along with a few physicians that stated that they were concerned about me. I didn't think that the meeting was to advance my stand before the community or the hospital, but to deal with me on their prejudicial issues. I wasn't sure, if seeking an attorney was in order, or if I should go alone and try to handle the matter myself. Dr. Evangelista took it upon himself to show me just how much he disliked me. I did not understand what his problem was. He wouldn't speak to me when I spoke to him. He was never polite or friendly. His attitude didn't stop me from speaking to him, and I think this annoyed him. I couldn't see myself being abrasive toward him.

I had "privileges" in medicine, pediatrics, surgery, obstetrics, and gynecology. Taking care of my patients in the hospital gave me a chance to practice a more intensive form of medicine. Sometimes I had as many as five or six people in the hospital at a time. Occasionally, a nurse would pull me to her side and tell me that some of the doctors were envious because I had so many people in the hospital. I never took those comments seriously because it appeared so ridiculous and immature for any physician to be resentful or threatened because I was doing well at what I had been trained to do.

It wasn't only Dr. Evangelista, who was acting out his own frustrations by taking it out on me, but Dr. Dizon, one of St. Croix's most well-known and respected internists. St. Croix didn't have a heart doctor at the time. Most people sought his care if their ticker was acting up. I respected him.

When I had a client who needed cardiovascular care, I encouraged most of them to see him. When I saw him, he avoided me like Dr. Evangelista.

I wasn't surprised when I walked in and saw Dr. Evangelista sitting at the beautiful rectangular wooden table amid a pile of charts in front of him. The Medical Director, of the hospital, Dr. King and the Assistant Commissioner of Health, Dr. Christian was sitting with him.

At first, I wasn't sure what their plan was until I noticed my charts piled in front of Dr. Evangelista. He didn't have a smile on his face, and the other two had half-smiles. Dr. King asked me politely to have a seat and Dr. Christian, asked me to relax. The Medical Director, told me that they had some concerns about the way I practiced medicine. I asked him what the concern was.

Dr. Christian replied, "Tommy [Dr. Evangelista] has some feelings that you're not practicing medicine correctly."

"Yes," Dr. Evangelista said, "he doesn't know how to read an EKG. He treats his patients the same way. He gives all these men the diagnosis of prostatitis and treats them all with ampicillin."

I asked Dr. Evangelista what was wrong with the treatment and questioned him if they got well or not. He said, "You even treat all your ulcer patients the same way."

I replied to him and said, "Don't they get well and leave the hospital better than when they came in?"

He said, "But you can't read an EKG." I sat before them feeling insecure and full of rage because they were saying, in effect, I was incompetent as a doctor. Dr. Christian said, "We're only trying to help you Wilbert," and Dr. King remained silent. I wanted to get out of there. Dr. Evangelista was still shouting in the air that I didn't know how to read an EKG. I left the meeting furious and determined to continue to treat my patients the best way I knew how.

When I went home that evening, I was emotionally drained.

Obstetrics Inferno

I was delivering babies in and out of the hospital. My first out-of-the-hospital delivery was done in my office. A patient of mine who recently moved onto the island from the States asked me to deliver her baby outside of the hospital because she had heard so many bad things concerning the delivery room. I assured her that she could have a safe delivery in the hospital, but she insisted on having it in my office. The delivery went OK except for unexpected bleeding. I had to drive to the hospital and get some medication in order to stop the bleeding. By the time I got back to her, it had stopped. I later found out from her that she hemorrhaged with her first delivery; she withheld that information from me. After that out-of-hospital delivery, we started getting calls from people asking if I would deliver their babies at home. I wasn't too keen on it, but my wife and I decided to try it. This time it was in the patient's home, and it went well. After my second delivery outside of our community hospital, I was sold on home deliveries. The clients kept coming, and I kept delivering. I continued to deliver babies inside the hospital.

Midwives controlled the hospital labor and delivery rooms. This was the first time for me working in such a setting. My experiences had been working with doctors who controlled the labor and delivery rooms. The St. Croix Hospital didn't have a doctor on call, so the midwives were making the judgment call, even concerning high-risk pregnancies and deliveries. It wasn't a good setup, and it concerned me; especially when they tried to make the judgment call on my patients. All of my patients were private, and they didn't appreciate the attitudes of some midwives walking into their room and pulling back the sheets, telling them to open up their legs.

When I went into the labor and delivery rooms with my patients, I'd stay all day or night with them. I could see the midwives steaming because they wanted the control over my practice in their domain, but I wouldn't surrender it. Therefore, they put out the "word" on me, told Dr. De Chabert, the director of Ob/Gyn (who was also the Chief of the department) that I was difficult to get along with, and didn't want any one of them treating my patients. Those midwives only gave half-truths when they spoke to him, and he believed them. He didn't help to improve the situation, and he could have. He protected the midwives no matter what. Each time I went into the delivery room some midwife would fabricate charges on me. That wasn't all; they would also behave as if half of me was there. When I asked for certain items for care to my patients, I was often made to wait, not to receive it. Many times, I had to get it for myself or do without it. When I asked for an intravenous set to start a glucose water drip, some of those nasty nurses would make some ugly faces. I tried hard to deal amid their attitudes. I continued to greet them morning, afternoon, and evening. Some of them were more than determined to let me know that they were out to get me. One nurse was very vicious, devious, and cunning. She was a bit quieter than the rest and sneaked around to talk about me, as various people on staff at the hospital told me. A few times, I caught her talking about me negatively.

Surrounded by Fire and an Impaired Doctor

Hell broke loose in the delivery room when a patient of mine had difficulty in the second stage of labor, and she just stopped at that point. Midwife Downs asked me if I wanted her to call in one of the Obstetricians whom she favored, and I said OK. When he came about one-half-hour later, he walked a bit unsteady with slurred speech. I looked at him in amazement; not wanting to believe what I was seeing. The three midwives in the room with me acted as if everything was normal. I couldn't believe their deliberate denial about the fact that this doctor was high on something. I previously asked the nurse to start a Pitocin drip which was running slow due to the seriousness of the medication. When he came in, he opened the valve and let the medicine freely run inside the patient. I looked on in horror while the midwives acted like nothing wrong had been done. When she failed to deliver her baby, he requested that we take her into the delivery room. He made a midline episiotomy to ease her delivery, then put the forceps on the baby's head which cut the vaginal wall. After the baby was born, yellow fat tissue was protruding from the vagina, and I looked at the midwife, who ignored my signals that all wasn't well.

Disbelief

I stood with that doctor and watched him in disbelief, knowing that he needed help. He sutured her like a Thanksgiving Day turkey, and no one said a word, including me. I didn't appreciate Nurse Downs's help because she didn't help my patient and I sure didn't appreciate the Ob/Gyn physician that didn't have the professionalism to be fully sober while practicing medicine.

That evening a nurse asked me how the delivery went, and I said, "Not good, the doctor who came in order to help ripped my patient up." I told her that I believed he was intoxicated. The following day the word was out in the labor and delivery room that I accused the doctor of being stoned. Nurse Downs stopped speaking to me. When I greeted her, she answered me with a grunt if she said anything at all.

I apparently had overstepped my bounds as far as loyalty and staying with the "medical pack" was concerned. I once again breached the fact that doctors are supposed to stick together, but I didn't care. My patients came first. They trusted me, and I wasn't going to let any secret honor code guide my principles or channel the way I practiced medicine. I didn't spend the time becoming a doctor, sweating, and crying tears in medical school, for acceptance by them.

My office practice was as busy as ever, and I had my hands full, spending at times ten to eleven hours taking care of the sick and dying while being a husband and father at the same time. Often I wondered if I had made the right decision to become a doctor in the first place. I wondered if it were worth the tension, anxiety, and outright depression at times to help people.

Chapter 25
Stealing Away

He refreshes and restores my life;
He leads me in the paths of righteousness for
His name's sake.

Psalm 23:3

I tried burying myself in other projects. A guy whom I knew from the church, which I was attending (Church of the Nazarene) was gifted with his hands. We were sitting down one day when he and his brother (who was my pastor) decided to embark on making a Hovercraft. It was agreed that I would finance the project and Steve, the pastor's brother, would build it. When the Hovercraft was finished months later, it functioned well on the ocean. Our plan was to start building them to sell, and it would be a way for me to quit medicine, but the plan never worked. Gary (my pastor), Steve's brother, along with Steve made the decision to leave our craft at someone's beachfront property, without consulting with me, and I objected. I told my pastor that it was none of his business, and Steve took offense and decided that he didn't want to follow through with our plans.

Our relationship became strained. I didn't stop my pursuit to leave medicine. I next tried the fishing business and purchased sixteen lobster cages with a guy whom I met in my practice. Again, I had promises of loyalty and dedication to a project that not only would benefit me, but the other person as well. The guy told me that he was starting a fishing business, and lured me with the promise of a boat, which he was buying.

It took him so long to get a boat that the lobster cages, which I purchased through a friend of his rotted in the sun.

I tried a third time in the fishing business with a guy, who made fish cages with my money. He had a ragged car with bald tires and doors that barely closed and a piece of a wooden boat, which he made. For a homemade job, it wasn't that bad, but he acted like he had a yacht, and he was doing me a favor. Every Saturday morning at 5:15 a.m., I awakened and met him at his house to go to the ocean and pull our fish traps. Our catch was usually minimal. I stayed with him many Saturday mornings in his yard while he sold fish. Sometimes I went home with no fish because I believed that he needed the money more than I needed the fish or the money.

After a few months of this, one Saturday he refused to speak to me. He wouldn't tell me what was wrong and the more I spoke with him the angrier he became. He wanted me to leave. He told me, "I done with you." I was very confused and didn't understand what, if anything, I did to upset him.

I spoke with Iris about what was happening in my life. She seriously told me with force that I would never be successful at any project where I wanted to leave medicine. She reminded me that I had begged God to help me to become a medical doctor, and I agreed to give it back to Him in service to people, and I was backing out. She said, "Medicine is the only thing you will do well because that's what God gave you." I listened to her more intently than she imagined. Her words continued to ring in my mind.

Pushing on

We continued to deliver babies outside of the hospital, and I began to hear the disapproval of some midwives. I once had a woman in labor at home, and she ceased to progress in her second stage of labor, and after futile attempts to deliver the baby, I took her to the hospital. I informed the midwife on duty that her labor had ceased, and I was sure she would need a C-section. The staff allowed her to stay in labor with the baby's head pounding against her pelvic bone for hours. When they got ready, they called in an Obstetrician who, with another doctor, did a C-section.

I was not asked to help in these cases and was ignored by the Chief of Obstetrics Dr. Ralph De Chabert and his assistant. This wasn't the first time it happened. I always felt very lonely at these times and questioned my worth and importance in Obstetrics, and this was their intent. Each time I had a hospital delivery most of the midwives, save a couple, would be apathetic to the needs of my patients, and had a bad attitude with me. Those midwives were mean as hell and made sure that they ganged together, right or wrong. I never once mistreated any of them, and they had no justifiable reason to deal with me the way they did. I felt sorry not only for my patients, but other patients who were less fortunate than mine because they didn't have a private doctor to stand up for them when some of the midwives leached out their terror on them. I experienced seeing women who were staff patients (having no private doctor) being talked down to as if they were some kind of low-life. Some of them were outright abused physically and verbally. A midwife would just slap on a surgical rubber glove and command the patient to do whatever she said. It disgusted me, but there was little or nothing I could do at the time to make their situation better. Those midwives did whatever they pleased, because they had virtually minimal check and balance.

I began to hate each time that I had to go there; my stomach would fill with gas, and I often had diarrhea. Sometimes a midwife or two would act as if I weren't even there.

Early one morning a midwife named Fredrick told the Nurse Supervisor that she couldn't work with me. I was difficult to get along with, and I didn't want anyone helping in taking care of my patients. I was shocked because I thought that she was neutral and was not a part of the gang of those other devious, nasty midwives. I spent over five hours with my patient, and I was tired, and Nurse Fredrick was there with her lying mouth talking badly about me. I looked at Nurse Fredrick in disbelief, and my heart was pounding against my chest so hard that my head was rocking, and I asked her why she said such a thing, and she didn't answer me.

I was so upset while my patient was in labor, I took a legal pad and wrote her a four-page letter, telling her that professing Christians are not supposed to lie and certainly not on each other, and she had no foundation to say what she did. I reminded her that I was also a Christian and her brother in Christ Jesus. I ended the letter by telling her I would pray for her, and that I loved her.

Almost all the conflicts with midwives caused some serious emotional and spiritual conflicts for me, and I was in a state of personal turmoil and agony. From that point on, Nurse Fredrick changed her outward behavior toward me. I, however, believed that I could never let down my guard with her.

Home Deliveries

The home deliveries were increasing, and the word was spreading through the Caribbean islands that I was doing them. As a result, my practice in obstetrics increased because women from other Caribbean islands sought my care. I didn't mind it at all, because I loved delivering babies. I enjoyed taking Iris along with me because she helped tremendously during the deliveries. She had a way of relaxing the patients, and she knew enough to deliver one if it were necessary.

Sometimes we packed our children in our custom van and headed for a delivery with excitement. We were all over the island. Many times, we traveled on bad roads into hilly areas and a few times; we had to travel through the rain forest. The children slept in the van while we delivered the baby. Most of my home deliveries went smoothly. I adopted a policy of trying not to deliver women who were pregnant for the first time. A few patients literally begged me to deliver their babies, and I complied with their requests. These deliveries were usually long and exhausting. Sometimes we were worried that a patient was going to need a C-section, but thanks to God, they didn't.

One time I went to a home delivery, and Iris decided to stay home in order to remain with our children. It was late at night, and I got in my car and rushed to the patient's house only to find her anxious and uncooperative. For two hours, I begged and pleaded with her to follow my instructions, and for the same two hours, she did what she pleased. I knew she was uncomfortable and in pain, but so were many other women whom I took care of. Because the deliveries were all natural, I wouldn't give anyone medication for pain and things usually worked out well. This time all seemed to go wrong. I was so tired of dealing with her that I did anything to relax, and as a result; I took off my shoes. She had to go into the bathroom, and I followed her to make sure that she wouldn't have the baby in the toilet bowl. She defecated on the floor, and I stepped in it. I took her to the hospital. After arriving in the labor and delivery room, within one-half-hour she delivered. When the midwife heard from the patient that she attempted labor at home she was upset. She complained to the other midwife about me delivering babies outside of the hospital.

After that delivery, I told Iris I was quitting obstetrics and didn't want to deliver any more babies. She assured me that by the time the next delivery came, I would change my mind and of course; I did. Sometimes when I went to the delivery room, I had patients on the medical ward, the surgical ward, and in the pediatric nursery. The staff frequently saw me going from one discipline in medicine to another. I took care of the babies whom I delivered and on occasion had to do a circumcision. A couple of the Pediatricians didn't exactly throw down the "welcome mat" for me in the nursery, in the pediatric ward or elsewhere. Sometime I went into the nursery and took pictures of my newborns with my Polaroid camera.

There were moments when I was complimented, and it made a world of difference to me. A pediatric nurse commented to me that she had never seen such a well-done circumcision before. A few people at the hospital were friendly and kind to me. I kept getting warnings from some of them to watch my back, because it was being said by a few important people that I was trying to do everything in medicine, and I wanted to do my own thing. I wanted to practice medicine without them telling me how.

My relationship with Iris and my children was reassuring because they showed me that they loved me dearly. I tried to please Iris because she had sacrificed so much for me and for the children. She had married me, and gave me five healthy beautiful children. Much of her time was spent trying to help me stay in balance and deal with adverse circumstances concerning my profession and my personal life. She watched me helplessly sometimes make mistakes because I wouldn't listen to her and follow her advice. I knew that she was right many times in her opinion, but I had to do what made me feel useful and alive.

Iris constantly talked to me about what she believed I needed to do in order to escape some of the pressure that I was under. Most of the time, however, I wouldn't listen to her. As a result, my response usually drained her of the energy. Iris understood when she married me that I was full of energy and strongly committed to loving and helping people. I tried not to display or have a selfish attitude about anything, which I did for people or my family. I just wanted to do what I did best, care and love people. I found things to do in order to take up the lonesome and depressed areas of my life. It was strange because in the midst of a loving family, and a couple of friends like Raymond and Michael, I felt lost and alone. It was like being without something necessary to sustain happiness and peace. There were times when I had no peace and no joy. I thought there had to be more to life than looking down people's throats and listening to their hearts and lungs, delivering babies and caring for the sick and dying.

Ostracism from the Medical Society

The process had begun for my ostracism from the medical establishment, and it wasn't my desire, but it was inevitable. I wouldn't conform to their rules because I didn't think that they were fair. Iris was again pregnant with our sixth child, only a few weeks from delivering. I was happy about the pregnancy, even though we had our hands full with the five children we already had. Iris as usual was doing fine and tolerating her pregnancy.

My troubles in the hospital became more intense. Dr. Evangelista continued to ignore me, and some of the nursing staff let me know that I was still disliked by a powerful few. I was ostracized from the medical community, and it hurt. I wasn't asking them to overlook what I had done because I didn't believe I had done anything wrong. I was not going to apologize for what I believed was right and true.

Chapter 26

Ostracism and Ob/Gyn

Insanity, Again

The Lord is my Shepherd
[to feed, guide, and shield me], I shall not lack.

Psalm 23:1

It was clear that I was ostracized from the medical community, and it hurt. One of my patients who was thirty-six weeks pregnant was involved in a car accident. When she told the Ob/Gyn staff that she was my patient and wanted me to be notified so I could care for her, they were offended. Dr. De Chabert was on call and was told that the baby was dead, and he refused to take care of her and told them to call me to deliver her baby. When I was called, I immediately went into the hospital. I delivered a dead baby, and I believe this gave the two midwives who were there satisfaction. No fetal monitoring was used prior to my arrival. The patient's husband, who was a police officer, was pacing up and down the hall talking about how he wanted to hurt someone for not caring properly for his wife. All I could do was try to console him and his wife. They sued the Department of Health and the St. Croix Community Hospital and won. I was happy that they got some compensation for the negligence, which they had to experience.

One medical crisis followed another, and I was expending energy as I tried to maintain my sanity. I delivered a patient of mine who was pregnant

266

for the first time and delivered a baby boy. The baby vomited in the nursery and was diagnosed as having an outlet obstruction to the stomach. The surgeons found that the food could not leave the stomach to enter the intestine, so they had to operate. After the success with the operation, the anesthetist placed an adult breathing bag over the baby's nose and mouth in order to help it in breathing during recovery. A few hours later the baby was bleeding from his mouth and nose. The surgeons were called back in, and they rushed the baby to the operating room and diagnosed five holes in the baby's stomach. After the operation, a few hours passed and the baby died. The conclusion concerning the holes in the baby's stomach was related to the bagging technique, which was done after the first operation. The surgeons repaired the stomach. The parents wouldn't have an autopsy done, unless I was present. It was mandatory in order to decide why the infant died. I reluctantly went. I saw five sutured areas in the baby's stomach. The father, in his distress over his first and only baby's death, went into the morgue and took his baby out of the hospital. He went to a friend's house and buried it in the back yard. He called me on Thanksgiving Day, cried, and told me that he wanted to kill somebody, and he didn't feel like living. I spoke to him and reassured him that he could still try to have another child. I told him to dig his baby's body up. He did what I asked and had a proper burial for his baby. He and his wife decided to sue the St. Croix Hospital and the Department of Health, and they won their case. I felt very sorry for them because they not only lost their first baby due to malpractice, but the father lost his desire to live. If it were not for his wife holding together, I don't think that he would have made it.

Iris knew about these tragedies and told me that there was nothing, which I could do that would be greater than the impact of the parents pushing for the system to change by being vocal and complaining to government officials. I, on the other hand, believed that I needed to do something constructive in order to help improve the conditions concerning medical care, but I didn't know what to do. The hospital officials didn't want to hear what I had to say, because as far as many of them were concerned, I was a troublemaker and needed to be silenced. Iris saw my frustration, anger, and depression each time that I had to deal with medical issues in regard to the system. It made her angry that I wouldn't follow her advice. She was tired of seeing me hurt.

Church Business

Our new pastor at the Church of the Nazarene was having challenges with some of the members, and he had confided in me. Some of the church members decided that he wasn't spiritual enough to be the pastor and decided to make their feelings known throughout the church. It overwhelmed him, and he got distressed and didn't know what to do. I promised him that I would stand by his side. I even fired a member at the church who worked at my office and had a few words with her about her attitude toward him and his wife. I was caring for the pastor's wife, who was pregnant and having a difficult time with her pregnancy. The baby died in her womb, and the uterus did not expel it. I sent her for a second opinion in order to decide if the baby needed to be aborted, but the physician decided to allow her to go into labor on her own. Usually within a few days, the baby will be expelled from the uterus. She got angry with me because she believed that I had kept the knowledge of her dead baby from her. I couldn't convince her that she was wrong. My relationship with the pastor and his wife was strained. I was in a painful position with people whom I loved.

I had engagements to speak in churches throughout the island. Sometimes two pastors would ask me to speak on the same day and hour. I was busy studying the Bible and practicing medicine while my mind and heart were under pressure in the hospital. It never dawned on me that it was my responsibility to say no when someone asked me to speak when I had something in medicine to do. I trusted and respected the pastors that sought me. I was immature as a Christian and I believe some of the pastors knew it and used me. I was entangled in the church pastor circle and preached around St. Croix, and my family followed me wherever I went. I gave my testimony and told everyone what God had done for me, how He saved my life from destruction, and I became a new person in Christ Jesus. I believed every word of it then, as I believe them now. The greatest miracle God ever performed as far as I was concerned was changing me.

I was loyal to my pastor because God had changed my life. When the pastor revealed to me that he was going to resign from the church, but before doing so would go on a pastor's conference and use the church's shallow bank account first, the loyalty abruptly halted. He had not told anyone else as far as I knew, but me. I was on the church board and when the topic came up concerning the pastor's plans to resign from the church, and some members said that they didn't understand why, I offered what

I believed was his reason. When the pastor heard what I said, he believed that I betrayed him, and he aggressively attacked me, and his wife called me a dog. When I asked him to control his wife and not allow her to continue her behavior, he wouldn't. The board meeting deteriorated, and I resigned from the Church of the Nazarene effective immediately.

Religion and Race

In a couple of weeks, we joined another church called Community Christian Fellowship. I previously heard of the church for years, but never had any desire to go there. The pastor met me at a Full Gospel Men's Fellowship meeting of businessmen. The pastor was from Birmingham, Alabama. I wasn't keen on being in a congregation that had a white minister, especially from Birmingham, Alabama. Iris and I attended the church and decided to visit a second time. We became members.

Deliveries and Conspiracy

My life in the hospital was draining and at times; I had to force myself to go there. Some of the midwives were still raising hell with me.

I had a delivery early one morning, and a midwife refused to speak to me when I entered the labor room where my patient was. After not addressing me professionally, she tried to take over my patient. I said good morning to her, and she wouldn't speak. When I repeated it, she yelled, "I said good morning to you didn't I." I was stunned, not knowing what to do, and I pretended as if nothing occurred. I was embarrassed and hurt. I tried to compose myself, and I only felt worse, so I asked God for strength. The delivery went well and as usual; I took care of the baby in the nursery. Each time I went into the nursery; the reception by some Pediatricians got colder, and some of the nurses were hesitant to be friendly with me. I didn't know what was happening.

Emotionally, I started falling apart after I delivered a baby of someone I personally knew and the baby died hours later in the nursery. The neonate developed respiratory difficulty. It had amniotic fluid in its lungs. It needed a respirator, but the hospital had no one trained to use the one they say that they had. I requested that the baby be transported to Puerto Rico or Miami, Florida, but the Pediatrician waited until dawn the next day. During the morning hours, the baby died. I was furious, and the family for the baby was devastated and in shock. They tried for eleven years to have a baby and finally had a baby boy, only to have it die. The word was passed that the baby's death was my fault because she was a high-risk patient, and I allowed her to be in labor too long. I felt partially responsible because I knew that she was high-risk, and I should have asked her to see another physician. I didn't because she begged me to deliver her baby. All the other Ob/Gyn physicians had abandoned me, and some of the midwives followed suit. I was in a vulnerable position. I was finally intimidated by the midwives and the Ob/Gyn physicians, and I dared not seek any help from them. It was the way they wanted it, and they made it hard for me to fight them fairly. I was wounded emotionally. Dr. De Chabert finally mustered up enough nerve to tell the midwives to tell me if I wanted any consultations done in his department, it wouldn't be given. I was to give my patients to his staff if they needed help. He sought my total humiliation and end in his department. This left my patients vulnerable where I could not help them. I wasn't sure how to deal with it all. I didn't know it at the time, but it was against the Virgin Islands' bylaws for the Ob/Gyn doctors on call to deny my patients consultations that they were entitled to under my care. He refused to inform me of what was being done to my patients. Each time I saw him in the hospital; I spoke to him politely, and he would grunt, if he did that. I felt like a fool trying to engage myself with him. I hid my emotion. It was eating me up inside. My commitment to face injustice and prejudice was what kept me fighting them. It was ironic that we were all so-called "people of color," and they were just as evil, if not worse than some white bigots whom I encountered throughout my life.

I believed that I was to remain in St. Croix and follow my heart and care for and love people through medicine. I never had in my heart or mind to hurt anyone. I unloaded a lot of my despair on Iris. She tolerated it well. I told her that I didn't want to go to work anymore and was finally going to leave medicine. I didn't believe that she understood why I felt the way I did. I don't think that anyone understood or felt to any degree my agony and pain. It wasn't anyone's fault. I realized that I was a complicated guy under the surface. I am the first to admit that I was fully committed to what I believed was right even when the odds were against me, and maybe this is what drove people mad. I wanted to hear someone tell me to fight and some people did, but not in the way; I wanted to hear it. One prominent physician, who Iris and I met in a shopping plaza, advised me to kiss Dr. De Chabert's behind, he said, it would do to make the amends. I wasn't going to bow down to Dr. De Chabert or anyone because he had a little power. The few times that I confided with those in authority were futile. I believe that it was a waste of time trying to confide in the system because it was feeding itself with its own greed and set of rules. Nurse Nethersaul, the Nurse Supervisor of the midwives, one afternoon listened to me patiently while I told her that Dr. De Chabert wouldn't speak with me or be professional as a physician. She asked me why I thought he behaved the way he did. I told her that I had no idea. She asked me if I wanted her to speak to him because she had a good relationship with him. I encouraged her to speak to him because I believed that she was neutral. After a few days, she told me that she found out from him that he believed we had a personality problem. I told her that I didn't have a personality problem with him, and I didn't understand what he was referring to. Much to my ignorance, Nurse Nethersaul was on his side. I was foolish in not realizing that these two people fed each other's egos. While the Ob/Gyn physicians were allowed to stay home, Nurse Nethersaul and her crew of midwives were in the delivery room working hard. There was never a doctor on call for the labor and delivery room while I was there, and patients were suffering medical trauma because of it. The midwives many times made critical decisions that physicians were trained to make. I and some other people understood that the labor and delivery room was left vulnerable to the whims of the midwives. When a baby in distress was born, there wasn't even a Pediatrician to receive it until hours later. A few times, I experienced a midwife calling all over the island trying to find a doctor and the operating room team when a patient needed an emergency C-section. It was irresponsible and unprofessional, and they all got away with it because they covered each other. One time I had two patients in labor at the same time, and both had C-sections. When the doctors arrived, one patient had escalated too critically, and a serious need prevailed to deliver the other because the baby was pushing against the pelvic bone with each contraction. After the operations, both patients needed intravenous antibiotic therapy and had lengthy stays in the hospital. I couldn't figure out what went wrong. Why were two patients who were operated on by the same doctors seriously ill? One of the patients considered suing the hospital. When these kinds of things occurred, very little was said about it and business went on as usual.

One nurse was on the warpath with me, full time. Besides her hating my guts, she wanted to see me professionally destroyed. She was determined to see the chapter closed on me, and she didn't care who had the honor of doing it. I continued to speak to her, and it made her more vicious. Not all the midwives approved of the treatment that I was receiving, but they were scared to speak out because their lives in the department might end like mine. One midwife who was white spoke her mind pertaining to other matters in the labor and delivery room, and a Black midwife smacked her. The midwife who smacked her got away with it, and the other midwife transferred to the island of St. John. One of the midwives, who knew I was a Christian, never spoke any words of encouragement to me while I was going through all the fire and brimstone in the labor and delivery room. I had fellowship with her in a Pentecostal church, occasionally. She had many opportunities to speak with me, and she at no time did. She knew that I was a Christian and was aware of what I was going through and many times witnessed ill-treatment of me and not once said a word to me. I received no words of encouragement or warning from her. She was old enough to be my grandmother, and her attitude hurt me the most.

Cilicia

Iris delivered our sixth child on September 24, 1985. We named her Cilicia. Cilicia is a city mentioned in the bible. Iris named Cilicia while she was pregnant. She would say, "Goodnight Cilicia." I often said we will be in trouble if this is a boy, but Iris knew that the baby was a girl. My mother and friends, Brother and Sister Singh were with us. My mother sang songs to comfort Iris while sister Singh repeated "Don't bite the pain, go with it." Brother Sing prayed in the living room. My mother and Sister Sing attended to Iris. I delivered our baby. She was 9 lbs. and 6 0z . . . She was a beautiful baby; she nursed until she was 4 years old. Cilicia was a good baby. Brother and Sister Singh became her Godparents. She loved to spend time with Brother Singh. He would bring bananas to church on Sundays because he knew how much she loved bananas. She was a loving child.

I Want Out

I wanted more than ever to leave medicine, and I called around the country in order to look for an airplane to become a professional pilot. I finally found one in Florida and arranged with a guy whom I knew, named John, to go with me in order to fly it back to St. Croix.

John lived in St. Croix. He spent many years in the South and had a strong Southern accent. John said that he took a liking to me the first time he met me. There was something about him that most black people can detect when they come up against it. I didn't know it at the time, but John was a bigot.

We went to West Palm Beach. Florida to a small airport called Lantana Airport. I had not forgotten Florida and that my friend Michael was called a big black "nigger" in Vero Beach. I was still frightened of the South. The first night in Florida, we stayed in a small motel, and the following morning got up at five o'clock in order to catch a taxi to the airport.

The weather was chilly, and we waited outside a small wooden shack where we would meet the person who was flying the aircraft, which I was to buy. As the early-morning sky got brighter from the rising sun, I saw a strobe light, in the distance, and it was the aircraft that I was to purchase. I had an $18,500 banker's check in my briefcase to purchase the plane. After checking the aircraft for any possible damage, I flew it with John, and I didn't hesitate to buy it. I was the only black person at the airport until a Black guy came in, grabbed a broom and started sweeping the floor. I got some serious stares from the pilots. John noticed them, looking at me, but he didn't address it. I was nervous. I felt intimidated by them.

We went into a restaurant where pilots often ate and had an old-fashioned breakfast with home fries. There were no Black people there. I felt uncomfortable being around all those white Southern people. While we were eating, I spoke with John about the stares, and he admitted that he witnessed it all, but I was not to worry about it. John did the best he could in order to change the course of my conversation. I appreciated his honesty by not covering over it, but I felt once again alone in the midst of company. John was prejudiced against Black people, but it was his best-kept secret from me for a while.

When we went back to the airport, I made sure that anyone who was looking at me saw the banker's check, which I handed the seller. We filed a flight plan with Miami radio and prepared to leave West Palm Beach, Florida for Freeport, The Bahamas.

I called Iris in order to let her know that we were on our way home. She told me that I had a patient in labor, and she asked Dr. Camoes, one of the Obstetricians who worked with Dr. De Chabert, to deliver the patient, and he refused. I felt terrible not being able to get assistance from colleagues to help my patients in Obstetrics. I should not have been surprised by his refusal, but I was because this doctor at least spoke to me. I had no known problems with him, and he never gave me any indication that I was on his black list. It was obvious to me that he felt threatened by me. When

I hung the telephone up, I knew for sure that I would quit medicine and leave that stress behind me.

Flying Home in My Airplane

As we were flying over the Atlantic Ocean to Freeport, The Bahamas, I hated having to make the decision as to whether or not I was to continue practicing medicine. My new airplane gave me a sense of accomplishment, and I tried not to care about anything, but my family. When I saw the island of Freeport, it looked beautiful from the air. I pulled back the throttle, put the aircraft in full rich position, and prepared for landing.

When we landed in Freeport, the black Bahamian custom agent walked to John and me and asked, "Can I help you?" and John arrogantly said, "No." The man just looked at us and didn't say a word. John felt threatened by that Black man in his uniform because it represented authority and power, and it was too much for him, to handle. John kept saying, "Who does he think he is, asking me if I need any help; if I needed help I would have asked him for it." It upset me to experience that. We were picked up by a missionary who was from South Carolina who took us to his house. It was a trying ordeal. A Bahamian who was a Christian stopped by. I was talking to the missionary's daughter, who was in her teens, about some of my experiences racially in the states and my journey to become a doctor. She was very friendly, but inquisitive about my background, being a Black doctor. I spoke with her about some of the racial things, which I went through. The black Bahamian, who didn't consider himself Black because of his light skin and British heritage, started talking about Black Americans. He said that they were lazy and didn't work hard enough in order to improve themselves. I was upset with him. I went into a church service where the Bahamians and Haitians worshiped with a wooden wall between them. These people really thought that they were serving God while they were practicing bigotry and racial prejudice. It was sad. After I spoke with the missionary I was convinced that he, along with his clan, besides his daughter and maybe his wife, who I spoke with in depth, were prejudiced. I couldn't wait to get out of that place. The following morning we went to a small restaurant with that bigot Bahamian, and I could hardly eat in his presence. I never wanted to see him again.

I flew the aircraft from Freeport, The Bahamas to Georgetown, then to South Caicos Island. We fueled up and flew more than 350 miles of the Atlantic Ocean to Isla Grande in Puerto Rico. I flew for over three hours. We hit a head wind of 20 knots and lost vital time, and our fuel was running low. It got dark and hazy. John was nervous and started poking his face with the pen, which he had in his hand. I was flying for over three-and-a-half hours in a haze, and it was raining and dark over the ocean. We were not able to contact San Juan radio in Puerto Rico, and we were running out of fuel. The gas gauge needles were registering 10 gallons in each tank. We had 2.5 gallons of reserved fuel in each one and had no idea how far we were from the coastline of Puerto Rico. I watched those needles touch the 5-gallon marks, then the 0-gallon marks. I prayed. John was saying, "I sure will be glad when we see the coastline of Puerto Rico." It was dark and all I could see was the strobe light flickering off the propeller blades. I watched the needles touch the empty marks for at least 15 minutes. I told God I wanted to see my family, and I didn't want to die in that ocean. When we saw the coastline of Puerto Rico, I put the throttle to the wall. When I landed at Isla, Grande Airport, I got out of that piece of metal, kneeled, touched the ground and thanked God for life.

Flying Fools and God's Grace

We were given a warning from customs because the guy in the tower at South Caicos Island didn't notify customs in Puerto Rico that we were en route, and to top it off, we arrived late. The gas station was closed, and they wouldn't accommodate us. John said that he didn't want to stay in Puerto Rico overnight. He asked me if I were willing to fly over a lake (lagoon) to the International Airport. I said, "You're the instrument pilot." He said, "Let's go." Like a fool, I started the aircraft with no fuel in the right tank, and we had to shake the wing to see fuel in the left. I put the throttle to the wall, roared down the runway and headed over the lagoon. I had the nerve to ask God to guide us safely. It seemed like we would never get there. When we finally touched down on the runway with our main wheels, I knew that God had hung out with two fools. When I arrived in St. Croix, I hugged and kissed my wife and told her about my foolishness.

I cut my practice hours down to three days per week and enjoyed the rest during the week flying and being with my family. For a number of weeks, I had less stress. The financial side of it was not as rewarding, but at least I obtained a greater peace of mind. I spent quality time with Iris, and we enjoyed each other more. Even the children were more relaxed, and that pleased us all.

Every chance I had to fly my airplane I did. Sometimes during lunch break from the office, I would fly to the small island of Vieques in Puerto Rico in order to get gas. It was my excuse to soar through the air and be free.

I wondered if I would survive mentally all the things, which I had allowed my mind to suffer. I really didn't know any other way to live, but to forge ahead in the face of resistance when it appeared. If I could have traded my medical license in for a professional airline pilot's license, I would have. Reality was that what I knew to do best; I was doing; practicing medicine.

Chapter 27
Testimonial Retribution

I will say of the Lord,
He is my refuge and my fortress:
My God: in him will I trust.

Psalm 91:2

I wasn't surprised to find out that as I went my separate way from the stress in the hospital, I was being trailed. My practice was busy, though I worked fewer hours. People made sure that they got their medical needs attended to.

I thought that some of those midwives had enough of my hide. They cooled down for a while, so I thought. I went into the delivery room late one evening. I had a patient in labor that was obese. A vicious midwife was working. She was quiet this evening; it was strange behavior in my presence because she was often aggressive with me. I figured maybe she had come to enjoy life and finally joined the human race.

The patient had difficult labor and for hours was pushing, and the baby was descending slowly. Early into the morning, she became fully dilated (10 centimeters, when the cervix is opened to a maximum diameter). The baby was now able to descend through the birth canal. I told the midwife that she was ready to deliver, and she took her into the delivery room quickly. It was about 2:30 a.m., and I had stayed with her the entire time. I informed Iris at intervals what was happening. After being in the delivery room for about 15 minutes, the baby descended through the canal, and I delivered it. The midwife took the baby from me in order to suction, the nose and mouth for amniotic fluid and vaginal secretions. I was busy trying to stop the bleeding from her uterus, which was heavy with blood clots. I delivered the placenta, and I put it in the stainless steel basin on the table behind me. The midwife was supposed to check it and tell me if it was missing portions, so I could give the patient Pitocin (medication to help the uterus to contract to stop the bleeding). She didn't say a word, and I didn't question her. The bleeding stopped and I congratulated the mother, and checked on the baby. I thanked the midwife for her help and went home. I was very tired. I had not slept from the night before, and it was almost 4:00 am . . . I couldn't wait to get home and get into my bed and sleep.

That morning I got up at 8:00 a.m. in order to go to work. My office was full, and I saw a number of patients. Iris told me that a midwife from the hospital was on the telephone line and wanted to speak with me. The midwife told me that I needed to come to the hospital right away. I asked her if it could wait until I finished seeing my patients, and she said I needed to come, then. When I got inside the delivery room, she pulled me into a little utility area and with a half-serious look on her face said, "Do you know that you left the placenta in the patient?" I asked, "What patient?"

She said, "The patient whom you delivered this morning." I stood before her in disbelief. I asked her how she knew that. "Because we got it out," she replied. "I just wanted to let you know you left the placenta in the patient, but we got it out." When I asked her where it was, she told me that they threw it away. I knew that they were doing it to me, but I had no proof that I got the placenta out. The midwife wasn't going to back me up. She was trying to cover her own behind because she was supposed to identify the tissue in the basin, and she said nothing. I believe she did this on purpose. I left the hospital depressed. I spoke with my patient, and she told me that she didn't know what they took out of her. They told her that it was the placenta. She was doing fine, and I discharged her from the hospital in a couple of days. I thought the matter was settled until I got a call from the Medical Director's secretary requesting I meet with Dr. De Chabert. I knew that if I did leave the placenta in the patient, it was not a benign matter, but there was no evidence. I had no proof that they were telling me the truth. They didn't show the placenta to me. Many Ob/Gyn physicians have at some time during their career left a portion of the placenta in a patient. The midwife had eased in the clear, and she had Dr. De Chabert protecting her.

When I walked into Dr. De Chabert's office, he was sitting behind his desk with a long white lab coat on. He hardly gave me a chance to sit before he said, "Why did you leave the placenta in the patient and deliberately leave the hospital?" I told him it was not consistent with my character to do that. He said, "But why did you deliberately leave the hospital, knowing you left the placenta in the patient?" I told him that I did not knowingly leave the placenta in the patient and leave the hospital, and please don't say that again. He repeated it a third time. I told him that if I did, the midwife was just as responsible because she was working with me and was supposed to check the tissue in the basin. He acted as if he never heard me. I told him that other doctors had done it. "Not the whole placenta," he said. He told me I would be hearing from him. They were doing it really well to me, and I had no way of stopping it. No one would verbally stand up for me.

After a couple of weeks, I was called into a meeting full of doctors with blood in their mouths. Like a pack of wolves, they cornered me. They had Dr. Hendricks, (a "Psychiatrist"), Dr. De Chabert (Chief of Ob/Gyn), Dr. Endriga, (a Pediatrician), Dr. Pedersen, (an Orthopedic Surgeon), a General Surgeon, and Ms. Safe, (the Medical Director's secretary). They were all sitting at the table looking blood thirsty. I was asked by Dr. Hendricks, the Psychiatrist, to sit, and then he pushed the button on a black tape recorder on the table. I said, "I thought I didn't need a lawyer." I spoke with the Medical Director's secretary a week before the meeting about getting one, and she told me that I didn't need one. Dr. Hendricks asked me if I had anything to say. I didn't know what to say. I didn't even know why I was there. However, it didn't take me long to figure it out. They wanted to destroy my credibility. Dr. Hendricks told me that there was a serious concern about how I practiced medicine. The situation of the placenta came up. I told them that some midwives were out to get me, and I felt that they set me up. I looked at the Dr. De Chabert and said, "For two years you refused to speak to me, and I have done nothing to you. Tell me what I have done, and I will publicly apologize." He didn't say a word. He tilted his balding head over the table edge. I told him that I loved him, and he was wrong for treating me the way he did. Everyone was silent except the Psychiatrist, who told that me; they weren't there for any purpose, but to help me. He was a liar, and he knew it, and they did. They wanted to Lynch me from the rafters of the hospital. Dr. Endriga, the Pediatrician presented a letter asking to have me removed from the nursery. I looked at her in shock because I used to attend Bible study with her. I reminded her that she could have talked to me about any problem, which she felt that I had because we were both Christians. She looked at me stupidly. Dr. Pedersen, the Orthopedic Surgeon, who I didn't even know, told the committee that I gave a patient inappropriate medication. I told him that the patient whom he was referring to was my private patient in my practice. He said that she was not my patient, and we argued. "You're wrong," I told him. "What is your problem with me, I don't even know you?" Dr. Hendricks asked me if I had anything else to say. I told him yes and held them for almost thirty minutes more until the tape in the recorder finished. I assured them that I knew they were lynching me.

Conspiracy Completed

A few days later, I was sent a letter by Dr. De Chabert. The letter stated that I needed an Ob/Gyn physician to back me up if I wanted to deliver any more babies in the hospital. I asked him to back me, and he said no. I asked all the Obstetricians, and every one of them said no. I wrote Dr. De Chabert and told him that he asked me to find back up and everyone refused, and would he consider doing it because he was the most experienced. He responded with, "No." He knew that he asked me to do something, which I couldn't accomplish. One of the doctors was Dr. De Chabert's associate; both doctors worked in the same office. The third Ob/Gyn claimed to be recovering from chronic ulcer disease, and he stated that he was already backing a physician and couldn't help me. The conspiracy was completed. The devil's work had been done, and I was put out of the Labor and Delivery rooms. It was the price, which I paid for telling them all that I would not bow down to their images, their hidden agendas, their secret codes of honor. I can't say that I didn't care because I did. Matter of fact, it hurt terribly, and it put me in a kind of grief and longing to be free from this earth. The only hope, which I saw was Iris and my sweet children and my love for all of them. I felt defeated.

It took me weeks to recover. I felt embarrassed though I had nothing to be embarrassed about and ashamed, though I did nothing dishonest to be ashamed of. In addition, I felt like a bastard child who had been kicked out of his house. I, then got mad. I told my wife, the next time I had a delivery; I was going into the delivery room. For two years, I defied them all and delivered babies in the hospital. Dr. De Chabert was his normal self, not speaking with me, and some midwives were angry concerning my insistence on being in the delivery room.

Chapter 28
Searching

Then I saw that human wisdom is better than folly,
as far as light is better than darkness.

Ecclesiastes 2:13

I started to cry in my car a second time. I didn't know what was wrong or what hit me. A patient was waiting for me in front of my office, and I couldn't stop crying. I tried to stop, but the tears continued to fall from my eyes. I wiped them away and more came. I said, "God, whatever you want from me; I'll give it. Oh God, why me? Why do I have to feel this way?" With the tears still wet upon my face, I got out of my car and greeted my patient. She didn't give me any indication that she believed there was something disturbing me.

I told Iris that I needed to go to New York again. When she asked me why, I told her that I needed to "share the word of God," and practice medicine free. She didn't understand any more this time why I needed to leave her and the children and go to New York then she did when I went to speak in the schools. I guess I appeared unstable to her, having come so far in our lives, sacrificing so much to become a doctor, and telling her that I wanted to preach God's word and give my learning away for free. We struggled over my decision, and she gave in to me.

I went to some of the elders at the church: Orlando, Michael, Bob, Joseph, and John and told them that I felt God wanted me to go to Red Hook and rent a motor home and park it on the main street where drugs were sold, and preach the gospel. They had to think hard about what they advised me, and they prayed, and told me that they believed God was with me.

I got in touch with my friend Raymond in New York, and we planned the journey. The night before I left a friend and his wife; the Singh's prayed for our family. He told me that he believed it was God's will for me to go. I trusted Bro. Singh's opinion because he was a man who trusted God's Word.

Murder in the Street

When I arrived in New York, Raymond and I drove to New Jersey the following day in order to pick up the motor home, I was to practice medicine in. I decided to finance the journey and brought $1,500 to handle expenses. It was great seeing my family and as always; they were happy to have me home again.

My first evening while sleeping in my mother's apartment, I heard gunshots all night into the morning. One particular shot was very loud. That morning a dead body was lying on the side walk behind the building where I was to practice in front of on that day and preach at that evening. I parked the motor home on Columbia Street where drug trafficking was taking place as usual. By 9:00 a.m., I was practicing medicine and people couldn't believe it was free until I took care of them. Some people asked me what was the catch, and I told them that there wasn't any. The people who knew me were proud to see me giving to Red Hook. It was a great feeling taking care of people who knew me while I was growing up. I enjoyed the entire day, and the fact that we were parked on a street, which was known for a lot of crime.

That night as it was getting dark, Raymond and I set up the PA system, and I was ready to speak. It was an emotional experience for me. My message was entitled, "The Word of God Will Set the Captive Free." I told the large crowd, who numbered a little over fifty people, that I traveled 1,850 miles from the beautiful Island of St. Croix in the Caribbean, to tell them that God wanted them to be free. "You don't have to be locked up in prison to be in slavery. You can be enslaved by drugs and crime. If you give God's word a chance to change your hearts, it will set you free, and you'll never be enslaved again. I encourage you today to let the Word of God set you free." I told them of God's love for them, and that God loved them. I told them that I heard guns shooting during the night into the morning, and I knew someone was killed. "One of you did it or knows who did it;

you need to ask God to forgive you, and He will. I don't care about my life, and you can kill me if you want to, but God's word will stand. He'll set you free. God loves you greater than anyone." I began to cry and I started praying for people, as I asked God to set them free.

When the meeting was over, my friend Raymond chastised me for becoming so emotional, and I didn't receive his criticism well, but he meant no harm. I appreciated and loved Raymond, and my heart was open to him.

That evening I didn't hear any gunshots. I asked my mother if she heard any, and she said no. I practiced medicine the following day the way I did the day before, and it went great. I saw some of my old friends. At night, Raymond preached. He was a bit quieter than I was and didn't cry. After he finished, I gave some parting words to the crowd. I told them that street crime, and drugs were killing us all, and it needed to stop. "God cares about you, and He wants to set you free." I drove the motor home to Raymond's house to park it. He lived in a better neighborhood, and I didn't want anyone to break into it in Red Hook. Raymond and I shared some intimate words and bid each other farewell for a while. He took the motor home back to New Jersey.

I asked my mother during the day of my departure if she heard any gunshots the previous night, and she said, "No." I didn't either. For two nights, I didn't hear any gunshots, and it was a confirmation that God was with me. I hugged my mother, kissed her, and told her that I would keep in touch. My sisters hugged and kissed me and gave me their support.

On my return trip to St. Croix, I relaxed in my seat. I felt better than I had in years. It was as if my soul was revived, and I was living again a productive life. I thanked God for His strength in me. For the first time throughout my life, I believed that I did exactly what God wanted me to do; believe, trust, and follow Him.

No More Tears

My life changed for the better after my journey to New York. The tears had dried up, and I didn't feel like an emotional wreck and lost. I made copies of "The message," which I gave on Columbia Street. When I listened to the tape, I realized Raymond was right about me being too emotional. I could at times barely understand what I was saying. During the latter third of the message, I was crying. Nevertheless, I gave copies to those people whom I believed would be honestly interested. I talked about it to Iris and let her listen to the tape, and I wasn't convinced that she believed I did my best. I didn't say anything to her because my going to Brooklyn, in her opinion, was not the greatest idea.

I was tired of all the challenges, which I was facing. Tired of fighting, tired of my anger, and tired of the pain of rejection. I was exhausted and wiped out. There was no more fight in me. The same thing that happened to me emotionally at Lutheran Medical Center had occurred again. I still cared about my patients. I wasn't going to forget about them as I did when I was a second-year resident in Brooklyn, but for now, I needed a rest.

There were major events taking place in my life, and I was trying to cope with them: First, I had my six lovely children to love and be affectionate with. Second, my wife was trying all she could to help me through my challenges, and she endured and loved me all the way. I appreciated her care of me and admired her strength once again. I was missing something in my life; I didn't know what it was, and I continued to feel exhausted.

I awakened one morning, looked at Iris and burst into tears. I didn't know why, but Red Hook was on my mind. She was not prepared for my outburst and wanted to know what was bothering me. Between the crying, I told her that the children in Red Hook were dying, and I needed to go there. She didn't understand why I believed I had to go. She reminded me that I didn't owe anything to Red Hook, and I paid my dues when I kept my promise working there after medical school. I told her that somebody needed to care for those children. I knew that Red Hook was full of crack addicts, pimps, drug pushers, and there were illegal guns being used by children who knew nothing about the destruction, which they could cause. I knew that there were shootings almost every night because my mother told me about it when I called her. Sometimes while speaking with her, she paused because of gunfire in the street. "Did you hear that?" she would say. "They're out there shooting again."

Red Hook was a war zone and my mother and sisters, and a host of relatives were caught in it. I wanted them to get out. They didn't see the urgency of leaving because it had become a part of their everyday life. It wasn't that they or anyone living there felt comfortable with the gunfire, but they felt helpless. The police knew who had guns and who sold drugs, but why should some of them care; they didn't live in Red Hook projects. I heard at least two gunshots each time I called my mother. I couldn't comprehend it all. It was as if the whole city had fallen to the lawless element, and the justice system failed to contain the convicted felons.

People were in, and out of jail before the next holiday rolled around. "Ma," I said, "how can you take what's happening in Red Hook, all the shootings, drugs, and crime?"

"What can I do, Buddy?" she replied.

I needed to visit Red Hook and try to encourage a change. Iris believed that it was foolish, and I understood why she felt that way. She was tired of seeing me trying to save the world, and she told me so many times. She'd say, "Buddy, you can't save the world." I knew saving the world was beyond my reach, but I needed to try to be a part of the solution.

Taking Care of My Wife

I wanted to do something nice for my wife. It was her dream to have a Mercedes-Benz, and I saw one in the car showroom. Iris was the hardest-working, loving wife in the world.

I went into the showroom and inquired about the Benz. It was a beautiful 190 E Mercedes with a beige interior. Iris was partial to black cars; she believed that they looked elegant. When I told her, I saw one at the dealer and was thinking about buying it, she didn't think that I was serious. We were driving a nice Subaru four-door sedan, and we traded it in, added $3,000 as a down payment, and drove the Mercedes home. Iris was elated over her dream car. It was her third brand-new car since my internship and residency. I felt great being able to please my wife. She was going through a lot with me and the least I could do was give her some things, which she wanted.

Tolerating My Situation

My medical practice was going well, and I continued to work long hours into the evenings in order to pay our bills and try to accomplish day-to-day tasks and succeed in being financially independent. I didn't trust the system and the people in it, and I realized that I needed to continue to work and support my family. I still wanted to leave medicine, but I didn't talk much about it because Iris got on my case each time that I mentioned it.

Red Hook was still on my mind. I told Iris that I was planning a trip there. I wrote letters to the public and junior high schools, which I attended, and asked if I could visit the schools in order to speak to the students about medicine and career goals, and determination. I received a warm response and was welcomed with open arms. I bought two-casual suits, two pairs of shoes, and packed my bags to leave. Iris was still trying to understand why I had to return to Red Hook, but she gave me her blessing. I knew that I was doing the right thing because the children of Red Hook were in my soul, and I had to speak to them. The three-and-one-half-hours flight to New York was different from other times. I had a butterfly sensation in my stomach all the way to New York, and it wasn't going to go away until I fulfilled my purpose to tell those children my story. When I arrived at Kennedy International Airport in New York, my sisters and my mother met me. I was happy to see them. I missed them so much. My first night in Red Hook, gunshots were fired all night into the morning. I couldn't believe Red Hook had become a battle zone. No one was safe on the street during the day or night. While I lay on the bed my first night there, I heard a few gunshots, and it startled me. I jumped from the bed and onto the floor. I slowly looked out the window and saw two young guys and one was pointing a handgun in the air. I saw him discharge a round. There wasn't a police officer in sight. This wasn't rare in Red Hook; gunshots were the norms each night. I crawled into bed again and looked toward the ceiling. "Oh God," I said, "I know you're in this place, and You can help these people." I prayed for Red Hook while my heart was weeping.

Red Hook wasn't just any place. It was the place I once adored and defended. It was my first home, my running ground, and it was still in my soul. When I awakened that morning, the shooting was fresh in my mind, and I told my mother about it. She said she heard it, and that's how it was almost every night. I put on my new white sport suit and pinned my name badge to it. I reflected on Red Hook and took an emotional journey looking for the places where I played, the basement and bushes that I hid in while playing with my friends, the broken benches, the red fire alarm box, which I pulled, the street that the "Kovons" marched on, and some of the same people whom I grew up with. They greeted me and told me how good I looked, and I was amazed that they were so excited to see me. It made me feel very special and important.

I had some mixed emotions and felt somewhat guilty that I had made it educationally and socially, but some of them didn't. It was the guilt, which Iris spoke to me about many times, but I didn't want to recognize it.

I walked slowly to the school, as I wondered had I stayed in Red Hook and practiced medicine would I have made a difference. When I arrived at the schoolyard, I remembered how Ronald stomped on me and hurt me really badly. I didn't hate him anymore. My mother told me that she heard that he was killed in California. She said that she wasn't sure, but she believed that he was dead. I felt sorry that Ronald and I never made it right between us. I would have gladly forgiven him if he had stopped messing with my mind. Even the beating he gave me would have meant little to me, if he had given me an honest hello. Nevertheless, it was too late and many years were between us and now a possible death. In some ways, it was a tragic finale, and it sealed a painful moment in my life. However, I was now able and strong enough to tell myself that I had nothing to be sad about, but it would have been great to understand and love Ronald.

Precious Seeds

Public School 27 had just opened its doors to the incoming students. I was greeted at the door by the hall monitor, who knew me and took me to the principal's office. When the principal arrived, she had a smile on her face and said, "You must be Dr. Williams." I told her that I was. She excused herself after telling me how busy it was trying to help the staff get their assignments for the day, and helping some students who seemed to be confused about why they were in school. I knew that she was being challenged while trying to be polite and respectful to me. I didn't mind the delay because the butterflies in my stomach were getting worse. When she came back, she apologized, and told me that the children were going into the auditorium in order to wait for my presence. When I got to the auditorium, it was loaded with children. My mother and my sisters were sitting in one row from the front.

The Speech

When I stood up to speak, a quiet hush fell over the room. Some of the students had blank stares on their faces. One student, in particular, kept eye contact with me. He may have wondered what I was doing invading his space and his life and trying to change the rules, which he was familiar with. I knew I had to say something to all of them that would affect their lives and change them forever. They needed to know the truth about me and hear as much of my story as I could give in the forty-five minutes, which they gave me to speak.

I began to tell them about my journey, and my mother taking me to a Psychiatrist when I was a little boy. The crowd broke into laughter. I looked at my mother, and she was laughing as if we had a private joke between us. The laughter permeated the room like thunder in the sky. I knew at this point they would listen to me and wait for me to tell them more. They were captivated by my bluntness. I prepared a lot of information to tell them, but I didn't have the time. I told them that I was left back four times during my thirty years in school, and in the fifth grade, I was accused of tripping a substitute teacher. They could hardly sit still from laughing. They didn't have a chance to recover from laughing because I kept telling them my story. I told them that I spent most of my summers in summer school because I kept failing courses. I boldly told them that I was never cited for any outstanding academic achievements; except one time when I was in high school on the honor roll for six months. When I finished college, I said, "I had eleven F's and nine Ds on my college transcript." I made eye contact with a little boy who was sitting in front of me distracting other students, and his eyes fixed on mine. I had at least one person who was absorbing what I was telling the students.

"I almost flunked out of medical school," I told them. "In the opinion of some of my professors, I didn't belong in medical school, and one professor told me that he and some other people were concerned if I ever got a license to practice medicine." I wanted them to know these things about me because they should believe that they could achieve anything, which they tried if they put their minds to it.

I paid a price to stand before them and tell them what I thought was best to secure their future. The price was paid by all the things that I went through in order to be successful in America. I didn't have the right to tell them what to become, but I was sure going to tell them about their great potential. I had an idea what they were up against because I grew up in their neighborhood. There were years between us, but they were faced by similar problems, which I faced when I was growing up: drugs, guns, and crime. The difference in their generation from mine and most of the generations I ever read about was, children killing each other.

Living in Red Hook for twenty-four years was not a liability to me, but an asset because at least I understood after seeing what was going on around me that I needed to get out. Not everyone needed what I needed, but it saved my life, and I did not become a victim to it.

I told them all these things and more, as much as they would allow me to and as much as my soul could reveal.

When they finally quieted down, they waited patiently to hear what else I had to tell them, and I paused. I paused long enough to see some of the teachers in a daze. Some of them looked tired, having listened to me for over an hour, but no one dared to stop me. I had not finished what I wanted to say, but I had to end my journey with them. I didn't believe that I gave them any solutions to achieve success. Therefore, I told them to believe that God loved them and made them well. "Look at yourself, you're beautiful. God made you that way. You're strong like a seed with great potential, and your soil is the place you live in, and every place you go, and everyone you allow to talk to you. Every now and then, you will be watered by circumstances, and the circumstances will be your life experience. There will be some dry spells in your life, but don't give up and die; be like a powerful seed and fight to live. Some of you might die before your appointed time, but you should never abandon your dreams and be committed at the end of your lives. You owe it to yourselves to reach your potential and be successful. You are not junk, but beautiful children who can become engineers, doctors, lawyers and educators." They stood upon their feet, yelled, and applauded, and I felt like weeping because I was convinced that I reached their hearts and souls.

I was fully confident with God's help and grace that they all would make it if they stayed focused on their dreams and faint not. My soul was assured that I did my earnest best to give them myself without fear that they would think of me less than I ought to be.

Junior High School Days Again

When I went to Junior High School 142, I had an emotional rush. I remembered Rosa and how I sang songs from "West Side Story" to her. I remembered Betty and when I put that note in her violin case, which my homeroom teacher intercepted. I was remembering all of my mischief there and how I would sit waiting for the bell to ring in order to go to the next classroom. Mr. Manfreddy, one of my teachers whom I had when I was in the eighth grade, surfaced in my mind. One day I was clowning in class, and he politely asked me to leave the room. Outside the classroom, he smacked me hard on my face and my whole body shook. I wanted to see him. I didn't want to say anything to him, in particular. I just needed to see how he looked. He was a big strong-looking man, and I was scared of him then and still was. I saw him, not long after I entered the principal's office. When he walked in, he had that same walk with his shoulders riding high and that serious look on his face. He didn't recognize me, and I spoke to him. "Hello, Mr. Manfreddy, how are you, I'm Wilbert. You were my teacher."

He had no problem recalling me and said, "Hi, how are you? It's good to see you."

"It's good to see you also, Mr. Manfreddy; I'll be speaking here today."

"Yes, I heard about it; I'll see you later."

When I arrived in the auditorium, there weren't as many students as I expected. The teacher responsible sat them together in the center section. The students looked at me with little or no excitement. There was something very different about them, something that frightened me; I couldn't figure what. Maybe the cares of life in 1987 made them appear dull and apathetic. I had a hard time getting prepared to speak. I wasn't sure what I was going to say and how I was going to say it. When I began to speak, I stumbled over my words and my trend of thought was not flowing. At one point, I didn't want to continue speaking because they wouldn't respond to me in a way that showed they were receiving my message. As I continued my talk, the students appeared as though they were tolerating me, so I ended it. When I finished, I was not satisfied that my being there was worthwhile.

Mr. Manfreddy stood up and told the students what a great student I was when I attended. He was lying through his teeth, and he knew it, or he never remembered how bad I was. I couldn't believe he forgot when he smacked me. I asked him to get me a school T-shirt, and he told one of the students to get it. I don't remember any of the students asking me any questions. I was glad it was over because I felt bad. Mr. Manfreddy thanked me for coming to the school and wished me well.

I did my part. I traveled 1,850 miles from the beautiful Caribbean island of St. Croix in order to give of myself to those students, and it was all worth it, even if the reception was dull at Junior High School 142. I had to face the reality that times had changed since I was there and would continue to change with every passing day.

The night before my departure for St. Croix, gunshots were ringing out in the streets, and it broke my heart to experience that kind of change in Red Hook. Life magazine did a story on Red Hook. It was called "Death of a Neighborhood." I read the article and looked at the familiar pictures of the project hallways and courtyard. It wasn't the same Red Hook, which I grew up in, but it was still the place I loved dearly. On my return trip to St. Croix, I saw those children at Public School 27 as clear as I could see the seat in front of me. "Oh God," I said, "Keep those children and give them strength to fulfill their dreams and goals."

When I arrived in St. Croix, the experience of being in Brooklyn, New York had changed me, and I felt strong and renewed, knowing that I did something purposeful with my life. I gave all that I could, and I felt confident it was exactly what I was supposed to give.

Iris, as always, looked beautiful as ever to me, and I was happy to see her. I squeezed her gently but firmly and told her that I loved her. She looked at me sincerely and said, "I love you too, honey." Iris was really my anchor and my confidante. She didn't agree with many of the things I did and some of my ways of thinking, but the fact that she loved me made a world of difference. Our children were at the airport, and they were the other part of me. I loved them more than I expressed. They meant the world to me, and I was glad that I had them. It was during the hard times during my life that I realized they were God's gifts to me and without them; my life would have been missing something vital for balance. There were times when having to care for them burdened me and created some anxiety; especially when I made a decision to challenge the system. That's when I saw their faces vivid before my mental eye. I loved my children with a passion, and I would never regret their being with me. I went back to work and all the stress that accompanied it was waiting for me as if it had missed a partner for a few days, and my patients were waiting for me to see them also. Some of them had needs while I was away and when they saw me, they without pain let me know that they needed me. One person asked me what she was supposed to do when I left the island. I looked at her and said, "I'm sorry, but I needed some time off." It always bothered me when my patients let me know life would be difficult for them without me giving them medical care. I didn't visit the hospital, unless I had a patient admitted; otherwise, I tried to keep it far removed from my mind. It was a source of pain that I wanted to forget about, but it wouldn't go away because I decided when a patient of mine was in labor, I would be there to deliver her. That time came and when it did, I boldly walked into the labor and delivery room with acid in my stomach, and the midwives who were there looked surprise. Their eyes opened wide, and they looked shocked. I hid my anxiety as usual. I wasn't going to let them take from me what I was entitled to have; the right to deliver babies in the hospital where I had privileges at. I had a permanent license to practice medicine in the Virgin Islands, and no one gave me a thing and therefore, I didn't owe them. I did owe the people of the Virgin Islands to practice good medical care and do the best I could. The midwife who was on call accompanied me during the delivery. All went well. I didn't detect any animosity from her. After the delivery, I walked out of there as boldly as I walked in. I didn't hear anything coming from the Chairman of OB/Gyn's desk. He was probably tired of dealing with me. Each time I had a delivery; I entered the delivery room and delivered my patients' babies.

Every opportunity I had, I was at the airport cleaning, polishing, or flying my Piper 180-G single-engine aircraft. That airplane was a major player in my life, and I was fascinated by its ability to help me fly like an eagle.

I started a flight club and called it the Agape Flying Club. I wanted to encourage the kids in St. Croix, concerning aviation, to become pilots. I put a sectional aviation chart and a sign in my office window in order to advertise the flying club. It caught the attention of many people. When the kids saw it, they stopped and asked. Some parents came in and inquired if I taught adults to fly an airplane. Before long, I had a number of children to teach; Dexter, Elroy, Elwin, Anthony, Richard, and Atom. We had one girl, but her stay was short because she moved to the States. Every other Saturday we met in my office for ground schooling, and I taught them what I knew. The other Saturdays we gathered at the airport, and the kids took turns; three at a time went up with me. I let the student in the copilot seat fly the airplane. Picking up the microphone, I'd say, "St. Croix ground, November 4496 Tango ready to taxi to active from east ramp parking, request permission to taxi to active runway."

The ground control would answer, "November 4496 Tango, permission granted to taxi to active."

It was great waiting for the take-off, speaking to the tower, and waiting to become airborne. "N-4496-T cleared for take-off."

I would tell the student to push the throttle to the wall, and the airplane pushed us reward in our seats and down the runway, we soared until the air speed reached 78 miles per hour. "Pull the yoke," I'd instruct, and off the ground, we lifted through the air. Each time we went through this procedure was just as gratifying as the one before. We would fly at the end of the island, called the East End, and do all kinds of crazy stuff like: sharp turns, steep descents and ascents, stalls (turn the engine down to idle speed and point the nose of the plane up until it started to shake and fall), and weightlessness. They went wild when I did this. I'd push the throttle to the wall and soar upward, and then suddenly push the yoke forward and our butts would lift out of the seats. I usually tossed a pencil in the air, and it would float until I couldn't take the empty-hole feeling in my stomach and leveled the airplane. It was great, and we had a grand time with that airplane. Sometimes, I took them away to another island like St. Martin, St. Thomas, or Puerto Rico. I liked those trips because it gave me quality time for the guys; especially the ones who wanted to follow aviation as a career. Dexter and Atom were two who put energy into moving in that direction. Dexter asked me for some information, and I gave him three pages of addresses and telephone numbers. Atom was interested in joining the Army in order to enter aviation school. Atom's mother died. She suffered a cerebral stroke. She was young and loved by many and she was our friend. She was cremated, and her husband asked me to take her ashes up in the airplane and release it into the air. Atom and I took my Piper 180-G and soared to four thousand feet. While he commanded the controls, I opened the side window and sprinkled her ashes into the air. I think some of Atom's pain was decreased when he saw his mother's ashes freely fading into the atmosphere.

Iris and I spent quality time together in that little airplane going to other Islands. We frequently went to Puerto Rico to shop and eat. We often visited my in-laws, who live in Corozal, near the mid-southern portion of the island. I loved being with them. They treated me well, and my mother-in-law fed me as if I were her own child. Being in the country of Puerto Rico was great, and I marveled at the acres of banana and plantain trees. It was a very relaxing time for me, and I never grew tired of going there.

One time I took Shoshanna and Taina with us to Puerto Rico in our airplane. On our return to St. Croix, I arrived at the airport while it was getting dark and hazy. I cleared with San Juan, Puerto Rico for our return to St. Croix. The flight to St. Croix was challenging. It was hazy and raining and Shoshanna, and Taina started vomiting. Sometimes I did stupid things like taking off in marginal weather, believing that we would be OK. I learned slowly from my hairy experiences while flying. One time I took off from Ponce, Puerto Rico and headed to St. Croix without an operating left brake. When I was twenty miles from the coast line of St. Croix, I radioed the tower and told them that I had no left brake. They cleared the runway and had a fire truck waiting to put out the flames if I crashed. When I stepped from the aircraft, a firefighter in a silver suit asked me if I were OK. I felt foolish.

My worst near-disaster came one Saturday on a return trip from St. Martin, the weather deteriorated down to instrument conditions, and I was not rated to fly in that type of weather. The instrument panel showed the plane was not flying in straight and level flight. I panicked, knowing that I couldn't fly well in that kind of weather. I lost altitude and was less than one thousand feet over the water, and the right wing kept dipping to a forty-five-degree angle. I called San Juan, Puerto Rico and told them that I didn't know where I was and should have reached St. Croix by then. They told me to hold on, and I lost contact with them. I called them back, and they gave me false information. Knowing the east end of the island had small mountains, I figured that I would hit one. I prayed to God as I did when John and I almost ran out of gas coming from South Caicos Island to Puerto Rico. "O God, I need your help. We can't die out here like this." Within thirty seconds, the haze broke and the mountain was in front of us; a few hundred feet away.

My Cocoon

The airplane became a part of my stable mental diet. It even became my friend because when I should have died in it, along with others, it never once fell apart or didn't do what it was created to do. It didn't fail me like some people had, and when I had the chance, I took the best care of it that I could.

In many ways, it was one of my escapes from all the fire and brimstone I was going through in St. Croix. Each time I climbed into it. It felt like a cocoon around me, and I'd sit in it and my soul would cry. It helped me to survive and in some way dance in the fire I was in.

I tried to spend more time with my children, and it was a major effort because there was always something that needed my attention. My children meant the world to me, and I know in ways I failed them, but I also failed myself, because they are an extension of me. I took them to the beach and played on the sand with them; we camped out in our yard and ran through the brush. We stayed in our custom van overnight and called it a sleep-out while the mosquitoes ate us alive. I built a playhouse for my daughters, so they could put their dolls in. I enjoyed the time that I spent with them, and I believe it was the highlight of their lives.

Iris was delighted each time she saw me giving to the children. She encouraged me to spend time with them. She realized it was best for the balance in all our lives because we were family. I spent quality time with Iris. I took her away many times in our airplane just to let her know that I did not forget her in the midst of all the confusion surrounding us because of me.

I decided to upgrade the instruments in the airplane, and I asked her to fly with me to Miami, Florida from St. Croix. I was a bit anxious about taking a long trip across the water even though we were island hopping. I got the information, which I needed in order to successfully make the trip, and plotted the course to three islands. We left our children with a baby-sitter and headed to Miami/Opa-locka, Florida. Our first stop was Isla Grande in Puerto Rico. We cleared customs and headed for Borinquen, which was at the northwestern tip of Puerto Rico. We stayed in a motel, and the following morning awakened with the rising sun and flew along the northern coast of the Dominican Republic to a place called Puerto Plata. I took a heading north that I thought would take me to the island of South Caicos. I went to North Caicos Island and had to be guided to the correct island. The Bahamas' islands were dotted throughout the beautiful water of the Atlantic and once again; it fascinated me. We cleared customs, went to the rest rooms and headed for Georgetown, Bahamas Island. It was a small airstrip with a dingy wooden reception building. We filled the Piper with gas and headed for Miami/Opa-locka in Florida. It seemed like a long haul from Georgetown to Miami. We flew over Andros Island, in the Bahamas. After flying over it, I called Miami radio and told them that I was coming in. They followed me all the way into Miami, as they spoke to me about air traffic and my position to them. When I reached Florida and saw all the tall buildings, I had no idea where to go. I didn't know where Opa-locka, Florida was. I told Miami radio I didn't know where to fly in order to reach "Hanger-1" at Opa-locka airport. They coordinated my exact position and guided me exactly to the tip of the runway at Opa-locka. After landing, an attendant came out and parked my airplane in a designated spot. They literally had a red carpet for us to walk on from the airplane to the hanger building, which had chandeliers hanging from the ceiling. I checked my airplane in as if it were going into a hospital and checked into a hotel. I didn't know it at the time, but my airplane's hospital bill would be $10,000.

When we returned to St. Croix via commercial airlines, our home was as we left it and our children were very excited to see us. The time that Iris and I spent together was very special to us, and we will never forget it.

When I wasn't practicing medicine, flying my airplane, riding my horse, scuba diving in the ocean, growing vegetables, or doing something childish with my children, I was thinking about my life and what I really wanted to do with it.

Every five years I took an assessment of the road, which I traveled and where I ended. It gave me an idea of the progress of my life, and if it was worth it to God to have made me. I wondered if it was deserving of my mother and father having labored over me, and if it was worth it to my wife to have married me. I usually came to some startling conclusions. I continued to plot my journey and find my place since that time, in my life. I needed to know who and what I had become, if I were a better person or a different individual, and if my life was worth anything in a world that needed so much. It was this world that I envisioned in flames that kept me focusing on my life. I didn't want to be consumed by it.

I was confused about my purpose. I knew I was important, at least to myself, my wife, my children, my mother, sisters, and a host of relatives, but something was missing in my life, and I didn't know what. I was beginning to show signs of stress and depression again, and Iris noticed it. One day I went to the Mercedes dealership in order to speak with the owners, who suggested that I look at a white Benz, which was due in the showroom in one week. It was a 300SEL four-door sedan. It was one of the largest made, other than the limousine. The owner of the dealership had one just like it, but hers was eight cylinders and the one coming in was a six. I told her that I wasn't interested, but she insisted that I look at it. "Buddy, you'll like it and you deserve to have something nice to drive around in. You work really hard delivering babies all hours of the night and morning. You need to treat yourself." I told her a Mercedes Benz wasn't me, and she asked me why, and I couldn't answer her. When the Mercedes came in, I took Iris with me to see it and Iris agreed with Carol that I should buy the car. I told Carol and Iris that I didn't want it. They tried to convince me to buy it. They said I would look good in it. Carol said, "Buddy, your patients would like to see you in a Mercedes." I told her I didn't think so. Iris later asked me what was my problem with having a Mercedes, and I told her it just wasn't me. After a week or two, they both convinced me to buy it, and I dug deep into my pocket and financed it for $54,000, which after bank interest, cost $74,000. I drove the car home, anxious that someone who knew me might judge me negatively for indulging in an expensive item. The reason why I didn't want the expensive Mercedes Benz was I didn't believe that I deserved it. It wasn't because it cost too much money, because I was making a lot. I felt guilty that I left the projects and made it, and so many of my friends didn't. I didn't think that a Black man with my beliefs was supposed to sport a luxury car while so many Black men were in jail or facing tremendous challenges. The system put us all at a disadvantage; here I am thinking that I owed my entire life to try to solve the problems of Black people because at least I had a piece of America's apple pie. As Black people, overall, we have to work harder in order to prove that we are entitled to all the rights that the United States spells out. Even as a professional, I was not able to escape the trauma of the system. I had a hard time fully enjoying my new car, as if it were borrowed. I gave people rides in it who were hitchhiking along the road. I didn't care what they looked like or how they were dressed and wanted to share that car with as many people as possible. I believed it would make me deserving of having it, because at least people who may have never had a chance to ride in a Mercedes Benz would ride in mine. I even offered some people whom I knew the opportunity to drive it. In spite of my personal problems, I did try to enjoy the 100-watt stereo cassette player. I blasted gospel music through the ten speakers while cruising with the windows rolled up and bathing in the cold air coming from the high-powered air conditioner. That car could reach 100 miles per hour with ease and feel like it was 35.

I had some emotional encounters in my Benz. I broke down and cried in it about four or five times. I went to a church service one evening at the New Testament Church of God. The service was nice, and I felt lifted spiritually when I left. I got in my Benz and turned on the air conditioner and blasted a gospel song by Helen Baylor entitled "The Anointed." When I was almost home, I switched the cassette player to the radio. The news reporter stated James Baldwin died in Port De Vince, France. I didn't have any great affection for James Baldwin, so I thought. I read some of his books: Giovanni's Room, another Country, Nobody Knows My Name, the Fire Next Time, and saw and heard him on a television program with the famous Anthropologist, Margaret Mead, rapping on race. I enjoyed listening to him speak because he spoke precisely, surely, and intelligently, spiced with big words. I sat in my car thinking of him choosing to live in France because of his need to feel like a real man because America had shown him her racist side. It was too much for him to stomach. He just couldn't deal with it and left his roots, his family, and his dream to be a full American with all the rights that the United States Constitution said he, and other Black Americans had. I thought about my father in Chesson, Alabama, my mother having worked hard doing domestic work, the unfortunate blacks in America. I thought of the starving children of the Sudan in Ethiopia. My father flashed through my mind again, and I could see his pain and agony being a Black man in America, and I broke down and cried. I cried so hard that I wept. My chest felt like it had a hole in it, and my heart would tumble out onto the carpeted floor. I said, "Oh God, what do You want from me? I hurt so much and I don't know what to do, what do You want?" I didn't get an answer from Him at that moment. I was confident that my journey was going to take me to a different level of life. I was tired of pain. I didn't know how to handle a simple rejection from anyone, not even an enemy. I didn't want any more emotional trauma, but it seemed to be with me.

Doing What I Did Best

My practice was busy I had enough work to take my attention off all my problems. I was delivering a few babies, and the midwives were tolerating me. The Chairman of Ob/Gyn as usual didn't have anything professional or social to say to me. I finally wrote him off as a mistake in my judgment. I believed that he and all people who behaved as he did fail to join the human race.

Thank God, I didn't have any problems with my patients, and they were pleased with my care. I admitted a few people to medicine and most of them got well.

One patient, in particular, slipped through my better judgment. She was about 47 years old. She came into my office for a routine exam with a chief complaint of a "rash" on her breast caused by mosquitoes. When I looked at them, they were clearly eaten away with deep pockets of infection. I asked her how long did her breast look that way, and she replied a couple of weeks. I diagnosed it as an infection and gave her an antibiotic. A few days later, she was admitted into the hospital for infectious cancer. I spoke with the surgeon who diagnosed it, and he told me he had seen that type of cancer many times before. That Sunday I visited her, and she couldn't breathe because of fluid accumulating in her lungs. I asked the nurse to give me a large-bore needle, and I drained over one quart of cancerous liquid from her chest. She thanked me for helping her. Within five days, she died, and the family blamed me for her death. I was devastated. I didn't believe her death was my fault. She had cancer for a while, but I was blamed because I missed the problem. I admitted to my incorrect judgment and took blame for it, but the family wanted me to take all the blame. One of her daughters was determined to get revenge, and in a way, she succeeded. When she was pregnant, she came to the office for prenatal care. After I delivered her baby, she refused to pay me. It was not the refusal to pay me money that hurt me. It was her attitude toward me.

Fellowship

Community Christian Fellowship had become a part of our lives, and we were going to church every Sunday regularly. Our pastor was a pleasant man who loved people, but his wife was a bit to the left of being sociable. The services at the church were encouraging and a blessing. The people were nice, and it felt like family being there. It helped me to believe that my life was worth something and there were people who loved me regardless of color and race. In many ways, the families in the church represented to me hope as far as racism was concerned, because many of them were white including the pastor and his wife.

Iris and I didn't spend much time with the families within the church other than at church gatherings. Michael and Paula invited us to their house for dinner, and we had a good time. We met Orlando and Annie, and Joseph and Bernadette, and they were friendly and open with us and our relationships would be tested. For the most part, our fellowship with these new people of our lives would be positive.

When I had the energy and the time, I called Michael and Margie in Albany, New York. It was so refreshing to speak with my friends. In many ways, I missed them because they were a part of my life. Michael and I talked about his job situation, the church, and his life at home. He was having some challenges in his life, and he shared them with me. He trusted that I would speak my heart to him as a friend and I did. He was still thanking me for encouraging him to do all he could to have a good relationship with his parents. It wasn't that it was poor; Michael was just concerned because they were getting older, and he wanted to be a good son to them.

Ephraim and Yoli were having some challenges in their lives. We loved them dearly, and it hurt us to know that they were not happy. Iris and I knew what type of challenges presented married couples because we had our own battles to win in our marriage. I encouraged all my friends to continue to seek the best in each other and keep the love alive between them.

Since Elder Mac Daniel died, the church seemed to have a greater struggle being a family. Yoli mentioned to me that she believed not having Elder Mac around caused a weakening in the church. Elder Mac was really missed by many people. Sis. Dix was still holding the banner up with the rest of the congregation, and she was doing a good job. Many others and I respected her and believed she would always do her best.

My life on St. Croix continued to be debatable. In one circle, I was considered one of the best physicians to come to St. Croix, in another circle a menace that needed to go back to New York. I wasn't going anywhere. My long-gone boss at the Frederiksted Health Center told me a number of times if I didn't like it in St. Croix; I needed to get some tickets at the travel agent to leave. It would have been so much better for some of my colleagues if I left, but there was no way I would. I had the right to live in peace in the Virgin Islands, just as much right as they had to live in peace and enjoy the benefits offered in the United States. I tried to maintain being happy, but considering happiness is a state beyond the mind and is subject to fluctuations depending on the cares of this life, I once again fell into depression. One morning while driving to work I, felt enslaved by my emotions, and just as I was entering the parking lot, I was thinking about Red Hook and my growing up there and now being a successful doctor, and I fell apart emotionally and wept.

Chapter 29
The Eye of the Hurricane

And there arose a great storm of wind,
And the waves beat into the ship,
So that it was now full.

Mark 4:3

I thought that the greatest storms in my life were over. I found peace with myself having given back to Red Hook what I thought I owed them. It was as if I had purged myself of all the guilt and pain, which I suffered through the years. I didn't know that I was the only one who believed that I owed anything to Red Hook, and if there were, a debt owed, Red Hook owed me as much as I owed her. In fact, we are all in debt to each other according to the Bible, because it says, "We are to bear one another's burdens." Whether we believe this to be true or not, I don't think that it ruins us or makes us, less than what we ought to be, but rather purges us of our own selfishness and greed. So in some way my journey set me free and pointed me in a direction away from myself, and I became a greater part of life.

If it were not for Iris, I would have been consumed by my challenges, because many times, I was confused and wounded, and she patched me up and tried to point me in the best direction. Without a doubt, we were meant for each other, and she was my greatest earthly asset.

Medicine had become something, which I had to do to be balanced, and it was grinding away at me because the problems in the hospital, although less, were before me. When I had a patient in labor, some of the midwives would wait until she was almost ready to deliver before calling

301

me. I would drive like a lunatic to the hospital, which was about three miles from my house on a winding road. It was impossible for me to arrive there in less than seven minutes, and each time they delayed calling me. I missed deliveries. I knew that they had delayed notifying me because my patients would tell me that they were in the labor room for quite a while before my being called. Sometimes they told me that they asked, pleaded, and begged the midwife on duty to call me, to no avail. These acts of deliberate unprofessional behavior hurt my patient and me, and I was disappointed each time it occurred. In spite of their behavior, I continued to deliver babies, and I guess some of them were angry. Each time I entered the labor and delivery area; acid poured into my stomach, and I felt sick. My heart would pound fast, and my legs felt weak. There wasn't a time that I didn't pray to God asking for strength, and He did. I continued to do what was best for my patients, and they appreciated my care for them. I was very active in the church ministry, telling people of God's great love and concern for all of His creations. I preached at a number of churches on St. Croix and was even invited to go to other islands in order to minister, which I never did. I had my hands full ministering on St. Croix. It got to a point where I was so drained with engagements. I typed a letter telling the pastors that I wouldn't be ministering for a while because I had other things to do. A couple of them approached me and told me when God called, I needed to answer, and I should never turn down an opportunity to preach the Word of God. Iris believed different because she saw some of what it took and cost me to stay up late at night and early into the morning in order to prepare a message. This was one of the times that I didn't have a hard time agreeing with her. As usual, I did what I believed was best but allowed some of these pastors to put a guilt trip on me. I continued to brave the preaching though my life was already busy, and I was tired. I did turn down a number of pastors, and I felt guilty when I did. One pastor approached me and said, "Come on. It's been long enough; come to my church and preach to my people. They would love it, Dr. Williams."

I respected a few pastors because I believed that they loved people as they preached the Word of God. I also respected their diligence and ability to deliver the Word a few times a week, take care of their families, and remain sane. I knew what it took to work through a preaching message, and it was no fun. It was tiring and anxiety provoking. Therefore, if not for anything else, I respected them for choosing to stick with their calling, for those that were called.

When I had the chance, I enjoyed scuba diving and spear fishing. I enjoyed being in the ocean. It is a very different world down there, and it fascinated me. When I was beneath the water swimming around, I didn't think much about what was taking place in the world. I understood that while the world had its challenges, the sea world was doing just fine, except for the vicious hands of men who tried to destroy it by killing the life in it. I believe that man is the most destructive creation made by God, and it was never intended to be that way, because He made us in His image and in His likeness, but we are bent on destruction, and that's why we kill each other without regard for life.

I called my friends John and Doris Belton in upstate New York. It was great hearing their voices. I was feeling down. I told them how good I knew God had been to me, and I was grateful, but I believed that all the things, which I had accumulated over the years, were not important. I told them that I felt separated from my airplane, my house, and my property. I told them that I just wanted to be in God's will. Both spoke with me. They didn't rebuke what I said, but I detected that they believed that there were some things, which I needed to understand. They were my friends. I respected their opinion, and I waited for them to respond to what I said. As usual, they were supportive of my being in Gods will and obeying Him. I did not know that I was soon to see them, and they would tell me personally how they felt.

St. Croix would suffer a traumatic experience, and the integrity and fiber of my life would be tested, and my family would look to me for answers, and I wouldn't have any. Life has many surprises, and if we live long enough we'll encounter some of them, and it will break us or make us stronger. Some of the encounters will point our lives in directions that we never intended to go.

It was August 19, 1989, and my life was set on the course that I desired. I earned $210,000 in the past twelve months. My Mercedes Benz car payments were one payment ahead. My mortgage was up-to-date. A two-acre piece of property was almost paid for. My airplane was paid for, and my practice was going well as usual. Iris was seven months pregnant with our seventh child, and my children were healthy and happy. Living in the Caribbean was different in many ways from living in New York. For one thing, I never had to worry about storms and hurricanes, but in the Caribbean, it was a yearly affair and highly unpredictable. My family and many families on the island of St. Croix and other parts of the Caribbean would experience the ravaging effects of a devastating hurricane. It would be one of the worst anyone in the Caribbean had experienced, called Hurricane Hugo. Everyone in the Caribbean knew Hurricane Hugo was on its way; to the eastern Caribbean, U.S. and British Virgin Islands, and Puerto Rico. The hurricane-tracking center in Coral Gables, Florida notified nationwide news companies and they, in turn, broadcast it throughout the world.

Cape Verde, on the southwestern coast of Africa, is the breeding ground for hurricanes, it birthed a monster of a hurricane that would tear St. Croix to pieces and drive its residents to its knees, and the island would never be the same again. The day during the hurricane, my family and I went to church. The wind was blowing hard enough to force us to close the two wooden doors in the back of the church while we had service. Each time the doors knocked against the doorstop; members looked toward the back of the church. When the wind became more intense, the service was quickly terminated, and we went home. I don't think that anyone had the slightest idea that within a few hours, we would be engulfed by a monstrous hurricane that would seem to have a mind of its own. The hurricane was one hundred miles in circumference, with an eye thirty miles wide, and packing 180-mile-per-hour winds. When it was about fifty miles southeast of St. Croix, it traveled at twenty-five miles per hour. When it reached the island, it dropped its speed to seven miles per hour and traversed the island, spending over ten hours chewing it to pieces and spitting it out like a dead carcass. My family and I were listening over the radio when our electricity shut off, and the house became dark. Iris and I looked at each other. We lit candles, and the children took out their Monopoly game as if nothing great had occurred, but Iris and I knew differently. The wind became more powerful, and it howled like a lone wolf in the night. I believed that we would have a harsh journey as the hurricane and the sand, which it picked up from the ocean, abraded the island like rough sandpaper. It was gripping, ripping, stripping, gouging the plant life to death, and blowing the earth. The coral within the sea was being destroyed, and some of the life in it was tossed onto the earth. We put the children to bed, and Iris and I lay on our bed as water poured down our walls and the roof lifted from the sides and corners of our house. We were being drenched with water and moved to our daughter's room until it too started to come apart. The roof was lifting, and we heard a loud bang in the boys' room. I jumped up from the bed and ran in there to find a large piece of concrete block near my son Jamal's head. I told everyone to get up and get out of the main part of the house and to go downstairs. They braved going outside in their pajamas and underclothes, while they tried desperately not to be blown off the steps, which led to our shelter. After we entered the bottom level of our house, someone remembered that our Rottweiler dog named Jemma was outside and I let her in. My horses were loose and they had the freedom to seek shelter, but Hugo stripped any possible shelter that there was.

Our shelter leaked from its concrete ceiling, while water accumulated in the main house. Iris cried all morning, and though I tried to console her, it did little to stop her tears. I slept in small spurts, and each time I awakened the wind seemed to increase its howl.

When I awakened in the morning, Iris was huddled next to me, and I looked at her. Her face was puffy from the crying. I looked outside and saw my horses on their legs stretched along the direction of the four corners of the earth like statues. The howl of Hugo was gone, and Iris didn't want me to go outside of the house. I touched her and told her I would be right back. When I went outside, I didn't recognize our property. It was as if something or someone had lifted our house like in the "Wizard of Oz," and sent it to another location. When I reached the top level outside the house, I saw our Mercedes-Benz, and they were not damaged. I turned around and looked over the roof, and most of the roof was off. I said, "Oh God, I praise your name." When I went inside the house, it was full of water and our piano and other contents were soaked. My heart began to race, but I maintained my emotion. It wasn't until Iris, and the children came out that I fell apart inside. I didn't cry outwardly, but my heart was slowly breaking. My children stood with Iris on a slab of concrete; they looked lost and weary. Their clothes didn't seem to fit them; it hung from their bodies, and I saw them without adequate shelter. I was supposed to provide for them, and it hurt me to see them destitute.

I took a picture of them standing next to our ravaged house minus most of the roof, and that picture has stayed on my mind; haunting me.

Bankruptcy

It was days before I could get in my office. The roads were blocked with debris, and everybody seemed to be going to the same place, even though there were few places to go to that weren't damaged. I tried going through the airport in order to check my airplane, but the National Guard and the police would not let me through. I told them that I was a pilot and needed to get to my aircraft. I needed to know if my friend that protected me from the world that was on fire made it, I needed to know if Hugo had mercy on it.

Days later when I arrived at my office, it was being robbed. Two people got out of a car, walked into my office as if it were theirs, and emerged with the cushions from the sofa, which my patients sat on. Iris asked one why they were stealing our things, and he responded, "You have insurance, what are you worried about?" She told him that we didn't have insurance and started to cry. I went in my car and pulled out of the glove compartment a brand-new stainless steel Smith and Wesson 5-shot revolver in its black Swede holster. I tucked it into my pants near my back pocket. A friend of mine was standing by named Daryl, who worked in the pharmacy next to my office, which had also been looted and destroyed. He told the guy standing by Iris that I had a gun and was going to shoot him. He looked at me, spread his legs, and said, "You going to shoot me, go ahead and shoot me." I looked up at the sky and said, "Oh God. These people are crazy." The things that were stolen from me weren't worth killing anyone for.

Though I had no insurance and almost all of my office equipment was stolen along with the furniture, and the office was trashed, I valued his life greater than anything, which I lost. It hurt me to know that people would take from me as those two people did. It hurt to keep on hurting, but I had no more tears to shed. I looked at Iris and said, "Let's get out of here."

God, What Is On Your Mind?

After a few days of begging and pleading with the police and the National Guard to let me through their blockade to the airport, I gave up. When things were more in order, they let me through. I prayed to God to allow my airplane to be spared damage. After parking, my car at the entrance to the parking area, I slowly looked in the direction where I had tied down my cocoon to the ground. I made sure that it was not near any other aircraft. It was upside down on its back. The propeller was bowed on each end like a pretzel, and the wings were bent along with the rudder and fuselage. I walked to it and said, "Lord; I don't know what you're doing in my life, but it hurts. God, I praise Your name." I had a Bible between the two back seats, and I looked for it. It was lying in the wet grass. I picked it up, and it was turned to the Book of Job. I told God that I loved Him. I went home and told Iris that the airplane was destroyed, and she told me not to worry; one day I would have another one. I returned to the airport and took my expensive instruments out.

I couldn't believe that we had lost so much to a natural disaster. I had no insurance on my house, no protection on my office, an under insured aircraft, and $ 3,400 in Chase Bank.

Iris was due to have our baby within two months, and to top it off; she was emotionally distraught. She was still intermittently crying, but I couldn't shed a tear. In many ways, I felt numb and unreal as if I were in a dream.

The U.S. Marshals, stateside National Guard, and the Federal Bureau of Investigation were on St. Croix trying to maintain order. The government let the prisoners out of jail because it was damaged, and crime was everywhere. We called my in-laws in Puerto Rico. They told us that we could go to Puerto Rico and live with them until we got our lives back together again. We went to Chase Bank, and they would only give us $500. We had a few hundred dollars in cash. We went to the travel agent and bought one-way compassion fare tickets in order to leave St. Croix.

Iris said that I lost it mentally. I burned most of her clothes; I left her with a bra and some panties. I burned furniture and gave most of our children's toys away. I gave our new small gas stove away, and our towels and sheets. Iris tried to stop me, but I wouldn't listen to her. I told people that I would never return to St. Croix to live again. I was finished emotionally, wiped out, and ready to retire from island life. One of my patients came into the house and told me, in front of Iris, how much she appreciated me, and I was a good doctor, who had helped her a lot. I broke down and cried. The tears flowed from my eyes like two rivers.

The Exodus

The day that we left St. Croix, the sun was shining bright, and we dressed in our best clothes and went to the airport early. Many people were there, as if most people wanted to leave. An exodus had begun weeks before; people who were afraid for their lives. John pulled out his gun into a crowd of people whom he said were harassing a woman on the street. From the way, he expressed it to me; I could tell that he was shaken and angry. He left St. Croix on a government airlift.

It was now our turn to be airlifted to the States, not by the government of the United States, but American Airlines. While we sat in our seats with the massive jet engines running, I wondered where I would go to practice medicine. We were heading to New York, but I wasn't sure that we would stay there. I was glad to be leaving for New York to be with family, and see familiar faces, but anxiety was high because I didn't know if I were ready for the fast pace. My other alternative was going to Florida. When the jumbo luxury liner lifted from the runway, I looked at Iris, and she was crying. I asked her what was wrong, and she told me, "I'm leaving my home." I didn't know what to say, so I said nothing. When we arrived in New York, it was chilly, and we were shivering from the cold. It was great seeing my family.

After a day or two, we visited Raymond and his wife Shauna. It was a moment of fresh air when I saw them because, as usual, they greeted us with smiles and hugs. Their children were happy, safe, and comfortable in their apartment. We all sat and Iris and I told them of our experiences, and they listened until we were finished. We were sitting on the couch. A video of Larnell Harris, the gospel artist, was on singing "Amazing Grace." Iris started to cry, and I followed. I sat with her; I felt vulnerable and helpless. I didn't know what to say to her, and the tears continued to flow. It was a very difficult time for us.

Raymond and Shauna took us to Sear's department store and purchased winter coats and hats for our children. Raymond was my best friend, and he and Shauna continued to share their love with us.

We visited Calvary Baptist Church. They were in a new church building that they built from the ground with hard-earned money. They got out of that bigoted neighborhood where the people called us "niggers." Calvary had not changed much except for a few key members dying, and Rev. Crayton was a bit older. They took up a collection for us, and we gladly received it.

I called the Florida and New York medical license boards in order to get information about working in either state. After thinking about Albany and Schenectady, I discussed our options with Iris, and we decided that Albany would be the best place for us to go. I told my family of our decision, and we left.

Raymond let us use his Dodge van. We packed the family comfortably in it and rode the New York State Thruway to Albany. Iris and I were content and sure that we were doing the right thing. We stayed at Iris's brother's house. I liked him because he was a gentleman and confident. He loved his wife Nancy and their two children. Tibbs, as he is affectionately called, was always nice to me and respectful. He never said anything to me out of the way, and things, which he knew that I didn't appreciate. I always liked him because he was confident. He was my idea of a good family man who showed himself responsibly. We stayed in his house until we could find a place to live.

We got in touch with Michael and Margie, and they were happy to know that we were in town to stay. That Sunday we went to Refreshing Springs Church of God and Christ. Refreshing Springs had not changed at all, and Sister Dix was still her beautiful self, calling people doll-babies. The people were delighted to see us. I sat through the service and cried. I remembered all the good times that I spent at Refreshing Springs and how it refreshed my soul. I felt as if a million pounds were released from my body; I felt revived again.

When the choir's turn came to give their selection, I couldn't believe what my eyes were seeing. My old girlfriend Gwen Newell was standing with the choir singing. I would have never missed her anywhere, with her full lips and crooked smile. My heart beat fast and I said to myself, "It can't be; she lives in Queens, at least that's the last place where I saw her." After church, I went to her, kissed, and hugged her. She told me that her father died, and her mother and sister were fine. Her last name wasn't Newell any more. She had been married twice, and she wasn't with her latest husband. She had two sons, and decided to move to upstate New York in order to work. It was nice seeing her again, remembering old times at New York City Community College and while we were dating. Gwen turned out later to be quite a surprise.

My next order of business was finding a job, and there were many available, being a physician. I went to the Whitney M. Young Jr. Health Center in Albany, by Arbor Hill. I wanted to practice as close to the inner city as possible and the predominantly black neighborhood of Arbor Hill was it. The Medical Director of the health center was an internist. He greeted me warmly and told me that they had an opening paying $75,000 ($65,000.00 cash and $10,000 in medical benefits). Considering I had very little money it wasn't bad. I told him that I would think about it.

Lies

I went to a health maintenance organization, and they told me that they had a few positions, and I would be paid the highest salary, which they offered because of my year's practicing and experience in Family Medicine; $110,000 was their quoted figure. They told me that they had a position available in Albany, and I told them that I would take it. They then told me that I needed to get letters of recommendation, my New York State license certificate, and my Drug Enforcement Agency certificate. Because they wanted tangible letters of recommendation, and the telephones were not operating for the private sector on St. Croix, I had to return to the island in order to speak with a few doctors who would write the letters for me. Though I had no colleagues on St. Croix, these three physicians were willing to help me: Dr. Garden, Dr. Sue, and Dr. Garcia. While I was on St. Croix, I went to our house and cleaned it the best that I could. I called the agency in Albany and told them that I was getting the letters, and the woman told me that we had a problem. I asked her what problem we had. She said that they needed three recommendations and needed to talk to the people who wrote them. I told her that wouldn't be difficult, and I would ask the ones involved to call her. She said, "We have another problem."

"What problem do we have now?" I questioned her.

"We need your Drug Enforcement Agency certificate, and a license certificate."

"That's not a problem," I told her.

"Well," she said, "we have another problem."

"What is that?" I asked.

"We don't have the spot available anymore."

After I hung up with her, I couldn't wait to get into the plane and head back to New York.

I went back to the agency with my letters, only to hear them tell me that they had nothing available for me. I may have been wrong, but I believed racism was staring me in the face again, and I was angry. They didn't have an acceptable reason to turn me down. I pushed them on the issue of them telling me that they had a job for me; then saying that they had none. They offered me a position in Glens Falls, New York, about 45 minutes north of Albany. I told them that I didn't want to go that far. They offered me a second position in Westchester County, New York. I didn't want to be that close to New York City. I told her that I didn't want it. "What about jobs within the area?" I asked.

"Dr. Williams, we don't have any available."

I thanked her and walked out of the agency.

White Fear and Black Pain

My second encounter with what I call racial harassment met me in a medical supply store on the main street in Schenectady. I was due to deliver our seventh child in November. I went into the store, and Iris waited for me in the van. There were about five customers inside. The owner of the business was a white woman. I walked over to the area where they had the diagnostic units and reached for a glucometer (device to check blood sugar) and the owner blurted aloud, "Can I help you, sir?" The people turned around and looked at me. I told her I was looking for suture material. She said, "We don't have any."

"Well, do you have a suture holder?" I asked.

"No, we don't have any suture holders."

I responded, "This is a medical supply store, and you don't have any suture material or a suture holder?"

"That's right," she said. The eyes of all the people in that store stayed fixed on me as if I were there to steal something or harm them. The owner wouldn't address their needs until I made a move to leave. I turned around and walked out. When I got into the van, I was shaking and angry. I told Iris what happened, and she didn't say a word. She knew that I was hurt, and I guess she felt as helpless as I did. I thought of going back to that store dressed in a three-piece suit; except that I didn't have one. I didn't feel that I needed to walk into the establishment with a stethoscope around my neck, or telling the woman that I was a doctor, who graduated from "their" prestigious private medical college in Albany. Too many times black professionals have to parade themselves around in order to get the same respect as their counterpart. I was sick and tired of having to answer to the establishment.

I thought about the Whitney Young Health Center. Perhaps I belonged in Arbor Hill, taking care of people and loving them. Maybe that was my place for now, but I didn't follow my heart.

I went to Ellis Hospital in Schenectady, where I did rounds with Dr. J.T. Henderson when I was a medical student. They were interested in placing a doctor in a neighborhood outside of Rotterdam, New York. They told me that the town had no doctor for about three years. The previous doctor died. They took me there and made me an offer. They would pay to set me up in private practice and support some of my salary for a while. The only problem, as they put it, was whether the people within the town would accept a Black physician. The hospital administrator took me to a doctor's office further out in the country in a small town. The doctor used to be a police officer; he quit the force and went through medical school. He had a nice comfortable practice. The hospital administrator asked him what he thought about my practicing in a small town with white patients. He said that he didn't think it would be a problem after they got to know me. He probably was right but by this time, I was sick emotionally and tired.

I also visited a doctor in his private office in Schenectady. I was told that he needed someone to join his practice. He spoke with me about my credentials; then, he told me that I needed more Continuing Medical Education hours and flatly turned me down, but not before making me feel inadequate for the position. I had it with their running me around. I believed that the only person who was honest with me was Dr. Bishop, at Whitney Young Health Center and the Administrator at Ellis Hospital. I believed that the Administrator respected me being a physician. I went to the Whitney Young Health Center, marched into Dr. Bishop's office, and asked if the job was still available. "Yes, it is," he said.

The Whitney M. Young Jr., Health Center

Whitney M. Young Jr., Health Center reminded me of the Family Practice program at Lutheran Medical Center. From my first day, it never felt right being there. When I was a fourth-year medical student at Albany Medical College, I did a clinical rotation at Whitney Young. A woman named Barbara remembered me from those days. When I spoke with Dr. Bishop the first time, I saw her, and she greeted me as if she didn't remember me, and I reminded her who I am. She smiled at me and said, "I remember you. You were a student here a few years ago."

"Yes," I replied, "I remember you also, how are you?"

Dr. Bishop had a secretary named Margaret. She was the one he referred me to before I was hired in order to sign documents and give copies of my certificates and diploma. Margaret looked benign, but she was sneaky and cunning. There were a couple of middle-aged women, Helen and Bernice. They worked in the blood lab. In many ways; they were like water in a desert to me. Janet was my secretary. She made life bearable at the center for me, and she was the life of my office. I looked forward to going to work in order to speak with her. We had some deep conversations. I met a young man named El-Wise, who turned out to be a super guy, who told me almost every day that he loved me, and I believe him to this day. He was a man who was bold, confident and wise. I never met a young black man like him. I learned that I could trust him with anything and not worry that he would harm me. He helped me build confidence in myself every day.

The doctors at the center were each unique in their own way. I was closest to Dr. Frank Brown, who was a Black Internist. He was younger than I was. He was intelligent, very fashionable and clean. I believe that I gravitated to him because he was precise, clear, and committed not to take, as he put it, "any of their crap, and stuff like that." He was talented and used to play the piano in church. Frank wasn't a religious person, but he respected me and never spoke ill about what I believed in. He was my strength outside of me; he helped me to focus on major issues in my life.

On my first day of work, the health center was active and stayed busy almost every day. My patients had various problems; most of them being high blood pressure, diabetes, stress or bronchial conditions. We took care of many immigrants from Russia. They were given sponsorship by various organizations, and given jobs.

I spoke a great deal to all of my patients and realized that I needed them as much as they needed me because I felt like I was in a wilderness. My secretary, Janet, was friendly, but professional. I asked her to "loosen up" a bit and smile. It took her a while to trust me because of "job politics" going on, and people were afraid to lose their job status. Without notice, people were switched to other job descriptions. Janet was smart enough to watch her back at all times, but sometimes she was paranoid, and it affected our relationship because she clammed up. She was having a few personal problems, and they too were taking a toll on her. We talked a lot about them. She was really a stronger person than she thought, if she weren't she would not have been able to help me with my problems. One day she came into the center and had a pair of shoes and some ties that she got from her boyfriend, and told me that she wanted me to have them. She really touched my core with her concern. I proudly wore the shoes and the ties.

I was using the van to get around. Though Raymond and Shauna needed it, they agreed to let us have it until our cars arrived from St. Croix. We left our cars with Orlando and Annie, who were friends of ours, until we had money to ship them. With the salary, I was making we weren't going to have enough money for a long time.

Being Grateful

Richard from Refreshing Springs Church found an apartment for us. His adopted daughter Jane agreed to let us stay at her house for $850.00 per month. He said that it was the deal of a lifetime, and we bought it. It was a nice three-bedroom red-brick house. The bedrooms were small, but the house provided a clean safe environment for us.

The insurance money for my airplane arrived for $14,500, and we were already $22,000 in debt. My aircraft was worth $30,000 when it was destroyed so I lost $15,500 from the start. We didn't have any money saved and all the money, which I was making had to be spent. We were shopping in the Price Chopper supermarket with coupons; we denied our family the things, which we could not afford to buy. We never had to select certain foods not to buy because of a lack of money since I became a doctor. I didn't feel degraded because I had to do it, but it made me feel inadequate as a provider. In some ways, it was therapeutic because it took me closer to the grass roots of how some people had to live.

Iris and I were tolerating our circumstances and having each other was a tremendous source of strength. We denied ourselves, purchasing clothes, in order to put food on our table. When Thanksgiving arrived, Refreshing Springs Church gave us a big turkey and the fixings. We enjoyed our Thanksgiving dinner, and it was an intimate moment for all of us, as we reflected on people's love for our family.

Ariana

Iris had our seventh child, on Sunday morning, November 26, 1989. Iris' brother Tibbs and wife Nancy helped with the delivery and taking pictures of the birth. She was beautiful. Iris named her Ariana. She was named after a Greek princess. I went to the church and announced her birth. Iris was a brand-new mother for the seventh time. Being the youngest (The baby) she demanded attention from everyone. Her siblings loved to care for her. She loved to dress up, be the princess. One of the things, Ariana liked was her hair blowing loose. She didn't like ponytails, hair ties, a bit of a wild child.

The first snowfall, I took the kids to the park, and we ran on the frozen lake and slid down the snow-covered hills. I had a lot of fun with them that day, and I forgot about my troubles. It was rare when I could do that.

I was elected to work with the teens in the church. As in most churches, the teenagers were to be reckoned with and the teens at Refreshing Springs were a handful. I really didn't want to get involved that way, but I agreed.

Gwen must have taken offense to my being elected; she suddenly would not support the functions that we had. One time we had a church camp-out, and she refused to let her boys get involved. She rounded them up to take them home. She walked by me and said, "What do you think you're doing?" She stopped, turned and looked at me with her crooked smile and lazy eye. She smirked at me and made a grunt sound. It hurt me to think so highly of Gwen and all she could think of to share with me was her arrogance.

Hidden Rage

Our cars arrived from St. Croix. They were in Ft. Lauderdale at Port Everglades. I asked Michael to accompany me to pick them up. I encouraged him to wear a suite, so we would not look suspicious, being Black and picking up two Mercedes Benz. We flew to Ft. Lauderdale, Florida, and met a preacher from the Church of God and Christ. Being a minister and having to do a funeral that day, he dressed in a suit. The three of us went into the port, and by mistake walked into the wrong door. We met a custom agent fooling around with a couple of women. The agent was highly upset and said, "Do you know you came through the wrong door?"

We looked at each other, and I said, "We're sorry."

He didn't say another word. We went to the front entrance and composed ourselves. When we were inside, he didn't see us, and one of the women looked at him and jerked her head in our direction. He walked over to us and said, "Can I help you?"

"Yes," I said, "I'm here to pick up two Mercedes Benz."

He took his time looking at my documents and said, "both of these cars are yours?"

"Yes, sir," I responded.

"What kind of gas do they use?"

"Regular," I said.

"We have a big problem here."

"What is the problem, sir?"

"You said these cars use regular gas, and they're not United States inspected."

"Sir," I replied, "they are U.S. inspected."

"But you already said they use regular gas."

"Sir," I responded, "I made a mistake."

"No," he said. "You already said they use regular gas."

At that point, I realized that he was jerking me around as if I were beneath him. My heart was pounding fast, and I said, "Sir am I going to get my cars? I came all the way here from New York, and I've been waiting months for my cars to arrive from St. Croix. They are U.S. inspected and use unleaded gas."

He looked at me and said, "I think there is a duty to be paid on these cars." The duty had already been paid on the cars when they were shipped to Montvale, New Jersey from Germany. He wanted to slap me with a $6,000 duty. I took out my documents, which verified that the duty was paid. Fortunately, I called Montvale, New Jersey and asked them to fax the duty-paid documents to me on the same day that I left for Ft. Lauderdale. After he finished tormenting me, and satisfied his sick craving to try to make me look small by harassing me, he said, "Come back at one o' clock." I looked at him seriously and said, "Sir will I get my cars?"

"Come back at one o'clock," he repeated. I collected my documents and walked out.

I hated the South, like my father hated it. I couldn't imagine what my father had to endure. At least, I had the passage of some key Civil Rights Bills in my favor, even if the whole place was a threat to every Black man who has to depend on the system. I couldn't wait to get out of Ft. Lauderdale. What I experienced in the medical supply store in Schenectady, New York was worse than what I experienced in Florida. Like a naive fool, I never expected northerners to treat me as if I were less than they were. I was aware of certain attitudes and understood anything could happen, given the wrong variables. When we arrived in Schenectady, I couldn't wait to show Iris her beautiful car. That night I told her what happened in Ft. Lauderdale with that custom agent. She didn't feed the conversation. We made love and went to sleep.

A few weeks prior to getting our cars, I asked Iris what she would say if I said, "Let's go back to St. Croix." She put a big smile on her face and said, "I was waiting for you to say that." We made up our minds to return to St. Croix, and we were positive that it was the right decision.

Richard and I spent time together sharing our lives. He talked about his past life and how he wasn't going to turn back to the world. I respected Richard because I always believed that he spoke from his heart. Even though he had that car accident, which crippled him slightly, he was handy with construction and was willing to help people. I especially appreciated how he encouraged and helped me at times.

Needing a Change

Iris and I decided to attend another church; we just needed a change. We went to a Charismatic church on the other end of town. The people were very friendly, and we enjoyed the services. On occasion, I went to Refreshing Springs at night and enjoyed their service.

John and Doris Belton were stable friends with us, and if it was not for them attending Refreshing Springs, I would have been long gone. They represented what was decent in this life. Their honesty, love, and devotion to my concerns won me. They never ignored me, not even while I was going through problems.

It Seemed Easy

On the day, we left Schenectady for New York City; I had ambivalent feelings. In one way, I knew that I needed to get away. On the other hand, I was going to miss my friends again, as I did before.

I made sure that I spent some time with Ephraim, Michael, Margie, and Bro. and Sis. Belton. There was a host of people I would miss spending time with. I was going to miss the many lunches I had with Michael, my talks with El-Wise, my intimate moments with Janet, and Dr. Brown's enjoyable smile. I would always miss refreshing Springs Church, because I had so many good times there.

We went to Queens, New York and stayed with my family for a couple of days. We had an enjoyable time. My mother was sad to know that we were returning to St. Croix. The day I told her I was leaving for the island, I said, "Ma, I'm going back home."

She replied, "You were born and raised in New York; this is your home." I understood why she was offended, but what she didn't understand was my desperation to get away from racism in New York. We drove to Ft. Lauderdale in our Mercedes-Benz, and we could appreciate our cars because they were engineered well. We made a few stops. With nine people, we were destined to stop almost every two hundred miles.

When we passed south of the Border, I got nervous. I felt out of my environment and couldn't relax in the South. I still didn't feel safe there. The customs agent at Port Everglades didn't help. I told Iris that I was concerned about going to the port again because I didn't want to meet up with that agent. I believed that he would give me a hard time. I didn't think that he would forget three black guys picking up two Mercedes Benz.

He represented a threat to me, my being Black. He had everything on his side, including race. When we finally arrived in the port, the agent wasn't there; instead, there was a woman. She told me that we couldn't ship Iris's car because it lacked the certificate of origin. I said to myself, "Oh, not again." I told her the car was mine, and we just shipped it from St. Croix a few months ago, and it was going back where it came from. She told me that she was sorry, but I needed the document. I stood motionless looking at her, and told her that the car was mine, and I purchased it in St. Croix. She looked at me and said, "OK; I'm going to let you by this time, but if you come through here again without the certificate, you're going to have big problems." We took care of the necessary documents, and sighed with relief.

Chapter 30

Home Again

Out of the depths
have I cried unto thee, O Lord.

Psalm 130:1

We boarded American Airlines at Miami International Airport. The flight to St. Croix was refreshing, to say the least. Iris and I kept looking at each other smiling; we were going home, to the place we loved and felt safe in. When the plane landed in St. Croix, my mind felt relieved. Iris said, "We're home."

"Yes," I replied, "we're home again." The warm air filled my lungs the way it did when I first arrived in St. Croix seven years prior.

When we arrived, home and saw our house, it looked terrible. The people who stayed there didn't take care of it; our daughter's cat died. My generator was destroyed, and our property looked like a bulldozer refaced it. I gave them thirty days to get out, and they got upset. I promised them when we left, that they could stay in our house for one year, and I wanted to keep my word, even if they didn't keep theirs. For the rest of their stay, they wouldn't help me do a thing about the house. When they saw me cutting grass or digging a hole, they either watched or got busy wasting time. Iris and I were glad when they left. We had to clean up their mess after they were gone.

That night we all slept as if we were in a castle, and I felt complete, content and safe.

My first order of business was following up on my privileges in the hospital. I applied before my return. I went to the hospital in order to speak to Ms. Safe, the Medical Director's secretary, but she was not there. I saw her in the bank, and I asked her about it. "Oh Dr. Williams, you're not going to believe this. Your application was the only application out of all the doctors who applied for privileges that was lost."

"What," I said, "you lost my application for privileges?"

"Yes, Dr. Williams, I'm sorry." I couldn't believe they lost my application, and only mine. "Come by and fill out another one," she said. I did fill another one out, and I told her not to lose that one. "Oh, we're not going to lose it, Dr. Williams. By the way, do you remember that nurse who gave you a hard time?"

I asked, "What nurse?"

"Nurse Downs, she died." I was shocked when she told me about Nurse Downs, but I wasn't surprised. That nurse created hell in the labor and delivery room. I felt sad that she died, and like Ronald, in grade school and high school that hurt me, I would have rather been her friend. The only difference between how I felt about her and how I felt about Ronald was, I hated Ronald for hurting me, but I felt sorry for Nurse Downs.

We had $11,000 cash when I returned to the island; $4,000 was borrowed, almost $2,000 was given, and the rest we saved in New York. I told Iris in two weeks we would not have any money. "How is that going to be possible, don't we have $11,000?"

"Yes," I replied, "God, revealed it to me." She didn't say anything else.

After we finished paying for another roof for our house, and building the interior of my office, which was housed in a mini mall, the money was gone. Iris called me on the telephone the second week after our return, and asked me for money to go shopping. I told her that I didn't have any and didn't know that I had one $100 cashier check in my wallet. "What happened to all the money, didn't we have $11,000?"

"I told you, Iris, in two weeks we wouldn't have any money."

A couple of hours later, Pastor Leomine went to my house and told Iris that she had $200 for us. She was one of the ministers I never let know that we needed money when we were in New York. I didn't have any particular reason, not to ask her; I just didn't. I thanked God for her.

Iris and I were going to the Pueblo supermarket that evening, but before going, I told her to take me by Bro. Bell's house, who was a brother at St. Croix Community Fellowship Church. He, his wife, and daughter were living in a government trailer home because Hurricane Hugo devastated the house, which they were renting. He told me that he had some furniture to donate to my office. Iris stayed inside the car, and I went into his trailer. He invited me to sit. "Where is your wife?" "She's in the car," I replied.

"Go get her, and bring her in."

"We have to get some food from the supermarket, and I can't stay long. I told her that I would be right back," I replied.

He asked, "Does your family eat rice?" He pulled a bag of rice from his closet. "Do you have any sugar?" He pulled a bag of sugar from the top cabinet and put it into a brown paper bag.

I stopped him. "Bro. Bell," I said, "I didn't come here to get food from you."

He said, "For years you have helped people in need, let God do something for you."

His wife Jackie walked in, looking tired after a full-day work. "Hi Hilarian," she said, "What are you doing?"

"Jackie," I said, "I didn't ask Bro. Bell for anything; he just started pulling food from the closet and giving it to me."

"Honey," she said, "did you give him any cookies for the children?"

I couldn't believe them. They were displaced from their home and living in a trailer; their clothes were rotting in a basement of a friend's house. I stood up in their living room, and cried. I told them that I was supposed to help them; not them me. Bro. Bell told me to accept the help. A few days later, he took me to the place where the furniture was, which he and his wife wanted me to have. The furniture was very nice. I saw big rats running all over their soaked, mildewed clothes, and I felt terrible. He helped me get the furniture to my office in a truck, which I borrowed.

The first day that I opened my office for business, no one came. The second day, two people came. As I was driving home, I was upset with God. "Lord," I said, "King David, said in your Word, 'I was young, and now I'm old, and I've never seen the righteous forsaken or his seed begging for bread.' Lord, my children are about to beg, and feeding them is Your business, and I expect You to do something. I know You did not allow me to return to St. Croix to be a failure." From that day, on my practice grew steadily, and we started satisfying our debts.

Our children were as happy as ever. I watched them run and play on our 7.5 acres of land, climb trees, and do whatever filled their time. I was happy for them. I saw a difference in Iris; she was relaxed and smiling. I knew St. Croix was the place where God wanted us to be without a doubt. I did not apply for privileges with the Ob/Gyn department; it wasn't worth the hassle. My family had gone through enough, and I didn't want to put them through anymore. I would have been entangled again with the midwives and Dr. De Chabert, the Chairman of Ob/Gyn; it would have taken time away from my family, and drained me of energy, which I needed in order to build my practice and enjoy my life. I didn't have my airplane anymore; my cocoon was gone, and the money from the insurance policy that I had on it was gone. It was my friend, and I dearly missed it. I didn't have it to protect me from the fire that I was in. It played its role well when I had it, but like all things, it was vulnerable to the cares of this life.

I didn't have any money except for what I was making daily in the office, and it was just enough to get by. Many people didn't know that we had returned to the island, and as a result, many of my old patients continued to see other doctors. Some of those patients I never saw again in my office. Some of my patients asked me why I abandoned them, and I explained my horrible journey to them, and they felt better about what I did. They understood that I had to do what was best for my entire family. One of my biggest worries was what people would think of me having left the island when times got rough. I think that it was my greatest fear; the fear of being rejected. I spoke with Iris about it many times before our return, and she said most people would understand.

My office was only 570 square feet of space. I had two exam rooms, an office, reception area, and a little waiting room. I bought a small air conditioner to keep us cool in the blistering heat of daily 87-degree weather. If too many people came in and stayed, the air became warm and muggy. I didn't change my approach to patients; I talked to them a lot and took whatever time I needed to take care of their needs. Their problems were the usual ones that most family doctors see: high blood pressure, diabetes, asthma, bronchitis, sinus infection, and skin problems. I did what I knew best to do, and they were better afterward. We had a couple of people who wanted us to deliver them outside of the hospital. We scheduled them in our office and delivered three healthy babies whose parents were happy. I enjoyed those deliveries; the first one was a mother who was having a baby for the first time. She literally begged me to deliver her. I told her that it wasn't my policy to deliver first pregnancies. I consented and did the delivery and Iris, and I stayed with her for twenty-three hours while she tried to deliver her baby. We drove her home.

The doctors at the hospital in Ob/Gyn knew that I was "back in town." Comments started coming to me via patients how some people in the hospital believed that I was not a good doctor. Each time that I heard these comments, it angered me, and Iris had to calm me down. I believed that I suffered enough. I was willing to let them be, and they needed to let me be. I wasn't asking them for anything except; my privileges in the hospital, which they were delaying. I continued to deliver babies, and I tried to ignore the negative comments, but I couldn't. Therefore, I was constantly in battle with myself to keep my mouth shut. I knew as soon as I said anything to them that it would give them pleasure knowing that they got to me.

Jewels in My Life

I needed Continuing Medical Education credit in order to renew my license. A conference was coming up in Chicago, Illinois, and I decided to go. It was a weeklong journey, and I wasn't crazy about being in an ice-cold conference room for hours at a time all day, but going would have served two things, which I needed: one, to get the needed credit and second, to see Michael and Paula St. John, who lived in Wheeling, Illinois. I missed Michael and Paula. I knew that they loved me with no regard to my color or race. I remembered Michael's kiss that Sunday at St. Croix Community Fellowship. When we spoke about race and color, I brought it up. I told Michael that I didn't understand what people's problem is with racial prejudice. He said, "Buddy, do you know what the real problem is with people who hate someone because of their skin color or race? It's not fear. It's not money. It's not houses or land; its sin, and the sin in people's lives are a spiritual problem, and only God can help those people." I listened to Michael that day intently, and I knew he not only spoke his heart, but he spoke the truth. I wanted to see them. When I arrived in Chicago, he picked me up and took me to his house. It was nice seeing Paula. Michael told their children to hug and kiss me, and they did, and it was exactly what I needed. I spoke with them my first evening there. I shared with them, my journey and how the hurricane turned our lives around for the worst, but God helped us through it. I talked to them about my battle with the medical establishment, and how tired I was. I talked to them about the church we went back to in St. Croix. They, as usual, responded to me in a careful way by telling me that they believed that I should share my concerns with a minister, we both knew who visited the church in St. Croix a few times and lived in Illinois. They called him over. When I saw him, we warmly greeted each other. He allowed me to share my concerns with him without interruption. We spent over three hours talking about race. He told me that he believed the races should not mix in terms of interracial dating and marriage. I told him that wasn't Gods will, and he quoted "scripture" from the Holy Bible in order to justify his position. I told him that he needed to get to his knees and repent of his belief. He disagreed. He had spent over the time that he intended to with me. He said his wife was waiting for him to return home, but if he left he guessed that I would classify him as I would any white man for getting up and leaving under such a conversation. I told him that he was right. He stayed around a while longer, said his good-bye and left. I never saw him again. Michael, Paula and I sat in their living room for a few moments, not saying a word. I told Michael that I was sorry for having that conversation in his house. I told them how much I respected and love them, and ask would they forgive me. They told me that there was nothing to forgive me for. They understood what I said, and they believed that it came from my heart. They knew that I wasn't a malicious person or one who got a charge out of hurting people or making someone look small. They fed my soul with love that night and told me they loved me very much, and God loved me. Every morning Michael asked me to take a walk with him. In the freezing cold weather, he was warm-hearted, kind and gentle. He talked to me about God, man and the universe. He told me every day in many ways that he loved me. The conference went well and before I knew it, the week was gone. On the day of my departure, I got up early in the morning, went into the bathroom, looked in the mirror, broke down and cried. My heart felt so heavy. I called for Michael and Paula. They came running in the bathroom, asking me what was wrong. I told them that I was very tired, and I couldn't take it anymore. They prayed with me and shared their love that came from God. Michael asked me to promise him, when I had an encounter with a person that was negative, to pray for the deliverance of that person, and ask God to help me through it. I told him that I would. I hugged the children, kissed them and Paula and I said good-bye. I told them that I loved them very much, and they returned the same.

I Wanted to Smack Him

No sooner had I left Michael and Paula; I had my first challenge with an elderly white man whom I sat next to on the plane. He complained when I asked him to excuse me so I could sit. He told me to wait and don't be in such a hurry. I sat next to him, and put my Walkman headphones on.

He told me to turn it down because it was disturbing him. He said some things after that with a tone, which I didn't appreciate. I got mad. I wanted to tell him to go to hell and caught myself; I remembered Michael's words to me. "Buddy, you're going to be challenged before you know it, call on God, brother." I prayed for that man, as I looked at him. He was so pitiful and full of everything that is wrong in this world.

On the return flight to St. Croix, I decided to stop in New York in order to see my family. I had a good time with them. I couldn't stop thinking about my encounter with that minister at Michael and Paula's house. I felt sorry for him. He was convinced that he wasn't prejudiced against Black people; he believed what he told me was right before God.

They Turned Up the Heat

When I arrived in St. Croix, it was refreshing. The children were happy doing what children do, and Iris was holding down the camp. I told her about my trip, and I shared with her Michael and Paula's love for me, and how beautiful their children were. The following day I went into my office and saw a load of patients.

My privileges in the hospital came through, and it was another factor in my life, which I had to deal with. Attitudes developed within the hospital concerning me. One nurse, in particular, Nurse Nethersaul, was creating hell. One morning I went into the hospital in order to see a patient, who was my private patient, but she was admitted under another doctor. I was standing across the room reading the chart, and a "student nurse" came in and asked me if she could talk to me for a moment. When I walked in her direction, she asked me to bring the chart. "Dr. Williams, I'm so embarrassed; Nurse Nethersaul told me to get the chart from you."

"Why?" I asked.

"She didn't say."

I looked at her and told her I was a doctor at that hospital with privileges, and it wasn't right for Nurse Nethersaul to ask her to get the chart from me. I asked her where was Nurse Nethersaul? "I don't know," she replied. I was steaming. I called the operator in the hospital and asked her to page Nurse Nethersaul, but Nurse Nethersaul never answered. I thought, "She is hiding like a snake." I did not forget when she went to Dr. De Chabert, supposedly to help resolve what he called later a personality problem between us. She was rotten then, and still was. What she did to me hurt and I found it hard to pray for her. She wanted to destroy me. No matter how hot she set the furnace, neither she nor anyone else would see me burn because God was with me.

I had a couple more deliveries in my office, and they went well. My patients were having their needs met, and I was content that I could help them. I started getting tired of the routine of medicine. My pilot's license was not current. It was over two years since I flew an airplane, and I couldn't afford to buy one. I thought of things to do. Sometimes I rode my horse or planted vegetables. I never got much from it, but a small watermelon and a few tomatoes, squash or zucchini.

Farming

My in-laws came to visit us, and my father-in-law discussed with me growing banana and plantain trees. I decided to go for it. We planted 1,600 trees on our property. It took two weeks to dig those holes, plant the trees, cover them with dirt and fertilize them. My father-in-law did most of the work by himself, because I had to work. I did help when I came home and on the weekend. I also hired a helper in order to assist him.

I also decided to become a poultry farmer. I purchased 500 baby chicks from Pennsylvania and was raising them. I had a sign made called "The Chicken Den," put it on my new red Datsun B2300 truck, built a cage to fit in the flat bed, went to my lawyer, and started a corporation. I thought; I was moving ahead; from the cares of this life. Every day, I walked through the field where my mini plantation was and marveled at its beauty.

I Didn't Start It

One day my son came home from school and told my wife a boy in his school told him his mother, who is the wife of a well-known obstetrician/gynecologist, said that I was a crazy doctor. My wife called her on the telephone, and she never denied it. Her husband developed a vicious streak in him concerning me. It may have had to do with the fact that I would not stop delivering babies out of the hospital. He had a successful practice, and some of my previous patients went to him for care. Many believed that he was very nice in the office, and they liked his way. I only heard good things about him. He did not have any reason to be threatened by me, except for the fact that I was cutting into the delivery business. However, not even that should have bothered him because he was making lots of money. After Iris spoke with his wife, we closed the issue.

I was having a ball driving about the island in my truck with that sign. I was selling frozen chickens, and became known as the "chicken man." It bothered my children to see me selling chickens, but it didn't faze me one bit. Iris was laughing at me in fun. When my children asked for money, I told them all I had was chicken money, and I thought they didn't want any of that stinking money because it was made selling those nasty chickens. Nine months later, the banana and plantain fruits were ready to pick and sell, and that is exactly what I did. Almost every day I took them to my office, put them outside, put a sign on the window and sold them. I sold them on the honor system. I let people take what they wanted to buy and trusted them to pay me. I made a good penny between my two businesses.

I moved my office into a larger one because I needed more space to adapt to my patients.

Who Cares?

My office was busy as ever, and a young woman about 21 years old came in for a postpartum check-up. I had never taken care of her, but her sisters were patients of mine. She told me that she was a clinic patient of Dr. Cranes. He took care of her during her pregnancy. She told me that she didn't want to see him as a patient because throughout her pregnancy, he gave her aspirin, knowing she was sensitive to it, and she had bled at that time because of it. I asked her why she didn't tell him she was allergic to it. She said that she did. It was hard for me to believe her story after that because it didn't sound like something a medical doctor would do; especially to a pregnant woman. I listened to her ramble on about her problem. I asked her if she had a pap smear. She told me that she didn't. I asked her if she had anything else to say, and she said no. I had her completely undress, and I examined her. The examination was unremarkable. I did the Pap test and sent it to California for it to be examined. Within three weeks, it was returned to my office. It stated that she had a Class-4 pap smear, carcinoma in-situ-3, with severe dysplasia (a precancerous result). I immediately called her into the office and read the results to her. She took it well; in fact, I made sure that she understood that it was a serious finding diagnosed by the pathologist in California. I told her that was all that they did at that company; they examine pap smears all day, and I trusted their diagnosis. I told her that she needed to be examined by a specialist. The referral was made for her to go to Puerto Rico to be examined by a doctor we confided in by my wife. Within a couple of weeks, she came back to my office, and told me that she couldn't afford to go to Puerto Rico. She went to the local clinic, where a visiting doctor looked over the pap smear results and examined her. He told her that she needed to go to Puerto Rico to see a specialist in Gynecology. He sent her to the head nurse, who in turn sent her to the social service department. The doctor in the clinic, the head nurse, and social service all signed a document, which gave her permission to leave the island to see a specialist. It needed a medical doctor's signature that was in the field of Gynecology. They sent her to another health facility on the island, and she saw Dr. Cranes.

Dr. Cranes examined her and told her that she had nothing wrong, and I was only upsetting her with the incorrect diagnosis. He refused to sign the document, which would give her permission to leave the island. He sent her home with prescriptions for an antibiotic, birth control pills, a hormone cream, and a cream to insert into her vagina for yeast infection. She came into my office a few weeks later, and told me that she didn't go to Puerto Rico, but she had taken the medication, and Dr. Cranes told her that there was nothing wrong with her, and stop letting me upset her. I was furious with him. I told her that she had a serious problem, and I reminded her that I did not make the diagnosis, but a specialist made it. She left my office the same way she did the first time that I saw her, with a bewildered look. I was furious with Dr. Cranes. I couldn't understand how he, being a well-respected Gynecologist, and knowing good medicine, could have done this to a 21-year-old black female. Cervical cancer can sometimes stay dormant for as much as five years before it expresses itself, and cause death. I pleaded with her to leave the island and get proper medical care. She told me that she didn't have the money. I took her to another Gynecologist on the island, and asked him to examine her. I paid her bill, which was $50. The physician suggested putting her in the hospital to do a procedure called a "cone biopsy." He wanted cash money for the procedure, and she didn't have it.

Iris called the Pap smear Company in California and told them that a doctor on St. Croix refused to accept their diagnosis. They responded, "Doesn't he know he can get sued?"

"I guess he does," Iris replied. The company agreed to pull the Pap smear slide and have it read again by two independent Pathologists. They wrote us a letter, which confirmed that the diagnosis was correct; as far as they were concerned; she had a precancerous pap smear and needed follow-up treatment by a specialist. I went to her house and told her what

I knew, and she didn't seem disturbed. I understood why later. Dr. Cranes sent a nurse to her house in order to tell her that everything was OK and not to let me disturb her anymore. I went into the clinic where Dr. Cranes worked when he wasn't in his private office or in the hospital. He wasn't there. I asked the head nurse to allow me to see her chart, and she refused. I told her if anything happened to the patient, she would have to answer for it. She asked me was I threatening her. I told her I was not.

By this time, I was fed up with Dr. Cranes and his unprofessional treatment of this client. She didn't know any better than to believe him and not the test results, but her mistake was in not getting a second opinion. Dr. Cranes put her life on the line; especially her being a Black female.

That week I went to the Medical Director's office, (Dr. Lloyd Henry) and asked the Director' secretary if we had a peer review committee. She told me that we didn't. I asked her whom do I speak with when there is a problem. She gave me the names of two well-known physicians. I went to one of them. He was upset with me and asked if I spoke with Dr. Cranes. I told him that I didn't. He suggested that I speak with him. I asked the operator to page him. When he answered, I identified myself and told him that I wanted to speak with him. He told me to meet him at the operating room door. When we met he told me that I had three minutes, I asked him why he told a 21-year-old black female who had a precancerous pap smear that there was nothing wrong with her. He replied, "Because there is nothing wrong with her." I asked him why he gave her antibiotics, anti-yeast vaginal cream, birth control pills and a hormone cream, knowing that the estrogen hormone, which was in birth control pills and the cream, could enhance an already possible cancer of the cervix in the patient. "I didn't do anything wrong," he said. I asked him why he spoke poorly to the patient concerning me. "You spoke badly about me," he replied.

I said, "Don't you realize she could sue you?"

"She's not going to sue me. She's going to sue the Department of Health." He told me that he didn't have any more time for me, and went inside the operating room. I was angry.

I wrote letters to a number of key physicians on boards: Commissioners of Health, the Chairman of Ob/Gyn, and the Medical Director of the hospital. For ten months, I sent certified return receipt letters to these people whom I thought cared about the quality of medicine in St. Croix. One well-known physician replied, asking me to take it up with Dr. De Chabert and Dr. Lloyd Henry, the Medical Director of the hospital. A doctor asked me, if I were willing to volunteer to do breast exams in a private Radiologist's office. I agreed. "By the way," he said, "how did things work out for you with Dr. Henry, the Medical Director?" I told him that I wrote Dr. Henry, and I didn't get a reply to date. I told him to tell the Medical Director that I wanted that meeting, or else I was going to take other steps in order to solve the problem pertaining to what Dr. Cranes did. He asked me if I wanted him to tell the Director exactly what I said because it sounded like a threat. I told him if the Medical Director wanted to take it that way it was OK with me, because I was fed up with the nonsense. The Director sent me a letter asking to have all of my documents pertaining to Dr. Cranes and the patient, and I did.

It took a month for Dr. Henry to set up a meeting with me, Dr. De Chabert and Dr. Cranes. I had to wait eleven months before the Medical Director agreed at that meeting. On the evening before the meeting, I was given a small tape recorder to record the meeting, if when I arrived, they decided to record it.

I walked into the meeting and the Medical Director, and the Ob/Gyn Chairmen were sitting. I greeted them diplomatically and sat. Dr. Cranes came in dressed in a nice island shirt, looking scared. The Medical Director, in a low tone, opened the meeting. Dr. Cranes pulled a small Radio Shack tape recorder from his pocket and placed it on the table. I pulled mine out and he jumped from his seat and said, "see." "I told you, you couldn't trust this guy."

Dr. Henry wouldn't continue the meeting until we put away the tape recorders. The Medical Director looked through the folder of documents he had before him, which he asked me to send, and said, "Well, Dr. Williams, you seem to have something to say; what is the problem?" Dr. Lloyd Henry sat there knowing exactly what the problem was. I painfully told him what he already knew. Dr. De Chabert sat in his seat and didn't speak a word. He asked me what I wanted them to do. "I want this young woman to be examined correctly," I replied. "I want her to have colposcopy [examination of the cervix with a high-powered lens to look for abnormalities] and a possible biopsy."

"What is colposcopy?" the Medical Director asked.

It almost became a joke to me. There he was, moderating an important meeting, and had no idea what colposcopy was, even though it was the main diagnostic tool used in order to diagnose her case. He said that they wouldn't do the biopsy, and would have Dr. Cranes do the colposcopy. I interrupted, and asked him how could he ask Dr. Cranes to do it when

330

Dr. Cranes was the reason we were there in the first place? I asked Dr. De Chabert to do it, and he flatly refused. I reminded him that he took care of patients of mine with fewer problems, and asked him a second time to do it. He said that he wouldn't. Dr. Cranes said, "Why don't you do the colposcopy, Dr. Williams?"

"I will, if you let me use the colposcope in the clinic."

"No, I won't," he replied.

The meeting degraded to who should do what. I looked at the Chairman and said, "If Dr. Cranes did to your wife or daughter what he did to this young woman, would you like it?" He said nothing. I looked at the Medical Director and said the same thing, and he said nothing; just like he did for eleven months while I awaited his response about Dr. Cranes's unprofessional behavior. I looked at Dr. Cranes, and started asking him the question. Before I finished, he jumped from his seat again as if he was on fire and said, "Don't you say anything about my wife." I still repeated the question. Dr. Cranes was angry. I stood up and walked out of the meeting. Halfway through the executive office I realized that I left my briefcase. I stormed back into the office, looked at Dr. Cranes, walked to him, put my finger in his face, and told him that he was one of the most dangerous doctors whom I knew, and he was a liar. The Medical Director grabbed me and said, "Please, Dr. Williams, don't do this."

I looked at the Medical Director and said, "But what about what he did to this 21-year-old black female, he was wrong, and he knew it."

"Please, Dr. Williams," he kept pleading. I picked up my briefcase and left.

After that meeting, I became an emotional wreck. I exerted so much energy that there was none left for myself. I couldn't even practice medicine without pausing throughout the day to think about my life. I was mad and full of fury. I wanted to hurt Dr. Cranes, and make him pay for his treatment of that young woman. Her life was now at further risk being Black and medically mismanaged, and in the next five years, she might develop cervical cancer. I told them all, if she did, I would make sure I personally walked into the courtroom with her by her side.

I didn't know what to do about my life. It was painful. I was discussing my journey with a woman I know and respect in a supermarket one day. I said to her, "These guys (the system) really did it to me."

She looked at me and seriously said, "You did it to yourself; you allowed them to do it to you." She didn't help to make my life any less painful, but she awakened me. I thought of her words, and I agreed. I left myself vulnerable to the system, and they took their best shots at me. I did what I felt I had to do. I stood up to them. I told them in more than one way that they were not worth the sacrifice of my principles and my character.

Chapter 31
Finding my Father

I cried unto the Lord with my voice;
With my voice unto the Lord, I make my supplication.

Psalm 142:1

I thought a great deal of my father. I missed him. I would have given almost anything to see him and tell him that I loved him. It was too late to do any of those things, so I grieved for him. I thought about my sister Janice when she told me once that she felt depressed and called out to my father to help her. I felt that way a few times. He was always willing to help me when I asked although he was firm and sometimes harsh with me.

My father took the history of his family to the grave with him. I didn't know anything about them. I had no idea where to find them until I spoke to my mother, and she helped me. I had a few leads that they were living in Connecticut. She told me about my father's brother, my uncle Louis. My Uncle Louis' wife, my aunt Queen, lived in Montgomery, Alabama. My mother gave me Aunt Queen's address, so I wrote her. Aunt Queen responded quickly with a Christmas card. We corresponded a few years by letter. One day Aunt Queen's granddaughter, Angela, called me at work. I was shocked when she called me. She addressed me the way my father had been addressed. She called me "cousin Wilbert." Her voice was soft and relaxed. "Cousin Wilbert," she said, "I was speaking to my mother, and she told me to give you a call. We just want to know you better." I told her that I wanted to see them and was thinking about coming to Alabama. She told me that they would love to see me. We had a wonderful conversation.

I told her that I would get back with her about tentative dates. When I told Iris about my contact with my father's relatives, she had a smile on her face. She knew that I was excited. I shared the conversation with her, and she said, "You really should plan to go to Alabama and visit your cousins." I didn't know until later, Iris believed that I needed to connect with my father's family for emotional reasons. She believed that some of my problems with restlessness were due to my search for my father's family and trying to fill a void.

I arranged to travel to Montgomery, on October 11, 1997. I was to stay five days with my father's sister in-law, my aunt Queen Williams, and her children and Grandchildren. Iris took me to the airport to catch my flight at 7:15 a.m. She was in good spirits. The ticket attendant was a patient from my practice. She greeted me with a warm smile. "So you're going to Alabama," she said.

"Yes," I replied, "I'm going to meet some of my father's relatives whom I've never seen."

"Oh, that's exciting; have a great time."

Iris kissed me at the custom's entrance. I told her that I loved her, and she said, "I love you too, honey."

Before I boarded the aircraft, my patient approached me, asked me for my ticket, and gave it to another agent. They gave me a first-class ticket. I was shocked. A man was sitting on the seat next to me. He greeted me warmly, and we mesh like bread and butter. I found out that he was a Christian businessman who lived in North Carolina. He was visiting his daughter on the island. We spoke about our lives and our past journeys the entire trip to Atlanta, Georgia. When we arrived in Atlanta, we planned to meet whenever he was in St. Croix. I caught the following flight to Montgomery, Alabama. The Alabama landscape looked beautiful from the air. When we landed, I recognized the tower building from some old civil rights pictures. I thought about the racial prejudice I experienced in New Orleans, Florida and Washington, D.C. when I was younger. A fear filled me. When we landed, I thought, "Gee, no ku klux klan's men to greet me." I expected a hostile attitude in the South, but I didn't find it. The stories and the documentaries that I had been educated and indoctrinated by over the years were almost a thing of the past, and my Cousin Orlando would prove it to me.

I waited for my cousin Orlando, Aunt Queen's grandson, to meet me. I saw a well-built guy walking toward me, and we greeted each other. We greeted each other cautiously because, he was looking for an older guy, and I had no idea what he looked like. He walked pass me; then, came back and looked at me. We pointed our fingers at each other and nodded our heads.

"Are you Cousin Wilbert?"

"Yes."

He helped me bring my luggage to the car. We hit it off well. I liked him from the start. He spoke with me about his job as a personal financial analyst with Primerica Financial Services. The knowledge that he had was what I needed in order to set my finances in order. He drove twenty-two miles to a place called Waugh in Montgomery County. Waugh is beautifully nestled in the country. I tried not to miss a thing. I scanned the countryside, and marveled at the woods. He stopped on a dirt road and said that he had to get the mail. There I saw four houses on top of a hill. The house directly facing me from the road was where my aunt Queen lived. My father's brother, my uncle Louis, built that house from the ground up with his hands. To the right of it was a second house, which my cousin Louis, my deceased uncle's son lived in. Next door about one hundred yards was my Cousin Katie's home, Orlando's mother. My cousin Elmira and Katie were taking turns caring for my aunt Queen, who was suffering from congestive heart failure.

I got out of the car and took a picture of Orlando standing next to the road sign named Queen Williams Road, which led to the property. "My God," I thought. I didn't have a road named after me, but I also didn't have her wisdom and experience or own sixty acres of land either. She deserved her name as a road sign and more. Cousin Katie met me on the porch at Aunt Queen's house. She had a pleasant smile on her face and hugged me. It was a surprise to her that I looked younger than my stated age. When I entered the house, I felt warm all over. I couldn't believe that I was standing in the living room of my father's brother. On the piano, I spotted a picture of my uncle Louis in his cap and gown taken when he graduated from high school. He and my father were spitting images of each other. Aunt Queen was lying in bed resting. She was not well for more than a year. This was the reason why I decided to expedite my trip in order to see her. Cousin Katie guided me to her room as I looked over every inch of the house with such contentment. I had corresponded with Aunt Queen for seven years and felt wonderful finally seeing her. "Hi Baby," she said. "How are you doing? You look so good, and it's so nice to see you."

"It is great seeing you, and I am so happy to be here."

"It's so nice having you here." I hugged and kissed her and squeezed my face against hers.

Cousin Katie gave me the room next to Aunt Queen's room to sleep. "Cousin Wilbert," cousin Katie said, "This room is yours."

I noticed the broad smile on her face and the brightness in her eyes while she spoke those few words to me. I would realize later that my cousin Katy was loving, kind and compassionate, and she would never change. I looked around the room and marveled at the handiwork of my uncle Louis. My uncle was a preacher and a builder. I sat on the edge of the bed and thought about my father and his ten brothers and his sister, Aunt Maggie, who lived and died in Indiana. My father told me that he used to be a mason builder, but decided to become a barber. My father's family was like a rainbow with different colors. Some were dark complexion like my uncle Louis, and my father and one was light complexion like my aunt Maggie, who had Indian features like her mother, my Grandmother, Meg. I was determined to find out why my father didn't want to tell me anything about his family.

In the evening, my Cousin Elmira came home from work. She greeted me with warmth and love. She told me that it was so nice for me to visit. Later in the evening, I met Angie, Oscar, Mira, and Jackie. I soaked their love in. I stayed up early in the morning talking with Cousin Katie and her children Angie and Orlando. I just could not stop talking about how important it was for me to find them. I told them about my journey, the difficulties growing up in Red Hook Projects, and racism and racial prejudice. I told them that I was afraid of the South. They listened to me patiently while I rambled on about my life and my family. I told them that I loved them dearly. I tried to stop talking, but the words continued to flow from my dry mouth. It was not until 2:30 a.m. that Cousin Katie went to bed when I stopped talking.

The following day I hung out with Orlando. I was so glad to be with him. He took me to a credit loan business where he visited to copy documents. When we went into the office, Orlando joked with three women behind the desk. I didn't think a black man could be out right, friendly with white women in the South. He was respectful, but to the point and polite. They joked with him, and I was shocked. I checked out their response to his joking, and the fact that he was black didn't seem to matter. I expected black people to find their place and shut up, but not my cousin. Orlando was bold. He took charge of his space and theirs also.

I enjoyed spending the day with Orlando. Unknowingly, he destroyed my first fear about the South, that a black man couldn't really be a man south of the Mason-Dixon Line. That evening I sat and spoke with Katie and Elmira about the South and my fears of being there. They assured me that the South had changed from the era of the civil rights movement. They let me know some areas were still holding on to the old ways, but Alabama had changed for the better. That evening I held them at bay again until early in the morning as I talked about my wife Iris and our children. We talked about their living in Connecticut before deciding to return to Alabama. On my third day, I spent a lot of time talking with Aunt Queen about my father. I wanted to know how she felt about him. I asked her if he was kind to her. She told me that he was good-hearted and sweet and was particular about himself. I assumed that she told me everything she remembered about my father, and it was all good. I was grateful and pleased that she shared some of my father's life with me. Her explanation helped me to understand some of the softer moments, which I had the opportunity to share with my father; especially the day that my father held a dead puppy in his arms and looked sad. She knew that I had written a biography of my life before going to Alabama, "Dancing in Fire." She made me promise that I would not write about my father's family. She didn't believe that it was right. She said, "Let it go honey, because the dead can't speak for themselves." I promised her that I would not write about my father's family in a book. I am grateful to my aunt Queen Williams for her openness and kind words about my father and his family.

Later, that afternoon I spent time with my cousin Louis, Jr., who lived next to Aunt Queen. His features were more like my fathers than anyone in the Williams' family was. I remember him coming to stay in our project apartment in 1972 for three months. I felt especially close to him because he reminded me of my father. He was just as interesting to spend time with as I spent by my father. He played the electric guitar for me and sang a blues song. I recorded the memorable moment with my 8mm Sony camera. As I watched him play the guitar, he seemed so content as if he had found his place of refuge in a comfortable "cocoon." When he finished playing, I didn't want to leave. Sitting with him was like being with my father. After, we sat down a while it was like talking with my family in New York. He didn't smile at all that day. I wondered what had stolen the smile from his strong face. I thought that it was the cares of this life. That's what it was; the cares of this life stole his smile. That evening I told my cousins Elmira and Katie how much I enjoyed being with Louis,

Jr. I told them how much he looked like my father. The following day I was with Orlando again. We traveled around Montgomery taking care of his Primerica paperwork and visiting clients whom he recruited. I asked Orlando if Alabama had many integrated neighborhoods. He told me that there were a few. Alabama didn't fit the picture that I had. I told Cousin Katie, I couldn't figure Alabama out. She told me things had surely changed. That evening, Orlando took me to a black attorney's office in the city of Montgomery. She was with her daughter, who looked about seven years old, and sat quietly. I felt as though we had invaded her office and her space because she had no idea that we were coming. I said to myself, "My God, I'm sure that she doesn't like this set up. At least, Orlando should have called her first." I watched a beautiful black woman who was an attorney speak with authority to the state of Alabama.

Orlando told her who I was, and she looked at me and smiled. "I want him to tell you his story," Orlando said. I sat thinking; she doesn't want to hear my story. She wants to continue her work, care for her daughter, and go home. It was dark outside, nearing late evening. She put her hand on her cheek, leaned back in her chair and listened. I told her where I grew up and how bad I was as a child. Her smile widened. I told her about my troubles academically and that medical school was very difficult. When I shared with her some racial things, which I encountered in medical school, she looked at me, tensed. I could tell that she was caught up with the things, which I told her. I spoke a bit about St. Croix and my family. She smiled again. Her smile was refreshing. It wasn't until I finished that she spoke to me. She shared her experience with me at the University of Alabama and Alabama Law School. She told me that the South's old racist boys' ways tried to mess her up. She didn't believe that they treated her fairly when she took her bar exam. "They unjustly failed me," she said. "I had to deal with them." She passed her bar, and the state of Alabama had to do right. I was fascinated and captivated by her. She encouraged me. I was glad Orlando believed my journey was important enough to share with his friend. She wished me well. Orlando told her that I had written a book about my life. She said she was looking forward to reading it. That evening I told Orlando I wanted to see Tuskegee University. He gladly consented. He was driving down route 80 on a two-lane road about seventy miles per hour. That road reminded me of the road in the movie, "Mississippi Burning." I thought, "A racist cop would stop us, and my worst nightmare would begin." I told Orlando that he was driving fast. I thought that he would slow down, but he didn't. We turned into a dirt road. It was pitched black, and a deer jumped in few of our headlights. It was beautiful. It reminded me of my hunting days in upstate New York. I thought again, "Some racist is going to kill us up in these woods." I looked at Orlando. He told me to relax and not to worry because he had driven that road often. We stopped at a client's house. He was a doctor of veterinary Medicine who was not at home. "Okay," he said. "Let's go to Tuskegee." We drove the route 80 East to Tuskegee University. I was fascinated with the university. I asked Orlando to take me to the airfield where the Tuskegee Airmen trained. He started in the direction, but it was getting quite late. I told him to forget going. I was not up to anymore after dark driving in Alabama.

Sunday I went to Macedonia Miracle Kingdom and Worship Center under the leadership of Bishop Leo S. Lewis. Macedonia Miracle Kingdom was where Oscar, Orlando and Angela worshiped. I was ready for church. I was filled to the brim with deep emotions concerning my father and what I believed Alabama did to hurt him emotionally. I had emotional pain that I couldn't describe, and I needed to bear my soul in music, prayer and song. I wanted to hear some good preaching down home style in the South. The church was beautifully decorated in bright colors and shadowed in gold trim. I felt a bit shy not knowing anyone, but Angela, Oscar and Orlando made me feel at home. I was in time for Sunday school. The class I was in was full of men with their bibles in hands as they listened attentively to the speaker. I was distracted during Sunday school. I kept thinking of my father in Alabama. I was thinking about Martin Luther King, Jr. and the civil rights movement, the bombing in Birmingham, Alabama, the Selma Alabama march across the Edward Pettish Bridge, and the brutal attacks on Black people. However, I was no better off, in ways, living in New York. The North perhaps was worse; although I believed that, my living situation was better. I was less fortunate than these Southern gentlemen who probably had a greater sense of whom they were than I did. The distraction took up the better part of the Sunday school lesson. Perhaps I learned that my state of stability was not steady at all. After Sunday school, we gathered in the main sanctuary for the main service. People flooded the sanctuary while the choir took their seats at the front of the church.

Suddenly, Pastor Lewis who was a handsome gentleman came out, grabbed the microphone and told the people to praise the Lord for their blessings. I sat looking at the beautiful people who waited patiently for the choir to sing while the band members tuned their instruments. Pastor Lewis prayed fervently, and it was most dynamic. I was surprised when I heard him speak because I thought that I was going to hear moans and groans of a black preacher in the South full of Southern pain. I listened for every word, which he spoke wondering if he would avoid speaking on race issues. However, he cut deep into the subject. He spoke about Blacks bowing down to white people on almost level, but hating their own skin color. He didn't hold his tongue about the need for people to be accountable for their actions. He told the congregation to get off their behinds and do positive things to help them and their race. Knowing that he spoke the truth, I settled into my seat, agreed with him, and gave the amends to the message. He told us that God was sick and tired of foolishness and our petty ways. He said, "If we are to be great and successful like God designed us, we need to wake up." When he finished preaching, my ignorant view about Southern Black preachers was changed. I felt as though I had missed a life of abundant positive values by living in the North. I believe that I would have been a stronger person, full of confidence and pride, if I had grown up in the South. I knew on my arrival at my Aunt Queen's home that I had missed not only family, but also priceless love. My aunt Queen, her children, and grandchildren confirmed their love for me by embracing me emotionally. I felt their depth of love each time words came from their mouths as they verbally said, "We love you cousin Wilbert." I must have told them a million times that I loved them. I couldn't help myself. In many ways, Bishop Lewis' message made me more confident that God can keep us in the South. His message of Blacks being accountable and prosperous led me to believe that even in the deep South where racism raised its ugly head and destroyed many of our black brothers and sisters, we didn't have to be afraid because God was with us. I enjoyed the church service and the fellowship with other Christians. I got away from the crowd, went outside the sanctuary and found an isolated area to stand and think. I reflected on being in Alabama, not believing I made it a part of my journey. I continued to think of my father and what my life would have been if he had taken us back to Alabama to live. I remember him telling me a few times, if he had stayed in Alabama, he would have been killed or killed someone. If not for any other reason, I am grateful that we were raised and lived in the North. Everyone needs freedom from overt and covert racism. Racism primes ones for social war. We need to love each other and appreciate our differences. Although, with my energy, I'm sure, I would have been on many battlefields for justice. My cousins were doing well, and they seemed comfortable and content living in beautiful Alabama. Sunday afternoon we had a wonderful dinner of turkey, collard greens, vegetables, and cornbread. I did not tell my family that a highlight of my coming to Alabama was to eat their Southern food. That evening I went back to church with Angela and Orlando. The service was a blessing. Bishop Lewis spoke again about making an impact on the world by doing something for God with our lives. He spoke about Black people needing to be prosperous because God endowed us with everything we need to be prosperous and successful. I listened to him as intensely as I did the morning service. At the end of the service my cousin Orlando told Bishop Lewis about my being his cousin from the Virgin Islands, and that I had a wonderful testimony. I didn't want Orlando to spotlight me. Therefore, when Bishop Lewis called me to the front of the church, I was surprised. The Bishop spoke directly to me and told me that God had his hand on me. Bishop Lewis told me that he was going to pray for me. When he put his hand on my head and began the prayer, I fell upon the floor. I didn't know what happened or why. He told someone to leave me on the floor and closed the service. While I lay on the floor, I was very relaxed as if I had been resting all day, feeling peace and being quiet. I must have lain there for five minutes before sitting in the same spot. I was self-conscious about what happened to me and wished everyone would go home or just vanish for the evening. After I composed myself, I wondered what Angela or Orlando would say to me about my experience. I didn't want to talk to anyone about what happened. Orlando mentioned how the spirit of God really moved in the service. He didn't have to tell me how it moved. I ended on the floor. He asked me how I felt, and I told him well. I told him my being prayed for and dropping onto the floor was my first experience. He asked me to tell Bishop Lewis about that being my first experience, and I did. Bishop Lewis asked me to continue to trust in God. During the ride home, I was very quiet.

That evening I spoke with my cousins Angela, Katie, Elmira, and Jackie. Orlando was there. I just started talking and would not stop. They listened to me tell them again about my life. I spoke about Red Hook Projects, my family, my hurts, racism, and finding my father through them. I spoke for a long time. They never interrupted me. Cousin Angela said, "Let's pray." She prayed and asked God to heal our family and release us from any generational curses, pain, hurts and wounds, which we encountered over the years. She prayed fervently. Everybody started praying. My cousins began to cry. Everyone was filled with joy. My cousins hugged me. I felt refreshed almost like I did when I gave my heart to God. I apologized for keeping them up early in the morning. I knew that they all had to go to work. They didn't want me to apologize. They wanted me to know that they loved me. I felt their love. I love them.

My trip to Alabama was wonderful. I will never forget it. I found my father through my loving family. I took pictures of them. I visited Lewis Jr. and told him that I loved him. He told me that he loved me also. I hugged him. I didn't want to leave him, but I had to go home to St. Croix.

On my last day, it rained. I visited my cousin Oscar and his wife. He lived in a beautiful house that he and his wife furnished beautifully. Orlando drove me to the Montgomery airport in Oscar's new car. Their brotherly love encouraged me. I spoke with Orlando on the way to the airport. I told him how I loved him and how grateful I was for his love toward me. He was a bit reserved, but told me that he loved me also.

When the jet lifted from the runway, I thought, "I found him. I found my father in all of them." Thank God.

Chapter 32
The World is Beautiful

In the beginning God
Created the heaven and the earth.

Genesis 1:1

The crises in my life stood still for a moment, and I could see the world and some of its beauty. I took my family on a cruise, and we were launched into the deep ocean of the Caribbean. We boarded a cruise ship in San Juan, Puerto Rico called the Festival with the Carnival cruise line. We had never been on a cruise before, and we were all excited like little children. It was a nice ship, a newly model of its fleet. As we cleared customs at the port, the children were going through their daily ritual of misbehaving, and Iris was doing what mothers usually do, telling them to shut up. I was my usual self, acting as nothing was going on. When we got aboard the ship, I couldn't believe how beautiful it was. It looked like a fancy hotel in some big city-like New York or Dallas, Texas. There seemed to be tons of people in that ship. We were directed to our cabins, which were small but cozy. The children were going crazy talking about who was going to sleep where. Iris and I just looked at each other for a while, and then Iris took over. "OK, I'm going to tell you who sleep where." The boys wanted me to sleep with them. She engineered the arrangement of sleep, and she and I ended up being in separate rooms. We didn't like sleeping apart, but the children won.

My first order of business was looking for all the food. I heard the food on cruises was fantastic, and I was determined to find out if it were true. We went to the top deck of the ship, and they were serving a small lunch of hamburgers, franks, potato fries, fruit and drinks. I ate until my stomach protruded; someone would have thought that I didn't have any food for days.

We enjoyed our first evening. The ship stayed in port until 10:00 p.m., at which time it departed for St. Thomas, Virgin Islands. We stayed up late that night and every night after. I ate food of all delights the whole day. They served us food 12 times per day every day. It was the highlight of the cruise for me. When we went to bed, we were all tired. I was up early for 7:00 a.m. and went to the main dining room to eat. I never saw so much food beautifully arranged in sections as it was.

They had a beautiful ice carving of an American Indian on the main table. I searched every line and curve of its artistry, and I thought that the person who created this is full of talent. That carving represented to me some of the finer things in this life, and they are available to us all if we search for them. I was searching on my journey and finding riches. Everything the cruise had to give that would help me see another side of life I wanted.

The kids kept us busy, finding things for us to do. They either wanted us to go into the cinema, jump into the pool, or just clown around with them in the room. I had lots of fun with the boys during the evening. They never wanted to go to sleep and constantly did things in order to make sure that there was time spent in laughter.

I wanted to do more with the boys than I did, but I needed to spend time with Iris. Our time came at night when the children were told to stay in the rooms. We went up on the top deck where they always had food and music, or down to the main dining room for a 1:00 a.m. buffet. Sometimes we went on the outside deck and acted like newlyweds. I tried hard to give Iris some special time, but I never felt satisfied that I did, because in some ways I was trying to make up for the times I spent with her that weren't special; those times when I was engulfed in my problems, sulking and complaining how bad I felt. I was at least determined not to waste the precious time that we had together, even if I felt inadequate to give her all that she needed. I knew for sure, no matter what I felt, or how she received the time that I spent with her, there was no doubt that she was my love.

We met a friend in St. Thomas named Pastor Benjamin, who took us around the island in a flatbed truck. He wanted to show us a good time, and I wanted the family to see the island. They did not see it in a long time. The island is so beautiful, but small and congested. We had a good time laughing and joking. I kept the children laughing, telling them we were like cattle being shipped to market in the back of that big truck. It was all in fun, and by the time he took us back to the ship, we were tired and content. I thanked him for showing us a good time.

When we got aboard the ship and settled down, my first order of business was to find the food. If we missed food in one spot, they had it in another. I had a ball eating, and my stomach was stretching on an hourly basis.

It was so nice and relaxing lying on the bed under the blanket tucked to my neck with the air conditioner blowing while the ship gently rolled from side to side. There was a gentle pressure on my body while the ship thrashed forward. I had never felt that relaxed before. I thanked God for His blessing in my life, and I thanked Him for Iris and the children. The island I enjoyed and loved the most was Dominica. It is so lush with vegetation. Banana trees were everywhere I looked. I purchased one of the largest pineapples I ever saw in my life and paid only $5 for it. It was funny standing before the owner of the business, which was nestled high up in the mountain, asking her how much it cost. She didn't know what to charge me. There was a kind of innocence in that woman, like the innocence of the forest that surrounded us all on that beautiful island. We stopped at another roadside stand; I tasted a new fruit, and my body enjoyed something brand new and fresh from God's precious earth. I delighted in all the things, which I saw and touched, and I felt a oneness with the earth and its innocence. We went to a waterfall in the midst of the forest. It was so beautiful, more beautiful than anything that I ever saw, flowing over rocks neatly fit together on a ridge. The water plunged into the pool below it and splashed, sending forms of pure water everywhere. I said to myself, "Oh God, You are so great and so wonderful. I love Your creation." I felt in my spiritual longing to become one with it, as if I were there alone having no responsibilities and no burdens. I felt free and clean, and I didn't want the feeling to flee from me, but I knew it would, as soon as I left the serenity of it. We climbed up to the level we descended from, and we were on the backside of a hill, and I saw a mist so beautiful caressing the mountain before me. It was a remarkable sight. I thought about the Black people living there and how rich they really are, but the cares of this life would prevent many of them from enjoying their riches from God. I was sure the pain of life's struggles to keep them well and protected was a daily exercise. The island represented the pure side of life, the side that was distant from the fire, not burning up like the rest of the world, but it too was in danger of being consumed because man had taken charge of it. When we left the island of Dominica, I prayed in my spirit that I would one-day return to greet it, and thank it, for showing me a purer side to this world. I didn't like Martinique and Barbados because they seemed to me to be caught up in the cares of this life. I didn't take well to the commercialism. We thoroughly enjoyed the trip from Barbados to San Juan, Puerto Rico. We spent a day-and-a-half at sea. We went to shows, participated in fun times, filled our bellies to near-stretch capacity and enjoyed the Caribbean. We never had so much fun as a family. The cruise was the best thing we could have ever done. I believe it served as a cocoon for us all, and protected us from some of the cares of this life. For me, it brought me a full circle to see myself without anger, without pain and without fear. I was better because of it.

The West Indies and all the worlds are the beauty of God's handiwork. It is meant to be enjoyed; not abused, not misused or destroyed. It was never meant to be taken for granted or ignored, but to be caressed and loved. It is one of God's gifts to us to enjoy and be blessed by. It is God's representative of what was made without a blemish and without scorn.

Chapter 33
Faith and Hope

Now Faith is the assurance (the confirmation, the title deed) of the things [we]
hope for, being the proof of things [we] do not see and the conviction of their
reality[faith perceiving as real fact what is not revealed to the senses].

Hebrews 11:1

When I think about the Juan Louis Hospital, I see a mind field of
challenges. There is not a hospital in the world that is not challenged
by its own record. Now that we are in the new millennium, I wonder
how we will meet the needs of our community. The Juan Louis Hospital
today is not the St. Croix Community Hospital where I had privileges
in more than ten years ago. In some ways, the Juan Louis hospital has
improved concerning hospitality, which is due largely to a changing of the
guards. Some health care staff from the old vanguard has left the health
care system. This changing of the guards has been healthy because many
health care providers have refused to change things for the betterment
of our community. Much of the refusal to upgrade our system relates to
hospital and community politics. There is a vast amount of favoritism and
monopolized power by a few prominent people. The system has obviously
worked among these people, but what about most of our communities that
belong to the less fortunate.

There are things, we should be proud of like, our efforts to make the
hospital a more suitable place to care for our sick neighbors. Even if our
efforts have been dwarfed, and we don't feel appreciated and powerless to
change some ills that plague us; at least, we have tried to progress. There

is still optimism. The hope for a better tomorrow is in all of us. We need to continue to be strong and courageous and stand firm for what we believe.

There is always room to improve even upon excellence. Excellence is just a measure of where we are and how far we have come, not a final resting place. In the midst of the hard, trying times, which I have experienced I could have done some things differently and perhaps better. I was challenged to do my best. Still, the trying harder could not satisfy me, but I continued to have hope. It is in this hope that I speak to you that we all have to excel, so I stand with all who push toward the higher goals with integrity, justice, and truth in God. I pray that my family and I are making this world a better place because we are here. I pray that peace be upon us all in and by the name of God.

I will always seek what is right no matter what prevails in this life. I know all that is good, perfect and beautiful comes from God, and the vicious fire that is raging; consuming mankind is not God's will for His creation.

The Core of the Fire

I stood in the core of the fire that was hotter than ever, and I refused to submit before the most influential images in my life. The system of this world faced me like a golden calf set high on a throne for me to worship as if it were my God. I saw the church before me, with its laws and bylaws, it's doing's and don'ts. It's bigotry and hate, its scorn and pride and told it, "I won't bow before your images." I saw the negative incidents in my life and every person who despised and hated me for being whom I am and standing firm with conviction, telling the system, telling the world that controls and destroys people's lives, "I won't bow down to you . . ." And I saw many people who helped, loved and encouraged me, standing before me like faces in a mirror, and I said, "Thank you for your love and for not being ashamed of me, but reaching out to me, without gain for yourself on this earth."

My cocoon was made before I was born, before the foundation of the world, and God is protecting me from the fiery furnace that this world is engulfed in. He promised me that he would never leave me, and I believe Him.

I understand like never before, like nothing else in my life, that it is more important to be willing to die for what is right, then to live for what is wrong.

I was dancing in Fire, but now I am "Beyond the Fire and the Rain."

Afterword

Therefore, I will not refrain my mouth;
I will speak in the anguish of my spirit;
I will complain in the bitterness of my soul.

Job 7:1

African Americans have faced racial prejudice and low self-esteem since slavery. As an African American, I have faced racial, social and personal walls. If it were not for God, my parents and my wife, I don't believe that I would have become a medical doctor. Physicians are not born; they are made. The ingredients that make a medical doctor are faith, hope, perseverance, determination, and study. My faith in God has become my shield that protects me from the blazes of the cares of life. Hope has pointed me in the direction of a bright tomorrow. Perseverance has kept my doubting soul company. Determination has been my staff on an unsure path, and study has quickened my mind. The success of my stormy passage across the dessert, over the rugged mountains, and across the choppy seas, has been the Creators grace. His grace is sufficient for me. God has never forsaken me.

I struggled against the odds to enter medical school, and become a successful physician. We will experience success if we stand as a foundation of love, truth, justice, forgiveness, and reconciliation. We can win every battle if we believe that we can with God who loves us, as He guides us.

"Beyond the Fire and the Rain" spoke to you about failure, triumph, and success. Failure, triumph, and success will prepare you to face your later years gracefully, humbly, and courageously. You will be blessed as you seek all that is just before God. We all need to be successful, and overcome challenges and prejudice from without and from within.

I pray that my journey has been inspirational for you, and you will soar like eagles, peering with your mental and spiritual eyes at the blazing challenges of your life. My hope and prayer are that you will gain strength and support from your parents, family, friends, and well-wishers, and that you will see obstacles as ridges to scale toward your dreams, goals, and aspirations. I sincerely desire that you have a lifetime partner who will be as loving and as dedicated to you as my wife Iris has been to me. Teach your children to face their challenges with hope, love, and courage with faith in God. Teach your children to fight the just battles against the enemy. Let us, share with them the weapons of warfare that are not carnal, but spiritual. God will allow His grace to be sufficient for you and your children. I am living proof that one can make it, "Beyond the Fire and the Rain."

Special Acknowledgment

To my special friend, Dr. Robert V. Vaughn who spent eight years and countless hours incubating my work inside your humble, kind and gentle soul. I decided to combine your engineering labor on my two books, "Dancing in Fire" and "Shouting at the Rain" into one book. I am sure you would not make a fuss over my decision other than to tell me as you told me 20 years ago to not do it. You know I have always followed your advice. I know you will forgive me. It is going to be okay. I am never going to change another thing about these books except to put the names of some people who you suggested I not mention because I might lose allies in St. Croix.

Bob, it does not matter to me anymore if I have allies or enemies. I am at peace knowing that the precious hours and your care of my emotions by your tender and firm words has finally awakened me. You spent countless hours, afternoons and nights laboring over me. Why you allowed me more than 26 years in your company I will never know. I know that your company and advice have made me a better man. You added to the foundation of my acceptance of me.

I know now that you planned your memorial and set me up months before you left to go home to be with God. You knew all along medical things that I as your friend and doctor did not know. You prepared me without telling me that you were going to die. I am still recovering from your departure.

I remember when you came to my office and gave me an envelope with documents. You personally handed me everything I needed to know about your history and journey. You selected songs through others that you wanted sung during the celebration of your departure. I should have known. You got the last one on me Bob. I should have never put it pass a B24 Bomber pilot to be prepared. You really laid it on me when after your departure; I was told that you wanted me to give your eulogy at your funeral. I am not sure, but I believed you said the same thing to me one evening while we sat in your living room and had a beer.

So, Bob you prepared me for many things about this life. Some of it was forced but needed. Thank you. Thank you for loving me. Thank you for sharing your life with me.

Bob, I really think I had the last earthly word concerning you. I told a church filled with people who love you about some of our secret talks. When I see you, I will tell you all about it, if you do not already know.

By the way, the new title to your great work is, "Beyond the Fire and the Rain." Thank you for helping me to arrive here.

Love, Buddy

Made in the USA
Monee, IL
24 April 2021